How to Do *Everything* with Your

iPAQ Pocket PC

Third Edition

Derek Ball
Dayton Foster

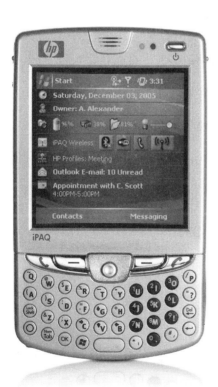

McGraw-Hill

New York   Chicago   San Francisco   Lisbon
London   Madrid   Mexico City   Milan   New Delhi
San Juan   Seoul   Singapore   Sydney   Toronto

McGraw-Hill books are available at special quantity discounts to use as premiums and sales promotions, or for use in corporate training programs. For more information, please write to the Director of Special Sales, Professional Publishing, McGraw-Hill, Two Penn Plaza, New York, NY 10121-2298. Or contact your local bookstore.

How to Do Everything with Your iPAQ™ Pocket PC, Third Edition

1234567890 CUS CUS 019876

ISBN 0-07-226092-0

Sponsoring Editor
Megg Morin

Editorial Supervisor
Patty Mon

Project Manager
Vastavikta Sharma

Acquisitions Coordinator
Agatha Kim

Technical Editor
Dax Games

Copy Editor
Sally Engelfried

Proofreader
Joette Lynch

Indexer
WordCo Indexing
Services, Inc.

Production Supervisor
Jean Bodeaux

Composition
International Typesetting
and Composition

Illustration
International Typesetting
and Composition

Cover Designer
Pattie Lee

*For Mom, words can never express how thankful I am for you
and all that you've done for me. You have made me into the
person I am today. I love you and will miss you dearly. Peace, Love.*

—Derek

*I would like to dedicate this book to my lovely daughter Avery.
Avery was born during the writing of this book and was instrumental
in keeping me awake all night (and all day, and all night) to help ensure
that the book was completed in a timely manner. As always, my gratitude
goes to Derek Ball, who doesn't take "I don't have time for another project"
for an answer and to my wonderful wife Kate for her love and support.*

—Dayton

About the Authors

Derek Ball is a leader in wireless technology and has been focused for several years on delivering solutions for handheld wireless devices such as the HP iPAQ. Derek has published ten other books on technology topics and has traveled the world speaking at conferences and seminars on emerging technology. In between trips, Derek lives in Calgary with his wife Lesley, daughters Jamie, Carly, and Devon, and golden retriever Casey.

Dayton Foster is an authority in the mobile technology space and has been involved with converged mobile technologies including BlackBerry, Windows Mobile, and Palm since 2000. In addition to coauthoring books on the Treo 600 and HP iPAQ, Dayton is the Director of Product Marketing with the Avocent Mobile Technologies division. Dayton lives in Calgary with his wife Kate and his daughter Avery.

About the Technical Reviewer

Dax Games is a Senior Systems Engineer with Avocent Corporation, the leading provider of keyboard, video, and mouse (KVM) switching, remote access, mobile device management, and serial connectivity solutions. He's also been a daily Pocket PC/Windows Mobile user ever since the first iPAQ 3600 was introduced in early 2000. He spends way too much time visiting many of the sites mentioned throughout this book to keep up on all the latest products, tips, and tricks available in the Windows Mobile world.

Contents

Acknowledgments

Writers are a strange lot. Technical writers perhaps even more so. We have had the tremendous opportunity (curse?) to embark upon several book projects in the past. However, as is typical with "selective memory," we often forget what a monumental effort it actually takes to complete a book, not only on the part of the authors, but of all the other people who are involved in the project and without whom no book would ever see the light of the sun through the bookstore window.

When McGraw-Hill asked us to produce the what is now the third edition of the iPAQ book, we realized that we had someone very important to thank. That important person is you, and all the people like you, who picked up this book to help you make the most of your iPAQ. The tremendous success of the first and second editions, and the great feedback we received from our readers have made this third edition of the book possible. We thank you and hope that with this book we can deliver to you information which will help enhance your mobile lifestyle!

There are a great many additional people we would like to thank, but thanks hardly seem to be enough. Megg Morin at McGraw-Hill has been amazing. We have been through many books together now, each with its own unique challenges, and Megg has been unwavering in her support and skill. Megg has actually toughed it out with us through all three editions of this book, which is an incredible testament to her perseverance! Megg, as with all the previous times we've said this, you have been a fantastic source of support, for which we are deeply grateful.

Special thanks also need to be extended to Agatha Kim. Agatha is the queen of organization, making sure that everything flows from the authors, through the technical review, copy editing, and so on. I can't even begin to guess at everything that she does behind the scenes to make this nicely polished finished product pop out at the end of the process. Thank you, Agatha!

There are many other people directly involved in the editing and production of the book that we haven't mentioned by name. Between the two of us, we have written many books in the past, and we are continually amazed at the high quality people that we have the opportunity to work with at McGraw-Hill. Thank you all!

Our technical reviewer, Dax Games, helped us to make sure our information is as accurate and up-to-date as possible. He was invaluable in validating and correcting our information. Thank you, Dax, for helping to ensure the quality of this book and for all of your great suggestions.

Special thanks are due to several folks at Hewlett-Packard, who went out of their way with the third edition of this book to make sure we had access to the necessary information, product samples, and people to make this book a success. Specifically, thanks go out to Jackie Dillemuth and Alison Connor.

There are many other individuals behind the scenes involved in the production of the book whose names we may not know but whose contribution to delivering this book into your hands is no less significant. Your efforts are also appreciated.

And finally to our families, who have put up with late nights and family activities where Dad couldn't go, for encouraging and supporting us through this process. Your love and support made all of this possible. Our deepest gratitude and love.

Introduction

When Compaq introduced the iPAQ Pocket PC to the world, it began a revolution that saw the pendulum of the existing PDA market begin to swing from the heavily Palm-oriented world to that of the Microsoft Pocket PC. To date, more than 10 million iPAQ Pocket PCs have been shipped, and they are selling more every day.

This remarkable device contains so much power that mobile individuals can now do things never before possible with a PDA. Beyond simple contact and calendar management, now people can send and receive e-mail, write MS Word documents, build spreadsheets, make presentations, surf the Internet, and so much more, all from a device that you can slip into a pocket.

The iPAQ Pocket PC has gone through many iterations of development, becoming more powerful and flexible with each release. The merger of Hewlett-Packard with Compaq energized the iPAQ platform with the introduction of even more powerful, flexible, and portable devices. The future of the iPAQ continues to grow more and more interesting as the power and battery life of these devices grow, and yet they become smaller and more portable ... and with the introduction of integrated wireless technology, more connected! More and more people are adopting this device and integrating it into their mobile lifestyles.

Who Should Read This Book

This book is intended for all iPAQ Pocket PC owners. If you're a new iPAQ Pocket PC owner, this book will help you understand how to get started using your new iPAQ properly. For the owner who has had an iPAQ for a while, this book will help you understand how to get more out of your investment.

Whatever your level of experience with the iPAQ, you will find relevant information in this book to do things with your iPAQ that you haven't done before.

You can follow along with the information in this book as it walks you through using built-in applications such as Word Mobile and Excel Mobile. In other sections of the book you can read about the potential of the iPAQ and future devices, and perhaps you will choose to integrate GPS or wireless connectivity into your mobility.

How This Book Is Organized

We have organized this book in sections to enable you to jump right into the area that is most relevant to you. Part I, "Meet Your iPAQ and Connect!" introduces you to the basic setup of your iPAQ and also explains how to connect your iPAQ to your PC, the Internet, or your telephone service.

Part II, "Get Personal with Your iPAQ," switches the focus to fun things like games, music, books, movies, taking photos, and navigating with GPS. Part III, "Work with Your Mobile Office," shows you the powerful software for working with documents, presentations, e-mail, calendaring, and advanced business applications. Part IV, "Optimize Your iPAQ for Maximum Productivity," deals with important issues for making your iPAQ run better, faster, and longer and also teaches you how to make sure that your information is safe and secure. The appendixes of the book are there to help you troubleshoot some common problems with the iPAQ Pocket PC, as well as to point you to other resources that you might want to investigate for more information on your device.

As you read through the text, you'll see we've included boxes for points of specific interest, so watch for the sections labeled How To, Did You Know?, Caution, Note, and Tip for special information about the section you are currently reading.

We hope that you will find this book helpful as you learn to live the mobile iPAQ lifestyle! We use our iPAQs on a daily basis, and they have almost become an extension of our arm. Our most critical information is never more than a moment away, and we can consolidate many disparate information sources into one location. We use them to find our way around foreign cities when we travel, give presentations while on the road, wirelessly stay connected to the office to manage our infrastructure and data, send and receive e-mail, and so much more! Your iPAQ Pocket PC can become as important a productivity tool to you as it is for us.

Part I

Meet Your iPAQ and Connect!

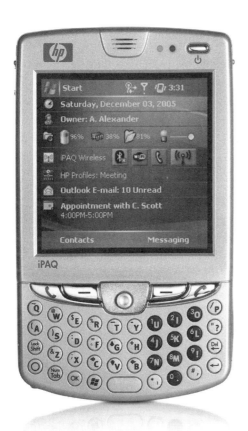

Chapter 1

Meet Your Pocket PC

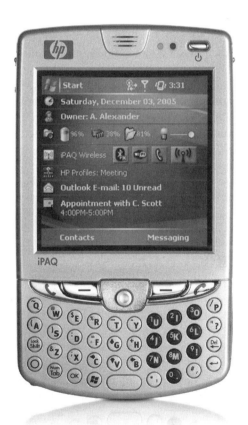

How to...

■ Tell one iPAQ from another

■ Live the mobile lifestyle

Ever since we humans learned to store information somewhere other than in our heads, we have been working on ways to not only make permanent records of our information, but also to take those records with us wherever we go. Over many millennia, this pursuit has taken us from crude paintings on cave walls to hieroglyphics on stone tablets to papyrus to the printing press to the day planner and now to the *personal digital assistant* (PDA).

We are no longer satisfied to simply carry our information with us. We are pushing for a new era of portable information. We want our PDAs to do even more than was even hinted at by early science fiction writers and television shows like *Star Trek*. We want our devices to become an extension of ourselves, to function as a personal secretary, travel agent, guide, doctor, communicator, and entertainment device.

Hewlett-Packard responded to this demand with the iPAQ family of Pocket PC PDA devices. With its sleek retro styling, powerful Intel processor, abundant memory, and ultra-bright and clear touch screen, this device is a bestseller. In its early days it was hard to find an iPAQ on store shelves, although increased production has eliminated this problem. HP recently passed a major milestone, having sold over 10 million iPAQs!

It used to be that a PDA was more of a status symbol than a truly practical tool, but this has changed, and they have become as ubiquitous as mobile phones (and in fact some even *are* mobile phones!). With the current release of Windows Mobile 5, we are getting closer to the ideal of a handheld PDA acting as an extension of ourselves.

The History of Pocket PC and Windows CE

Many years ago, Microsoft realized they would need to develop a lightweight operating system (OS) for non-PC devices. Without a clear picture of the kind of device that would use the new OS, however, it was difficult for Microsoft to move forward. At the time, futurists prognosticated a great deal about the impact of multimedia on our culture. This resulted in one group at Microsoft wanting to push the new OS to become heavily multimedia oriented for use in television set–top boxes. A different group wanted to strip NT down to its bare bones and use that as the new operating system.

In an attempt to bring some unity of vision to this area, Microsoft brought these groups together in 1994 under the direction of Senior Vice President Brad Silverberg. This team realized that what was really needed was an operating system that would be compatible with the existing and future Windows operating systems but would not necessarily be just a subset of them. This resulted in the development of Windows CE version 1, which appeared on the market in late 1996.

The team knew that if they were going to be successful in building a new operating system, it was critical that users not feel they were using a strange, new OS. This meant that the user interface had to mirror the already popular Windows 95 and use a similar desktop of icons as well as the Start menu toolbar at the bottom of the screen.

Such devices at this time were called *handheld personal computers* (HPCs). They were extremely limited in capacity, with very little memory (usually 4MB or less), a small grayscale screen, and a very limited processor that ran between 33 and 44 MHz.

The limited power and storage capacity led to only meager adoption of the initial Windows CE device except among the most hardy computer enthusiasts. The average business user instead tended to adopt the more portable and easy to use competitor to the Windows CE platform, the Palm OS devices, such as the well-known Palm Pilot from 3Com and the Visor from Handspring.

The next generation of the CE platform was version 2, which came out in 1998. The devices that ran this operating system generally had double the CPU power and RAM of the earlier devices, and on top of that many of them featured color screens.

Microsoft hoped that this new version of CE would provide greater competition to the successful Palm Pilot line of PDAs. Unfortunately, this wasn't to be, as sales of the Windows CE 2 operating system were also very slow. Microsoft had also anticipated the accelerated adoption of portable computer systems in cars. The company hyped its Windows CE 2 operating system as its answer to the expected surge of "Auto PCs" (a handheld computer installed in any car in place of an existing stereo). Through a voice interface, drivers could request directions to any address in their Pocket Outlook contact list. The adoption of the Auto PC never happened (although some still think that this is yet to come).

Microsoft followed up Windows CE 2 with version 2.1, which was primarily aimed at embedded developers. These developers were building applications to run on specialized devices, with the operating system embedded directly within their hardware. Examples of places where developers would use an embedded version of Windows CE are customized gas monitors, handheld inventory tablets, or point of sale (POS) systems.

While all this development on Windows CE was going on, Palm OS–based devices continued to gain market share. Things were not looking good for Microsoft's vision of a handheld version of Windows.

Then in January 2000, Microsoft released Windows CE version 3. This product was dubbed the *Pocket PC* operating system. It overcame many of the limitations of the previous versions and also had the good fortune to come into existence when a new line of powerful processors was poised to come out of the gate. Intel's Strong ARM processor gave the new devices running the Pocket PC OS several times the CPU power of the most powerful Palm device at the time. Many of these devices were also equipped with at least twice, and sometimes as much as eight times, the memory of the most well-endowed Palms.

Sales of these Pocket PC–equipped devices began to pick up. The HP Jornada took an early lead, but the release of the Compaq iPAQ handheld set a new standard. Sales of the iPAQ have soared ever since.

The next chapter in the Pocket PC saga occurred in October 2001. Microsoft released the next version of their Windows CE operating system dubbed *Pocket PC 2002*. The Pocket PC 2002 operating system featured an improved user interface, better character recognition options, enhanced Pocket Outlook features, expanded Pocket Word and Pocket Excel features, Pocket Internet Explorer enhancements, Terminal Server client, and more. A Pocket PC user could now expect more functionality than ever on such a compact device.

In 2002, something amazing happened. The two leaders in the Pocket PC field, HP and Compaq, merged. A great deal of confusion and concern arose among Pocket PC enthusiasts as to what this would mean. Would the HP Jornada line survive? What about the Compaq iPAQ? Would the two lines be "blended"? This confusion was enhanced by competitive offerings that were now hitting the market from Toshiba, NEC, Dell, and a host of other companies. The result of the HP/Compaq merger was that HP chose to keep the iPAQ line and rebranded it the *HP iPAQ*. With barely a hiccup, while the merger was occurring, HP shipped the new and improved 3900 series iPAQ. Before year's end, they shipped the lineup of the 1900 and 5400 series, demonstrating their continued dominance in this market and their ability to deliver superior products even in the face of increased competition.

In May 2003, Microsoft released the next version of their Pocket PC operating system, called *Pocket PC 2003*. It featured enhanced wireless support, improved integration for hardware with integrated cellular phones, more games, and personal software. In addition, many features were designed to make the Pocket PC platform more appealing to enterprises, such as remote provisioning, e-mail configuration, sync setup, device locking, and more.

In late 2005, Microsoft released the current version of the Windows CE operating system called Windows Mobile 5. This operating system was designed to improve areas such as battery life, usability, and more. All the new Windows Mobile 5 devices are shipping with a different kind of memory called Flash memory which means that if your battery dies, you no longer lose your data or application. It also means that your battery will last longer in an equivalent Windows Mobile 5 device because it doesn't always have to run an electric current through the memory to keep it alive. Like previous versions of the Pocket PC operating system, Windows Mobile 5 was designed to merge a mobile phone with the iPAQ into a single device, but Windows Mobile 5 did it much better.

It has been 10 years now since Microsoft's entry into the mobile marketplace and the improvements and innovation continue. What will the future hold for the iPAQ? We will look into the crystal ball later in this chapter. The entry of many other players into this space with their own Pocket PC offerings has many analysts expecting a price war between these vendors. Such competition usually benefits the consumer, as the companies increase the pace of innovation (to differentiate themselves from the competitor) and at the same time drive prices down. You can expect that, at a minimum, you will continue to see increasingly powerful machines—with longer lasting batteries, better screens, and more expansion capability—for lower prices.

This book will focus primarily on the most recent versions of HP iPAQs that run the Windows Mobile 5 or Pocket PC 2003 operating systems.

Pocket PC vs. Palm OS

Now that you are a proud owner of a shiny HP iPAQ, you might find yourself being approached by owners of Palm OS-based devices who will try to engage you in debate about your device versus their own. The relative merits of each OS are hotly contested among many PDA users and can be dangerous territory for any author. Traditionally, the Windows devices had more powerful processors and more memory but were less efficient than their Palm OS cousins. Over time, the

Palm OS devices became more powerful and the Windows devices more user friendly. Recently, Palm Inc., the largest maker of Palm OS devices has also started offering Windows Mobile 5–based devices too, bowing to public pressure for the powerful Microsoft OS.

The variety and power of the hardware platforms that are available for the Pocket PC is impressive. On this handheld device you can now perform processing that until recently was the exclusive realm of *Star Trek*, such as speech recognition and 3-D modeling. Many of the devices are well adapted to the wireless world, which will be the next major wave driving the handheld device space. The number of applications available for the Pocket PC is growing daily and includes many of the titles that you are already accustomed to using on your desktop.

This doesn't mean that the Pocket PC platform is perfect. The hardware tends to suck battery power quickly, can be bulkier than the Palm (although the H19*xx* series again proves that a Pocket PC can be sleek and lightweight), and definitely presents a more complex environment than a Palm. The Palm was an early entry in the PDA market and secured a significant market share. It is well liked by users for its simplicity of operation, light weight, long battery life, and voluminous catalog of third-party applications. However, the Palm faces declining popularity because of its limited hardware expandability, limited wireless support, and limited processor power.

The Pocket PC, in formats like your iPAQ, offers the best opportunities for the future of handheld computing.

The iPAQ Family

The term "iPAQ" has come to refer to the sporty handheld unit with the familiar PDA style running the Pocket PC software. That unit is the focus of this book. However, it is important to point out that iPAQ was originally much more. Compaq produced an entire line of consumer devices and Internet appliances all bearing the iPAQ moniker. This short section will explain what these other devices were and where they fit into the Compaq universe. With the HP merger, the only iPAQs still around today are the Pocket PC devices. The rest of this book will be dedicated to only the handheld Pocket PC device, but watch for the other iPAQ devices in museums!

Internet Appliance

Compaq aimed their iPAQ Internet appliance offering at the home market. These devices were essentially stripped down PCs running MSN Companion, which allowed you to access the Internet and receive e-mail. The Internet appliance came in two configurations; the IA-1, with a 10-inch display and a wireless keyboard, and the IA-2, with a 15-inch display but fewer gizmos to play with. Both came with six months of free Internet access from MSN. These devices were not well received in the marketplace and were short lived.

Audio Players

Compaq released two audio players under the iPAQ name, one a portable unit and the other a home unit to hook into your stereo.

The portable unit was much like other MP3 players on the market. It used a 64MB MultiMediaCard (MMC) to provide up to two hours of music and supported both the MP3 and WMA music formats.

The home unit was designed to plug into your home stereo system and provide digital music playback for your MP3 and other digital format music files. It came with a CD tray and converted your audio CDs to MP3 files and stored them on its internal 20GB hard drive. Approximately 400 audio CDs could be stored on the unit. Through a network connection, it could connect to Internet radio stations as well as online sources to decode the artist and song names of any audio CDs you inserted.

BlackBerry

The Compaq iPAQ BlackBerry is a Compaq branded version of the popular BlackBerry two-way pager from Research In Motion (RIM). This device was intended as a less expensive option to the iPAQ handheld with an expansion sleeve (a hardware accessory available for earlier iPAQ models) and CDPD card (the popular wireless option for iPAQs before GPRS, 1xRTT, EDGE, HSDPA and EV-DO networks became common). The BlackBerry is first and foremost a two-way pager that handles e-mail through a direct e-mail link or through a Microsoft Exchange or Lotus Notes gateway. This device has some limited capability to run third-party software but generally is only used as an e-mail device with a calendar and contact database.

This device came in two versions; the pager-sized W1000 (aka the RIM 950), and the larger H1100 (aka the RIM 957).

Compaq Residential Gateway Products

The iPAQ family of products also included networking components designed to allow home users to build shared networks in their homes that could communicate through and share a single Internet connection. This included a variety of wireless base stations, wireless cards, Ethernet cards, HomePNA (phone line–based networks) access points, and hubs. This technology competed with a host of other home networking technologies that still dominate the market, including solutions from 3Com, Linksys, and others.

Home PCs

If that isn't confusing enough, Compaq released a line of desktop PCs called the iPAQ. This line of products was aimed at the home user and was tagged as being low cost and easy to install.

Handheld Pocket PC

Finally, we come to the line of handheld PCs for which the iPAQ label has become a one-word description. This prestigious family continues to grow as HP builds more and more into their iPAQ package.

Most iPAQ models have at least two model numbers. The last two numbers of your iPAQ model generally refer to the geographic region or channel that the device was sold through. The units themselves are identical but may feature different software on board.

The iPAQ lineage includes dozens of different models, so we won't list them all, but the most recent devices feature wireless radios for getting data through wireless networks, mobile phones, digital cameras, and much more.

Adopting the Mobile Lifestyle with Your Pocket PC

As PDAs have become more popular, many people seem to be carrying them around in their briefcases or pockets. However, amazingly, many people also still carry around paper-based day planners and files of business cards or keep that trusty paper phone book by the telephone (although it always seems to have been moved by someone when you need it most).

To get the most out of your handheld device, it is important to adopt habits that will centralize all of your information in your device. You will never make effective use of your handheld if you keep some of your appointments in a paper calendar and some in your Pocket PC.

Tips for Adopting the Mobile Lifestyle

Here are some suggestions to help you integrate your handheld device into your life:

- Pick one point during the day, usually at the beginning or end of the day, where you will enter any business cards that you have picked up into your Outlook Contacts folder. This will keep your Pocket PC business contacts completely up to date. Then you can discard the business cards, or, if you feel compelled to keep them, place them in a binder to be kept in your office.

- Whenever someone gives you personal contact information such as a phone number, resist the urge to scribble it on a piece of paper and stuff it in your pocket or briefcase. We all have drawers of unidentifiable scribbled phone numbers that are of little use, and these scraps of paper don't tend to be in your hand when you need to call that person back. Instead, take the extra 45 seconds to put that person's information into your Pocket PC where it will be permanently preserved and available to you anytime you need it.

- When you book an appointment or plan an event, even in the distant future, always immediately enter the event into your handheld calendar. If you are consistent with this behavior, you will learn to trust the calendar in your Pocket PC. If you aren't consistent, you will find yourself missing appointments or double booking as you try to organize yourself with both a paper system (or worse, your memory) and a Pocket PC.

- If you use your Pocket PC for expense management, use the same diligent technique of once a day entering all your receipts or financial information into your system.

■ Whenever you think of something that you need to do, personal or professional, instead of "making a mental note," put it into your task list. You can categorize it, prioritize it, and assign a date to it.

■ Every morning when you get up, look at your calendar and to-do list. If something that you know is happening that day isn't in your calendar, enter it. If there is something you need to get done that day, put it on your task list. Not only does this help you keep track of your tasks and appointments, it helps you feel that you've accomplished something when you look back on your day. Instead of that "where did the day go, and did I actually get anything done?" feeling that sometimes comes at the end of the day, you will be able to look at your list and see all the activities and tasks that you knocked off.

■ When a special event such as a birthday or anniversary occurs, record it in your calendar as a recurring event (the technique for doing this is described in detail in Chapter 12). That way your Pocket PC will become a true personal assistant by reminding you to make a dinner appointment or pick up a gift well in advance of the date! Try to find things that you are already doing that you might be able to do better with the Pocket PC. For example, I work out at the gym regularly and am an avid runner. I use software from **www.vidaone.com** to help me track my workouts and fitness goals. If you are watching what you eat, check out their diet tracking software. If you are an avid wine connoisseur, you can load databases of different wines, and so on. The amount of software now available for the iPAQ is impressive.

Keeping Your iPAQ with You

Making the best use of your iPAQ also means that you need to keep it with you as you live your mobile life. The iPAQ, although small and lightweight, isn't quite small enough to slip into your shirt pocket or the back pocket of your pants like a wallet (with the exception of the H190xx series which will fit nicely into a shirt pocket), especially if you are using any add-on accessories!

As future versions of the product are released, you will likely see the two form factors exhibited in the current lines continue. The integrated WiFi and Bluetooth also remove the need for bulky expansion sleeves to enable wireless communication. We can hope the form factor will continue to get smaller and the overall weight lighter; right now the best method is to carry it in a briefcase or purse when you move around. But what about those times when you don't want to carry your briefcase or purse?

Your iPAQ doesn't weigh any more than a conventional portable CD player or mobile phone and is as easy to carry with you. In fact, you will probably find your iPAQ works as well or better than your CD player while you run, work out, or perform any such activities. What's more, with MP3, you will never again experience that annoying skipping that even the very best "skip-free" CD players are prone to.

For casual walking around, cargo pants with the side pockets can be very useful places for storing your iPAQ. For more of a business-casual appearance, Dockers has released a line of casual pants called "Mobile Pants," which contain a special pocket for holding your iPAQ. This idea is a good one; unfortunately, Dockers' execution wasn't great. The pocket (specifically identified in advertising for fitting an iPAQ) is too small. It is possible to squeeze in the iPAQ with no expansion sleeves or accessories, and the H19xx fits, but the fit is extremely tight. Unless you are standing at just the right angle, the bulge of the iPAQ is still obvious, and don't you dare sit down! Dockers has the right idea; let's hope other clothing manufacturers will actually try putting an iPAQ into the pocket and using it before they tout their clothing as "Mobile" wear!

NOTE   *If you're constantly on the move, finding the right cases and bags to hold all your gear is critical. RoadWired (**www.roadwired.com**) has produced the most durable and lightweight range of bags, portfolios, and cases for your iPAQ and accessories. We have been using them for several months now. The portfolio pockets aren't quite big enough for the iPAQ, but the briefcases are excellent. For a thorough review of the various bags, cases, and accessories, refer to the website **www.pocketpcmag.com**.*

One popular method for carrying the iPAQ is to get a case with a belt clip. However, you will need to search through third-party offerings because the cases that came with the older iPAQs were generally of poor quality, didn't fit the expansion pack, and did not feature a belt clip and so are mostly unusable. The current iPAQ lines don't even have cases included. On the **www .pocketpcmag.com** website you will find reviews of many of the cases available from third-party manufacturers that will give you the pros and cons of each one.

There are other carrying methods as well, such as the secret agent–style under-the-jacket holster, or the multipocketed vest. One of the vests specifically targeted to the PDA owner is the SCOTTEVEST (SeV) (see **www.scottevest.com**), which is a lightweight water-repellent vest that looks like a safari vest. It is loaded with pockets for all your wireless toys and has a unique feature: Velcro-enclosed conduits to hold all the wires that connect your devices together and keep the cords tucked safely away. They call this a *personal area network* (PAN). However, the vest isn't something you could wear to a business function, and for personal recreational wear, the $160 price tag is rather steep. For those of you who like leather, SeV has also introduced a leather jacket with the same integrated pockets and personal area network features.

Wrap It Up

The iPAQ has a long and interesting history, which continues to build as HP advances their mobile technology. It is a powerful tool which, if used properly, can enhance and enrich your life!

Chapter 2

Get Started with Your iPAQ Pocket PC

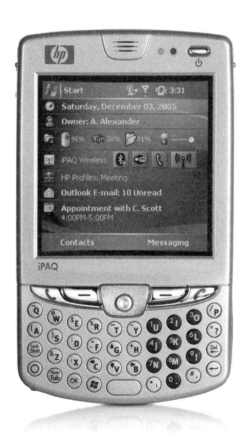

How to...

- Unpack your iPAQ
- Use your iPAQ for the first time
- Use the iPAQ controls
- Set up owner information
- Use and customize the Start and New menus
- Use the companion CD
- Enter data by hand
- Connect your iPAQ to your PC
- Set up ActiveSync
- Beam data between devices

We know how it is—you've got the box in your hands and you can't wait to open it! But before you can jump into scheduling appointments with Outlook Mobile or analyzing data with Excel Mobile, you'll need to get to know your iPAQ. This chapter will help you understand the basics of getting your iPAQ set up and ready for use, as well as what software you should add to the iPAQ from the companion CD that comes with it.

> NOTE   *Prior to the release of the latest Windows Mobile 5 OS and application suite, Microsoft referred to the built-in applications with a "Pocket" prefix (e.g., Pocket Outlook, Pocket Excel, Pocket Internet Explorer). They changed this with Windows Mobile 5, eliminating "Pocket" and replacing it with a "Mobile" suffix (e.g., Outlook Mobile, Word Mobile, Media Player Mobile). We will use the latter method in this book.*

Unpacking Your iPAQ

Different versions of the iPAQ come packaged differently; however, what is inside the box varies only slightly from model to model. Your iPAQ should come with the following:

- Your iPAQ (of course!).
- A carrying case—maybe. A case is a must-have accessory to help protect your iPAQ from damage. However, the case that ships with your iPAQ is rather basic. Many third-party cases provide better protection and a lot more style, but discussing all the case manufacturers is beyond the scope of this book. A full review of cases and case manufacturers can be found at **www.pocketpcmag.com** and other websites referenced in Appendix B.
- A synchronization cradle ships with many iPAQ models, but to keep the price of some of the models as low as possible, you may have only received a sync cable.

- An AC adapter for charging your iPAQ
- Quick Start Guide
- iPAQ companion CD-ROM (more on this later in the chapter)

> **NOTE** *When you first pull the iPAQ out of the box, there will be a thin film covering the screen. This is to protect the screen during shipping, and you should peel this off before using your iPAQ. Similar plastic adhesive overlays are available from HP and third-party vendors that you can place on your screen to protect it during use. Many users swear by these. You can purchase these accessories directly from **www.hp.com**. Other commonly recommended screen overlays are WriteShields, available from **www.pocketpctechs.com**.*

> **NOTE** *To synchronize your iPAQ with your desktop PC, you'll have to first install ActiveSync on your PC and then connect your Pocket PC to your desktop PC using the sync cradle or sync cable. We'll discuss ActiveSync setup later in this chapter.*

Hardware Orientation

The various models of iPAQ can all vary considerably in their hardware configuration, but there are several elements that are common between them.

As in Figure 2-1, most of the following controls can be found on your iPAQ but you may need to refer to your specific manual to discover exactly where they are located:

- **Microphone**   The built-in microphone is useful for voice dictation and voice control software. It is hard to see—look for a little hole on either the top or bottom of your iPAQ.

- **Power on/off button**   This button turns the device on and off. Some models feature LEDs that show when the iPAQ is connected to an AC adapter by glowing orange while charging and glowing green when fully charged.

- **Wireless alert light**   Some iPAQ models are equipped with WiFi and/or Bluetooth wireless communication abilities. On-board LEDs will usually show when one or both of these are active. The WiFi LED usually flashes green when WiFi is turned on, and the Bluetooth LED will flash blue.

- **Screen**   The touch-sensitive transflective screens are usually capable of displaying 65,000 colors. The size of the screen will vary, with most models sporting a 240×320 pixel screen (called QVGA). Some models such as the 4700 have a 480×640 pixel screen (called VGA), and the Mobile Messenger devices have smaller 240×240 screens.

- **Application launch buttons**   There are four programmable buttons set two on each side of the navigation button. These buttons do different things on different iPAQ models. Most of the newer Windows Mobile 5 devices include a Windows key that opens the Start menu and an OK button to help speed navigation through the device and its menus. On pre-Windows Mobile 5 models, these buttons were usually set to launch some of the most commonly used applications such as Calendar, Contacts and e-mail.

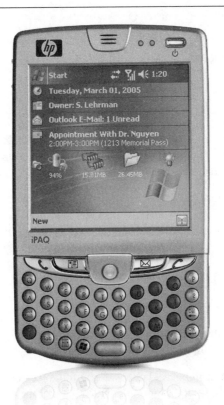

FIGURE 2-1 Most of the controls you'll use are located on the front of the iPAQ. These include the on/off button, navigation disk, application launch buttons, and the touch screen.

- **Navigation disk (bottom center between application launch buttons)** This is a multiposition disk for navigating through applications and data. The center button acts as a select button.

- **Speaker** Notification beeps and voice messages are played through the iPAQ's built-in speaker. On most models this is located inside the device, behind the navigation disk. It is not visible from the outside.

- **Headphone jack** Use this jack to plug in stereo headphones and listen to any of the sounds the iPAQ produces. (A nice set of stereo headphones turns the iPAQ into a great MP3 player). iPAQ devices that do not have a telephone will generally have a standard 3.5mm headphone jack; however, the phone-equipped devices will usually feature a 2.5mm headset jack that is standard for mobile phones.

- **CompactFlash (CF) slot**   If your iPAQ is equipped with a CF slot (such as the 2700 series), this will be the larger of the two expansion card slots on the top of the unit. This slot allows you to insert standard Type II CompactFlash cards to expand the capabilities of your iPAQ. For example, you can use this slot to add file storage, a GPS receiver, an FM radio, and more.

- **Secure Digital (SDIO) slot**   This is the smaller card slot on the top of most models of iPAQ (although a few of the economy models are not SDIO-compatible, meaning that the slot can only be used for memory storage). You can use this to add file storage and other hardware features to the iPAQ.

- **Stylus "silo"**   This is the hole to the extreme right on the top edge, which stores the stylus you use with the touch screen. Slide your finger or thumb in an upward motion on the right side of the iPAQ to make the stylus top pop up where you can grab it.

- **Infrared port**   Also found on the top edge of the iPAQ is the infrared (IrDA) port, which is used for sending and receiving information to and from other infrared devices. You can transfer business cards, contact info, appointments, and more with users of other handheld devices, including Pocket PCs and Palms. See the "Beaming Data for Easy Transfer" section later in this chapter for more information.

- **Sync port**   This is the port that connects to a sync cable or your data sync cradle. Accessories such as external keyboards also use this port to communicate with your iPAQ.

- **Application launch button five**   This additional button is often located on the left side of the iPAQ and may be set to launch the Notes application, voice recorder, or camera but can be set to launch whatever application you choose. Pressing this button will open the Notes application (if so configured), but if you press and hold this button down, you can also record a voice memo. Each voice memo is stored as an audio file with the default name Recording 1, Recording 2, Recording 3, etc. The iPAQ microphone has limited sensitivity and is useful primarily for voice memos, not recording music. It produces reasonably good results up to five feet away in a quiet room. You'll have to hold it closer to your mouth in noisy environments.

- **Soft reset button**   This is located in a small hole hidden somewhere on your iPAQ (usually the bottom). When you press the point of your stylus into this hole, you perform a "soft reset" of your iPAQ. This closes down all running applications, but no data is lost.

Turning on Your iPAQ for the First Time

When you power up your iPAQ for the first time, the iPAQ will initialize and walk you through some initial configuration procedures. You must tap on the screen in various positions to calibrate the touch screen. If you ever find that the places you tap on the screen register inaccurately, you can rerun this screen setup utility from the Settings area.

The initial setup will also prompt you to select your time zone (be sure to set this to the same time zone as your PC, otherwise your appointments will be off!). Once you have worked through these initial screens, your iPAQ is ready to use.

Setting Up the Owner Information

After you've run through the initial setup procedures, you're taken to the Today screen. This screen displays the date and time, upcoming appointments, unread messages, and more. The second line at the top of this screen reads "Tap here to set owner information."

Tapping this line will open the Owner Information dialog box, as shown in Figure 2-2. This is very important to set up, as it will ensure that if someone finds your iPAQ, they can get it back to you.

NOTE   *On this screen you will enter your name, company, address, telephone number, and e-mail address. You can also set an option that causes your information to be displayed every time the device is turned on. That way anyone turning it on will immediately know who it belongs to.*

CAUTION   *The option to show your owner information when the device is turned on is especially important if you decide to set a power-on password for your device (discussed in Chapter 16), because it is the only way someone finding your device will know who it belongs to.*

FIGURE 2-2   Set up the Owner Information dialog box to make sure that if your iPAQ is lost the person who finds it knows where to return it.

> TIP
>
> *One way to ensure that your lost iPAQ gets returned is to offer a reward. In the Notes tab of the Owner Information screen, place the words "REWARD IF RETURNED" and include your phone number. If someone calls, arrange a meeting in a public place, give them the reward, and thank them.*

Using the Start Menu

As in the desktop versions of Windows, in Pocket PC you launch applications from the Start menu. Tapping the Start menu at any time will open the drop-down list shown in Figure 2-3. Note that when an application is launched, the Start menu is replaced by the name of the program that you are currently running, but tapping on the program name will always cause the Start menu to appear.

Listed in the top portion of the Start menu are the most commonly used programs that you can launch. This list can be customized (discussed in the "Customizing the Start Menu" section later), but initially provides links to the Today page, Calendar, Contacts, HP's Home screen, Internet Explorer, Messaging, and Windows Media Player.

The next section of the Start menu lists the most recently launched applications, but only if they are not in the first part of the Start menu.

The final section of the Start menu contains links to the Programs and Settings folders, and to the Help feature. Programs will take you to the folder where shortcuts to programs loaded on the Pocket PC are stored. Note that if you customize the Start menu so that one of these applications appears in it, the application icon will disappear from the Programs folder. Likewise, if you

FIGURE 2-3   The Start menu is the primary launching point for applications on the HP iPAQ.

remove it from the Start menu, the icon will reappear in the Programs folder. The Settings folder contains a variety of setup and configuration utilities for the iPAQ. The Help utility is context sensitive. If you are in Pocket Word and you tap the Start menu and then tap Help, you will receive Help for the section of Word that you are in. This aspect of Help makes it particularly handy while you're getting to know the Pocket PC applications.

Customizing the Start Menu

The top portion of the Start menu can be modified to meet your specific needs. From the Start menu, select Settings and then tap on the Menus icon. This opens the Menus dialog box from which you can customize the Start menu, as shown in Figure 2-4.

The Menu dialog box displays a list of all applications installed on your iPAQ, including programs installed in subfolders (e.g., the Games subfolder in the Programs folder). To add programs to the top portion of the Start menu, simply tap and check the boxes next to the programs or folders you want to appear. Tap on boxes that are already checked to remove programs from the Start menu.

You do not delete programs from your iPAQ when you remove them from the Start menu; you simply move the program launch icon from the Start menu to the Programs folder. You can only have seven items listed in the top part of the Start menu. If you want to get around this, put programs in folders and select the folders to appear in the Start menu.

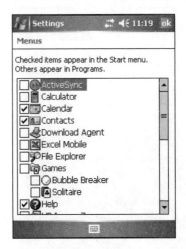

FIGURE 2-4   You can customize the Start menu from the Menus utility in the Settings folder.

What's on the Companion CD?

With every iPAQ you receive a CD-ROM from HP that contains some tools to help you make the most of your iPAQ.

   To make sure that you can synchronize e-mail, the CD includes a copy of Outlook. Earlier versions of the iPAQ came with Outlook 2000, but the more recent editions ship with Outlook 2002 (although neither of these is the most recent version of Outlook, Outlook 2003). If you are going to upgrade your Outlook installation, you should do this before you install ActiveSync.

 If you need to install ActiveSync or upgrade ActiveSync, do not plug in your sync cable or cradle until after ActiveSync is installed.

   After these basic essentials, the CD contains a set of applications (or links to downloadable applications) that can enhance the use of your iPAQ. Some of the programs on the companion CD are full versions and others are trial versions that let you use a program for a limited amount of time to see if you like it. The CD also contains a comprehensive Owner Manual in Acrobat (PDF) format. The actual programs will vary between the different iPAQ models, so you should check your specific CD to see what goodies are available to you.

Entering Data by Hand

The iPAQ is designed to have data entered in a variety of formats. Most iPAQs in circulation do not feature a built-in thumb keyboard, but rather use the screen as an input mechanism. Built in to the device is handwriting recognition capability and a "soft keyboard," the image of a QWERTY keyboard that can be displayed on the lower third of the screen, allowing you tap on keys to enter characters. Optional near-full-size external keyboards are also available, allowing you to type in text.

   If you have the iPAQ Mobile Messenger line, you will have a small thumb keyboard built in to the device which is very convenient for typing while on the go.

Mastering Handwriting Recognition

The most common way of entering data into the iPAQ models without a built-in keyboard is to use the stylus to write characters that are interpreted as text. All current iPAQ models come loaded with three handwriting recognition modes for text entry: Letter Recognizer, Block Recognizer, and Transcriber.

   Only one method of character recognition can be used at a time. In devices using the Windows Mobile 5 operating system, an icon at the bottom-center of the screen indicates the current method of recognition that you are using. This icon appears in the lower-right corner of the screen on devices with previous versions of the OS. Tapping on the up arrow beside the icon will open a pop-up menu that allows you to change your input method, as shown here.

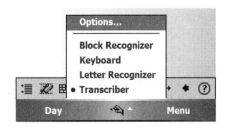

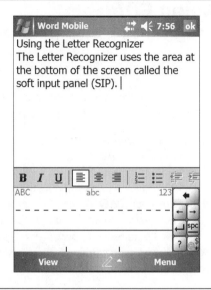

FIGURE 2-5 The Letter Recognizer divides the soft input panel into three vertical sections.

Using the Letter Recognizer

The Letter Recognizer uses the area at the bottom of the screen called the soft input panel (SIP). This area is divided by vertical hatch marks into three sections, as shown in Figure 2-5. The left third of the SIP is reserved for drawing uppercase characters. The middle section is for lowercase letters, and the right third is for numbers, symbols, and punctuation marks. The far right of the SIP contains buttons for Backspace, Cursor Left, Cursor Right, Return, Space, Help, and Special Characters.

The Letter Recognizer will interpret any characters that you write in the SIP area and enter the translated character into the currently running program wherever the cursor is, just as if you were typing on a keyboard. The dashed line through the middle of the SIP is used so letters can be correctly interpreted. For example, because the uppercase and lowercase forms of some letters look the same when handwritten, to write a lowercase *o* or *c* you should write them below the dashed line, as shown here.

Parts of characters that descend below the normal printed line are called *descenders*. Letters such as lowercase *p* and *q* are examples. You should draw them below the dashed line, with the descending part extending below the solid line, as shown below in the left illustration. Similarly, letters with parts that extend above the dashed line, like *b* and *d,* are called *ascenders*. These should be drawn with the body below the dashed line and the ascender above the line, as shown in the right illustration.

Punctuation can also be entered anywhere in the SIP Letter Recognizer, but we found it more effective to use the Special Characters button on the right of the SIP. This button is labeled with three small symbols as its icon: @, *, and $. Tap on the Special Characters button and a soft keyboard pops up, with a wide variety of punctuation marks and symbols, as shown next. You can select the character you want to insert by tapping it with the stylus. As soon as you have selected your character, the panel returns to normal Letter Recognizer mode.

The odd thing that you will need to get used to is that when you are using the Letter Recognizer, you always enter letters as lowercase, even if you want an uppercase letter. To get an uppercase *A,* you enter a lowercase *a* in the leftmost section of the SIP. This is a little counterintuitive and can make the Letter Recognizer difficult for new users.

You can change the way Letter Recognizer behaves and tweak it for your own uses from the Input Options screen. To open this menu, tap the up arrow next to the Input icon in the bottom center of the screen. Make sure the Input method is set to Letter Recognizer and then tap on the Options button.

The first option is Quick Stroke. Checking the box next to this item will allow you to write letters with a single stroke of the stylus. This is different from the Graffiti language that is used on the Palm operating system devices and requires you to learn new ways of writing letters.

The second option is Right To Left Crossbar. Check this box if you are in the habit of putting the horizontal line in letters like *t* and *f* from right to left instead of left to right.

The third option is Allow Accented Characters. Check this box if you want to enter characters that use accents, such as *è* (*e* with a grave accent) in French.

When you've selected the desired options, tap on the OK button to return to the application you're working in.

Using the Block Recognizer

The Block Recognizer is similar to the Letter Recognizer in that you write letters on the SIP one character at a time. This method, however, uses a method identical to the Graffiti language that is standard with Palm hand-held devices. If you are migrating to your iPAQ from a Palm, this option makes it easy to use the same input method that you are used to on the Palm. The SIP is divided into two entry sections. The left section is for letters (both upper- and lowercase). The right section is set up for numerical entry, as shown in Figure 2-6.

The keys on the right side of the SIP do the same as they do in the Letter Recognizer. If at any time you need help figuring out what strokes to use to make a character, tap on the Help (?) button on the right. It will launch a Demo that will show you how to draw any strokes you require.

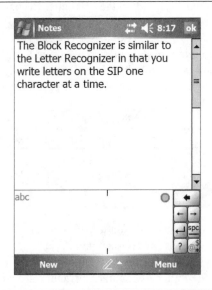

The Block Recognizer is similar to the Letter Recognizer in that you write letters on the SIP one character at a time.

FIGURE 2-6   The Block Recognizer allows you to use a Graffiti-like method to enter text.

Using Transcriber

Transcriber is our favorite way of entering text into the iPAQ, particularly when writing e-mail messages or documents. Transcriber allows you to write anywhere on the screen in cursive, print, or mixed handwriting styles and enters your handwritten text into a document interpreted as words and phrases. Figure 2-7 shows an example of writing with Transcriber.

When using Transcriber, don't write too small. The larger your text, the easier it is to interpret. On the other extreme, don't write so large that you can't fit your text on the screen. Also, remember that you can write anywhere, so use the full screen. Don't worry about writing over whatever is currently displayed; what is shown on the screen will not impact your Transcriber input. Try not to rest your palm on, or allow anything else to come into contact with, the screen.

Another advantage to Transcriber is that it works with any Pocket PC application, but doesn't take up screen space, giving you the maximum view of your application.

Fine-tuning Transcriber   Transcriber can be fine-tuned to improve the accuracy of the handwriting recognition and speed it up, using the Letter Shapes Selector. You access this utility by tapping the Transcriber icon in the tool bar at the bottom of the screen. (In Figure 2-7, it's the second icon from the left—the one above the letter "V" in "View.") The Letter Shapes Selector screen is shown in Figure 2-8.

FIGURE 2-7   Transcriber allows you to write words anywhere on the screen and have them translated into text.

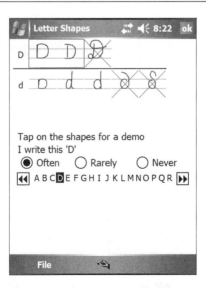

FIGURE 2-8   The Letter Shapes Selector allows you to fine-tune the way Transcriber recognizes cursive and printed writing.

The Letter Shapes Selector window is divided into three parts. Near the bottom of the screen is a horizontal character list with double-arrow icons on either end of the list. You select the letter, number, punctuation mark, or symbol you want to fine-tune from this list by tapping on it. If it's not currently displayed, tap on the double-arrow icon until you see it.

Once you've selected a character from the list, the various ways you can write the character are displayed at the top of the screen. In Figure 2-8, the letter "D" was selected; the top of the screen displays the three ways you can write a capitalized "D" and the five ways you can write the lowercase version of the letter. Now comes the fine-tuning.

Between the character list on the bottom and the handwritten characters at the top of the screen are the words "Tap on the shapes for a demo." Tap once on any character at the top of the screen to select it and tap again to see a brief animation that will show you how to write the character.

Below the words "Tap on the shapes..." are the words "I write this 'D'." Below this are the Often, Rarely, and Never buttons. You can select each character variation at the top of the screen and tag it as being one that you use often, rarely, or never. Any letter you select as rarely used will appear with one slash through the letter, and any that you mark as never used will appear with an *x* marked through the letter.

By default, Transcriber has every variation of every character tagged as being used often. Customizing this list serves two purposes. First, by eliminating letters that you never write, Transcriber has fewer letters to search through each time in order to find a match. This can speed up the handwriting recognition process. Second, there are a number of characters that are written in a similar manner; for example, "2" and one variation of the cursive "Q." If you tag that version of "Q" as never used, Transcriber will never mistake it for a 2.

If you customize Transcriber as just described and share your iPAQ with someone else, it might not recognize their writing. Fortunately, the Letter Shapes Selector lets you set up two profiles: Master or Guest. By default, it assumes you are editing the Master profile. To change that, tap on File at the bottom of the screen and select Guest from the pop-up menu. You can also use this menu to save any recognition profile you've created and open it at a later time.

Selecting Text with Transcriber You need to be able to select letters, words, and phrases in any document to delete them, move them, or apply a font to them. Selecting text is a bit tricky with Transcriber. For example, when you move the stylus over a word on the screen to select it, Transcriber assumes that you are entering a word and attempts to interpret the mark as a character. There are three ways to make sure Transcriber knows you're selecting text.

In the first method, you tap and hold the desired text until the text is selected (usually about two seconds). The text will appear highlighted to show that it is selected. The tap and hold method is fine for selecting text in Calendar or Contacts, but it doesn't work very well in applications like Notes and Word Mobile, which have a tap-and-hold shortcut menu. For example, in Notes, if you tap and hold on a word, a shortcut menu appears, which allows you to insert a date, paste text already saved in the clipboard, or look for alternate words.

The second method to select text is to tap your stylus to the left of the first word in the text you want to select and then drag it to the right, drawing a line across all the text you want to select. Then, without lifting the stylus from the screen, hold the stylus in place at the end of the selection until the text is highlighted.

The third method for selecting text is to suspend Transcriber temporarily by tapping the hand icon in the bottom center of the screen. The Transcriber tool bar and the faint white background around the hand icon will disappear. You can now tap on words and drag your stylus across phrases to select text without it being misinterpreted by Transcriber. When you've selected the text you want, tap on the hand icon to return to Transcriber. Suspending Transcriber enables you to drag and drop, select, and carry out other stylus activity that can be difficult with Transcriber active.

Using Drawn Gestures for Special Characters and Commands   To use Transcriber effectively, you will need to know how to use your stylus to input letter spaces, press ENTER, access commands, and perform other tasks by drawing. The sign you draw on the SIP is called a *gesture*.

- **Enter**   (Equivalent of pressing ENTER on a keyboard) Draw a line straight down and then turn 90 degrees to the left. Make sure the horizontal line is at least twice as long as the vertical line.

- **Space**   (Equivalent of pressing the SPACEBAR on a keyboard) Draw a line straight down and then turn 90 degrees to the right. Make sure the horizontal line is at least twice as long as the vertical line.

- **Backspace**   (Equivalent of pressing BACKSPACE on a keyboard) Draw a line straight to the left.

- **Quick Correct**   (No keyboard equivalent for this gesture) Draw a line straight down and then straight back up. If a word is selected, this will open the alternate words menu (discussed later). If not, it opens the symbol/number soft keyboard.

- **Case change**   (No keyboard equivalent for this gesture) Draw a line straight up. This will change the capitalization of the letter, word, or text block that is currently selected. If a word is selected and it is in mixed upper- and lowercase or lowercase only, it will be changed to all uppercase. If the selected text is all uppercase, it will be changed to lowercase.

- **Undo**   (No keyboard equivalent for this gesture) Draw a line straight up and then back down again. This will undo your last action.

- **Copy**   (Equivalent of pressing CTRL-C on the keyboard) Select text, then draw a line to the right and back again to the left. The selected text will be copied into the clipboard and can be pasted somewhere else later.

- **Cut** (Equivalent of pressing CTRL-X on the keyboard) Select text, then draw a line to the left and back again to the right. The selected text will be removed from its current location and copied into the clipboard so you can paste it somewhere else.

- **Paste** (Equivalent of pressing CTRL-V on the keyboard) Draw a line up and to the right at a 45-degree angle, and then back down to the right at a 45-degree angle. Any text in the clipboard will be pasted into the document at the cursor's current location.

- **Tab** (Equivalent of pressing TAB on the keyboard) Draw a line straight up and then turn 90 degrees to the right. Make sure the horizontal line is at least twice as long as the vertical line.

- **Correction** (No keyboard equivalent for this gesture) Draw a standard check mark, drawing from left to right. This will open the Transcriber correction window.

Transcriber's Alternate Words Menu If a word has been entered poorly or was recognized incorrectly by Transcriber, you can go to the Transcriber correction window to fix the problem. First, select the word that was incorrectly recognized (the fastest way is to double-tap on it). Then open the Alternate Words menu by drawing the vertical down-up Quick Correct gesture, as shown previously.

The alternate words menu pops up, displaying a list of similar words. Tap on the correct word, and it replaces the highlighted word automatically. You can also use the alternate words menu to add a word to the built-in spelling dictionary.

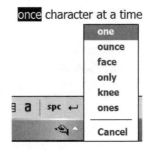

Built-in Calculator and Help Transcriber has a built-in calculator that you can use to solve simple equations by writing them on the screen. For example, if you need to know the answer to 4×3, simply write $\mathbf{4 \times 3 =}$ on the screen, leaving the answer blank. Transcriber will fill in the answer when it transcribes the equation into the application, as shown in Figure 2-9.

Finally, at any point you can tap on the Help icon—the ? on the extreme right of the Transcriber toolbar—to go to the help area and learn more about the options on the toolbar.

Configuring Transcriber Options You can configure Transcriber using the Transcriber: Options setup screen shown in Figure 2-10. To access this screen, tap on the Options icon, which is the leftmost icon on Transcriber's tool bar at the bottom of the screen.

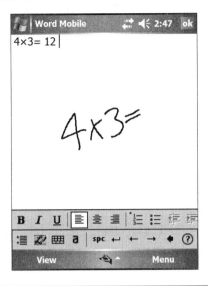

FIGURE 2-9   Transcriber recognizes and carries out simple handwritten calculations.

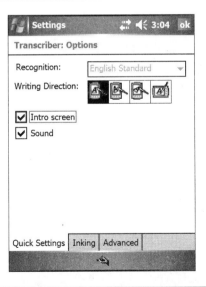

FIGURE 2-10   The main Quick Settings tab of the Transcriber: Options setup screen.

The Transcriber: Options dialog box has three tabs: Quick Settings, Inking, and Advanced. On the Quick Settings Tab there are four options you can set, as shown in Figure 2-10:

- **Recognition** This lets you select handwriting for different languages, but only if those language options are installed on your iPAQ.

- **Writing Direction** This lets you adjust Transcriber so that it recognizes writing in different screen orientations.

- **Intro Screen** Selecting this check box causes the Transcriber introduction screen to be shown each time Transcriber is started. This screen gives basic instructions and also shows how to draw gestures that aren't intuitively obvious like Enter and Backspace.

- **Sound** This option turns Transcriber's sound effects on and off.

The Inking tab is shown in Figure 2-11. It has three options:

- **Recognition Delay** This sliding bar lets you adjust the speed at which Transcriber recognizes words. The shorter the delay, the faster it recognizes words, and the less accurate it is. The longer the delay, the slower it operates, and the more accurate it is.

- **Add Space After** Check this if you want Transcriber to add a space after each recognized word.

- **Pen** This option lets you set the width and color of the handwritten "ink" as it appears on your screen.

FIGURE 2-11   The Inking tab lets you set recognition delay, accuracy, and more.

2

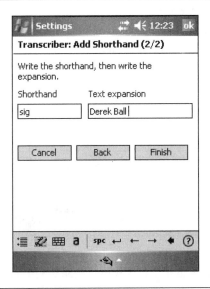

FIGURE 2-12   Transcriber lets you create shorthand that allows you to enter blocks of text, insert dates and time, and even launch applications by writing a few letters or characters on the screen.

The Advanced tab lets you add specialized dictionaries to Transcriber. It also lets you create shorthand to speed up your writing. For example, if you always sign your full name and title to the end of a letter, you can set it up so that whenever you enter "sig" (short for "signature"), Transcriber will enter your full name and title, as shown in Figure 2-12. You can also use the shorthand feature to launch programs, enter the current date and time, your phone number or e-mail address, and more. This is a great feature that will save you a lot of time.

TIP   *If you like Transcriber, check out Calligrapher from Phatware (www.phatware.com), which expands the feature set of Transcriber with functions such as more sophisticated recognition for both cursive and printed text, different pen colors, and faster recognition.*

Using a Keyboard to Enter Data

Another way to enter input into your iPAQ is through a keyboard. You can use the built-in virtual keyboard, the thumb keyboard of the iPAQ Mobile Messenger, or an external keyboard.

Using the Virtual Keyboard

The virtual keyboard, also referred to as a *soft keyboard*, is accessed from the Input Selection menu. Open any application that accepts text input and, at the center of the very bottom of the screen, you'll see an icon indicating the input method being used. To the immediate right of this icon there should be a small up arrow. If it's not there, tap on the icon and it will appear. Next, tap on the arrow to display the input selection menu, and tap on Keyboard to display the virtual QWERTY keyboard as shown here.

You can tap any of these keys, just as you would with a real keyboard, to insert that character where the cursor is in the text. Tap on the 123 key at the top left of the keyboard to display a keyboard with numbers, symbols, and punctuation marks, as shown here. Tapping 123 again will return you to the regular keyboard.

Tapping on the áü button, located on the bottom row of the QWERTY keyboard next to the Ctl key, opens a keyboard with special foreign characters, as shown here. Tapping this key again will return you to the regular keyboard.

Changing Virtual Keyboard Options

You can modify the settings for the virtual keyboard. Open the Input Selection menu as just described and select Options to display the Input Method tab of the Options dialog box, as shown in Figure 2-13. Make sure Keyboard is selected as the input method. By default, the

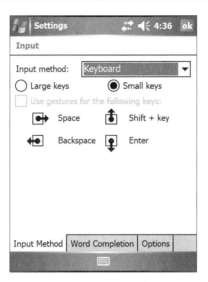

FIGURE 2-13   The Input Method tab of the Keyboard Options dialog box lets you display a keyboard with small or big keys.

Small Keys button is selected on this screen. This causes a complete QWERTY to be displayed, with a number row on the top and directional arrow keys. If you select the Large Keys option, an abbreviated QWERTY keyboard will be displayed with larger keys that are easier to read and tap. However, this keyboard lacks the top number key row, the arrow keys, and a few other function keys.

When the Large Keys option is selected, your are also allowed to select the "Use gestures for the following keys" option. This allows you to use stylus gestures on the screen to enter a space or backspace, to activate the SHIFT key (for a SHIFT+key combo), and to press the ENTER key.

The Word Completion tab shown in Figure 2-14 lets you activate or deactivate the feature that suggests a list of words after you have entered a few characters. By default, this feature is activated and set to suggest one word after you have entered two letters. You can change this to suggest up to four words after entering up to seven letters. You can also select or deselect the Add A Space After A Suggested Word and Replace Text As You Type options on this page.

The final Options tab lets you set the voice recording format, set the zoom level for writing and typing, capitalize the first letter of a sentence, and scroll reaching the last line.

Using an External Keyboard

As adept as you might become with the other handwriting and input methods, they will never equal the speed of a touch typist using a full keyboard. You can purchase a compact collapsing external keyboard from HP directly. Alternatively, third-party accessory manufacturers offer

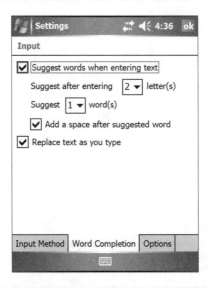

FIGURE 2-14 The Word Completion tab lets you activate or deactivate this feature, as well as configure it.

portable keyboards for the iPAQ. For example, ThinkOutside offers infrared and Bluetooth keyboards, as shown in Figure 2-15. Check out **www.pocketpcmag.com** for reviews of keyboards as they become available.

When attached to the keyboard, the iPAQ is propped up efficiently by a small stand at the back of the keyboard. Most keyboards draw their minimal power requirements from the iPAQ, but some will use an external battery.

FIGURE 2-15 The Stowaway Bluetooth Portable Keyboard communicates wirelessly with Bluetooth-enabled iPAQ Pocket PCs.

In order to make the keyboard work, you must install a keyboard driver onto the iPAQ. This driver can be found on the CD that is supplied with the keyboard (if your CD is missing, you can download the driver from the HP support site at **http://support.HP.com**) or from the third-party vendor's website.

Connecting Your iPAQ to Your PC

There are a variety of ways to connect your iPAQ to your PC for synchronization and connectivity:

- ■ USB (universal serial bus) cable
- ■ Infrared port
- ■ Bluetooth

The most common method is to connect with a USB cable. Your iPAQ will have arrived with either a cradle with a USB cable that plugs into your PC or a sync cable that plugs into the bottom of the iPAQ and into your PC. If your PC doesn't have a USB port, you can get a serial cable from HP, but you must order it separately. Serial syncing is also very slow, so it is not recommended. It is important not to connect your cables to your PC until after you have installed ActiveSync (described in the next section).

Also included in your iPAQ kit will be an AC adapter for charging your batteries. This adapter will plug into the back of your cradle (or into the sync cable if your iPAQ is so equipped). It comes with an adapter that will let you plug directly into the bottom of your iPAQ if you only want to charge the device and not sync. Third-party vendors like Belkin (**www.belkin.com**) offer sync/charger cables that let you charge your iPAQ from the USB port on your PC. If you travel, it saves having to take your adapter with you on the road. In addition, it comes with a cigarette lighter adapter that allows you to charge your iPAQ in your vehicle, which for road warriors is invaluable. As a final bonus, this cable is very reasonably priced—an excellent value for the money. Another popular cable is the miniSync cables put out by BoxWave (**www.boxwave.com**), also available at **www.pocketpctechs.com**.

You can also sync your iPAQ with your infrared port. Many laptop computers have infrared ports that allow you to sync with your iPAQ if the ports are aligned and the port on your laptop is active. You must also first activate the IR ActiveSync settings on your iPAQ by going to ActiveSync | Tools | Connect Via IR. Desktop PCs rarely have infrared ports. This is also a slow sync method and is rarely used. However, it is useful to know that it can be done if you are on the road with your laptop and have forgotten your cable.

If your PC is equipped with Bluetooth and your iPAQ is likewise equipped, you can pair your PC and your iPAQ so that they can ActiveSync over the Bluetooth connection. To do this, you set up a Bluetooth connection as described in Chapter 3 then select ActiveSync | Tools | Connect via Bluetooth to initiate the ActiveSync connection.

Setting Up ActiveSync

Once you have determined how you will connect your iPAQ to your PC, you must configure the software so you can synchronize information and load new software onto the iPAQ. This is accomplished using software provided by Microsoft called ActiveSync. You can install ActiveSync from the CD that came with your iPAQ. The program installs very easily and doesn't need any information from you to get it installed.

ActiveSync lets you synchronize data from the desktop PC version of Outlook with the Pocket PC. It does not synchronize data from third-party Personal Information Managers like ACT!, Lotus Organizer, etc.

If your PC has trouble seeing your iPAQ, it may be because you are running a software firewall on your PC. There are many known issues with the various software firewalls that often will block communication with USB ports in order to protect the integrity of your computer. You will need to check your firewall manual to ensure that your USB ports are not blocked.

Do not connect your iPAQ to your PC with the sync cable until after you have installed ActiveSync on your computer. If you do, the install may not work properly.

Setting Up an ActiveSync Sync Relationship

Once ActiveSync is installed on your PC, you can physically connect your iPAQ to your PC. This will initiate a "conversation" between your iPAQ and the PC as they attempt to establish communication. The first time you connect a new iPAQ to your system, a wizard will open, asking whether you want to set up a Standard Partnership" or a Guest Partnership with the device, as shown in Figure 2-16. A standard partnership is required if you want to allow your iPAQ to synchronize Calendar, Contacts, Notes, e-mail, and other Outlook Mobile data with your PC. If you only want to use the cable to load software or files onto your iPAQ, you can select a guest partnership.

If you chose to establish a standard partnership, the next screen gives you the option of synchronizing directly with a server, as shown in Figure 2-17. Select this option if your company uses Microsoft Exchange Server. If you do select this, you'll need to have the server address and your login credentials available. This feature is great for the mobile corporate professional and allows for syncing Calendar, Contacts, and Inbox of your iPAQ from remote locations over a wireless or wired connection.

If you choose to sync your data using Microsoft Exchange Server, you cannot sync directly with your desktop PC. You can do one or the other, but not both at the same time.

If you just want to sync with your desktop PC, select the Synchronize With This Desktop PC option and click Next. This brings up the Synchronization Options screen, as shown in Figure 2-18. This screen prompts you to choose the information you want to synchronize with your iPAQ. Check the boxes next to the programs you want to sync, and uncheck those you don't want synced.

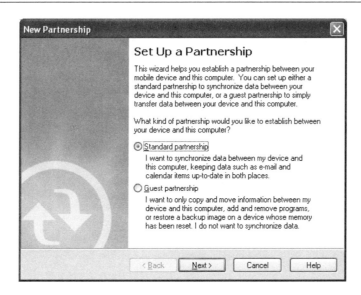

FIGURE 2-16   ActiveSync's Welcome screen gives you the option of establishing a "standard" partnership with your PC or a simple "guest" connection that lets you install programs on the device from a PC.

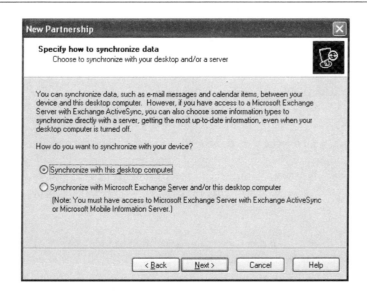

FIGURE 2-17   ActiveSync's initial setup procedure gives you the option of choosing to sync with a Microsoft Exchange Server.

FIGURE 2-18 The Synchronize Options screen lets you select the data you want to sync with your iPAQ.

A list of the Synchronization Options follows, with a brief description of how you can customize ActiveSync to sync only the data you need.

Contacts Option

Check this option if you want to sync your desktop PC's Outlook Contacts list with your Pocket PC. No sync options are available.

Calendar Option

Check this option if you want to sync your desktop PC's Outlook Calendar appointments with your Pocket PC. If you double-click the Calendar option, you are presented with its Settings screen, as shown in Figure 2-19. This screen allows you to specify how far into the past you synchronize appointments. By default, it is set to synchronize the past two week's appointments.

E-mail Option

Select this if you want to sync e-mail between your desktop PC and Pocket PC. Double-clicking the E-mail option displays the E-Mail Synchronization Settings screen, as shown in Figure 2-20. This screen allows you to configure your iPAQ's Inbox to synchronize past e-mail (you can include e-mail from 1 day ago to all past messages). It also lets you specify the size of e-mails synchronized and whether or not you want e-mail attachments synchronized (and how big they can be). Tap on the Select Folders button to specify the Inbox folders you want synchronized.

FIGURE 2-19   The Calendar Synchronization Settings screen lets you specify how far into the past you want to sync appointments.

You can only sync e-mail with the first PC you set up a partnership with. There is no option to change which PC you sync e-mail with after you set up the first partnership.

Tasks Option

Check this option if you want to sync your desktop PC's Outlook Tasks with your Pocket PC. No sync options are available.

FIGURE 2-20   The E-Mail Synchronization Settings screen lets you control what e-mail messages are synced with your iPAQ.

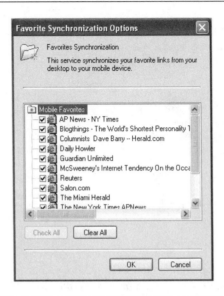

FIGURE 2-21 The Favorites Synchronization Options screen lets you specify which of your Mobile Favorites links are synced with the iPAQ.

Sync Notes

Check this option if you want to sync your desktop PC's Outlook Calendar appointments with your Pocket PC. No sync options are available.

Favorites Option

Check this option if you want to sync your desktop PC's Internet Explorer Favorites list with your Pocket PC. Double-click the Favorites option to display the Favorites Synchronization Options screen, as shown in Figure 2-21. This allows you to select which of your files you would like to synchronize with your iPAQ.

Files Option

Check this option if you want to sync files between your desktop PC and iPAQ. When you check this option, ActiveSync will ask you if it's OK to create a subfolder in your PC's My Documents folder. A link to the folder is also placed on your PC's desktop. Any documents in this folder will be synchronized automatically with the My Documents folder on your iPAQ every time you synchronize your Pocket PC. In the File Synchronization Settings dialog box, shown in Figure 2-22, you can choose not to synchronize specific files that are in these folders by selecting them and clicking the Remove button. You can add additional files to the list by clicking the Add button and selecting the file from the File Selection dialog box.

FIGURE 2-22   The File Synchronization Settings screen lets you specify which files you want to sync with your iPAQ.

Media Option

Click this box if you want to sync media content with your iPAQ. You need version 10 of Windows Media Player on your desktop PC to use this option. If you don't have version 10 on your PC, then the first time you try and sync, you'll get a message in ActiveSync's main screen next to the Media icon, telling you that "Setup must be completed," as shown in Figure 2-23. Click that, and you'll be asked if you want to install it on your PC. Answer OK and you'll be directed to the Media Player web page, where you can download and install the latest version of the program.

When Windows Media Player 10 is installed on your desktop PC, you're prompted to establish a media partnership between your desktop PC and Pocket PC. To be able to do this, you must have a 32MB or greater SD or CF storage card in one of the iPAQ's card slots. With the card in the slot, open Media Player on your desktop PC, click the Sync tab, and follow the instructions to establish and configure the partnership. You can also use the Sync tab to modify the settings.

Resolving Synchronization Conflicts

You can also fine-tune how ActiveSync handles synchronization conflicts. These rare events occur when changes are made to the same Outlook item on both the Pocket PC and desktop PC while the two devices are not connected. Occasionally, ActiveSync won't be able to figure out which change takes precedence.

FIGURE 2-23 To use the ActiveSync's Media sync feature, you need Windows Media Player 10 installed on your desktop PC. If it's not there, you'll receive a "Setup must be completed" message when you try to sync.

By default, ActiveSync expects the data on the desktop PC to be correct, but you can tell it to favor the Pocket PC change. To do this, go to ActiveSync's Options screen and select the computer with which you are synchronizing (it should be either Windows PC or Exchange Server). Then click the Settings button to bring up the Desktop Computer Settings screen, as shown in Figure 2-24. The second data field on this screen, If There Is A Conflict, lets you tell ActiveSync to Replace Item On Device or Replace Item On Desktop. This screen also lets you tell ActiveSync to sync the iPAQ's date and time with the desktop PC.

Converting Files between Your Desktop and Pocket PC

If you have an older iPAQ (prior to Windows Mobile 5), by default, ActiveSync automatically converts certain files when you copy them from your desktop PC to your Pocket PC, or vice versa. For example, when you use ActiveSync to copy a worksheet created by Excel Mobile from the Pocket PC to the desktop PC, ActiveSync converts it from the Pocket Excel Workbook format (.pxl) to the Microsoft Excel Worksheet format (.xls). You can change these conversion settings or disable them completely from the Conversion Properties screen shown in Figure 2-25. To open it, go to the ActiveSync Tools menu, select Advance Tools, and click the Edit File Conversions Settings option. From this screen, you can disable ActiveSync's file conversion capabilities. You can also access the Device To Desktop or the Desktop To Device conversion tabs, which allow you to change the way documents are converted.

NOTE

The Pocket Word converter is no longer installed with AS4. However, if you install 3.8 and upgrade, it is still supported.

2

FIGURE 2-24   You can tell ActiveSync how to resolve conflicts between it and your desktop PC or Exchange Server.

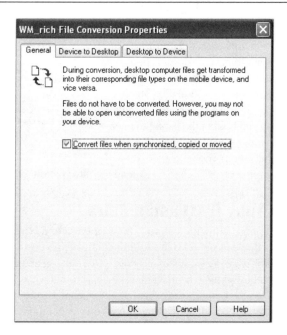

FIGURE 2-25   In the Conversion Properties dialog on the General tab, uncheck the Convert Files When Synchronized, Copied Or Moved box to disable ActiveSync's file conversion capabilities.

Disabling the file conversion feature ensures that files copied to the iPAQ remain in their original format. This allows you to use the iPAQ as a portable hard drive to move files between your work and home computers.

Scheduling ActiveSync Data Synchronization

By default, ActiveSync 4 will synchronize data as soon as you connect your iPAQ to your PC, and it will immediately synchronize any changes you make to Outlook while the PC and iPAQ remain connected. In previous versions of ActiveSync, you could change this. With 4, however, this is the only option available for a direct connection between the Pocket PC and desktop PC.

Beaming Data for Easy Transfer

There is a very convenient way for people who have Pocket PC devices to share data: beaming information back and forth through the infrared ports that are standard on most Pocket PCs and all iPAQs.

Beaming Between Two Pocket PCs

To beam between two Pocket PCs, you simply align the two infrared ports, and, on the device that is sending information, choose the information you want to beam. You can choose to beam contacts, appointments, notes, tasks, or files. For example, say you want to beam contact information about a particular individual to another Pocket PC. Find the individual in your Contacts list. Then tap and hold in the listing to open the Editing menu, as shown here. To send the contact, select the Beam Contact option from this menu. The sending iPAQ will immediately begin searching for another Pocket PC to send the information to.

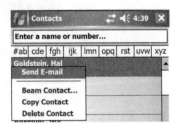

Beaming Between Your iPAQ and a Palm

All iPAQs include OBEX support, allowing you to beam to a Palm or a Nokia cell phone. There are also third-party products that can improve the beaming ability on your iPAQ. One of these is Peacemaker from Conduits Software. Peacemaker has both a free version and a more sophisticated full version. The free version allows you to beam contacts to and from devices one contact at a time. The paid version allows you to select multiple data sets (multiple contacts, appointments, files, and so on) of information and transfer them all at the same time. You can get more information from Conduits directly at **www.conduits.com**.

Wrap It Up

The iPAQ is a very easy device to start using right away, and once you master the basics and get it configured, you are ready to begin doing much more! Have fun exploring the possibilities of your new tool with the rest of this book.

Chapter 3

Connect Wirelessly with Your iPAQ

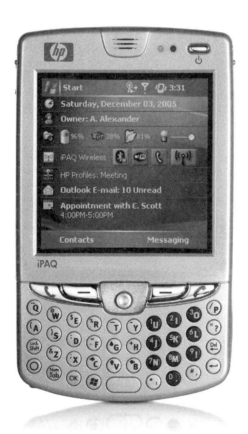

How to...

- Configure your iPAQ for wireless data
- Identify when to use the different wireless networks
- Connect your iPAQ using a cellular data connection (GPRS/CDMA)
- Connect your iPAQ using WiFi
- Connect your iPAQ using Bluetooth
- Browse the Web using Pocket Internet Explorer
- Use third-party wireless applications

The most useful and, arguably, the most interesting features of your iPAQ involve wireless connectivity. Obvious examples include the using the phone, sending and receiving e-mail, and browsing the Web, but there are many other things that you can do using the wireless capabilities of your iPAQ. This chapter includes topics such as configuring your iPAQ for wireless connectivity including cellular, Bluetooth, and WiFi; using Multimedia Messaging Service (MMS) and using Short Messaging Service (SMS); and also includes a selection of other wireless options and third-party wireless applications designed for your iPAQ.

TIP   *What happens to your data connection when a phone call is coming in on your iPAQ? For most wireless networks and iPAQ models during a voice call or text messaging, any data services such as e-mail or Internet browsing are suspended until you are finished with the phone; then they automatically resume.*

The setup to connect using a wireless network depends on the type of wireless connection you want to make. iPAQ devices are capable of several different types of wireless networking, including cellular (GPRS or CDMA), WLAN (WiFi/802.11), Bluetooth, and infrared. Because each type of wireless connection uses a unique technology, each one requires specific configuration and depends on the availability of other networking components.

- To make a cellular data connection (GPRS or CDMA):
  - Your iPAQ must have a service contract with a wireless service provider (WSP).
  - You must be in range of a cellular tower.
- To make a WLAN (WiFi/802.11) connection:
  - You must be no more that 100 feet from a WLAN access point.
  - If the access point is protected from open access, you will also need to have the privacy key.
- To make a Bluetooth connection:
  - Your Bluetooth must be turned on and must be no more than 30 feet from another Bluetooth capable device, in any direction, that you want to connect to.
  - Both Bluetooth devices must share the same profiles and optional PIN to connect.

■ To use infrared:

   ■ Your iPAQ infrared port must be aligned with the infrared port on another device no
     more than 7 inches apart.

This chapter covers all of these wireless networking topics.

Use Your iPAQ in Both Wireless and Nonwireless Modes

Your iPAQ essentially uses two independent modes: organizer mode, also called offline mode,
and wireless (phone, SMS, e-mail, web browsing) mode. While the wireless mode is turned off
you can still use all of the functions that don't require wireless connectivity such as the organizer,
contact list, calendar, music, camera, and so on. One reason you may want to leave the wireless
mode off when you are not using it is that is significantly improves how long you can go without
recharging your iPAQ battery. You may also want to turn the wireless mode off while continuing
to use the nonwireless features on an airplane, where wireless mode may interfere with the
airplane navigation systems—although you may still hear comments from flight attendants when
they see you using your iPAQ on the plane.

Making Sense of the Various Wireless Networks

You have likely noticed that there is a lot of industry-specific technical jargon regarding the world
of wireless: GSM, 802.11b, Bluetooth, WLAN, CDMA, CDPD, VoIP, GPRS, GPS, Quad-band, and
so on. And yes, there is a fair bit of it in this book. However, while each type of wireless network
technology is technically different and each offers advantages and disadvantages, many are very
similar from the user's perspective. The fastest wireless network right now is still WLAN, at around
11Mb per second, but it is limited to relatively short range so you can't be more than around 100 feet
from a WLAN access point. Bluetooth is an even shorter range wireless technology—about
30 feet—but tends to take a lot less power than WLAN. There is also a wide range of wireless
service provided by various cellular carriers or wireless service providers (WSPs) such as CDMA,
GSM, GPRS, EvDO, and Edge. These technologies usually offer much more range and some are
available in virtually every part of the world. They are the only real choice for the globetrotting user
of mobile phone and e-mail technologies. The most common types of wireless networks offered by
wireless service providers are listed in Table 3-1; the types of wireless network technologies that
don't require a wireless service provider are listed in Table 3-2.

Connect Wirelessly Using a Cellular Data Account

The wireless networking technologies that offer the widest physical range and give you the most
mobility while still being connected are certainly the cellular networks such as CDMA (including
EvDO and CDMA 1xRTT) and GPRS (including EDGE and GSM). In addition to technical
differences, the cellular networks differ from other wireless networking technologies in that you
have to pay to use the networks. This means that you sign up with your local wireless service
provider such as Sprint, Bell, Rogers, Orange, Cingular, AT&T, T-Mobile on a service contract,

Protocol	Bandwidth	Specifics
GSM	9.6Kbps–14.4Kbps	GSM (Global System for Mobile) communication is the most widely deployed wireless technology in the world. If your iPAQ uses a GSM provider, you will be able to travel virtually anywhere in the populated world and still get coverage.
GPRS	56Kbps	GPRS (General Packet Radio Service) is an upgraded version of GSM and is widely deployed throughout the world.
EDGE	70–135Kbps	EDGE (Enhanced Data for Global Evolution) is one of the latest wireless technologies. It is an evolution of the GSM standard, and claims are often made that it is three times faster than GPRS; we say 'claims' only because theoretical and real-world performance can be quite different and is highly dependent on many factors.
CDMA	14.4Kbps	CDMA (Code Division Multiple Access) is network technology that is beginning to be superseded by CDMA 1xRTT and EvDO and is limited to North America. CDMA data connectivity functions like a dial-up modem, so you need to configure the dial-up information to browse the Web and send and receive e-mail.
CDMA 1xRTT	56Kbps–384Kbps	CDMA 1xRTT, also known as CDMA2000 and IMT-CDMA Multicarrier, is a first-phase 3G wireless network technology and is a faster version of CDMA.
EvDO	500Kbps	EvDO (Evolution Data Only or Evolution Data Optimized), also abbreviated as EVDO, EV-DO, EvDO, 1xEV-DO, or 1xEvDO, is a wireless radio broadband data protocol that is being provided by CDMA mobile phone providers such as Verizon and Sprint because it is much faster than CDMA.
CDPD	19.2Kbps	CDPD (Cellular Digital Packet Data) was formerly the most widely deployed wireless data and voice transmission technology, but it has been superseded by some of the more recent and faster technologies such as EDGE, CDMA 1xRTT, and GPRS.

TABLE 3-1   Carrier wireless networks

Protocol	Bandwidth and Range	Specifics
Bluetooth	720Kbps data transfer within a range of 30 feet	Bluetooth began as a global initiative by Ericsson, IBM, Intel, Nokia, and Toshiba to set a standard for short-range cable-free connectivity between mobile phones, mobile PCs, handheld computers, and other devices such as printers and headphones.
WLAN	11Mbps with a range of up to 100 feet	WLAN, also known as WiFi or 802.11, is a short-range wireless technology that connects a wireless device such as your iPAQ to an access point that is connected to a wired network.

TABLE 3-2   Noncarrier wireless networks

and you receive monthly bills for the amount of voice, data, and other network services that you use in that month. This section talks specifically about using wireless data over a cellular data network. Other wireless data technologies such as WLAN, Bluetooth, and infrared are discussed later in this chapter.

Using Wireless E-mail, Web Browsing, and Data Applications on Your iPAQ

Your iPAQ is essentially two wireless devices in one: a cell phone and a wireless computer. The wireless computer component of your iPAQ requires different wireless services than the phone. It is important to understand that wireless services providers—the company you pay to use your iPAQ phone—tend to view wireless voice and wireless data separately. Ideally, your service contract and iPAQ were both set up correctly when you purchased your iPAQ and you were immediately able to use the mobile phone and take advantage of advanced features like SMS, MMS, e-mail, and the Internet. But be aware that not all wireless service providers offer data services, and data services are not automatically included in your phone plan.

Make sure that your service contract includes data service and that your service has been activated. Some providers even separate data services into Internet, MMS, and SMS, so you will have to ensure that all are included in your plan in order to take advantage of all of the features of your iPAQ. Some of the brand names for data services are listed later in this chapter.

Set Up Your Cellular Wireless and Data Connections

As mentioned earlier, many iPAQs offer more than one wireless connectivity technology for you to use. Each technology—Bluetooth, WLAN, infrared and cellular—has its own pros and cons. In this section, we will discuss cellular technologies such as GPRS, CDMA, EDGE, and EvDO. If your iPAQ features a built-in cellular phone, it is equipped with cellular technology.

Your SIM Card (GPRS/GSM/EDGE Only)

If your iPAQ is hosted on the Sprint or Verizon wireless network, you don't need a SIM as the settings are downloaded directly to your CDMA radio and are specific to each carrier. For instance, the same settings that work on the Sprint CDMA network will not work on the Verizon network. If your iPAQ is a GSM/GPRS/EDGE version and is hosted by Cingular, T-Mobile, or AT&T, and depending on where you purchased your device, the SIM card may have already been inserted into your iPAQ. In order to use the phone, e-mail, or web features of your iPAQ, you will need an activated SIM card. If a SIM card did not come with your iPAQ, you need to contact your mobile service provider to subscribe to a GPRS data plan and you will be given a SIM card that you insert in to the SIM slot on your iPAQ. In this case you can even use the same SIM card with any GPRS phone that has a SIM card slot.

NOTE *SIM stands for "Subscriber Identification Module" or "Subscriber Identity Module." SIM cards are small smart cards based on the GSM technology that fit inside phones. Your SIM card contains personalized information about you, including your network activation, phone number, and voice mail access number. Your wireless service provider uses the SIM information to register and track your iPAQ on the network.*

Brand Names for Wireless Data Services

When dealing with a wireless service provider—also known as a carrier—it is helpful to be aware that each has their own marketing names for wireless data services. Some examples include:

- Cingular: Data Connect
- Fido–GPRS: GPRS Access
- Rogers AT&T: GPRS Data Access
- Sprint PCS: 1xRTT*- PCS Vision
- Nextel: Web Plan
- Verizon: NationalAccess, BroadbandAccess, or PDA/Smartphone E-mail
- T-Mobile: Wireless data and text/instant messages

What if My Wireless Service Provider Does Not Offer Wireless Internet Service?

Some wireless service providers offer wireless data but not wireless Internet, although this is becoming less common. If your wireless service provider does not offer wireless Internet service for your iPAQ, you may also need an Internet Service Provider (ISP). Because some wireless service providers offer data services—the ability to send/receive data wirelessly—but will not act as a gateway to the Internet. In this situation, you may need to use a separate ISP to access the Internet with your iPAQ.

Another option is to change your service contract to another wireless service provider that offers full voice, data, and Internet service. However, this may not be a realistic option if you live in an area where there is only coverage by one wireless service provider, if you are locked into a long-term contract, or if your iPAQ is "SIM locked" or on a CDMA network and permanently linked to a particular wireless service provider.

Connect Your iPAQ to Your Wireless Service Provider

It is usually a good idea to leave your iPAQ settings at the automatic network settings, but there are times when you may want to manually select a different wireless network to use.

Getting Connected with Your Wireless Service Provider   Ideally, this is something that should be taken care of by your WSP. The various networks, different iPAQs, and different WSP configurations can make getting set up challenging for the average user, especially since there is so much information you need to gather before you can begin configuring. You may find that some wireless service providers don't want to share network information and will insist on configuring your iPAQ automatically when it connects—this is a good thing—or they may insist that you take your iPAQ to a service center where it can be configured. A major reason you may need to configure your cellular data settings is if you are roaming outside of your normal coverage area where your normal WSP may not have a network.

Keep in mind that your iPAQ user documentation covers the more technical tasks of getting connected and is always a great reference point. Before you get started there is some information that you need. If you don't have this information, you will need to either look at any paper work that your received when you signed up for service or contact your wireless service provider directly (also known as a carrier). The information that you need is

- The name of your wireless service provider (the company you pay for cellular phone and data service, for example, Nextel, Verizon, T-Mobile, Cingular, Sprint, Telus, Rogers, Orange)
- The name of the data access point, also known as the APN (Access Point Name)
- Username and password
- DNS address
- IP address

Other information that you will need, depending on the type of connection you are making, includes:

- To make an MMS connection:
    - MMS center address
    - APN for MMS server if it is different than the APN for the Internet connection
    - Username and password
    - IP address and port
- To make a WAP (Wireless Application Protocol) connection:
    - IP address and port

Windows Mobile 5

When you have the IP address and port, follow these steps to set up the connection:

1. Select Start | Settings, then select the Connections tab and select Connections.
2. Select the Advanced tab, then select Networks.
3. To connect to a private network, select the drop-down Menu and select My Work Network.
4. Select New, then select the Modem tab.
5. Enter a name for your connection; this name can be whatever helps you remember the connection name.
6. Select a modem from the drop-down list. It's important to select either Cellular Line or Cellular Line (GPRS, 3G) to connect through your wireless service provider and tap Next.
7. Enter your access point (if you don't have this information you can get it from your wireless service provider) and tap Next.
8. Tap Finish, then select OK.

Windows Mobile 2003 SE (GSM/GPRS/EDGE Networks Only)

When you have the IP address and port, follow these steps to set up the connection:

1. Select Start | Settings | Connections tab.
2. Select the GSM/GPRS Manager.
3. Tap the down arrow under Country and select the appropriate country name.
4. From the Operator drop-down menu, select the Create New option.
5. Enter the new service provider name.
6. Tap Next.

Send and Receive E-mail on Your iPAQ

Your iPAQ likely arrived with a preinstalled version of Microsoft Outlook Mobile (earlier version was called Microsoft Pocket Outlook). Outlook Mobile is a great e-mail client and will work with most types of e-mail accounts; it is covered in detail in Chapter 12. If you want to use your iPAQ with a corporate e-mail account, this topic is covered in detail in Chapter 14. But what if you don't already have an e-mail account and you want to be able to send and receive e-mail on your iPAQ? Fortunately, you have several options, and they are covered in this section.

If you don't already have an existing e-mail account and don't need to connect to a corporate account, your options are a little simpler because you don't have to worry about corporate e-mail solutions like Exchange or Lotus Domino or the bureaucracy that can be associated with corporate IT and security people. With corporate e-mail out of the picture, your best alternative options are POP3 and web-based e-mail.

Set Up a New POP3 E-Mail Account

POP3 (Post Office Protocol 3) is a common e-mail standard that is widely supported, so it is relatively easy to find a service provider that offers POP3 e-mail accounts.

If You Have a Home Internet Connection

If you already have an Internet service provider that provides your home with Internet access, the company supplying your connection can likely set you up with a POP3 e-mail account. In fact, the cost is often included in your Internet fees. Contact the company to find out how to get set up, and then get the POP3 setup.

If You Don't Have a Home Internet Connection

If you do not have a home Internet connection, there are organizations that provide free POP3 e-mail accounts. As with most things, you get what you pay for, so if you choose to use a free provider, don't expect high reliability or top-notch service. Examples include **www.hotpop.com** and **www.gmx.co.uk**, but a quick Internet search will produce several others. The most reliable

POP3 option is to purchase e-mail service from a web-hosting company. The cost of POP3 service is reasonable (about $20 per year in North America) and will vary between providers, so shop around and make sure you find a provider that is both reasonably priced and that will provide quality customer service when you need it. E-mail is transported on the Internet, so the physical location of the company hosting your POP3 account is relatively unimportant. This said, though, service may be slower if your e-mail server is located on a different continent.

Set Up a New Web-Based E-Mail Account

The fastest and simplest way to set up an e-mail account is to use web-based e-mail. To do this, just use your iPAQ web browser to open a web page and log on to view and send e-mail using the web page. Before you decide whether web-based e-mail is right for you, take a look at the following sections that describe some of the advantages and disadvantages of using it.

Advantages of Web-Based E-Mail

There are pros and cons associated with each of your iPAQ e-mail options. Here are some of the best features of web-based e-mail:

- **Cost-effective**   In fact, web-based e-mail is usually free.
- **Easy to set up**   Just fill out a form and you're registered.
- **Easy to use**   Web-based e-mail typically has simple user-friendly interfaces.
- **Accessible**   Web-based e-mail can be accessed easily from any device with a web browser, including your home, office, or neighbor's PC. (Note that POP3 e-mail can also be accessed from other computers and devices, but it's not nearly as easy to set up.)

Disadvantages of Web-Based E-Mail

While web-based e-mail is the easiest option to set up, there are some limitations you should be aware of:

- **Screen size**   Browsing web pages that are generally designed for a much larger screen can be trying. (Note, however, that an increasing number of web-based e-mail providers provide specific pages that are formatted for mobile devices such as your iPAQ.)
- **Slow speed**   Browsing web pages on most wireless networks can be too slow for many users, so you may want to first try out web-based e-mail to make sure it's not too slow for you. However, many users don't find speed to be a problem.
- **Having to check for e-mail**   One of the advantages of POP3 e-mail is that you can set up the client software to check for new messages at timed intervals and to alert you when new messages are received. When you use web-based e-mail, you have to log into your e-mail to see if there is anything new. This means that important e-mail may go unnoticed for long periods of time until you check you account.

Some examples of organizations that offer free web-based e-mail include the following:

- Yahoo! Mobile Mail: **www.yahoo.com**
  (mobile site: **http://mobile.yahoo.com/mail**)

- Hotmail Mobile: **www.hotmail.com**
  (mobile site: **http://mobile.msn.com/hm/folder.aspx**)

Ultimately, you may need to try a few different e-mail options to find the best one for you.

Use Online Support Resources

If you're more of a figure-it-out-yourself type of person, many service providers have excellent online knowledge bases that can supply you with all the information you need. If you know the company that provides your e-mail, go to their website and find the Support section. Microsoft also has an excellent Support and FAQ section at **www.microsoft.com/windowsmobile/**.

Use Pocket Internet Explorer

Many are regular users of PC Internet browsers such as Firefox, MS Internet Explorer, Netscape Navigator, and others. The web browsing experience on an iPAQ is certainly a little different due to the reduced screen size and generally slower network connections. Your iPAQ likely has MS Pocket Internet Explorer built in to your ROM and your iPAQ user documentation covers all of the features of the Pocket IE browser in detail. In this section, we will discuss some of the features that make the biggest difference to the user experience as well as features and functionality that are significantly different than PC-based browsers.

Generally, the MS Pocket Internet applications are very similar on both Windows Mobile 5 and Windows Mobile 2003 SE, with the primary difference being how the menus are arranged. The features that are new in Pocket IE for Windows Mobile 5 include the ability to save images from a website, a full-screen mode, and a download status bar that keeps you informed of a page that is currently downloading. Fortunately, there are not so many options that you'll get lost, and most screens and functions can be easily located by viewing the menus.

The following are the Pocket IE features that are similar to PC web browsers:

- **Favorites** Allows you to save the URLs of websites you visit often.
- **Properties** Allows you to view the properties of specific web pages such as size and encryption.
- **Home page** Allows you to set a specific page to load whenever you launch Pocket IE.
- **Memory settings** Allows you to clear your History of visited websites and cached web content saved from previously visited web pages.
- **Cookies and Security settings** Allows you to set whether or not you want the browser to save cookies and warn you when you are viewing a page that is not secure.

The following are some differences that will help to make your iPAQ wireless web browsing experience better:

- **Layout**   Due to the diminutive screen on your iPAQ, you can change how you want to view pages, including full screen, desktop (you will have to scroll around to see the entire page), and one column that renders the page as one long thin page but minimizes the need for horizontal scrolling.

- **Show images**   Because most wireless networks are slower than wired networks and most of the download size of web pages tends to be the images, you may want to choose to not download the images to make browsing quicker.

- **Show Address bar**   To give you more screen real-estate you have the option of hiding the Address bar.

- **Text size**   You have the option of changing the size of text to either get more text on the screen by choosing small text or increase text size so that it is easier to read.

Intranet Specific Features in Internet Explorer Mobile

If your company has an Intranet that you would like to view using your iPAQ, there are some specific steps you need to take to help your iPAQ deal with loading a page that is not available on the public Internet. By default, when you enter a URL web page address in the Address bar on your iPAQ, it will try to find the page on the Internet. We won't go into detail about network idiosyncrasies, as there are many different configurations. but it is important to know that if an Intranet address that you want to browse has a period in the address (for example, **intranet .company.com**), you need to add it to the Exceptions list in MS Internet Explorer Mobile. To access the Exceptions list, follow these steps:

1. Select Start | Settings | Connections tab.
2. Select Connections | Advanced tab | Exceptions.
3. Tap Add New URL.
4. In the Work URL field, enter the Intranet URL. If you use several URLs that share the same root company name (for example, **sales.company.com** and **hr.company.com**), you can avoid entering each one individually by entering ***.company.com**.

Instant Message and Chat on Your iPAQ with MSN Messenger

If you are already familiar with MSN Messenger for the desktop PC, the mobile version is very similar. If you are new to instant messaging, you'll find it easy to learn and surprisingly useful. You need to be running the MSN Messenger on your iPAQ and you will need an active Internet connection for the MSN Messenger to work.

What Is So Great about Instant Messaging (IM)?   There are many ways to communicate with an iPAQ: voice, text messaging, e-mail, MMS, and so on, so what is so great about something like MSN Messenger? Well, there are several scenarios when instant messaging makes more sense than other types of communication, and sometimes it is just more fun. The best feature is the interactivity of instant messaging. Communication is much more like a real-time conversation that involves text instead of voice, and you can even have instant message conversations with multiple people at the same time. The real-time factor is important because it really cuts down on the delayed response involved in other types of communication such as e-mail. IM is also an excellent choice because it tends to be less expensive than phoning someone. For example, if you lose a friend at the theater, instead of phoning their mobile, you can simply begin a conversation with them using IM:

> "Where are you?"

> "I am getting popcorn"

> "Ok, meet U at theater 8 in 5 mins"

> "Cool"

To download the latest version of MSN Messenger for Windows Mobile–powered Devices go to **www.microsoft.com/windowsmobile/downloads/msnmessenger**.

MSN Messenger offers many features. You can

■ Maintain a list of other MSN Messenger users.

■ Receive alerts if others are trying to contact you.

■ Use the My Text feature to quickly type frequently used messages instead of typing the entire message out.

■ See when the person you are Instant Messaging is writing back to you so that you know that a message is on its way, which makes the conversation more interactive than e-mail.

Connect Your iPAQ Using Infrared

Infrared is a short distance line-of-sight wireless technology. Most iPAQs support slow infrared (SIR). SIR is also defined as IrDA 1 and has a maximum data transmission rate of 1.15Mbps (megabits per second) with a maximum infrared (IR) transmission distance of 7.8 inches (20 centimeters). Check your iPAQ documentation to find out exactly which IR specification is implemented on your iPAQ.

ActiveSync Using Infrared

A great use of infrared technology with the iPAQ is synchronizing your iPAQ with a laptop that is equipped with an infrared port. We will use that example here because connecting your iPAQ to any infrared-capable device is similar.

*If your PC isn't equipped with an infrared port, there are third-party USB infrared ports that you can add to most PCs that have a USB port. To see what is available, USB Gear (**www.usbgear.com**) offers several options.*

Instead of using a wired cradle or sync cable to ActiveSync your iPAQ to your PC, you can use infrared to accomplish the same thing wirelessly. One limitation is that this only works on computers running Microsoft Windows 98 SE, Me, 2000, or XP operating systems. To set up an infrared connection to your PC follow these steps:

3

1. Synchronize your iPAQ with your PC using the desktop cradle or sync cable before trying to establish an ActiveSync connection via infrared.

2. If your PC infrared port is not already configured to receive connections, you will have to follow the PC user manual to correctly install and set up your infrared port.

3. Remove your iPAQ from the cradle and line up the infrared port with your PC infrared port so that there is nothing in between them and they are no more than 7.8 inches (20 centimeters) from each other.

4. To launch a connection and start synchronization using infrared, on your iPAQ, select Start | Programs | ActiveSync | Tools | Connect via IR.

5. When the sync is finished and you want to disconnect, move the iPAQ away from the PC or tap the "X" in the upper right of the screen to end the connection.

Beam a Contact Using Infrared

Another useful thing you can use infrared for is to beam a contact to another infrared-capable device. This allows you to save your business cards and avoid having to write down your information for people; beam it to them instead. For example, you meet someone at a conference and want them to follow up with you later on. If they have an infrared-capable iPAQ, you can simply transfer your contact information from your iPAQ to theirs using infrared. To do this follow these steps:

1. Launch your phone and select Contacts.

2. Find the contact that you want to beam—in this example, it is you.

3. Select the menu button and select Beam Contact.

4. Line up the infrared ports on each iPAQ at 6 inches or less apart.

5. Once the ports are aligned, the name of the receiving device will show up in the list. Select Tap to Send and the contact will be beamed to the other device.

At first this might seem less intuitive than writing someone's contact down on paper, but remember, if you do that, they will still have to manually enter your info into their PC or iPAQ contact list. The beaming process only takes about 10 to15 seconds, including tapping through menus and aligning the devices.

Connect Your iPAQ Using WLAN

WLAN (wireless local area network), also known as WiFi and 802.11b, is a short range wireless technology that connects a wireless device such as your iPAQ to an access point that is connected to a wired network. WLAN operates at a speed of 11Mbps, which is very fast in the world of wireless data, and has a range of up to 100 feet. If your iPAQ has built-in WLAN capability, you can utilize WLANs, hotspots, and access points on your iPAQ. If your iPAQ doesn't offer built-in WLAN capability, there are add-on cards that you can use with your iPAQ to allow you to utilize WLAN networks. A few options are listed later in this chapter in the section, "Expand Your iPAQ Connectivity with Expansion Cards."

Configuring WLAN settings to connect to a WLAN can be quite confusing if you are not already familiar with computer networking concepts. For this reason, if you don't have experience with computer networks and you would like to use a WLAN at your job, this is a good time to enlist the help of your friendly neighborhood IT professional. If your iPAQ has built-in WLAN capability, your iPAQ user documentation is generally very helpful in describing the more technical aspects of configuring your iPAQ WLAN settings. To understand the settings, however, you'll first need to get up to speed with WLAN specific terminology:

- **Wireless access point (also known as a wireless router or wireless hub)**   For most WLAN configurations, a wireless access point is a critical component. It is a device that connects into an existing network and sends and receives data from other wireless devices such as a WLAN-capable iPAQ to gain access to a network or to go out onto the Internet.

- **802.11 standard**   802.11 is a more technical name for wireless LAN and is the approved standard specification for radio technology from the Institute of Electrical and Electronic Engineers (IEEE) used for WLAN. The great thing about a standard is that any hardware that adheres to the standard will generally interoperate with other devices that adhere to the standard. This means that your iPAQ WLAN will work with virtually any WLAN component.

- **Device-to-computer or ad-hoc**   Generally, most WLAN connections are set up so that a WLAN device such as your iPAQ connects to a WLAN access point (wireless router), but you can also set up a connection to another WLAN device without using a WLAN access point to facilitate the connection. Connections made in this mode are called device-to-computer or ad-hoc connections. Using this mode allows you to connect peer-to-peer; for example, you can use WLAN to connect your iPAQ directly to your WLAN-capable PC.

- **Encryption**   The concept of encryption is highly important for wireless data communication. Encryption involves an algorithm that scrambles information then reassembles it when it has been received to prevent against unauthorized access. WLAN uses encryption most of the time.

- **Hotspot**   This term has become a buzz word for the cappuccino crowd—it refers to a public or private area where you can access a WLAN. Some places, such as libraries, hotel lobbies, or coffee shops, may provide a WLAN hotspot and may or may not charge for access.

3

■ **Proxy server**   In some instances, you will need to connect through a proxy server, which is a server that acts as an intermediary between a PC or iPAQ user and the Internet. The proxy server helps ensure security and administrative control by separating the enterprise network from the outside network and a firewall server that protects the enterprise network from outside intrusion. If you are connected to your ISP or private network during ActiveSync synchronization, your iPAQ should download the proper proxy settings from your PC. However, if these settings are not on your PC or need to be changed, you will need to set them up manually.

■ **Internet Protocol (IP)**   Every computer on the Internet has a unique number assigned to it. This number is its IP address. The IP address is a 128-bit number that identifies the sender and receiver of information that is sent across the Internet. For example when you send an e-mail message, the Internet Protocol part of TCP/IP includes your IP address in the message to identify your computer or iPAQ the sender and/or receiver of the e-mail.

■ **Media Access Control (MAC) Address**   This is similar in concept to an IP address but with some differences. Each computer or iPAQ (also a computer) has a unique hardware number in a network. The MAC address can be used for wireless security. If a WLAN uses a MAC table, then only the WLAN/802.11 devices that have had their MAC addresses added to that network MAC table will be able to access the network.

■ **Domain Name System (DNS)**   DNS refers to the way that Internet domain names are located and translated into IP addresses. A domain name such as HP.com is easy to remember, but when you type it into a browser, a DNS system translates that name into a numeric Internet Protocol (IP) address, such as 192.6.234.17. Every website has its own specific IP address on the Internet, and DNS resolves the domain name with the IP address.

■ **Security Set Identifier (SSID)**   An SSID is another network security feature and includes a sequence of 32 characters that uniquely identify a WLAN. If a WLAN is protected by an SSID, you will need to know and configure the SSID in the WLAN settings in order to connect to the network.

■ **Wired Equivalent Privacy (WEP)**   WEP is basic WLAN wireless security that uses an encryption key that automatically encrypts outgoing wireless data; the same encryption key enables the receiving computer to automatically decrypt the information. This effectively scrambles the information that is sent over the air, preventing someone from intercepting data packages and getting readable information from them.

There are certainly other terms that can be important for WLAN, such as WiFi Security Protocol Utilities, 802.1X Certificate Enroller, WINS, and so on, but the preceding terms will be the primary important terms to most users.

Turn on Your iPAQ WLAN Radio

As you likely have already noticed, there are often multiple ways to navigate to a specific function or screen on your iPAQ, and we don't usually mention every possible way. The simplest way to turn on your iPAQ WLAN radio is to show the Today screen by closing all other screens

Today screen WLAN icon.

and simply tap the WLAN icon, as highlighted in Figure 3-1. This will open the iPAQ wireless screen. Then tap the WLAN icon again to turn on WLAN.

Manually Add a New WLAN to Connect to

The terms WLAN, WiFi, and 802.11 refer to the same thing and are used interchangeably in this section. One way to add a wireless network is when the WLAN is detected; this happens when the Network Indicator icon shows in the Navigation bar. Another way to add a network is to do it manually by configuring settings. Before you get started, however, you will first need to find out how your corporate WLAN is configured. Specifically, you will need to find out:

■ Whether authentication is required

■ Whether data encryption is enforced and if so, what the network key is

■ Whether the network uses IEEE 802.1x Network Access Control, and if so, what kind

Once you have gathered this information you can manually add a wireless network. Follow these steps:

1. Ensure that WLAN is powered on, as covered in the previous section.

2. Select Start | Settings | Connections tab, and select the iPAQ Wireless icon, as shown in Figure 3-2.

3. Select the WiFi tab.

4. Select the View WiFi Networks link. If the network that you want to connect to shows up in the list, select it; if it doesn't, select the Add New option, as shown in Figure 3-3.

5. On the General tab, as shown in Figure 3-4, you have a few configuration options. Filling in Network Name is mandatory (if the network was detected you cannot change the name), and the Connects To option depends on the configuration of the network you are connecting to. If you are connecting to an office network, select the My Work option.

FIGURE 3-2 iPAQ Wireless icon.

FIGURE 3-3 Add New WLAN.

FIGURE 3-4 WLAN General tab.

FIGURE 3-5   WLAN Network Key tab.

6. On the Network Key tab, your network configuration determines how your network is set up. You will require help from your network IT people to provide you with authentication, data encryption, and possibly network key information, as shown in Figure 3-5.

7. Your corporate WLAN may use IEEE 802.1x network access control. To choose which type of access control to use, select the 802.1x tab, as shown in Figure 3-6.

FIGURE 3-6   WLAN 802.1x tab.

Use Bluetooth on Your iPAQ

Bluetooth wireless technology is a short-range wireless standard and specification sometimes called a PAN (personal area network) that is intended to replace the multitude of cables that connect digital devices together. HP, among many other product manufacturers, has built Bluetooth into their products. In doing so, HP produced the Bluetooth-enabled iPAQ in compliance with the industry standard. However, it is important to keep in mind that each product manufacturer tends to integrate Bluetooth in their own unique way, although you can usually get two Bluetooth devices from different manufacturers to "talk." Technical details of the Bluetooth standard include:

- Bluetooth is an open standard governed by the Bluetooth Special Interest Group (SIG).
- The majority of mobile devices are Class II devices that have a range of up to 33 feet.
- The most commonly supported Bluetooth specification is Bluetooth version 1.1.
- One of the advantages of Bluetooth is that it requires very low power. It uses less than 1 milliwatt, which is important for your iPAQ battery.
- Bluetooth operates in the 2.4GHz frequency band, also known as the Industrial Scientific Medical Band (in case you were wondering).

As Bluetooth is a short-range wireless network, the most common uses for Bluetooth on mobile devices such as your iPAQ include using Bluetooth headphones to talk on the phone and listen to audio without wires; printing to a Bluetooth capable printer; connecting to a PC to transfer files or to ActiveSync; and connecting to keyboards, mobile phones, and Global Positioning System (GPS) kits.

When Would You Use Bluetooth Rather than WLAN?   If your iPAQ offers both Bluetooth and WLAN connectivity, you may be wondering when to use one over the other. Bluetooth and WLAN are complementary technologies rather than competing technologies, despite the fact that both are relatively short-range wireless options. The difference is that WLAN is the 802.11b standard used for wireless networking and is intended to replace wired local area networking, while Bluetooth replaces the cables between individual electronic devices such as your HP iPAQ and a keyboard, printer, or headset. Here is an example of Bluetooth and WiFi complementing each other: in your office, you use Bluetooth to set up a network between your personal computer, printer, and keyboard so that no cables are needed between these devices. Then you use WiFi to connect the same computer to a local area network where information and other devices can be shared among coworkers.

Bluetooth Terminology

Many technologies have specific terminology to describe unique concepts, and Bluetooth is no exception. In this section, we will discuss some of the Bluetooth concepts and terms that are important to understand. Many of these concepts will be discussed in more detail later on.

- **Authentication**   Verification of a numeric passkey, a similar concept to a password, needed before a connection can be made.

- **Authorization**   The process of approving a connection or activity before it can proceed.

- **Bonding**   The process of creating a trusted connection between two Bluetooth devices; after a bond is created, the two devices are "paired."

- **Device address**   The unique electronic address of a Bluetooth-capable device.

- **Device discovery**   The wireless process of searching for other Bluetooth devices; your iPAQ must be enabled for discovery to allow other Bluetooth devices to find your iPAQ and to allow your iPAQ to find other devices within range.

- **Device name**   The name that is provided by a Bluetooth device when it is discovered by another Bluetooth device. You can configure your iPAQ with whatever device name you want—for example, Dax's iPAQ.

- **Devices in range**   During discovery, a Bluetooth-capable iPAQ searches an area of no more that 33 feet.

- **Devices not found**   You will see this error message when no Bluetooth devices are discovered within the 33 foot range.

- **Discoverable mode**   In order for another Bluetooth device to find and connect to it, your iPAQ must be in discoverable mode.

- **Pairing**   If you intend to use two Bluetooth-capable devices together on a regular basis, it is a good idea to pair the devices so that you don't have to re-enter authentication information every time you want them to connect. For example, if you plan to use a Bluetooth-capable printer with your iPAQ on a regular basis, pairing allows you to save the device name, passkey, and other information to enable the devices to automatically connect when you need them to. Some types of Bluetooth devices such as Bluetooth headsets require pairing in order to connect at all.

- **Personal identification number (PIN) or passkey**   A PIN can be required to authenticate incoming connections in the process of pairing two Bluetooth devices. This helps prevent unauthorized Bluetooth devices from connecting to your iPAQ without your knowledge.

- **Profile (service)**   In Bluetooth, a profile is the technical definition of how a device manufacturer must implement Bluetooth wireless technology for a particular user scenario. For practical user purposes, profiles and services are essentially the same thing. In order for two Bluetooth-capable devices to connect and function, both devices must offer the same profile. This topic is covered in more detail next in this chapter under the heading "Bluetooth Pairing versus Bluetooth Profiles."

Bluetooth Pairing vs. Bluetooth Profiles

The concepts of pairing and profiles can be a little confusing, but they each serve a specific purpose. Pairing, also known as bonding, is a concept that was introduced to create a first-time recognition of which devices are allowed to communicate with each other. The initial pairing process is required to allow each Bluetooth device to recognize each other and begin communicating. It is a security feature embedded in Bluetooth that effectively prevents a nonauthorized Bluetooth device from connecting to your iPAQ. Now, profiles are different: every Bluetooth capable device such as a printer, laptop, and headset supports specific Bluetooth profiles. A profile is a unique way to describe the Bluetooth functionality of different devices. The Bluetooth wireless technology is used for many different types of applications, and it is necessary to describe how the different devices and their applications should connect and function together. This description is called a profile. The supported profiles will be listed in the user manual for each device. For example, a Bluetooth mouse that supports the HID (Human Interface Device) profile will not work with your iPAQ because iPAQs do not currently support HID. It is important to ensure that whichever Bluetooth device you want to connect your iPAQ to supports at least one profile that is the same as your iPAQ.

Make a Bluetooth Connection with Your iPAQ

Probably the most common use of Bluetooth on an iPAQ is the use of Bluetooth headphones and headsets, so that's the example we'll use. However, the steps are similar to connect to any Bluetooth capable device. If you don't have a Bluetooth headset and want one, HP (**www .hp.com**) offers a model that matches perfectly with their iPAQ so you won't have to worry about incompatibilities. To pair a Bluetooth headphone or headset with your iPAQ, follow these steps:

1. Set your headphone or headset to discoverable or pairing mode as specified in the user documentation. Make sure to find the passkey that is in the headset documentation, as you will need it in a future step. On both Windows Mobile 2003 and Windows Mobile 5, select Start | Settings | Connections tab | Bluetooth icon | Accessibility tab, as shown in Figure 3-7. Ensure that the Paired Devices Only option is selected.

FIGURE 3-7   Pairing with Bluetooth settings.

FIGURE 3-8   Turn on Bluetooth.

2. To turn Bluetooth on, select Start | Settings | Connections tab | Bluetooth icon. If Bluetooth is not already on, select the Turn On button, as shown in Figure 3-8.

3. To pair your iPAQ and your Bluetooth headset on a Windows Mobile 2003 SE:

   a. Select Start | iPAQ Wireless | Bluetooth Manager | Tools | Paired Devices, then tap the Add button.

   b. On the Bluetooth: Device Pairing screen, as shown in Figure 3-9, select the Lookup or Search icon. This will discover any Bluetooth capable device within range, including your Bluetooth headphones (provided they are turned on and Bluetooth is enabled), which will show up in the list.

FIGURE 3-9   Bluetooth pairing.

or

To pair your iPAQ and your Bluetooth headset on a Windows Mobile 5:

a. Select Start | Settings | Connections tab | Bluetooth icon. Select the Bluetooth Manager link.

b. Select the New menu at the bottom of the screen, then select the Hands-free/Headset Setup option | Tap Next and tap Next again, and your iPAQ will try to discover the Bluetooth headset.

4. When the headphone or headset is discovered and appears in the Select A Bluetooth device list, select it and enter the passkey that is in the headset documentation, then tap OK.

5. If all went well (Bluetooth is turned on for both your iPAQ and headset; your iPAQ is set to pairing mode, and you entered the passkey on the iPAQ correctly), your headphones should now be paired with your iPAQ and you can begin using them.

More about Bluetooth: Configuring and Connecting

Your iPAQ user documentation covers a lot of ground regarding Bluetooth, so we'll just talk about the things you are most likely going to need to configure.

■ **Change the Bluetooth Device Name on your iPAQ**   You want to use a different name for Bluetooth than your iPAQ device name. To change it, go to Start | Settings | Connections tab | Bluetooth Settings | Accessibility tab. Ensure that the Use Pocket PC Device Name for Bluetooth checkbox is unchecked and enter a new name. That's it. Now that name will show up when another Bluetooth device detects your iPAQ.

> TIP
>
> *If you know that the Bluetooth device that you want to connect to is within the 33 foot range and you still get the Devices Not Found error message or no devices show up in the Bluetooth browser, the device may not be in discoverable mode. If it is in discoverable mode, there is a small possibility there is interference from other radio devices using the same radio frequency. Devices such as microwave ovens, some cordless telephones, and certain WLAN products, among other things, can interfere with Bluetooth. If you can, turn off these devices and try the discovery again.*

■ **Put your iPAQ into Discoverable mode**   It is a good idea to leave discoverable mode turned off on your iPAQ to help avoid unwanted connections. However, if you need to turn discoverable mode on, go to Start | Settings | Connections | Bluetooth Settings | Accessibility, and select Other Devices Can Discover Me, as shown in Figure 3-10.

■ **Configure your Bluetooth services**   "Services" is essentially a different name for a profile described in Bluetooth terminology. You can view your services and change their attributes such as Enable Service, Authorization Required, Authentication (Passkey) Required, and Encryption Required, as shown in Figure 3-11.

FIGURE 3-10   Set Bluetooth to discoverable mode.

End a Wireless Connection

Your iPAQ has limited resources, so it is important to know what is running at any one time. Shutting down the functions that you are not using will improve the performance of what you are actively using. It is also important to close network connections to prevent unauthorized access. If you are running Windows Mobile 5 on your iPAQ, you can disconnect any of the wireless network connections from the iPAQ Wireless screen, as shown in Figure 3-12.

To disconnect the different types of network connections:

■ When connected via a modem or Virtual Private Network (VPN), select the Data Connection icon on the title bar and tap Disconnect.

■ When connected via a cable or cradle, detach your device from the cable or cradle.

FIGURE 3-11   Bluetooth services.

FIGURE 3-12   iPAQ Wireless screen.

■ When connected via infrared, move the device away from the other computer or device.

■ When connected via Bluetooth, either move the devices away from each other or select Start | Settings | Connections tab | iPAQ Wireless and turn off the Bluetooth radio by selecting the appropriate link.

Voice-Over-IP

You may have heard all of the hype about Voice-Over-IP (VoIP) technologies, and you may have even used it as it is becoming more and more commonplace. Your iPAQ utilizes voice-specific technologies (not VoIP) to allow you to make and receive phone calls as well as send and receive MMS and SMS/text messages. VoIP, on the other hand, is voice communication that is transmitted over the Internet. One of the reasons VoIP is becoming so popular is that it uses data connectivity and technology in much the same way that e-mail and browsing the Web uses data connectivity, also known as the Internet. Therefore, if you have an Internet connection you can use VoIP to "phone" someone else who has an Internet connection. All you need is an appropriate client software agent on whatever Internet-connected device you are using to make the call. The Internet-connected device does not even need to be a phone for VoIP to work—it can even be as simple as a PC equipped with a speaker and microphone.

The major advantage of using VoIP instead of a land line or a cell phone, especially for long-distance phone calls, is that your phone company or wireless service provider won't be billing you for the call on your monthly statement. However, keep in mind that your Internet connection likely has a limit on how much data you can use in a given period (usually a month), so you will need to be sure that you are not going over your monthly limit or you will be paying for the overage.

Expand Your iPAQ Connectivity with Expansion Cards

Depending on which model your iPAQ is, you may want to use a type of wireless network connectivity that isn't built into your device. For example, you might have a 6500 that features cellular voice and data connectivity but only offers Bluetooth as a secondary option. What if you want to use a WiFi connection when you are in the office or with your home wireless network? Fortunately, there are several companies that make wireless cards that allow you to expand our iPAQ capabilities.

- Third-party WiFi cards:
  - Socket Wireless LAN CompactFlash card (**www.socket.com**)
  - Symbol Wireless Networker, 802.11b CompactFlash (**www.symbol.com**)
- Third-party cellular cards:
  - **Sprint PCS Vision CF 2031, Sprint Network CDMA** A PCS Vision–enabled CompactFlash (CF) card that comes packaged with a lithium-ion battery, PC card adapter, A/C charger, CD-ROM, and a Start Here guide. This card is designed for wireless data communication speeds of up to 144Kbps. To purchase a card and set up a plan, call HP Wireless at 1-877-261-6066.
  - **Audiovox Tri-band GSM/GPRS** CompactFlash card that provides wireless data and no voice and includes a GSM/GPRS CompactFlash card, software CD-ROM, and an owner's manual. To use this card, you will have to purchase the card then arrange for a service plan from a GSM/GPRS wireless service provider such as Cingular/AT&T, or T-Mobile. (**www.audiovox.com**).
- Third-party Bluetooth cards:
  - Socket SDIO Bluetooth card for Pocket PC (**www.socket.com**)
  - Ambicom CompactFlash Bluetooth card (**www.ambicom.com**)
  - Belkin CompactFlash Bluetooth PDA and PC adapter combo card (**www.belkin.com**)

What Are Other Wireless Uses for the iPAQ?

This section is designed to provide a brief cross section and overview of some of the ways you can use your iPAQ. One of the great things about Microsoft-powered devices such as your iPAQ is that the Microsoft developer community is extremely active. New products, and therefore new uses, for your iPAQ are constantly being introduced. The latest HP iPAQs have evolved significantly from earlier models and perhaps the most exciting additions are the wireless data and voice capabilities.

Download and Install Applications over the Air

Many applications have a small enough file size that you can download them over the air and install them directly on your iPAQ without the ActiveSync installer. There are many software developers that offer shareware and freeware applications that you can download from reseller and company websites.

 *Shareware is software that you can download and use without immediately paying for it. It is a great way to try out software before you buy it. If you decide that you want to use the software on a regular basis, simply purchase a license key, usually online, with your credit card. Most shareware applications are functionally limited to encourage you to pay for the software to get the fully functional version.*

There are several websites that sell applications for your iPAQ. Many of these sites allow you to pay for, download, and install applications and games and allow you to do it all over the air straight to your iPAQ. A prime example of a website that allows you to do this is Microsoft (**www.microsoft.com**).

 *Some applications require a conduit application that runs on your PC to facilitate application data synchronizing during ActiveSync. Any conduit applications need to be installed locally on your PC.*

Use Your iPAQ to Connect to a VPN

Remote workers and telecommuters have used VPN technology with PCs for years to allow them to securely access company computer networks over long distances. You may have heard of a wide area network (WAN), which is a generic term for a computer network that is spread out over a large area—possibly all over the world—and this is really what we are talking about when we talk about VPNs. The truly useful characteristic of a VPN is that it uses public networks, such as the Internet, to connect a remote user to a corporate network, and it does it securely. This is important because organizations and, increasingly, individuals are concerned about Internet security, and anything that can help minimize the risk of using the Internet is a good thing. Fortunately, there are software vendors that know that a wireless mobile device such as your iPAQ presents unique security challenges and that have developed technology to address these problems and allow you to use your iPAQ on a VPN. VPN tools for your iPAQ are covered in more detail in Chapter 16.

Other Wireless Topics Worth Mentioning: Dial-up and Roaming

Wireless technology is changing rapidly and will continue to do so for quite some time. While it doesn't make sense to learn everything about wireless just to make the most of your iPAQ, there are a few additional wireless connectively topics you may want to be aware of with regard to your iPAQ: Dial-up and Roaming.

What Is Dial-up?

Dial-up is a term that you will occasionally see relating to wireless data on your iPAQ. You may remember the old computer dial-up modems that allowed computers to communicate using phone lines; dial-up for your IPAQ is similar. Dial-up uses the iPAQ phone for data communications instead of using the data channel. It is generally a secondary mode of communication used only when regular wireless data connectivity is unavailable; for example, when you are roaming and your iPAQ is unable to connect to the primary means of connectivity, where the primary is usually GPRS. Dial-up connections also allow you to access the Internet using the iPAQ phone.

Why Dial-up May Be Important to You

There are a few reasons dial-up mode may be important to you:

- **Cost** Some wireless service providers charge extra for time spent in dial-up mode. If your wireless service provider is one of those, and you have your iPAQ set to switch to dial-up mode when you are roaming, the difference will show up on your next bill.

- **If your wireless service provider does not offer wireless Internet** You can use dial-up mode to access the Internet by allowing your iPAQ to connect to an ISP account.

Roaming

Roaming describes the situation where you are outside of your primary coverage area but are still connected to a wireless network. Your ability to roam outside your coverage area is dependent on the relationships between wireless service providers in other areas and on the details of your service contract. You can roam and use another carrier's wireless network as long as your wireless service provider has a roaming agreement with the other carrier to allow your iPAQ to connect to that carrier's network. There are two main reasons roaming is important:

- **Dollars and cents (or, euros, francs, yen, etc.)** You pay your wireless service provider for service. If you move into an area where you are using another wireless service provider's network, someone has to pay for that service. There must be a business agreement between the two wireless service providers so that the WSP providing your roaming can bill your WSP, who in turn bills you. Therefore, many wireless service providers charge you more when you are roaming to cover the associated extra accounting costs.

- **Performance and dollars and cents** In areas where normal service in not available, some carriers may resort to a back-up plan and allow you to use a dial-up connection to access the Internet. The performance of dial-up is slower, and there may be an added charge for using the service. If you don't want to use this dial-up option when roaming, be sure to disable any automatic Internet connections you may have set up, such as in your e-mail application.

3

Configure Your iPAQ for International Roaming

When you are planning on traveling abroad or otherwise out of your normal coverage area, you will be able to use your HP iPAQ by setting it up for international roaming.

It is important to do this at least 24 hours before you leave home so that you don't experience any time gaps in connectivity. Contact your carrier and:

- Ensure that your iPAQ phone is activated for international roaming. Depending on your mobile phone service provider, there may be an additional charge to activate this feature.

- Ensure that your HP iPAQ will work in the country you are going to and find out what kind of coverage you will receive. If your iPAQ is a CDMA/EvDO device hosted by Sprint or Verizon, your roaming options will be limited because many countries do not offer these networks. If you have a GSM/GPRS/EDGE iPAQ then your options will be better.

- Find out if you need to purchase another SIM card (only possible with some GSM/GPRS/EDGE devices) with the correct international format on it. Your mobile phone service provider may also be able to reformat the SIM card that you already have.

- Ask your mobile phone service provider for an up-to-date list of foreign operators that enable you to use data functionality abroad and added costs for the service plan.

- Find out if there are specific instructions that you will need to follow to configure your iPAQ once you arrive at your destination. Sometimes all you need to do is soft reset your iPAQ when you arrive to get it to connect to the local network, but you may need to take extra steps to get it to work properly.

- It is also a good idea to bring along the phone number of the technical support number of your wireless service provider just in case you need it.

IP Dashboard Network Monitor by Hudson Mobile

There are several tools that can improve your iPAQ wireless data experience and one example of a useful tool is IP Dashboard Network Monitor by Hudson Mobile Technologies (**www .hudsonmobile.com**). IP Dashboard is a Today Screen plug-in that enables you to monitor your wireless network connection and track your network usage, including WLANs. Some of the features allow you to:

- Monitor WLA, GPRS/CDMA, and sync cable data connections
- See inbound and outbound traffic activity
- View and edit current network settings, including IP address and DHCP configuration
- Configure a meter to track bandwidth usage with graphical display of current data rates
- Allow network administrators to release and renew DHCP IP addresses, see DNS and WINS information, and ping to test connectivity to other computers

Useful Websites Formatted for Your iPAQ

It is getting more common for websites to offer alternative web pages that are formatted specifically for wireless mobile devices. The major differences between these specially formatted pages and the web pages that are designed to be rendered on a PC is that they are formatted for a much smaller screen. Some examples include the list below but there are many, many more and the numbers are growing:

- Mobile MSN (**mobile.msn.com/pocketpc/**) The MSN search engine formated for your iPAQ screen.

- Google SMS (**www.google.com/sms/**) The Google SMS service allows you to search the web for stores and businesses in a specific neighborhood, and find the names, addresses, and phone numbers of businesses in any zip code across the U.S. For example, you could search for "pizza 10013" and the web page will provide you with a list of pizza vendors in that zip code; or, to find the address of a particular store you could query "spatulas R us new york ny."

- Edmunds (**pda.edmunds.com**) A web site designed for car buyers that features information on new and used vehicle pricing, insurance, a loan calculator and dealer locator.

- Major League Baseball (**mobile.mlb.com/**) This site allows you to use your iPAQ to get information about games, get wallpaper and ringtones and even watch game video.

- PocketOptimized (**www.PocketOptimized.com/pda**) this site is an exceptional resource that lists many sites that are optimized for you iPAQ screen and offers categorized websites including finance, games, health and many others.

Wrap It Up

Long gone are the days of the disconnected PDA. It's all about wireless and "mobility" now. HP has done an excellent job of incorporating highly useful wireless technologies into your iPAQ. Depending on the model of your iPAQ. you may have any combination of built-in cellular (GPRS/CDMA/EDGE/etc.), WLAN, Bluetooth or infrared wireless capabilities, and you also extend wireless capability by purchasing third-part CompactFlash or Secure Digital cards.

You may have noticed that this chapter is one of the longest in this book. There are several reasons for this, but the two primary reasons are that wireless data on your iPAQ is tremendously useful and you can use it for many things and wireless is technically complex to set up and each type of wireless technology requires other components to work properly. We could easily write an entire book on wireless data, but the focus of this chapter is to give you a 30,000 foot view of the topic. Your iPAQ user's manual certainly covers more information, and there are many websites if you want to find out technical details about the different technologies. Be mobile!

Chapter 4

Use Your iPAQ Phone

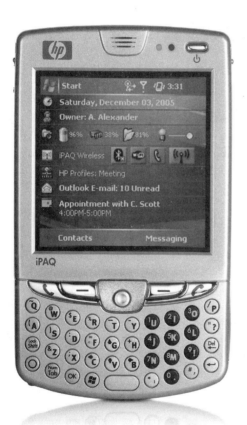

How to...

■ Configure and use your iPAQ phone

■ Send an MMS message

■ Send a text message

■ Use your iPAQ as a speaker phone

■ Record an audio "note" to yourself

If your iPAQ features a built-in phone, you have one of the best "smart" mobile phones on the market. You have likely already used your iPAQ as a phone. It is simple to operate because it is a heck of a lot like most telephones that you have used in the past. Simply push the phone button, type in a phone number, and select the Talk button. This is the simplest scenario of making a phone call; that said, there are a bunch of great features that your iPAQ phone has that just are not available on your average land-line phones.

Connect Your iPAQ to Make and Receive Phone Calls

Your iPAQ has several different ways to connect to wireless networks. This chapter discusses the phone setup and functionality specifically, including MMS (Multimedia Messaging Service) and SMS (Short Messaging Service); the more data-focused networks are discussed in Chapter 3. Depending on your iPAQ model, it may have any of the following types of radios:

■ Cellular voice

■ Cellular data

■ Bluetooth

■ WLAN/802.11/WiFi

Each data connection type requires different technology, generally speaking, and each is configured slightly differently. Cellular data, Bluetooth, and WiFi are generally used for data such as e-mail, applications, and the Internet, while voice phone calls use a separate voice radio similar to the old-fashioned cell phones of 1999. While it's true that the advent of Voice-Over-IP (VoIP) is blurring this distinction because it uses a data connection rather than a voice connection, we will keep this chapter focused on the stock iPAQ. VoIP is discussed in Chapter 3.

Connect Your iPAQ Phone

Wireless data connectivity is covered in detail in Chapter 3, and if you are already using your phone and browsing the Web, you may choose to skip this section. However, if you are just getting going with your iPAQ phone, this section covers some of the things you will need to know to get started.

What Is a SIM card?

If your iPAQ is on a CDMA or EvDO network such as Verizon, Nextel, or Sprint, your iPAQ does not have a SIM card. However, if your iPAQ is on a GSM/GPRS/EDGE network such as Cingular or T-Mobile, you do have a SIM card. SIM stands for "Subscriber Identification Module" or "Subscriber Identity Module." SIM cards are small smart cards that fit inside phones based on the GSM technology. Your SIM card contains personalized information about you including your network activation, phone number, and voice mail access number. Your wireless service provider uses the SIM information to register and track your iPAQ on the network. You can also seamlessly swap your SIM card between multiple devices while retaining the same phone number. The SIM card must be inserted into the SIM slot under the battery on the back of your iPAQ in order for voice or data calls to work, with the exception of emergency calls such as 911.

Ensure that Your Service Contract Gives You the Right Features

When you arrange your cellular voice and data service, it is important to understand what your iPAQ is capable of so that you can ask for the features you want to be enabled for your account with the carrier network. Your iPAQ, depending on the model, will have all or a subset of these features and you will need to ensure that your carrier enables the functionality you want. Of course, they will likely charge a little extra to enable each feature, including any or all of the following:

- Voice mail
- Caller ID.
- Call forwarding.
- International dialing.
- International roaming.
- Internet access with a data package (it is important to keep in mind that data is relatively new to carriers who are used to selling and providing service to cell phones and not all service contracts automatically include wireless data so you can use applications such as e-mail, Internet, and others that require the transmission of data to and from your iPAQ). This topic is covered in more detail in Chapter 3.
- Text messaging, also known as SMS.
- MMS, which enables you to send media such as sound clips, video clips, and photos to others without needing to use e-mail.
- Virtual Private Network (VPN), a network security option; this is covered in more detail in Chapter 16.

4

What is a PIN?

You're probably familiar with the concept of a PIN (Personal Identification Number) because they're used on automated teller bank cards, home security systems, network IDs, and other places where you want to restrict access. This same concept applies to keep unauthorized persons from using your iPAQ phone. Once your iPAQ has been activated on the network, you can protect it with a PIN. It is important to know that dialing an emergency number such as 911 doesn't require a SIM card and the call may be made even if the iPAQ is locked with a PIN.

Set a PIN on Your iPAQ

You are responsible for your phone bill, so if you should misplace your iPAQ you'll want to protect it with a PIN so that others cannot make calls. You can disable your PIN, but it is a good idea to keep it enabled for security reasons.

When the PIN is enabled, you will have to enter your PIN every time you turn on your phone features. Keep in mind that after three consecutive incorrect PIN tries, your iPAQ will lock to prevent further use. If you see the letters PUK (PIN Unblocking Key) displayed on your HP iPAQ screen, your iPAQ phone is locked and you must enter your PIN Unblocking Key on the screen to unlock it. If you don't have a PIN Unblocking Key, you will have to contact your wireless service provider to unlock it for you.

To enable your PIN, follow these steps:

1. Launch the phone by selecting the Phone button.

2. On the Phone keypad, select Tools | Options and ensure that the Phone tab is selected, as shown in Figure 4-1.

3. Select the Require PIN When Phone Is Used check box.

FIGURE 4-1   Set PIN.

4. At this point, there are two things that could happen depending on when you are doing this process:

- You will be prompted to enter a PIN number given to you from your mobile phone service provider along with the SIM card, or you will have to enter the default PIN code of 1234.

    or

- If your wireless service provider isn't enforcing the PIN and you want to add one to protect your phone, enter a PIN that you will remember.

5. Press the ENTER button to enable your PIN. Your phone is now protected from unauthorized use.

Inserting and Removing Your SIM Card

NOTE   *This section applies to GSM, GPRS, and EDGE iPAQs only.*

Since your SIM card is removable, you may need to insert and remove it yourself. To do so, follow these steps:

Insert Your SIM Card

If your SIM card is not already inside your iPAQ, you need to remove the battery cover and the battery from the back of your iPAQ and slide the SIM card into the SIM slot. Align the notched corner on the card with the notched corner in the SIM slot, then push the SIM card into the SIM slot. On some of the iPAQ models it isn't overly obvious just how the SIM card should go in, but keep in mind that you should position the SIM card in the battery cavity and then slide it in from there. The gold side of the SIM card should be facing down when it is inserted into the SIM slot. If it still doesn't make sense, your user manual should have illustrations of how it should look.

Remove Your SIM Card

Remove the battery cover and the battery from the back of your iPAQ, and use the stylus to push or slide the SIM card out. Remember not to touch the metal contacts, especially if you are using something metal with which to extract the SIM card.

Activate Your Phone Service

If you haven't already arranged for wireless service from a carrier such as Verizon, T-Mobile, Cingular, Sprint, Rogers, Telus, Orange, or any of the smaller carriers, then you will need to arrange for a service contract with a carrier in your area before you will be able to use the phone features of your iPAQ. If you purchased your iPAQ directly from a carrier or carrier reseller then it is likely already activated, or you may have been given instructions on how to activate your iPAQ yourself. Your iPAQ won't connect to the network until it has been activated. If you can make a phone call from your iPAQ, then it is obviously already activated.

FIGURE 4-2 GSM/GPRS parameters.

Once your phone is activated, the first time you use your phone the GSM/GPRS or CDMA Manager automatically detects the phone network and operator and sets up the GPRS or CDMA connection information for you. If your phone is a GPRS/GSM/EDGE phone, you can modify these settings to your own preference or create your own network settings if you like. To access the GPRS settings, select Start | Settings | Connections tab, then select the GSM/GPRS Manager icon. If your carrier name appears in the drop-down list, as shown in Figure 4-2, it is a good idea to use that connection because it is likely preconfigured, although you can edit settings if you need to.

Edit Your Network Settings (GSM/GPRS/EDGE)

 *Editing Network Properties is not recommended unless you are being assisted by a service provider support professional.*

Opening the Edit Network Parameters functionality on the GSM/GPRS Settings screen, as shown in Figure 4-3, gives you access to three different areas:

- **Internet Connection Information** Walks you through the different settings for GPRS (General Packet Radio Service) and CSD (Circuit Switched Data) connections.

- **MMS Multimedia Messages** Allows you to modify the Multimedia Message Service Center (MMSC) address.

- **WAP (Wireless Application Protocol) Information**

Accessing the Internet, MMS and WAP information on the iPAQ isn't as intuitive as it could be; to do so, follow these steps:

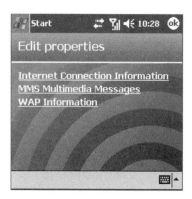

FIGURE 4-3   Edit Network Properties screen.

1. Select Start | Setting | Connections tab, then select the GSM/GPRS icon, as shown in Figure 4-4.

2. On the Connections tab, select the Edit Network Parameters button, as shown in Figure 4-5.

3. To modify your Internet, MMS and WAP settings you will need information from your wireless service provider.

4. Edit Your MMS Settings: If your voice connection is set up and activated (if you can make a phone call from your iPAQ), the only network setting that we are going to discuss in this chapter is MMS. MMS is also discussed in more detail later in this chapter. This section deals specifically with ensuring that your iPAQ is set up correctly for MMS. The MMS screen, shown in Figure 4-6, requires several pieces of information and, if it is not

FIGURE 4-4   GSM/GPRS icon.

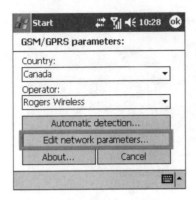

FIGURE 4-5 Edit the MMS center.

already configured, you will need to get this information from your carrier. The MMS Center Address and the APN (Access Point Name) are both web server addresses (URLs) because the server that your iPAQ will use send MMS messages is similar to a web server.

NOTE *Other network connections that are used specifically for data are discussed in Chapter 3.*

TIP *Not all wireless service providers offer MMS and SMS services, and if yours does then your wireless service provider needs to activate the specific functionality that you want to use on your iPAQ. Be aware that they tend to charge for each feature. If MMS is not configured on your iPAQ, it may be because your wireless service provider doesn't offer the service or that your contract does not include MMS and you have to add it to your package to be able to send and receive MMS messages.*

FIGURE 4-6 Edit Network Parameters button.

Use Your iPAQ Phone

Your HP iPAQ phone is a very powerful piece of technology that does much more that just allow you to make and receive phone calls. HP has done a great job with their user manuals and guides, and it doesn't make sense to copy and paste the content, so see your user guide for specifics. However, it does make sense to talk about the most useful functionality and what you'll probably use everyday.

The list of features includes:

■ Several different ways to dial a call:

   ■ Making a call from your contact list (covered later in this chapter)

   ■ Making a call using speed dial

   ■ Making a call from your call history

   ■ Making a conference call

■ Sending an MMS message (covered later in this chapter)

■ Sending a text message (covered later in this chapter)

■ Using a Bluetooth hands-free headset (Bluetooth is covered in Chapter 3)

■ Making notes while on a call, including the ability to record a call (covered later in this chapter)

In this chapter, we will discuss a few of the most useful and interesting features of your iPAQ phone. Information regarding other functionality is available in your iPAQ user guide.

Make a Phone Call from Your Contact List

On your iPAQ, you can first find a contact then simply press a button and your iPAQ dials your contact. This assumes, of course, that you are storing contacts on your iPAQ, but why wouldn't you? To dial a contact from your contacts list, follow these steps:

1. Launch the phone by pressing the green Phone button, or select Start | Phone.

2. Select the Contacts icon, as shown in Figure 4-7.

3. Find the contact you want to phone by either scrolling through the list or beginning to type in the search box, as shown in Figure 4-8.

4. Once you find and select the correct contact, if the contact has more than one phone number, select the phone number that you want to dial, as shown in Figure 4-9, and your iPAQ will automatically dial the number.

The process seems a little lengthy when it all written out but it actually goes very quickly. If you have numbers that you call all the time, you can make the process even quicker by adding those numbers to your Speed Dial list.

FIGURE 4-7   Dial from the Contacts icon.

FIGURE 4-8   Dial from the Contacts search.

FIGURE 4-9   Dial from your Contacts list.

If your iPAQ supports conference calling, you can create a three-way conference call between yourself and two other people. From the Phone keypad, dial the first number. After the person answers, dial in other people by pressing the Talk button and selecting Hold, then dial the second number, select Talk, and then select Conference.

Use the Notes Feature

The Notes functionality on your iPAQ is another feature that stretches the concept of what a phone should be able to do. The Notes feature allows you to take standard text-based notes while you are on the phone, in much the same way you used to scribble on the pad of paper beside the phone. Notes also give you the ability to record audio dictation and even record the phone call. To access the Notes functionality, follow these steps (you can do this even while you are on a phone call):

1. Launch the phone by pressing the green Phone button or selecting Start | Phone.

2. Select the Notes icon, as shown in Figure 4-10.

3. Select either the Text option (the pencil icon) or the Voice option (the cassette tape icon) option, as shown in Figure 4-11.

   a. When you select the Text (the pencil icon) you can either write or draw directly on the touch screen or type on the keyboard. Figure 4-12 shows both.

   b. When you select the Voice Note option you can record a phone call or anything else (such as dictation or a song on the radio that you want to remember) using the iPAQ microphone. To begin recording, press the Record button and press Stop when you are finished, as shown in Figure 4-13. The clips that you can record are relatively short, but you can record many of them, so keep that in mind.

After you have saved your note (voice or text), you have several options. Among other things, you can e-mail a note or beam a note to another infrared capable device.

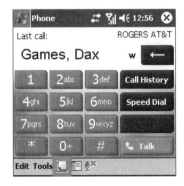

FIGURE 4-10   Notes icon.

FIGURE 4-11   Notes icons: Text or Voice.

FIGURE 4-12   Notes text.

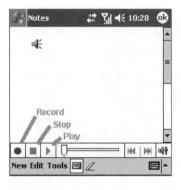

FIGURE 4-13   Notes Voice buttons.

FIGURE 4-14   Selecting ringtones.

Ringtones

Your iPAQ includes several different ringtones, and you can switch between them in the Phone Options screen (from the Phone screen, select Tools | Options), as shown in Figure 4-14, You can hear each ringtone by selecting it from the Ringtone drop-down menu and pressing the Play button.

To use downloaded ringtones such as WAV, MID, or WMA files, download them to your PC and use ActiveSync to copy the file to the My HP iPAQ\Windows\Rings folder on your HP iPAQ. Then, select the sound from the Ring Tone list as just discussed. Or, download a ringtone from the Internet using your iPAQ browser, but be sure to save them in the My HP iPAQ\Windows\Rings folder so that they show up in your ringtone list.

TIP   *Ringtones have become big business and you can download both paid-for and free ringtones or even create your own ringtones for your iPAQ. The key thing to remember is that your iPAQ will only play files of specific types such as Polyphonic MIDI, WMA, and WAV. Different iPAQs have different capabilities so you need to understand which files your iPAQ is capable of using as ringtones before you download ringtones. This information is available in your iPAQ user guide. Of course, most file types can be converted to other files types using third- party conversion tools; if you are prepared to do that then you can have any personal ringtones you want.*

Send an MMS Message

MMS (also known as Picture Messaging) has been gaining popularity as an easy way to share short messages consisting of images, text, and sounds, and the content can be presented as one or several messages. In order for MMS to work, both the sending and receiving devices must be MMS-capable. MMS is a standard, but the specific file types that you can send with

MMS depend on the MMS service used by your wireless service provider and the MMS client used by the sender and the receiver. Generally, the types of content you can in send in an MMS message include:

- **Ringtones**   MIDI, up to 16-voice polyphony; standard or SP-MIDI format, up to 64KB per sound file
- **Sound clips**   AMR, up to 30 seconds playback time, 64KB per sound file
- **Pictures**   JPEG, GIF, WBMP, BMP, PNG, up to 640 × 480 pixels, 64KB per image file
- **Video**   H.263 baseline and MPEG4 simple profile wrapped in video format such as MP4, 3GP, and 3G2

What is MIDI (Musical Instrument Digital Interface)? It is a type of sound file—more specifically, a communications protocol that allows electronic musical instruments to interact with each other: most ringtones are MIDI files that are played by your iPAQ when you receive a phone call. MIDI requires software to create MIDI files and client software to read/play MIDI files.

Caution: Not all iPAQs ship with MMS software installed. For example, Sprint iPAQ handhelds do not ship with MMS capability. That said, Sprint iPAQs do ship with a similar service called Picture Mail that allows you to send MMS types of messages.

MMS vs. E-mail

Depending on the type of e-mail account you have, you can send the same content by e-mail that you can with MMS. So, why would you use MMS? The primary answer is that MMS is designed for mobile devices, while e-mail has been adapted for mobile devices, with the result that MMS is easier and faster to use. E-mail and MMS are based on similar technologies, but MMS messages are sent straight to the receiving handheld while e-mail messages are sent to the receiving person's e-mail account. There's a delay between sending and receiving e-mail because it is not downloaded until the e-mail server either pushes the message to the recipient's handheld or the recipient's handheld checks the e-mail server for new messages. This is less of an issue when you use MMS to send messages; many carriers claim that an MMS message will be delivered in about 30 seconds from the time it is sent, provided the recipient's phone is connected.

Of course, all of this depends on both the sending handheld and the receiving handheld having MMS capability. At this point, MMS has not yet been as widely adopted as e-mail, so e-mail is still the most common way to send content-rich messages.

Get Ready to Send an MMS Message

You will have to have MMS enabled on your iPAQ and in your service contract with your wireless service provider before you can send an MMS message. You may have to contact your mobile service provider to add MMS to your account and, of course, there is an extra monthly

service charge for MMS. For example, you can add MMS service to your Cingular account
online; the prices at Cingular.com as of this writing were as follows:

- **20 MMS package** $2.99 per month; includes 20 messages, $0.25 for each message
  after that
- **40 MMS package** $4.99 per month; includes 40 messages, $0.25 for each message
  after that
- **MMS Pay-Per-Use** $0.25 per message

Of course, pricing is up to your wireless provider so you will need to check. It is not uncommon
for a user to send many MMS or SMS messages not realizing that their carrier will charge them,
resulting in a shocking monthly bill.

Send an MMS Message from Your iPAQ

Your iPAQ user manual has much more detail regarding the MMS client, and we don't want
to duplicate content, so here are the fundamentals and cool stuff regarding sending an MMS
message on your iPAQ. If your service contract includes MMS service and you are ready to send
a multimedia file to someone, follow these steps to send an MMS message:

1. Open the Phone screen by pressing the green button on your iPAQ.
2. Select the Tools | Send MMS, as shown in Figure 4-15.
3. Select one of the stock MMS pictures; for this example, you will see the Compose MMS
   screen, as shown in Figure 4-16.

   a. If you chose to send a Custom MMS on the previous screen, on this screen you will
      have the opportunity to browse to a file that you want to send.

   b. If your iPAQ has built-in MMS media files, you'll see what the recipient will see
      when you press the Play button.

FIGURE 4-15   Send MMS menu.

FIGURE 4-16 MMS Compose screen.

4. Find the recipient in your contact list by selecting the To button, or enter the phone number of the person you want to send the message to.

5. Enter a subject in the Subject line.

6. Enter a message, if you like, in the field below the picture.

7. Press the Send button.

This is the simplest MMS message scenario, but there several other things you can do with MMS, including:

■ Add an audio clip

■ Include a vCard or vCalendar file with the MMS message

■ Configure how you want your MMS messages handled. You can access the MMS Send Options screen by selecting the Options menu then selecting the Send Options menu, as shown in Figure 4-17.

FIGURE 4-17 MMS Send Options Menu.

FIGURE 4-18 MMS configuration.

You can also use MMS Send Options screen, as shown in Figure 4-18, to take advantage of several choices:

- You can either send the message immediately (check the Send the Message Now box) or schedule when you want the MMS message to be sent by unchecking Send the Message Now and changing the date and time.

- You can set the MMS message to expire after a specific period so that, in the event that the message cannot be delivered within the expiration period, it won't be delivered at all.

- You can set a priority for the message: low, medium, or high.

- You can request a delivery report by checking the Delivery Report check box.

- You can send the message anonymously by checking that option.

> TIP
>
> *You cannot use your iPAQ phone and send an MMS message at exactly the same time, so before you try to send an MMS message you need to end the phone call.*

Third-party MMS Applications

There are some software vendors that offer other MMS applications for your iPAQ if your iPAQ doesn't already have an MMS client or you are looking for different features.

Pixer MMS (www.electricpocket.com)

Pixer MMS allows you to send photos, animations, and picture messages to e-mail and mobile phones from your iPAQ using MMS. More information about the software is available on the

Electric Pocket website (**www.electricpocket.com**); the product is available for sale from Handango (**www.handango.com**).

EzWAP 2.5, MMS client for Phone Edition 2.5 (www.ezos.com)

This application allows you to create, send and receive MMS messages on your iPAQ and features the ability to send messages containing graphics, sound and text and you can use the integrated tools, EzPAINT and EzMELODY to create your own images and sounds.

Send Text Messages

SMS has been around since 1991 and has been significantly popular in Europe and Asia since then, but SMS has only recently become popular in North America as a common form of communication.

What Is Text Messaging?

Text messaging is known as SMS everywhere in the world except the United States and is basically a mechanism to deliver short, text-only messages using mobile wireless networks. SMS is a universal text messaging system; it has come to be associated more with GPRS/GSM/EDGE wireless networks than CDMA networks, but CDMA carriers have their own text messaging services. When you send a text message, it is sent from the sending wireless device and stored in a central short message center, which then forwards it to the intended recipient wireless mobile device. This way, if the recipient is not available, the short message is stored and can be sent later. Messages longer than 160 characters are split into multiple messages. You need to refer to your service plan for per-message costs and availability on your wireless network.

What Is So Great about Text Messaging?

Why would you use text messaging? As with all technologies, there are specific uses that make text messaging more valuable than other ways of accomplishing the same thing. For example, text messaging is well suited for exchanging small messages like, "See you at 8:45 tonight at the theater," because text messaging is much less expensive than calling someone on your iPAQ phone to give them the exact same message. In fact, calling the person to give them the exact same message almost invariably takes more time and costs more.

Another feature that many text messaging users like is that it is an excellent technology for "chatting." If you have ever used instant messaging applications on your PC, the concept is very similar. With text messaging, you type and send short text messages, as well as appropriate smiley face icons, back and forth with another text message user. One of the advantages of text messaging, similar to e-mail, is that all of the major wireless mobile networks support text messaging, so it is becoming a universal standard that can be used across a wide variety of wireless mobile devices and networks.

What You Need to Send and Receive Text Messages

Text messaging does not require a specific account as e-mail does, but a few things need to be in place for text messaging to work properly. Your iPAQ is text messaging-capable right out of the box, but in order for SMS to work, both the sending and receiving mobile devices must:

- Be SMS or text message-capable—not all of the available wireless mobile devices and cellular phones are capable of sending and receiving SMS or text messages.

- Be hosted on a SMS or text message-capable wireless service provider wireless network—not all wireless service providers have made the necessary technical upgrades for SMS or text messaging.

- Have SMS or text messaging included in their service contracts—it is not necessarily part of the default wireless contract.

4

TIP   *How big can an SMS message be? The size limit of an SMS is 160 characters if Latin alphabets such as English, French, German, and Spanish, -are used. If non-Latin alphabets such as Chinese, Korean, or Arabic are used, the limit is shortened to 70 characters.*

Send a Text Message

Now that you have a firm grasp on what text messaging is and why you would you use it for communication, here's how to send a text message. The steps are fairly straightforward:

1. Open the Phone screen either by selecting Start | Phone or pressing the green Phone button.

2. Select Tools | Send Text Message, as shown in Figure 4-19.

FIGURE 4-19   Send Text Message menu.

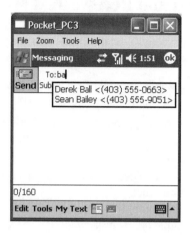

SMS Contact List.

3. Select the To field and either enter the phone number, including the area code of the text message recipient, or begin typing the contact's name and your iPAQ will match contacts from your address book so you can select the appropriate contact, as shown in Figure 4-20.

4. Select the Subject field and type in your subject.

5. Select the message body area and begin typing your message. You can even reduce your typing by selecting an option from the My Text list, a list of "canned text" that you might use often. The My Text list is shown in Figure 4-21.

6. Once you complete your message, select the Send button. That's it—your text message is now on its way to the recipient.

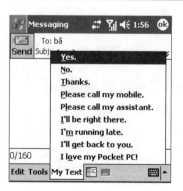

SMS My Text.

Configure Your Text Message Options

Your iPAQ user manual discusses all of your configurable options, but some of the highlights that you'll probably use include:

■ **My Text**   To help you minimize typing and allow you to quickly compose a text message, you can store a few messages that you use on a regular basis. My iPAQ allows me to store 9 different My Text entries. To access your My Text list:

1. Go to the Phone screen and select Tools | Send Text Message.

2. On the Messaging screen, select the Tools menu again and select the My Text option to access and edit your list.

■ **Spell Check**   It has become commonplace to abbreviate words and use slang to save on typing, but you also have the option of spell checking your message before you send it.

■ **Request message delivery notification**   You can request that you receive a notification when a message has been successfully received by the recipient. To turn this feature on:

1. Go to the Phone screen, select Tools | Send Text Message.

2. On the Messaging screen, select the Tools | Options to bring up the Request Message Delivery Notification screen.

3. On the Options screen, ensure that the check box is selected, as shown in Figure 4-22, and tap OK to save the setting.

FIGURE 4-22   Request Message Delivery Notification.

Use the TTY Functionality for the Hearing or Speech Impaired

An incredibly useful technology that was designed specifically for the hearing and speech impaired is TTY (tele-typewriter) and TDD (telecommunications device for the deaf), which allows a person with speech or hearing difficulty to communicate with a telephone. This is an ingenious innovation, although not a new one, in which the sending TTY device converts text input to a series of distinct audio tones for every supported character. These tones are then decoded and converted back into text on the receiving TTY device so that the receiver can read the message. Depending on the model, your iPAQ likely included TTY software on the companion CD that came with it that allows you to use your iPAQ with a TTY device. If you don't have the TTY software, contact HP to find out if software is available for your iPAQ operating system. There are also hardware connectors available directly from HP that connect your iPAQ to an external TTY or TDD device. In order for a TTY conversation to work, both of the connected phones must be capable of TTY or TDD communication.

One of the challenges for TTY/TDD on cellular networks is that the networks use digital audio compression "codecs" that may unintentionally distort the TTY audio tones while being transmitted through cellular telephones. Therefore, in order for TTY devices to work properly in cellular networks, your iPAQ must be set to a mode that optimizes the compression codec to handle TTY tones instead set to optimize transmission of the human voice.

The term codec *is an abbreviation for Coder-Decoder and functions as an analog-to-digital (A/D) and digital-to-analog (D/A) converter for translating the signals from the outside analog world to digital and then back again. There are many different types of codec agents that deal with different data formats.*

Enable TTY Support on Your iPAQ

Before you connect a TTY device to your iPAQ, you first need to enable TTY support. To do so, follow these steps:

1. Select Start | Phone | Tools | Options.
2. Select the TTY tab, as shown in Figure 4-23.
3. Check the Enable TTY Support check box and select OK.
4. When TTY is active, you will see a TTY icon in your navigation bar at the top of the screen.

Make a Call Using TTY

If you are used to using a TTY device to communicate over phone lines, this is probably fairly obvious, but just to show how simple it is:

FIGURE 4-23   TTY configuration.

1. On your iPAQ, press the green Answer/Send button.

2. Dial the phone number of the TTY call recipient, and when the person answers, begin your conversation by typing a message.

3. When you are finished with the call, press the red End Call button on your iPAQ.

Obviously, using TTY isn't difficult to use once you have everything configured correctly.

Wrap It Up

Do you remember the days when some people used to say, "Cell phone? Why does anyone need a cell phone? There are pay phones everywhere, what could be so important that you need to carry a phone with you?"

Yup, I do. In fact, I actually felt that way at one time but now I feel totally lost if I am not carrying my iPAQ. I need to be perpetually connected to the world via e-mail and mobile phone. This chapter covers a lot of topics regarding your iPAQ phone, including using the phone and all of the great features, as well as sending MMS, text messages, and even using your iPAQ for TTY communications.

Part II

Get Personal with Your iPAQ

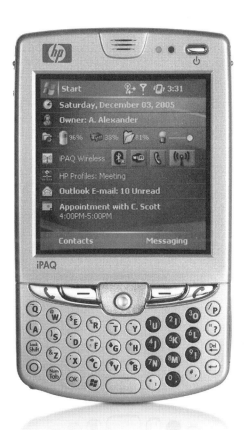

Chapter 5

Games, Music, Books, and Movies on Your iPAQ

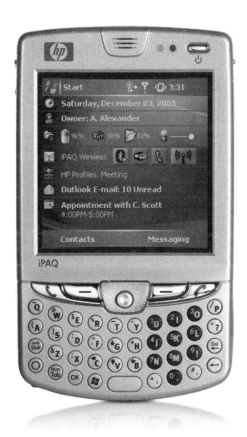

How to...

■ Use your iPAQ to listen to music

■ Use your iPAQ to listen to the news or other radio programs

■ Copy digital media from your PC to your iPAQ

■ Use your iPAQ to watch movies and videos

■ Play games on your iPAQ

■ Read books on your iPAQ

■ Choose some entertainment accessories

Use Your iPAQ as a Digital Music Player

In addition to being able to use your iPAQ as a cell phone, organizer, e-mail device, Internet browser, video game console, camera, and SMS/MMS/IM messaging device, you can also play music on it. In fact, most iPAQs do this so well that you really don't need to buy a separate portable music player. Unless, of course you just can't stop yourself from jumping on the iPod bandwagon.

You're probably familiar with the various versions of the Sony Walkman or similar types of portable radios, tape players, and CD players that allow you to listen to music or radio while you are walking around, jogging, or avoiding listening to advice from your friends. You are carrying around your iPAQ anyway, so why not use it to listen to your favorite music?

One of the advantages of listening to MP3s compared to listening to CDs or tapes on a portable device is that there is virtually no skip or sound interruption if you are moving while you are listening to your music; for example, your music won't skip if you are listening to music on your iPAQ while jogging or doing other mild impact sports. Of course, there are some logical limits. If you are listening to music during a motorcycle crash after nearly landing a 100-foot backflip, you just may hear a skip, but on the bright side it may not be the most important thing on your mind at that moment.

About Sound File Formats

There are several different types of files that can be played by electronic devices such as your iPAQ. Standards have evolved to help software and hardware manufacturers agree on formats that can be generated and played on a variety of different platforms. Many of the standards use similar technologies, and it is important to understand what file types your software can play so you use the correct file formats. If you need to, you can also convert your music files to the appropriate formats. The major file types of digital music are MP3, Ogg Vorbis, WAV, WMA, FLAC, AIFF/AIF, and streaming audio/video. These technologies are discussed briefly here, and much more information is available on the Web if you want to find out more. Later in this chapter we discuss converting your CD library to digital music files you can play on your iPAQ in the section "Convert Media File Types for Use on Your iPAQ."

What Is an MP3 File?

MP3 has become a relatively common term to most of us and is an absolutely essential part of the teenaged vocabulary. MP3 files are sound files that can be played by computer hardware running the necessary software to read and play the files. MP3 technology evolved primarily because of the need to reduce file sizes to make file transmission over the Internet faster and more efficient. It also allows minimizes how much memory is needed to store music files on your iPAQ. MP3s allow for smaller file sizes based on sophisticated file compression technologies. Music that you buy on CDs at your local music store is uncompressed, and therefore requires a lot of memory.

When uncompressed music from a CD is converted to an MP3 file, compression is applied that can reduce the file size to 10 percent of the original. How is this possible? The MP3 compression technology is mathematically complex so we won't go into too much detail, but if you are interested there are some great books and websites devoted to the more technical aspects of MP3 technology.

On the basic level, uncompressed files on your music CDs store more data than your brain can realistically process. For example, if two notes played simultaneously are very similar, your brain may hear only one note. Or, if one note is much louder than another, your brain may perceive only the louder of the two. MP3 compression removes any data from the file that you are not likely to notice as missing. This allows for much smaller file sizes. There are different levels of compression and, obviously, the more data that is removed from a sound file, the more the quality is reduced, so there is some tradeoff.

One of the advantages of MP3 files is that additional information is stored at the beginning or end of an MP3 file, such as the artist's name, track title, album title, year recorded, genre, and even personal comments. This is very useful for storing and tracking your MP3 collection.

What Is a WAV file?

WAV files are noncompressed audio files that can be played by a computer such as your iPAQ or PC. Most CD-burning software that converts music CDs to be stored and played on a PC converts them to WAV format. WAV files are noncompressed, so the sound quality tends to be better than compressed audio files like MP3 and Ogg Vorbis. However, the drawback is that WAV files can be very large—many megabytes—so storage space can be a problem on memory- and processor-restricted devices, which is why the MP3 and Ogg Vorbis files are more popular for devices such as your iPAQ.

What Is Ogg Vorbis?

Ogg Vorbis is a compressed audio format that is similar to MP3 (see the "What Is an MP3 File?" section for more information on audio compression); the same general principles apply to both. Ogg Vorbis is designed to provide better audio quality than MP3 while producing smaller files sizes. One of the advantages of Ogg Vorbis is that the technology used to create the audio files is not restricted by patents therefore users may use Ogg Vorbis compression technology for free provided that the user owns rights for the media being compressed. More information about Ogg Vorbis can be found at the Vorbis website (**www.vorbis.com**).

5

Other Music File Formats You May See

There are many different types of file formats, and to make it more confusing some of the file types are used for both music and video. Some of the formats you may see include MPEG/MPG, VCD, DIVX, AVI, WMA, FLAC, AAC, AIF, AAIF, AIDD, Audible.com spoken-word formats and Apple lossless files. Some of these files are more common for video, which is covered in more detail later in this chapter. The important thing to know about the various file formats is that each media player is capable of playing certain types of files and not others. However, there are utilities that you can use to convert most file formats to other formats on your PC before you move files to your iPAQ. File conversion is covered a little later in this chapter in the section "Convert Media File Types for Use on Your iPAQ."

What Is Streaming Media?

Most music and video files are stored in memory on your iPAQ and then played from memory. Even when you download an MP3 file from the Internet, for example, the entire file must be downloaded and saved before you can play it. Wouldn't it be great if you could begin to play the music before it is fully downloaded? That is essentially what "streaming" media is all about. When you select a file to listen to or watch, the file starts playing a few seconds after you begin downloading it and, as long as your Internet connection is steady, it will keep playing. Real Player or Macromedia Flash are examples of technologies that leverage streaming media.

How does streaming audio sound? Generally speaking, especially over relatively slow wireless connections, it tends to work better for talk radio than streaming music. However, as connection speeds improve, streaming media will continue to improve. The best way to find out what streaming audio sounds like on your iPAQ is to try it out for yourself. Fortunately, you can use the SHOUTcast (**www.shoutcast.com**) service. SHOUTcast offers thousands of radio stations, with almost any type of music and talk/news channels you can think of. Steaming radio is covered later in this chapter under the heading "Play Streaming Radio Using GSPlayer."

Use Windows Media Player to Rip Your Music CDs for Playback on Your iPAQ

Because your iPAQ likely shipped with a version of Microsoft Windows Media Player Mobile, we will discuss this process using the Windows Media Player that is installed on your PC to convert a music CD to something that you can play with on your iPAQ.

Get Windows Media Player for Your PC and Your iPAQ

If you don't already have the Windows Media Player installed on your PC or your iPAQ you can download the players for free from the Microsoft website:

■ For Microsoft or Mac PCs:
www.microsoft.com/windows/windowsmedia/default.mspx

■ For your iPAQ:
www.microsoft.com/windows/windowsmedia/player/windowsmobile/default.aspx

TIP

Mac users, don't let the Windows label scare you away: Microsoft provides Mac-specific Windows Media Player software for free.

You probably have music CDs that you would like to play on your iPAQ. You may even have video DVDs that you would like to play on your iPAQ. The process of converting CD/DVD files to files that your iPAQ media player is capable of playing is essentially the same, although the software that you will use will likely be different. We will discuss only music CDs here to help keep it simple.

NOTE

Ripping is MP3 jargon commonly used when talking about encoding. Basically, ripping is the process of extracting raw audio files from a music CD and is the first step in making a digital file. When you rip a CD, the result is a bunch of WAV files that are generally larger in size than you would like. The next step is to convert the WAV file to digital format that is smaller and playable on your iPAQ. This is accomplished with an encoder. Other names for software that allows us to rip CDs are referred to as CD grabbers or digital audio extraction (DAE) tools.

5

To rip tracks from an audio CD using Windows Media Player, follow these steps:

1. Insert the CD you want to rip into your PC CD drive.

2. On your PC in Windows Media Player, select File | CDs and Devices | Rip Audio CD, as shown in Figure 5-1.

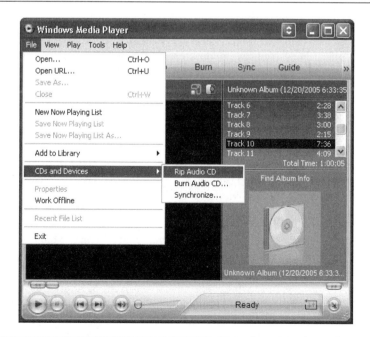

FIGURE 5-1 Windows Media Player's Rip CD menu.

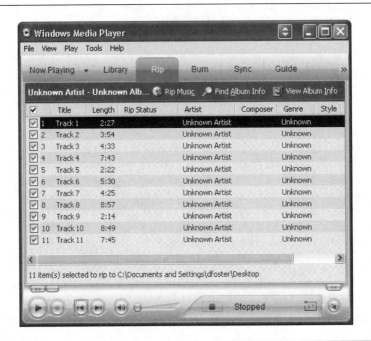

FIGURE 5-2   Windows Media Player's Select All Songs screen.

3. The Rip tab will be displayed, as in Figure 5-2, with all of the songs checked. If you only want to rip certain songs, uncheck the ones you don't want to rip. You can also select and deselect all tracks by clicking the check box at the top of the check box column.

4. Once you have selected the tracks that you want to rip, click the Rip Music button, as shown in Figure 5-3.

5. By default, the music files are ripped to the My Music folder on your PC and displayed in the Library feature in the Windows Media Player. The labels for the files will likely be default names, so you may want to rename the files with the name of the artist and album so that you can easily find the songs when you want to play them. If you are connected to the Internet while ripping a CD, Windows Media Player will name the files by artist and album for you.

Windows Media Player rips your music CD into a format called WMA, which is short for "Windows Media." The Windows Media Player Mobile player can play WMA, ASF, WMV, and MP3 files, so you can move your newly ripped WMA music files to a memory card and play them on your iPAQ. The process of moving your music from your PC to your iPAQ is covered in section "Transfer Your Music and Other Media onto Your iPAQ." Since the WMA files are relatively large in size, you may want to convert them to reduce the file size so you can get more songs onto a memory card. This topic is covered next.

FIGURE 5-3   Windows Media Player's Rip Music button.

Convert Media File Types for Use on Your iPAQ

1. If you use Windows Media Player Mobile on your iPAQ, you can play WMA files on your iPAQ, but there are at least two reasons that you may want to convert your newly ripped WMA music files or other file types before you put them on your iPAQ: Your iPAQ media player may not support a particular file type so you'll need to convert the file to a format that your media player can play.

2. You want to reduce the song file size so you can get more songs onto a memory card for your iPAQ.

NOTE   *You should know the types of media files that the media player on your iPAQ is capable of playing. For example, RealPlayer plays RM or RMJ files while most other players do not. Another popular group of media player–specific file formats is the Apple music file types such as AAC, AIF, AAIF, and AIDD.*

There are many websites that allow you to download music and video for free and many more that allow you to purchase media for download. Although you can usually find music already in a file format you can play on your iPAQ, what if it isn't? You'll need to convert it.

The process of converting files is pretty simple. The first step is finding the correct conversion tool. There are a lot of file conversion tools available on the Web. Many of these are shareware and offer free trial periods before you have to purchase the software. It is always a good idea to try out software before you enter your credit card number to be sure you are getting software that will work for what you need.

NOTE   *Digital Rights Management (DRM) and license protection is a hot topic in the press, mainly because there has not yet emerged a clearly better way to protect copyrighted digital files. Obviously, media companies that make their money from selling movies or music have a vested interest in ensuring they get paid for all of the hard work that goes into producing the entertainment that we enjoy. Generally, if you rip your own music CD, the resulting files will be unprotected. However, you may find that when you purchase music on the Internet that DRM protection is in place that will prevent you from converting or burning the media onto a CD/DVD. If you get protection or licensing errors when you try to burn or convert files, this is likely why.*

Convert WMA-encoded Files to MP3-encoded Files

Once you have ripped your music CD to WMA files using Windows Media Player, as discussed previously, you can either move the WMA files to your iPAQ for playback or convert them. The most common digital media type is MP3 so we'll focus on converting WMA to MP3.

There are so many types of encoders out there that we hesitate to recommend one over the other but many are available for you to try before you buy. Some great online resources to help you find WMA-to-MP3 encoders include:

- **www.wmatomp3.com-http.com**
- **www.mp3-converter.com**

Transfer Your Music and Other Media onto Your iPAQ

In order to play music on your iPAQ you must get the music to the iPAQ. There are several different ways to move files to your iPAQ:

- Synchronize your iPAQ with your PC to move files
- Download music files over the air using an Internet connection
- Transfer music files from your PC to a Compact Flash or Secure Digital memory card. Different iPAQs use one or both of these types of memory cards. Memory cards are covered in detail in Chapter 15.
- Stream music over the Internet to your iPAQ in much the same way that music is played on the radio. Steaming is covered in this chapter under both of the headings: "What is Streaming Media?" and "Play Music and Video with Windows Media Player 10 Mobile."

Play Music on Your iPAQ

Now that you can use your iPAQ as a music and audio player by storing music on memory expansion cards, you essentially have a portable CD collection! Instead of packing your CDs around between your house, car, office, and weekend cottage, you can store all of your favorite music on SD/CF memory cards and play them on your iPAQ wherever you happen to be, including through your car or home stereo.

Play Music and Video with Windows Media Player 10 Mobile

Your iPAQ likely shipped with a version of Microsoft Windows Media Mobile player to allow you to play MP3 music files. The iPAQ 3500 and 3900 models ship with Windows Media Player Mobile version 9. For this reason and because it is a capable media player, we will spend most of our time discussing Microsoft Windows Media Player. Additional media players and tools are also discussed in this chapter.

There are at least a couple of reasons why using software that is preinstalled on your iPAQ is often the best alternative: first, it is free with your iPAQ so it won't cost you anything extra to use it, and second, it has been thoroughly tested with your iPAQ hardware and software. There are a lot of freeware and shareware applications that you can download and try out, but although many of these programs are quality products, keep in mind that you run the risk of installing poorly designed and built software that may cause device instability and headaches.

At the time of publication, the latest iPAQ Pocket PCs—the 6500 and 6900—both come equipped with Windows Media Player 10 Mobile. Version 10 of the player offers quite a few more features than previous versions. Version 9 is relatively basic and offers simple playback and playlist functionality as well as a few "skinning" options.

Skinning essentially means that you can change the way an application looks by changing its "skin." Different skins use different colors, buttons, and layouts, and you can choose what you like best. Not all applications have changeable skins, but it has become relatively common.

iPAQs running Windows Media Player 9 Mobile on the following devices are upgradeable to Windows Media Player 10 Mobile:

- HP iPAQ rx3100
- HP iPAQ rx3400
- HP iPAQ rx3700

Windows Media Player 10 Mobile took version 9 and added a media library for browsing content stored on the device, album art display, better playlist support, easier controls, and the ability to play back more media types, including content encoded with DRM.

Microsoft Windows Media Player 10 Mobile is the first PDA-based software to offer lossless audio playback due to the support of WMA Lossless. Windows Media Player 10 Mobile is capable of playing back 640 × 480 video with stereo sound, although there are very few devices that are capable of this right now.

Windows Media Player 10 Mobile can also play audio and video content purchased or subscribed to from services like MSN Music (**www.music.msn.com**), Napster (**www.napster .com**), or the many other Windows Media–compatible online services now available. At the time of printing, iTunes (**www.itunes.com**) was not yet available for Pocket PC devices such as your iPAQ, but this excellent service will likely be available for Pocket PC and Windows Mobile soon.

Copy Music and Other Media to Your iPAQ Using ActiveSync

By using the desktop version of Windows Media Player 10 on your PC and the process of synchronization, you can easily copy music, recorded TV, video, playlists, and digital photos to an external memory storage card for your iPAQ.

Windows Media Player 10 currently only runs on Windows XP, so if you are running a different operating system you must use Windows Media Player 9. The steps for each are listed separately below.

CAUTION   *Your iPAQ has limited onboard memory, so it is always a good idea to store media such as music, video, photos to an external memory card. The type of memory card you can use depends on the model of your iPAQ; some types of media players will only play files that are stored on a memory card.*

Media Synchronization with Windows XP Desktop Computers

In Windows Media Player 10, all of your synchronized music, recorded TV, video, and playlists will appear in the Windows Media Player 10 Mobile library on your device. Note that Windows Media Player 10 Mobile cannot be used to view pictures, but most iPAQ handhelds ship with a picture viewing program.

The following procedure describes how to configure your computer to synchronize content to your iPAQ. After you complete this procedure, subsequent synchronizations will either occur automatically or with minimal intervention from you.

1. On your desktop computer, install Windows Media Player 10 for free from **www.microsoft.com/windows/windowsmedia/download/**.

2. If your iPAQ did not come with a CD including the latest version of ActiveSync, download it for free from **www.microsoft.com/windowsmobile/downloads** and install it.

3. Start Windows Media Player 10.

4. Right-click the title bar and select Tools | Options.

5. On the Player tab, select the Enable Picture Support for Devices check box.

6. Insert a storage card into your iPAQ and connect your device to a USB port on your computer by using the cable that came with your iPAQ.

7. If this is the first time that you have connected your device to your computer, the ActiveSync New Partnership Wizard will start up. Select Standard Partnership and follow the instructions.

8. If this is the first time that you have used your iPAQ with the desktop version of Windows Media Player 10, the Windows Media Player Device Setup Wizard starts. You will need to choose either the Automatic or Manual synchronization method:

   ■ **Automatic**   With this option, the desktop player will synchronize content with your iPAQ device automatically when you connect your iPAQ to your computer or when you change your synchronization settings. If there is enough free storage space on your iPAQ, the desktop player synchronizes all of the content in your desktop library to your iPAQ. If there is not enough free space on your iPAQ to synchronize all of the content in your desktop library to your iPAQ, the desktop player synchronizes the highest priority (that is, your favorite) content first. Note that automatic synchronization is not available unless there are at least 32MB of free storage space available on one of the iPAQ storage locations, such as on a removable memory storage card.

   ■ **Manual**   This setting enables you to choose what and when you want to synchronize your iPAQ with your PC. Synchronization will not happen automatically every time you connect your iPAQ to your computer.

9. Click Finish.

10. Once you have clicked Finish, depending on how you configured your synchronization method, one of the following will occur:

   ■ **Automatic**   The player will begin synchronizing media content. The next time you connect your iPAQ to your computer while Windows Media Player 10 is running, your content will be synchronized to your iPAQ automatically.

   ■ **Manual**   No items will be automatically synchronized.

   You can change your settings at any time. For more information on how to use the Sync feature, launch the Help system on the desktop version of Windows Media Player 10 by pressing the F1 key on the top left of your keyboard.

Media Synchronization with Non-Windows XP desktop computers

The desktop version of Windows Media Player 10 is available only for computers running Windows XP. If you are not running Windows XP on your desktop computer, you can use Windows Media Player 9 to accomplish essentially the same thing.

Windows Media Player 9 offers two free download versions:

1. For Mac OS, go to
   www.microsoft.com/windows/windowsmedia/software/Macintosh/osx

2. For Microsoft Windows 98 SE, Windows 2000, or Windows ME, go to
   www.microsoft.com/windows/windowsmedia/player/9series

With Windows Media Player 9 you can use the Copy to CD or Device feature to copy your audio files and video files to your iPAQ.

For more information on how to use the Sync feature, launch the Help system on the desktop version of Windows Media Player 9 by pressing the F1 key on the top left of your keyboard.

Transfer Music to Your iPAQ Using a Card Reader

Your iPAQ likely has an external memory slot for either a Compact Flash (CF) card or a Secure Digital (SD) memory card or both. If so, an invaluable tool is an SD/CF card reader. Card readers are widely available; you can find them for under $20 online or in specialty stores (SanDisk is one of many manufacturers: **www.sandisk.com**). Some card readers, such as the Lexar Media (**www.lexar.com**) Memory Card Reader, can read multiple types of memory cards: CompactFlash (types 1 and 2), Smart Media, Memory Stick, Memory Stick Pro, MultiMediaCard, SD Card, xD-Picture Card, MicroDrive, MS Duo, MS PRO Duo, and miniSD. Memory cards are becoming more common on a wide variety of devices so you can use the reader with your other electronic devices: using a USB cable to connect your PC to the card reader, you can copy a file from your digital camera, video camcorder, MP3 player, as well as your iPAQ. The SD/CF card reader attaches directly to your PC and allows you swap your SD/CF card from your iPAQ to the card reader to quickly transfer pictures, music files, applications, and other files to and from your iPAQ, without needing to synchronize. If you have an SD/CF memory expansion card and a card reader, follow these steps to transfer your music from your PC to your iPAQ (we assume your card reader allows your PC to view contents of the memory card as simply another drive on your PC):

1. Insert your SD/CF memory card into your card reader.

2. Open the folder where the files you want to copy or move to your iPAQ are located.

3. On your PC, open My Computer and double-click the drive that represents your memory card.

4. Once both folders are open, click and drag to copy or move your music files—WAV or MP3 files, for example—from that PC folder to the memory card folder.

5. Replace the memory card into your iPAQ. Now you will be able to select the files you want to play on your iPAQ

Play Streaming Radio Using GSPlayer

There are several streaming media players, including Windows Media Player Mobile, but we will briefly discuss another option to show how easy it is to install and begin using third-party software. There are certainly many different types of media players that are available for download, and if you like trying different things to see what works best for you, you have a lot of options. Many media players are inexpensive to purchase, but we'll talk about GSPlayer because it has a lot of features and it is free. The downside of freeware is that it often lacks user documentation and technical support but—did we mention?—it's free.

> **TIP**   *Before you download GSPlayer, you may want to refer to the earlier section earlier in this chapter, "What Is Streaming Media?" Also, it is important to realize that streaming relies on an Internet connection. If your iPAQ does not have wireless capability, you can still stream when it is connected to an Internet connected PC with a synchronization cable.*

GSPlayer is a free, small, open source MPEG audio player built by GreenSoftware (**http://hp.vector.co.jp/authors/VA032810/**) for Pocket PC devices that allows playback of SHOUTcast radio streams, MP3s, and other formats. Follow these steps to download, install, configure, and begin listening to streaming radio on your iPAQ:

1. Connect your iPAQ to your PC with a synchronization cable.

2. Download the GSPlayer (**http://hp.vector.co.jp/authors/VA032810/**). If you use the direct download link, you will get versions for different versions of Pocket PC, Windows Mobile, and Windows Operating Systems. The alternate download link allows you to choose the correct download by your iPAQ processor if you know it.

> **TIP**   *You will need an unzip program to unzip the file on your PC. WinZip software is available as a free download at **www.download-it-free.com/winzip/;** there are other available unzip programs as well if you search the Web.*

3. After you download and unzip the file, there will be at least one file in the folder you chose to download the zip file to. Drag and drop all files to your Pocket PC.

4. The GSPlayer interface has many options, but the ones you have to set up are all shaded purple. It is an interesting, simple way to guide you through the setup—you can play with the other settings later on. Follow the purple shaded menus to configure your player to play SHOUTcast stations.

5. Select Tools | Options, as shown in Figure 5-4.

6. On the Preferences tab, you can modify your preferences by ing the appropriate check boxes as shown in Figure 5-5.

7. On the Associations tab (Note: you may need to select the right arrow button at the bottom of the screen to scroll to the right so that you can see the Associations tab) select All as shown in Figure 5-6.

FIGURE 5-4 GSPlayer Options.

8. On your iPAQ, launch Internet Explorer and browse to the SHOUTcast homepage. You will see a list of the most popular stations or you can search for a specific type of music.

9. Choose a radio station and click the Tune In icon.

10. You will be prompted to download the SHOUTcast-playlist.pls. You can change the name of the station to anything you like by selecting the Change button, renaming the playlist, and selecting the OK button.

11. You should now hear the radio being played on your iPAQ.

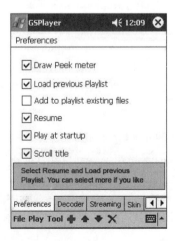

FIGURE 5-5 GSPlayer Preferences.

FIGURE 5-6   GSPlayer Associations.

Download MP3 Files from the Internet to Your iPAQ

In addition to being able to copy and move files between your desktop PC and your iPAQ, you can download music directly from the Internet using the wireless Internet capabilities of your iPAQ.

Some clever hackers have figured out ways to embed viruses into MP3 and movie files, so it is very important to use antivirus software on your iPAQ if you are going to be downloading media files directly to your iPAQ over the wireless Internet. More information about securing your iPAQ is covered in Chapter 16.

There are many websites from which you can download MP3 and other media files—just do a search from your favorite Internet search engine. Be aware that there are royalty and legal issues with downloading protected music.

Use Your iPAQ to Play Music through Your Car Stereo

There are several ways to play your iPAQ music through your car stereo. Most of the following options for your car stereo apply to your home stereo as well:

■ **Use an RF modulator (Radio Frequency Modulator, also called an FM modulator)**
This option likely has the highest "cool!" factor. It allows you to connect your iPAQ to your car stereo wirelessly using the FM capabilities of your car stereo and a little device you plug into the earphone output jack of your iPAQ. Once the RF modulator is hooked up to your iPAQ, tune your car radio or any FM radio to one of the digitally

tuned FM stations that are supported by your modulator. For example, the Arkon (**www.arkon.com/sf.html**) Soundfeeder FM modulator allows you to use eight different FM frequencies: 88.1, 88.3, 88.5, 88.7, 107.1, 107.3, 107.5, 107.7, so you have a high likelihood of being able to find a frequency that a radio station in your area is not using. Some users have reported great success with this approach, but others have reported that it can be difficult to get static-free sound. An RF modulator solution is relatively inexpensive, about $30 to $40. Two vendors that manufacture and sell FM modulators are:

- Radio Shack (**www.radioshack.com**)   product name: iRock
- Arkon (**www.arkon.com/sf.html**)   product name: Soundfeeder

- **Replace your car stereo**   Obviously, this option is not always practical, but if your current stereo doesn't have a 3.5mm input jack, you should know there are some models that do. This jack allows you to plug your iPAQ directly into your car stereo using an inexpensive patch cable that you can buy at Radio Shack. Some of the manufacturers that offer car stereos with this capability include JVC, Aiwa, and Pioneer. You can also connect your iPAQ to a home stereo this way, as many home stereos have input jacks; however, you may need an adaptor cable or two to make the connection.

- **Use a cassette adapter**   If your car has a cassette tape player, you can easily use an adaptor that allows you to plug directly into your cassette player. The adaptor looks like a cassette tape with a wire attached. Insert the mock cassette into your player and plug the cable into your iPAQ. This type of hardware is generally available at electronics stores; Radio Shack is a good place to start.

Use Your iPAQ to Make Your Car Stereo into a Speaker Phone

Being able to use your iPAQ as a speaker phone while sitting in your car is useful and, perhaps more importantly, a great way to impress your friends. There are currently no manufacturers that make products specifically for this, but the same technology that allows you to use your iPAQ to listen to music through your car stereo speakers works great at converting your car stereo into a speaker phone (your iPAQ hands-free microphone is still the input for your voice).

You will need an RF modulator to do this. Hook your RF modulator up to your iPAQ and make or receive a phone call on your iPAQ. The voice of the person that you are speaking with will be played through your car stereo and—remember to use the speaker phone option, covered in Chapter 4—your voice will be picked up by the phone microphone. There are some great car mount kits that allow you to mount your iPAQ to your dash for easy and accessible operation and keep your iPAQ in close proximity to the stereo.

As mentioned earlier, there are two vendors that manufacture and sell FM modulators.

Watch Video and TV on Your iPAQ

Yes, you can watch TV or movies on your iPAQ. Sure, the screen may be a tad smaller than your average 60-inch flat-screen high-definition entertainment system, but it can be a blessing when you are strapped into a tiny seat on an overbooked regional jet trying to forget about the unconscious football player drooling on the shoulder of your new suit jacket.

TIP *Video files tend to be large, so it's important to manage your onboard memory and memory cards so you have enough room to fit the video files. The good news is that if your iPAQ has an external memory card slot, memory cards with 2GB of data capacity are available.*

5

There are two ways that you can watch video on your iPAQ:

■ Load video files locally onto your iPAQ or onto the memory card in much the same way you store your music. This allows for offline viewing when you don't have an active data connection, such as when you are on a plane.

■ Stream video over a wireless connection through your cellular carrier or through WiFi/802.11/WLAN. Your network connectivity options are dependent on the model of your iPAQ and are discussed in detail in Chapter 3.

NOTE *Depending on the iPAQ model you have, the size of user-accessible internal memory will vary (see the chart of available memory by model number in Chapter 1). If your iPAQ doesn't have enough free memory to save video files, your next best option is to load video files onto an external memory card. If your iPAQ doesn't have a memory card slot or if you don't have a memory card, streaming video may be an option. Memory cards and streaming video are discussed next.*

Streaming Video

Streaming video is essentially the same as streaming music or radio. The video signal is not stored locally on your iPAQ. Streaming media can be either audio or video sent in compressed form over the Internet and displayed by the viewer software as it arrives. The advantage to streaming media is that you don't have to wait to download a large file before seeing the video or hearing the music. In order for streaming to work, you need a program installed on your iPAQ that decompresses the file and sends video data to the screen and audio data to the speakers. Streaming media plug-in applications are available for most web browsers, and some are available as separate applications. Some options are discussed next.

TIP *Remember, streaming means that video and sound data is sent over the Internet in real time, so the quality of your viewing and listening experience is highly dependent on the speed of your Internet connection. Cellular connection speeds tend to be faster and more reliable during off-peak hours.*

Streaming Video and Audio Viewer Applications

As Internet and wireless speeds continue to increase in speed and performance, streaming video is becoming a compelling reality. A few vendors that have embraced streaming video include Real Networks' Real System format (**www.real.com**), Microsoft's Media Player format (**www.microsoft.com**), and Apple's QuickTime (**www.apple.com**).

 *If you are streaming video or music/radio over a cellular connection, it is counted against your overall data usage. Overage charges can be very expensive, so if your data plan is not unlimited, make sure that you are not going over your plan limits.*

Microsoft Windows XP Media Center Edition

One of the most interesting media technologies to come around in a while is Microsoft's Media Center PC. Before you buy your next home PC, you owe it to yourself to look into this system. It is based on Windows XP, so you can do all of the things that you would do on your regular PC, but it has many other features designed to allow you to manage and enjoy all of your digital media including movies, music, photos, and TV. The Media Center PC is covered in detail in Chapter 7, but here are some of the features:

- Progressive-scan DVD playback with online chapter lookup.

- The My TV view, which offers a simple way to browse, watch, and record TV, even on multiple channels at the same time in both analog and over-the-air digital. The TV features work with an antenna, cable, or satellite TV signal and have a fast and easy setup. My TV includes live TV, recorded TV, the program guide, guide search, and the new Movie Finder2 service. You don't even need to pay a monthly fee for this functionality.

- My Music, which offers access to both your personal and online music collection. You can play a music CD, copy it into your library, burn it to a CD, create playlists, and edit album details.

- My Video, which lets you see an alternate view of your My Videos folder in Windows XP, organize files and folders by date or by name, and display a thumbnail image for each clip. Common video types are supported, including AVI, MPG, and WMV files.

- My Pictures, which provides an easy way to view and share your digital photos. You can download pictures from your digital camera; view your pictures and graphics; quickly create a slide show; and touch up, print, and burn photos to CD.

- The ability to copy to CD/DVD including creating CD menus, burning recorded TV to CDs and DVDs, sharing or archiving digital pictures and home movies, and burning CD mixes.

- Online Spotlight, an online guide that accesses the world of on-demand entertainment, including music and radio services; movie download and on-demand services; and customized sports, news, and entertainment programming.

■ Sync to Device functionality that allows you to transfer your favorite media to your iPAQ Pocket PC.

■ Applications such as Orb with which you can stream your digital media over the Internet from your Media Center PC to your iPAQ. Orb and the Media Center PC are both covered in detail in Chapter 7.

NOTE

*As of early 2006, Sprint (****www.sprint.com****) and MSpot (****www.mspot.com****) launched a service that allows subscribers to watch unlimited full-length movies, television shows, concerts, and comedy specials for a flat monthly fee of $6.95, plus the regular data charges. The service allows users to watch the movies in segments, much like a DVD setup. Sprint said their initial trials showed that most people have shorter attention spans when viewing on the handset. The initial list of movies were* Night of the Living Dead, Short Circuit, Angel and the Badmen, *and* One-Eyed Jacks; *Sprint plans to add seven films a week.*

5

Listen to Nonmusic Audio on Your iPAQ

In addition to music, there is a wide variety of audio that you can store and listen to on your iPAQ, such as:

■ Audio books

■ Audio magazines

■ Audio newspapers

■ Public radio programs that you can download from websites

One service that allows you to download this type of audio content to your computer so you can transfer them to iPAQ is Audible.com (**www.audible.com**). An Audible.com membership allows you to download over 18,000 audio books and programs to listen to on your iPAQ.

Read an E-book on Your iPAQ Using Microsoft Reader

Your iPAQ probably didn't arrive preinstalled with Microsoft Reader, but Microsoft Reader is available free directly from the Microsoft website (**www.microsoft.com/reader/downloads/ ppc.asp**) (they also offer some other excellent software for your iPAQ).

With Microsoft Reader you can download and view e-books in Microsoft's LIT file format. Microsoft Reader uses ClearType display technology that makes onscreen text onscreen easier to read. Microsoft Reader features include the ability to:

■ Change the font size from small to large

■ Highlight and bookmark text

■ Insert your own notes or drawings

■ Go to the last page you read

Microsoft Reader allows you to view commercial LIT-formatted books protected with Digital Rights Management Level 5 Security. Before you can read any of these files, you must first activate the software through the Microsoft Passport authentication system. This process must be done over the Internet, so if your iPAQ does not have wireless connectivity, you will need to hook your iPAQ to a PC that has Internet connectivity with a synchronization cable. Once your iPAQ is connected to the Internet, you need to launch a web browser on the iPAQ and open the Microsoft Reader Activation web page from **http://das.microsoft.com/activate/en-us/**

Microsoft Reader does not require activation to view e-books published in DRM1 or DRM3 standards.

Where to Get E-books

E-books are becoming increasingly popular and there are several places that offer free e-books or allow you to purchase e-books for your iPAQ. Some examples include:

- A list of e-book vendors is available online on the Microsoft site at **www.microsoft.com/reader;** there you will also find a link to the Microsoft online e-book catalog.
- You can also find nonprotected books on the Internet by searching for "free e-books."
- *Pocket PC* magazine offers list of e-book-related topics on their "Best Sites" page on their website (**www.pocketpcmag.com/bestsites.asp**).

Other E-book Reader Programs for Your iPAQ

Other e-book reader applications available for your iPAQ include:

- TomeRaider (**www.tomeraider.com**)
- Mobipocket Reader (**www.mobipocket.com**)
- eReader (**www.ereader.com**)
- Adobe Reader for Pocket PC 2 (**www.adobe.com**) (allows you to view PDF files on your iPAQ)

Play Games on Your iPAQ

As I am sure you are aware, like the drive-in movie and one-cent candy, the days of playing Pong on your TV and going to the video arcade to plug fistfuls of quarters into arcade games are long gone. Fortunately, your iPAQ is equipped with a bright color screen and stereo sound, which makes it an excellent choice for gamers. The Windows Mobile operating system also happens to be the platform of choice for many mobile game development companies, which means that there is a huge selection of games available for your iPAQ. Many of the available games are shareware and freeware, so you can be a gamer without spending a fortune on new games as they come out.

A Games Overview for Your iPAQ

There are so many different games for your iPAQ to list them all here would be to create a catalogue of games. Instead, we'll give you a brief cross-section of some of the games that are out there. Many games, including video games, card games, and board games that you know and love, have been adapted for the Pocket PC, so if you have a favorite game you can likely find it online.

To get a more complete idea of the games available for the Windows Mobile OS on your iPAQ, you can search the following websites:

- Microsoft (**www.microsoft.com**)
- PocketGear (**www.pocketgear.com**)
- Handango (**www.handango.com**)
- Handmark (**www.handmark.com**)
- Tucows (**www.tucows.com**)

Other great resources are iPAQ fan site discussion boards on which iPAQ users rank and review the most popular games; a list of some of these websites is available in Appendix B.

Board Games

There are some great iPAQ games based on familiar traditional board games. The following games are just a selection; all games listed here are available at Handmark, **www.handmark.com**):

- **Chess**   Award-winning PocketChess Deluxe about $20 has everything to challenge and entertain new and returning chess players (available at Handmark, **www.handmark.com**), as shown in Figure 5-7. Choose your difficulty level and personalize your game play. With the PGN support, you can add new games and problems to your chess library.

FIGURE 5-7   PocketChess Deluxe.

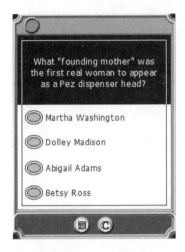

What "founding mother" was the first real woman to appear as a Pez dispenser head?

○ Martha Washington

○ Dolley Madison

○ Abigail Adams

○ Betsy Ross

FIGURE 5-8   Trivial Pursuit for Pocket PC.

- **Tetris Classic Game Pak for Pocket PC**   Available for around $30 Tetris isn't a board game, but the other games in this bundle do fit into this category. Some of us get a little bored of playing one game all of the time and game packs or game bundles are a great way to keep from getting too bored on those multi-hour trans-Atlantic parasailing journeys, or slightly more practically, while sitting in your doctor's waiting room. the Tetris Classic Game Pack for Pocket PC includes:

  - **Tetris Classic**   The Handmark version of Tetris Classic contains four different game types including Marathon, 40 Lines, and timed games.
  - **PocketChess**   Discussed earlier in this chapter as a standalone product.
  - **Handmark Checkers**
  - **Handmark Backgammon**
  - **Handmark Colors**   Match colors or symbols to clear out rows and quickly earn points.
  - **Solitaire**

- **Trivial Pursuit for Pocket PC**   around $20. Whether you are just bored or have a secret desire to annihilate your in-laws at Trivial Pursuit after turkey next Christmas, this is a great game for your iPAQ: see Figure 5-8 for a screenshot of a question card as it looks on the iPAQ. Some of the more interesting features include:

  - Over 1600 questions in seven categories: Sports and Leisure, Arts and Entertainment, History, Science and Nature, People and Places, and Wild Card.

- There are several modes:
  - Classic mode emulates the board game with the benefits of automated card selection, rolls of the die and token movement.
  - Flash mode offers a ladder-style version of the Trivial Pursuit game in which up to six players take turns answering questions. Players move up the ladder with every correct answer; the first player to reach the top rung and answer the final questions is the winner.
  - Single player–mode or against two to six opponents in local hot seat–mode and multiplayer.

Puzzle Games

Games that are classified as Puzzle games tend to involve thinking and strategy rather than action and focus on solving a problem rather than playing against an opponent.

Bejeweled 2 by Astraware (www.astraware.com) $19.95

Bejeweled is a popular game that has been available for several years and was adapted from an online game. In Bejeweled 2 players must match the colored jewels in lines of three horizontally or vertically to clear them from the board. Lines of four jewels are awarded with a Power Gem whilst lines of five award the much sought-after Hyper Cube. Both special jewels trigger their own unique jewel-clearing devices. A screenshot of the game is shown in Figure 5-9.

| FIGURE 5-9 | Bejeweled 2. |

FIGURE 5-10   Myst PPC 2.01.

Myst PPC 2.01 by CyanWorlds (www.cyanworlds.com) $24.95

Myst is an adventure, puzzle game that features original rich graphics, sounds and music. It has excellent review and has even won awards from the likes of Pocket PC Magazine. Figure 5-10 shows a screenshot of the Myst graphics to give you an idea of what it looks like. More screenshots and product information is available from www.cyanworlds.com

Action Games

This category can be open to interpretation, because one Gamer's backgammon is another Gamers "action" game.

Snails 2.6 by PDA Mill (www.pdamill.com) $19.95

We like a game that doesn't take itself too seriously, and this one certainly fits the bill. Check out this award-winning action-strategy game featuring "sheer stupidity and snails fighting for world domination"—how can you go wrong with that? The latest version for Windows Mobile includes local network (LAN/WLAN) and Internet multiplayer features to allow you to play against other iPAQ users. Some of the more interesting features include:

- Special effect eye-candy, such as smoke trails, flames, vectors, alpha-blended sparks, explosions, and weather effects.
- audio, including professional music, sound effects, and voices tailored specifically for the Pocket PC, with or without headphones.

- Three different snail races: the Moogums, Lupeez, and Nooginz, each with their own personality, including special animations, voices, texts, root beer preference, and culture. Extra add-on races for registered users.

- 10 unique levels ranging from the ancient desert sands to the chilly snowfields up into outer space, and down below the sea.

- Humorous weapons, including the cartoon anvil drop and the infamous exploding toad, Monsieur Frog!

Essential Entertainment Add-ons for Your iPAQ

Add-ons and accessories for your iPAQ are scattered throughout this book, but here we focus on some great accessories that relate more to entertainment than anything else, including Bluetooth stereo headsets, vehicle mount kits, and some ideas to connect external speakers to your iPAQ.

Bluetooth Stereo Headsets

Your iPAQ has an audio out that allows you to use a wide variety of stereo headsets, but if your iPAQ has built in Bluetooth wireless technology you can use a wireless headset to talk on the phone or listen to music. We will focus only on headsets for music and video here.

The key benefits to Bluetooth headsets are that they are wireless so you don't have wires to get caught up on things as you move around, the headphones take up less space when not in use, and you will look incredibly good walking around. Bluetooth allows you to listen to music or other audio up to 30 feet away from your iPAQ.

There are a few manufacturers that make Bluetooth stereo headsets and one of the best for your iPAQ is HP's iPAQ Bluetooth Stereo Headphones, as shown in Figure 5-11. These headphones have a design that HP calls "behind the head" with the key benefit being that your headphones won't mess your hair up when you wear them; or they will look good while wearing a baseball cap. The retail price is currently around $100 according to the HP website.

FIGURE 5-11   HP Bluetooth stereo headphones.

Some of the other features of the Bluetooth headset include:

- Easy access to controls—the volume controls, power on/off, play/pause, and track forward/back controls are conveniently placed on the ear piece.
- A carrying bag and charger are included, and each headphone charge gives you up to eight hours of listening with rechargeable batteries.

To learn more information about HP iPAQ Bluetooth Stereo Headphones or to purchase on the Web, go to **www.shopping.hp.com**. Another vendor that offers compatible Bluetooth headsets is Logitech (**www.logitech.com**).

Vehicle Mount Kits

There are several types and brands of vehicle mount kits; the right type for you depends on your vehicle and your needs. Arkon (**www.arkon.com**), for example boasts 14 different models; Figure 5-12 shows an example of an HP model. Vehicle mount kits are one of those accessories that you won't think you need until you try one out.

The process is simple: when you get into your car you take your iPAQ out of your pocket or off of your belt and place it in the mount kit. The main advantages of vehicle car mount kits include:

- It prevents your iPAQ from sliding around in your car and being damaged, or alternatively, flying out an open window as you round the corner.
- Some vehicle mounts are powered, so you can charge your iPAQ while you are in your car.
- It allows you to easily view appointments and scheduling.

FIGURE 5-12   HP vehicle mount kit.

- If your iPAQ is a phone model, the mount makes for an excellent hands-free tool when used with the speaker phone feature or phone headset. A great way to turn your iPAQ into a great speaker phone with your car stereo is covered in the section "Use Your iPAQ to Make Your Car Stereo into a Speaker Phone."

- If you use GPS on your iPAQ, you can easily see the screen and interact with the application as conveniently and safely as possible—a heck of a good alternative to gripping the iPAQ between your knees as you drive down the highway! GPS is covered in detail in Chapter 9.

- If you use your iPAQ to play music in your car you can use your iPAQ to play music through your car stereo (covered in this chapter under the heading "Use Your iPAQ to Play Music through Your Car Stereo").

Many vendors produce vehicle mount kits for your iPAQ, including:

- HP (**www.hp.com**)
- Arkon (**www.arkon.com**)
- ProClip (**www.proclipusa.com**)

Wrap It Up

You should now have a pretty good grip on some of the things that your iPAQ can do to help you ensure that you are not taking life too seriously, including listening to music and streaming radio, watching video, and playing games on your iPAQ.

5

Chapter 6

Take and Send Pictures with Your iPAQ

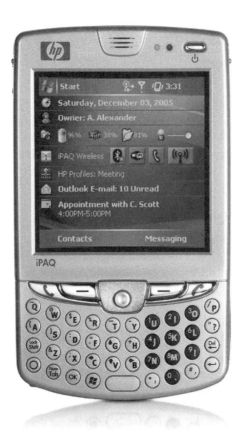

How to…

- Take a photo
- Record video and sound
- Take a photo with an HP accessory camera
- Send photos to others using e-mail, MMS, Bluetooth, and infrared
- Download your iPAQ photos to your Windows PC using MS ActiveSync
- Download your photos to your Mac PC using third-party software
- Use HP Image Zone software to view, manage, and send your photos
- Share your photos with others online
- Use third-party software to manage your pictures
- Use third-party software to edit your pictures
- Print your photos

One of the most significant recent advances in consumer electronics, besides your fantastic iPAQ, is the evolution of digital photography. And, as if your iPAQ doesn't let you do enough already, it also allows you take digital snapshots, save them, print them, and send them to others.

What if Your iPAQ Does Not Have a Built-in Camera?

The majority of iPAQ models don't have a built-in camera, but if your iPAQ has a slot for a Secure Digital (SD) card, you can purchase an HP Photosmart Mobile camera that plugs into the top of your iPAQ using the SD card slot. The HP Photosmart Mobile camera is discussed in the section "The SDIO Photosmart Mobile Camera iPAQ Accessory."

Technical Information about Your iPAQ Digital Camera

The iPAQ camera is not intended to capture monumental sweeping mountain landscapes to hang on your wall or to record your wedding reception for generations to enjoy—although you certainly can use it for that if you like. The camera is really intended as a fun toy with which to take snapshots anywhere and share them with friends. The technical specifications of your iPAQ camera depend on your model number; look at your user documentation to find out the details.

Examples of some of the iPAQ Pocket PC handhelds that do have built-in cameras include but are not limited to the 6300 series, 6500 series, 6900 series, and 3700 series, among others.

NOTE   *Your iPAQ photos are saved as JPEG files. The JPEG file format is named after the Joint Photographic Experts Group and is pronounced, "jay-peg." JPEG is the most popular format for digital photographic images.*

Camera Flash—or Not

Depending on your particular iPAQ, you likely won't have a built-in flash, although a few models such as the 3500 series have a light that helps illuminate close-ups. However, the light still doesn't do the job of an actual camera flash when taking photos in low light. Photos taken in low light will tend to turn out to be grainy and of poor quality.

> **TIP**   *Your iPAQ screen resolution may be lower than the capability of the camera. This means your resulting photos will likely be higher quality when you view them on your PC than what you see on the screen when you view photos on your iPAQ.*

Digital Zoom

Several iPAQ models feature a digital zoom that functions like a regular camera to allow you to get closer to your subject. The zoom functionality is covered in more detail in the section "Take a Picture and Record Video with Your iPAQ." Refer to your user manual to find out what the specifications of your iPAQ are.

The SDIO Photosmart Mobile Camera iPAQ Accessory

If your iPAQ does not have a built-in camera and is one of 1930, 1940, 2200, 3900, 4000, or 5000 series iPAQs, you can add an HP Photosmart Mobile Camera to your iPAQ, as shown in Figure 6-1.

6

FIGURE 6-1   HP Photosmart Mobile Camera.

The HP Photosmart Mobile Camera plugs directly into the SD slot of your iPAQ. If you are not sure your iPAQ has an SD slot, check your user documentation before you purchase the camera. With the HP Photosmart Mobile camera iPAQ accessory you can

- Use its 1.3 megapixel total resolution and 4x digital zoom
- Directly print from your Pocket PC using Bluetooth technology, WLAN/WiFi, or infrared connectivity
- Capture still images and add audio messages
- Capture video with audio
- Automatically synchronize your images from your Pocket PC to your desktop
- Edit and resize images with HP Photo Center software
- Use integrated photo sharing over the Web on HPphoto.com
- Use its 1-bit SDIO interface

A quick web search will show some of the many online stores that sell the HP Photosmart Mobile Camera if you decide it is a good choice for you.

Advantages of the HP Photosmart Mobile Camera vs. a Dedicated Digital Camera

If your iPAQ does not feature a built-in camera, why would you buy the HP Photosmart Mobile Camera as an add-on accessory to your iPAQ? The answer is relatively simple. The HP Photosmart Mobile Camera may make sense for you if you see value in any of the following:

- Sharing your photos directly from your iPAQ through e-mail
- Printing a photo directly from your iPAQ through the infrared or Bluetooth wireless connection with a Bluetooth-enabled printer such as the HP DeskJet 450
- Automatically moving photos from your iPAQ to your PC when your iPAQ is docked in the cradle connected to your PC
- Its small size (1.1 ounces)—if you are carrying your iPAQ anyway, the HP Photosmart Mobile Camera is much easier rather than packing a full size camera
- Its low cost—the accessory now sells for around $100

Tips for Taking Photos with Your iPAQ

You likely are not surprised your iPAQ does not produce photographs as fine as a Hasselblad 501 or a 9 megapixel digital SLR does. However, there are steps you can take to help ensure you are able to produce good quality digital photos with your iPAQ. In fact, thanks to the HP Photosmart technology, the camera is pretty darned good. In this section, we'll go over some ways to make the most of your iPAQ camera. If you already have a good working knowledge of photography, some of these suggestions will be basic, but they are important to maximizing the quality of your photos.

NOTE *To see some examples of great photos taken with iPAQs, search Google by typing "iPAQ camera" (**www.google.com**) to get a list of sites where iPAQ users showcase their photos.*

Use Good Light

Depending on your iPAQ model, it may or may not be equipped with a flash/light, so the quality and source of light on your subject is one of the most important factors to consider when taking photos with your iPAQ. Of course, in many situations the source and location of the light source is beyond your control—it usually isn't very practical to wait for the sun to move across the sky so that the daylight illuminating the squirrel is coming from just the right angle. Low lighting will be obvious on your iPAQ because you will see little blue pixels on the screen.

6

Ensure That the Main Light Source Is Behind You, Not the Subject

If you take a photo of a person with the sun shining from behind them, your resulting photo will often be more of a silhouette of the person rather than a detailed likeness. Your photos will turn out better if the sun is behind you, facing the subject, when you take the photo. This will provide more of the light your iPAQ needs to capture the image.

Move the Camera Until You Don't See Washed Out Areas

When looking at the screen in camera mode, you may notice that areas of high contrast and very bright or reflective areas appear to be washed out or whiter than they should be. Moving the camera slightly to change the angle of the shot will often allow the camera to recompose the image to more accurately reflect what the image looks like.

Take a Picture within Two Seconds of Launching the Camera

Some users have reported that taking a picture within two seconds of launching the camera—before the screen has had time to compose the image—improves their picture quality. The success of this technique seems to depend on the user and the individual iPAQ. You may find that it doesn't make much difference, but it is worth trying as part of your bag of iPAQ tricks.

Take Multiple Pictures of the Same Subject

If you have the time, it is always a good idea to take a few photos of the same subject from different angles and distances. One of the best things about digital photography is that you can delete any photos you don't want, and it doesn't cost you a thing, unlike film photography where you had to pay for film development before you were able to find out whether a photograph of your thumb was worth keeping or not.

Keep the iPAQ Still While Taking a Picture

Keeping your iPAQ still while you take a picture is another very important aspect to taking good photos. If you can, steady your arm on a table, tree, or parking meter, and your shots will improve. You will notice that even a little bit of movement will cause blurring in the photo. Of course, if you want a little blurring in your photos for artistic effect, that's easy to do.

Take a Picture and Record Video with Your iPAQ

If you are the type of person that likes to press every button and play around with your new electronics before reading about the features and how they work, then you may have already taken some photos of your pets, office, friends, big toe, etc. But, if you haven't yet ventured into the world of iPAQ digital photography, here is where you can get started.

The Simplest Path to Taking a Photo

To take a photo in the least number of steps possible:

1.   Choose something to be your photo subject.

2.   Select Start | Programs.

3.   Select the HP Photosmart icon, as shown in Figure 6-2.

4.   Your iPAQ screen now becomes your camera view finder. You will notice that the screen is presented sideways, or in landscape mode, so turn the iPAQ on its side with the keyboard facing you and to the left. When you are looking at the screen in camera mode, you see what the camera is seeing—this feature also means you don't have to hold the camera up to your eye to see where the camera is pointing. You can hold it any way you want; as long as you can see the screen, you can see what the photo will look like, as shown in Figure 6-3.

FIGURE 6-2   HP Photosmart application icon.

FIGURE 6-3   Camera view finder.

6

5. Point the camera at your target—as a rough guideline, the target should be at least 18 inches away from your iPAQ.

6. When your target is framed on the screen, while holding the camera as still as you can, press the camera button on the top right corner of the iPAQ or press the Capture button on the screen, as shown in Figure 6-4.

7. After the image has been captured, you will see it on the screen with three buttons: Don't Save (trash can icon), Send, or Save (OK), as shown in Figure 6-5. You don't have to select a button. If you don't select a button the photo will be saved and the camera will revert back to a ready state where it is ready to take another photo.

FIGURE 6-4   Onscreen Photo Capture button.

FIGURE 6-5   Camera Don't Save (trash can), Send, and Save (OK) buttons.

The Simplest Path to Recording Video

If your iPAQ, such as the 6500 series, has a camera capable of recording video, the steps to do so are very simple:

1. Press the Start | Programs and launch the HP Photosmart camera application.

2. Ensure that the camera is in video mode, as shown in Figure 6-6; if the button shows the camera icon simply press it to change it to video mode. In video mode, the time you have left to record is shown on the screen and depends on the resolution setting (changeable in the Settings menu) and the amount of free space you have available to store the video file. In addition, you can turn on or off audio recording, which is also configurable in the Settings menu.

FIGURE 6-6   Camera Video Mode toggle button.

3. When you are ready to begin recording, press the Capture button on the screen (the large round button), or press the physical button on the top right of the iPAQ.

4. When you are finished recording the video, press the Capture button again or the physical camera button to stop recording. You can now launch the HP Image Zone application to view your video and move it to your PC or share it with others.

CAUTION   *Video and audio requires significantly more memory than static digital photos, so memory management is important.*

After the First Photo and Video, What Else Does Your iPAQ HP Photosmart Camera Do?

As you are looking at the main camera screen, depending on your iPAQ model, there are a host of buttons with sometimes not-so-obvious purposes, as shown in Figure 6-7.

1. Zoom in (up to four times digital zoom, depending on iPAQ model)

2. Zoom out

3. Menu—this launches a series of menus that allow you to configure your camera settings (see the section "Customize Your HP Photosmart Camera Settings" for more detail)

4. Review—this launches the HP Image Zone application on your iPAQ

5. Flash (light) activation

6. Video Record button

7. Photo Capture (does the same as using the hardware button)

8. Ready light

9. Help

10. Close the camera application

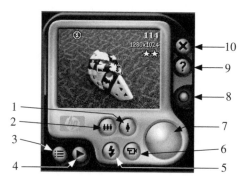

FIGURE 6-7   Camera buttons.

Some of the more advanced camera settings are covered next. Even if you don't intend to take a bunch of photos with your iPAQ, you may want to browse this section to get an idea of the power of this handy little camera.

Customize Your HP Photosmart Camera Settings

For most of you, the default settings will work fine for everyday use, but HP provides an impressive number of ways to change the camera behavior to suit your needs. Access the settings by launching the HP Photosmart application and selecting the Menu button. By selecting different tabs and options on each tab, you can customize your camera configuration. You can browse through your options yourself, but here is an abbreviated list of configuration highlights:

- Settings tab
  - **White Balance**   Offers different settings for different types of light including Sun for outdoor photos and Tungsten and Fluorescent for indoor photos. The default setting is Auto, which presumably will choose the correct setting for you.
  - **Color**   Settings include:
    - Color for normal color photos
    - Black & White
    - Sepia, which makes a photo look like an old black and white photo that has aged to a brown and black
    - Negative, which makes the photo look like a film negative
    - Cool, which captures the photo in blue and white
  - **Compression**   Settings include:(see the section later in this chapter called "What Is Digital Compression?" for an explanation.)
    - Good gives you high compression, making for a smaller file size but reduced picture quality.
    - Better, is the medium, default setting.
    - Best is low compression, creating a larger file size at the best quality.
  - **Resolution**   These four settings determine how physically large a photo is onscreen. The higher the resolution, the better the photo and the bigger the file size. You can fit a lot more photos on a memory card at low resolution than high resolution. Also, depending on what you want to do with a photo, you may want to change the resolution. For example, if you just want to e-mail a funny snapshot of a friend, you may want to choose a low resolution to keep the file size down.
  - **Flicker Filter**   This setting attempts to deal with flicker that can be caused by indoor fluorescent lights. Most of you won't have any reason to change the setting from Auto, but the power is yours.

- Setup tab—the Capture menu
  - **Camera sound (off/on)**
  - **Instant Review**   Allows you to set how long an image is displayed after a photo is taken. Tip: if you want to take photos quickly one after another, turn Instant Review off.
  - **Self -timer**   A timer that delays the photo from being captured either two or ten seconds after the Capture button in pushed. It is good for group shots you want to include yourself in, provided you can prop your iPAQ up and get yourself into the shot within ten seconds.
- File tab—allows you to change how you want your photos saved
  - **Filename prefix**   Call the files whatever you want, "iPAQ-Pics," for example, and each photo file will have that name plus an incremental number.
  - **Current counter value**   Allows you to set where you want the incremental numbers to start; for example, iPAQ-Pics01.jpg
  - **Save Pictures In**   Allows you to set the file location where you want your pictures to be saved on your iPAQ
- Video tab
  - **Video format**   You probably only have one format in the list.
  - **Video size**   You can set how large captured video appears onscreen; a lower setting means smaller screen size as well as a smaller file size.
  - **Record audio check box**   If you choose to record audio, when your record video your file sizes will be larger.
- Info tab—displays software and firmware version numbers for your HP Photosmart camera

What Is Digital Compression?

When a photo file is compressed, any data that is duplicated or is unnecessary is removed. This allows for the file to be squished, or compressed, into a minimal file size. For example, if large areas of a photo are white—snow, for example—the value of a single white pixel is saved along with the locations of the other pixels that share the same color. When the compressed image is opened for viewing or editing, the compression process is reversed. JPEG images are stored using a type of compression called lossy compression. The higher the compression settings, the more quality and sharpness is reduced, because similar colors are all changed to one color. For example, a highly compressed photo of a field covered in snow will show all of the snow as one color of white whereas in reality that snow may be thousands of different shades of light gray, blue, and yellow. High compression loses the visual subtleties of what the snow-covered field really looks like if you were seeing it with your own eyes, but for most purposes compression makes little difference to the visual quality of a photo, especially at lower resolutions.

Automatically Save Photos to a Memory Card

Your iPAQ is likely equipped with a SD and/or CompactFlash (CF) card slot(s) that allow you to use removable memory cards. Your iPAQ has a limited amount of available onboard memory for files, applications, and pictures, so the ability to expand the memory is extremely useful. In fact SD/CF cards are commonly available in sizes as small as 64MB and as large as 8GB. Another advantage to them is if you ever have to perform a hard reset on your iPAQ, all of the memory will be wiped out, but anything stored on your SD/CF memory card will remain intact. Memory cards are covered in more detail in Chapter 15.

There are at least four reasons storing photos and other data on memory cards is a good idea:

- You will almost certainly be able to store more photos on a memory card than in local memory on your iPAQ, especially since large cards of several gigabytes are constantly coming down in price.

- You can easily swap memory cards when one gets full, or use them to organize photos into different categories.

- Memory cards are more stable than onboard memory. If for some reason there is a problem with your iPAQ and you lose data, photos and data stored on a memory card will likely not be affected.

- If you have a card reader for SD or CF cards, you can easily pop out the memory card from your iPAQ to read the photos from the card without needing to synchronize your iPAQ. This can be a much faster method of transferring photos.

To configure your HP Photosmart camera to automatically store photos to a memory card, follow these steps:

1. Ensure you have a memory card inserted into your iPAQ.

2. Select Start | Programs.

3. Select the HP Photosmart application.

4. Select the Menu button.

5. Select the File tab, as shown in Figure 6-8.

6. At the Save Pictures In drop-down menu, select the File Folder button.

7. Browse the iPAQ folders and select the appropriate CF or SD card from the list.

8. Select the OK button at the top right of the screen.

Now every photo you take will be stored directly to the card you selected.

FIGURE 6-8   Camera Save Pictures In setting.

6

Use HP Image Zone on Your iPAQ to View, Print, and Send Your Photos

Most iPAQ devices ship with HP Image Zone software installed. To check whether you have the software on your iPAQ, simply tap the Start button, and select Programs to browse through the program list to find HP Image Zone. HP Image Zone software includes two software components: one that runs on your iPAQ called HP Image Zone for iPAQs, and one that runs on your desktop PC, called HP Image Zone for PCs. The version that runs on your PC is available on the companion CD that came with your iPAQ. If you don't have the companion CD or would like the latest version of Image Zone, it can be purchased from HP for about $50 at **www.shopping.hp.com**.

TIP   *If your iPAQ did not ship with HP Image Zone, HP Photosmart Essential is an excellent software program that is a scaled down version of HP Image Zone and available for a free download from HP.com (**www.hp.com/united-states/pse/download.html**).*

HP Image Zone for your iPAQ allows you to:

- View photos that are stored on your iPAQ or SD memory card
- Share your photo using HP Instant Share, infrared, or e-mail
- Print your photos using HP Mobile Printing or HP Instant Share (both topics are covered later in this chapter)
- Create your own slideshow on your iPAQ

- ■ Play your own recorded video
- ■ Edit your photos right from your iPAQ and even add drawings
- ■ Record sound clips to attach to your photos

HP Image Zone 5 for your PC allows you to:

- ■ Remove red eye, crop, and resize
- ■ Restore color, enhance black-and-white images, bring out detail in shadows using HP "adaptive lighting technology," and add special effects such as sepia and antique treatment
- ■ Organize photos by date or folder and search your photos using keywords
- ■ Add your photos to greeting cards, calendars, album pages, CD and DVD labels, flyers, and brochures
- ■ E-mail your photos directly from Image Zone
- ■ Upload your digital photos to HP's Snapfish.com so your friends and family can see your photos and even order photo gifts such as photo books, calendars, mugs, shirts, and posters
- ■ Watch videos and print freeze-frames
- ■ Use Image Zone to view photos in a slideshow accompanied by music.

You may view your saved photos on your iPAQ at any time by selecting Start | Programs and launching the HP Image Zone application. From there you can view a slideshow of the photos and videos stored on your iPAQ or browse to find a particular photo.

Send a Photo to Others from Your iPAQ

When you are browsing your photos, or immediately after you have taken a photo, you can choose to send the photo to someone else using either e-mail or Multimedia Message Service (MMS is covered in Chapter 3 and is dependent on the capabilities of your wireless service provider network and on the details of your service contract). After you have taken and saved a photo you can also transfer the photo to others using Bluetooth or Infrared which are both covered in Chapter 3.

Send a Photo from Your iPAQ Using E-mail, Bluetooth, MMS, or Infrared

Before you can send a digital photo using e-mail, you need to have an e-mail account that is correctly configured on your iPAQ. E-mail is covered in depth in Chapter 12. Whether you want to use e-mail, Bluetooth, MMS, or infrared to send a photo stored on your iPAQ from your iPAQ, the steps are similar:

1. On your iPAQ, select Start | Programs.
2. Select the HP Image Zone application.
3. Browse through your photos to find the one you want to send and select it.

FIGURE 6-9   Send Photo button.

4. Select the Send button, as shown in Figure 6-9.

5. You will see a menu with your options, as shown in Figure 6-10.

6. Select one of the following options and then select Next; each option requires other supporting conditions to work properly:

   a. MMS (Multimedia Messaging Service)   Only available if your iPAQ has phone capability; MMS is a service similar to SMS (Short Message Service) that is provided by your carrier and allows you to send messages and photos through the carrier without using e-mail.

   b. E-mail attachment   Primarily available if your iPAQ has phone capability. You will need e-mail set up on your iPAQ; e-mail is covered in Chapter 12. If you don't have e-mail on your iPAQ, you can move your photos to your PC and e-mail from there.

FIGURE 6-10   Send Photo menu.

What is Bluetooth Pairing?

Bluetooth pairing is what happens when two Bluetooth-enabled devices agree to communicate with one another and the two devices join what is called a "trusted pair." When one device recognizes another device in an established trusted pair, each device automatically accepts communication from the other, bypassing the discovery and authentication process that normally happens during Bluetooth interactions.

   c. Bluetooth   A short-range wireless networking standard; 30 feet or less. If your iPAQ has Bluetooth capability, you can use this method to send photos and other data to another nearby Bluetooth-capable device. Bluetooth and Bluetooth pairing is covered in detail in Chapter 3.

   d. Infrared   A line-of-sight, short-distance wireless networking protocol limited to only a few feet. If your iPAQ has an infrared port, you can place it next to another infrared-capable device with the ports facing each other and transfer data such as photos. Infrared is covered in detail in Chapter 3.

Move Your iPAQ Pictures to Your Windows PC with MS ActiveSync

Microsoft and HP have made this task exceedingly simple, provided your PC is running a Windows operating system. If have a Mac, some of your options are discussed in the next section.

To move your iPAQ pictures to your Windows PC, all you need to do is install Microsoft ActiveSync on your PC and connect your iPAQ to your PC with a synchronization cable or cradle. Microsoft ActiveSync is included on the companion CD that came with your iPAQ and is available as a free download from Microsoft.com at **www.microsoft.com/windowsmobile/ downloads/activesync41.mspx**.

After ActiveSync is installed on your PC and you synchronize your iPAQ with your PC, your pictures will be moved to your PC. Whether this happens automatically or requires you to start the synchronization process manually depends on your ActiveSync settings. ActiveSync configuration is covered in detail in Chapter 2. Once your iPAQ is synchronized with your Windows PC, you can easily browse to your photos on your PC by following these steps:

   1. Open MS ActiveSync and select the Explore button, as shown in Figure 6-11. A file explorer window will launch, as shown in Figure 6-12.

   2. Open the My Pictures folder to see your iPAQ photos. From here, you can view, move, rename, e-mail, edit, and do anything else you want to with your photos.

FIGURE 6-11   ActiveSync Explore button.

FIGURE 6-12   ActiveSync Mobile Device folders.

Move Your iPAQ Pictures to Your Mac Using Third-party Tools

Unfortunately, Microsoft has not yet come out with their ActiveSync software for the Mac platform, but there are some enterprising software developers that have made it possible to sync your iPAQ with your Mac PC. Two of your choices include:

- PocketMac Pro 3 from PocketMac, available for around $42 (**www.pocketmac.net**)
- Missing Sync 1 for Pocket PC from MarkSpace (**www.markspace.com**), available for around $40, works with the Apple iSync conduit (**www.apple.com/support/downloads/ isync.html**)

If for any reason your iPAQ pictures don't launch an image viewing applications when you try to open them, you can always use your web browser. JPEGs are supported in virtually every web browser. To do this, open your browser—Internet Explorer, Netscape Navigator, and Mozilla Firefox are the most common—then click File | Open and browse to the iPAQ picture you want to view. When you click Open, your picture will show up in your browser window.

Use Third-party Software to Edit Your Digital Pictures

Another significant difference between digital photography and film photography is you don't have to be an expert or own thousands of dollars of film equipment to edit your digital photos. Your iPAQ produces photos and allows you to send them to others and copy them to your PC so there isn't anything you *must* do to your pictures to enjoy them. But if you want to edit and work with your photos, there are some options.

Imaging software has come a long way in the past few years, which has lead to a proliferation of image editing software on the market. While choice is rarely a bad thing, it can also present an overwhelming number of alternatives. Most software office suites that include word processing and spreadsheet applications also include some kind of imaging program, so you may want to find out if you already have something installed on your home or office PC that you can use.

If you are unsure whether you already have image editing software, try to open one of your iPAQ pictures after you have copied it from your iPAQ to your PC. Double-click one of the JPEG files and see what application launches. You will have at least an image viewing application. If you are not familiar with the application that opens, check the help file to see what it is capable of and whether or not it will do what you want. A good first check is to see if it allows you to resize images.

Although, many of the built-in tools may be fine for rudimentary image manipulation, you may want a more sophisticated option. You choices may be somewhat different depending on whether your PC runs a Windows or Macintosh operating system, but either way there is lots of choice:

- HP Image Zone and HP Photosmart Essential software is included with your iPAQ or is available for download from HP.com. Both of these options are discussed in the previous section "Use HP Image Zone on Your iPAQ to View, Print, and Send Your Photos."

- Adobe Photoshop Elements 4 (**www.adobe.com**) is available for around $90. This program is a trimmed down version of the more powerful and much more expensive Photoshop versions and is available for both Windows XP and Mac; you can download a trial version to try it out before you buy it. Elements allows you to do a lot of things to help you enjoy and share your iPAQ digital photos, including:

    - Remove red eye automatically as you download.
    - Create composites.
    - Create slideshows with pan and zoom effects, voice narration, and multiple music tracks.
    - Order prints online with one click.
    - View photos on your TV.
    - Share your photos online.
    - Easily isolate objects from backgrounds.
    - Organize your photos.

- Adobe Photoshop (**www.adobe.com**) is comparatively expensive—around $900—but if you need more than red-eye reduction and slideshows, you may enjoy this full professional image editing standard for both Mac and Windows. Photoshop is an industry standard for graphic designers and professional photographers and is a powerful application. Be aware that it can be challenging to learn, but you likely won't be limited by the software capabilities.

- Paint Shop Pro (**www.corel.com**) is a powerful image editing application for Windows that offers a lot of functionality and costs around $100. (You may remember that this was formerly a Jasc product.) You can download a trial version before you buy and view an extensive list of its functionality on the Corel website.

- Microsoft Digital Image Pro (**www.microsoft.com**) is Microsoft's consumer digital imaging and editing software and is available for around $100.

This is a small selection of some of the more popular imaging products that are on the market, but there are many more you can find by doing a web search for "image editing software" or a similar search phrase. If you have time to try a few to see what works for you, great. If you don't, you can't go too wrong with Adobe or Corel products.

Use HP Instant Share to Share Your Photos via E-mail

HP offers a service called HP Instant Share that works in conjunction with Snapfish (**www.snapfish.com**) and allows you to share your photos via e-mail but eliminates the need for large attachments. This is accomplished by sending recipients an e-mail that contains photo thumbnails. When the recipient clicks a photo thumbnail, they are taken to a secure website where they have the option of printing or saving your photos, creating online albums, and ordering prints.

To use either HP Photosmart Essential or HP Image Zone software on your desktop PC, select the Share tab , as shown in Figure 6-13. Once you select a photo or group of photos, you have several ways to share the photos:

- E-mail with MS Outlook
- E-mail with HP Photosmart Share

FIGURE 6-13   Photosmart Share tab.

- Order prints
- Create a web album
- Create an Online project

Select any of the options and you'll be walked through the steps to help you share your photos.

Use Third-Party Software for Your Digital Pictures

Although your iPAQ camera is primarily a fantastic tool to share fun pictures with friends, it is also a great way to get into digital photography for very little money. In fact, the camera is really a free gift that HP simply threw into the deal when you bought your iPAQ. Digital photography is a booming business driven by both professionals and hobbyists alike. The digital nature of your iPAQ photographs means that the types of things you can do to and with your photos on your PC is only limited by your imagination. Besides the HP software that is discussed earlier in this chapter, there is a wide variety of software and tools that allow you to do some very imaginative things to your photos as well as practical tools to allow you to work with your photos. This section provides a cross section of some of the different types of software available to allow you to modify your iPAQ pictures on your PC. Where appropriate, also included is whether or not the software works on Windows or Mac platforms.

 Digital photography can be addictive.

Get Focused Using Third-Party Software

Some photos may be blurred beyond the point of no return, but many times when a great photo that can't be easily recreated—the fantastic back-flip that Grandma successfully landed off of the garage roof on her BMX bike, for example—you just want to minimize the blur as much as possible. There are some inexpensive software tools that are available to allow you to sharpen your digital photos. The success rate of these products is reported to be good, but you may want to try them out yourself to ensure that they meet your expectations.

Focus Magic

Focus Magic (**www.focusmagic.com**) allows you to improve the quality of photos. It is available for both Windows and Mac platforms, and you can try the software before you buy it. This product is slightly different than Sharpen or Unsharp Mask filters, which increase the contrast at the edges of an image. Focus Magic uses "Forensic Strength" technology to give you as much of the original 'in-focus' image as possible.

Unshake 1.4

Unshake (**www.hamangia.freeserve.co.uk/Unshake/**) is a freeware tool for Mac, Windows, and even Linux that is designed to improve blurred and "shaken" photos by programmatically determining the form of the blurring and deducing what the picture would have looked like if it had not been blurred. The author of the software originally developed the software for his own use and now shares it for free with others for nonprofessional use. Isn't the Internet great? To run this program, you will need to run software called the Java Runtime Environment, which can be downloaded for free from Sun Microsystems (**http://java.sun.com/getjava**).

*If for some reason the Unshake website link does not work, you will probably be able to find the product by using a website search engine such as Google (**www.google.com**).*

Tips for Improving Your Photos after You Have Taken Them

You can modify and edit your photos on your PC after you have moved them to your PC using ActiveSync. Your iPAQ produces image files called JPEGs, as mentioned in the section "Technical Information about Your iPAQ Digital Camera." Because JPEG is the most popular format for digital photographic images, it is easy to find image editing software that allows you to edit your iPAQ pictures.

Reduce the Picture Size Using Imaging Software

Using an image editing application, you can resize your photos from a larger iPAQ size, 1280×1024 for example, to 500×400. JPEG images do not scale up very well—that is, you will likely not be happy with the results of increasing the size of a JPEG image using an image editing application— but, JPEG images *do* scale down well. One way to improve your images is to reduce the size using an image editing software package, as discussed in the section "Use Third-party Software to Edit Your Digital Pictures."

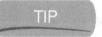

Most image editing applications have an option called Unsharp Mask that you should use whenever you downsize a JPEG image. Applying this filter after you have reduced the size of an image will reduce some of the blur and sharpen the edges. You can usually find out if your image editor has this feature by looking in the application help files.

Organize Your iPAQ Photos

When you get to the point where you have collected a large number of photos over a longer period of time, you may find organizing your photos and finding what you want quickly has become a bit of a challenge (some statistics state that family's are taking over one thousand digital photos per year!). Organizing thousands of photos becomes unwieldy quickly. Luckily, there are software applications that allow you to view, track, and manage digital photos. Generally, the way these applications work is to automatically scan your existing photo directories and create a database. Then you simply add information about the files into the program by selecting one or more images and assigning keywords like "family," "reunion," and "vacation" to them. According to your keywords, you can search your quickly search and locate the pictures you want to view. Some of the applications that offer these features include:

- **HP Image Zone or HP Photosmart Essential** (Windows only)   Available on the iPAQ companion CD or by download from HP.com. Both of these products are discussed earlier in this chapter.

- **Photo Manager by ModTech** (**www.mt-ac.com**, Mac and Windows)   Allows you to create musical slideshows and add animated clips, effects, and captions. You can upload your slideshows for free for 30 days to **www.photoshow.net**; publish it to HTML for your website; burn it to a CD, VCD, or DVD-ROM; or make a self-running executable file or screen saver.

- **Adobe Photoshop Album** (**www.adobe.com**, Windows only)   Adobe has been the leader in digital imaging products for a very long time. This application allows you to see all of your photos; access your entire collection of photos—even your video and audio clips—in one place, no matter where they're stored; locate photos by the date it was taken using the sliding timeline or Calendar View; view your pictures by day, month, week, or year, use keyword tags; and even touch up your photos.

Make a Digital Photo Album or Slideshow

The digital world, in some respects, does a fine job of emulating the nondigital world. People have been sharing, reminiscing, and embarrassing each other by showing off family photo albums for decades. The idea of an old-fashioned photo slideshow has been significantly updated. The idea of sitting around watching Uncle Wally's holiday slides while he explains in stunning detail exactly what each slide is about is already pretty darned exciting, but now you can combine sound and animation with your photo slides and run the whole thing on your PC.

There are two primary methods to putting your pictures into a photo album or slideshow format: locally on your PC, or on the Web. There are applications that allow you to easily show off your pictures; the online approach is discussed in more detail later in this chapter under the heading "Publish Your iPAQ Photos on the Web Using an Online Picture-hosting Website." Here we will discuss a couple of options to allow you to easily put your iPAQ photos together in a digital photo album on your personal computer.

Create Digital Photo Albums and Slideshows   As mentioned earlier, another convenient thing about digital photos is that there are many vendors that provide software that allows you to create multimedia shows such as digital photo albums and custom slideshows. Here is a short list of a few of the vendors that provide software for these purposes but there are certainly others.

- **Adobe Photoshop Elements** (www.adobe.com)   Discussed earlier in the section "Use Third-party Software to Edit Your Digital Pictures."

- **Simple Star PhotoShow** (**www.simplestar.com, Windows and Mac**)   The Deluxe version of Simple Star costs about $40, but Simple Star offers an Express trimmed down version for free. The application allows you to create and share multimedia shows using your own photos and music. You can choose photos, a soundtrack, and transitions and effects, then drag and drop animated clip art and captions to create PhotoShows. These can then be shared online, burned to CD-ROM, used as a screen saver, or published to a website.

■ **SmoothShow Slideshows (www.smoothshow.com, Windows)**   This application is about $20 and offers a free trial so you can check it out before you buy. SmoothShow 3 allows you to export your shows as digital movie files (AVI or MPEG) for making DVDs, VCD, streaming video website, or other video applications. There are also web templates, pan and zoom effects, unlimited overlays, and digital video transitions,"

■ **SWF 'n Slide by Vertical Moon (www.verticalmoon.com, Windows and Mac)**   At about $50, SWF 'n Slide is a program that allows you to take both digital images and music and create a slideshow. Your final slideshows are rendered in Flash (SWF) format, which is an easy standard format to e-mail, web publish, or burn onto to a CD-ROM.

■ **Paint Shop Photo Album 5 (www.corel.com, Windows)**   At about $49, Paint Shop Photo Album makes it easy to enhance and edit your photos. It can fix photo imperfections, add a fancy frame or photo border, or, for the antique look, add a sepia tone, frames, photo edges, and borders to your photos. You can also give yourself or your friends a slim new look with Photo Album's unique Thinify tool and you can also add captions and sound.

Back up your photos. Many people unexpectedly lose documents and other information from their PCs and handhelds. This may happen for a variety of reasons, such as hardware or software failure or "pilot error," but, if you are not in the habit of backing up your PCs and handhelds, you permanently lose your files. This can be a painful experience. It is even more important to back your digital photos up. The most common way to back up your photos is to copy or move them to a writeable CD/DVD, a Zip drive, or tape drive. Another way is to copy your pictures to a few different computers or network hard drives so that if one fails, you have a back up. There are even online services that allow you to back up your files using the Internet. There are too many to recommend one or two but if you use an online search engine with a phrase like "online backup service," you will likely be able to find something to suit your needs.

Use Special Effects with Your iPAQ Pictures

There are a ton of effects you can apply to your iPAQ pictures. Some are just plain fun and some add more of an artistic flavor. Of course, as with anything, beauty is in the eye of the beholder. Most image editing software packages have special effects or filtering options. Examples of some relatively common effects include the ability to transform a digital image to simulate stained glass, a charcoal drawing, or a painting. Of course you can also touch up imperfections and even change colors. Be sure you look through the users guide or help documentation of any software you choose to make sure you're aware of all of the functionality. There are a few applications on the market that perform specific effects. One example of such an application is Fractal-Explore from Eclectasy (**www.Eclectasy.com**). This application is discussed next.

Use Fractal Effects

What the heck is a *fractal*? There are a lot of definitions out there and most are verbose mathematical descriptions, so you may just want to try it out to see if the effect is something useful to you. An example of a photo that has received fractal treatment is shown in Figure 6-14.

FIGURE 6-14   Example of a fractal effect.

Many high-end image editing applications feature fractal effects. One application dedicated to converting pictures to fractal images is Fractal Explorer (**www.eclectasy.com/ Fractal-Explorer/index.html**). This program allows you to generate polynomial and iteration sets such as Mandelbrot, Julia, and Newton fractals as well as—just in case you have an aversion to Julia fractals—orbital fractals.

Publish Your iPAQ Pictures on the Internet

Yet another great thing about digital images, as with your iPAQ pictures, is that it is easy to share them with others by publishing them on a web page. This way, your friends and family, and the general public if you like, can view your iPAQ pictures from any PC or device using only a web browser. Once you your photos up on a web page, you can e-mail all of your friends the website address. They will be able to appreciate your photos with virtually no effort on their part—they'll just need to click a link.

There are two primary methods to publish your digital photos on the Internet: use a picture hosting service, or publish your pictures on your own website. The easiest way is to use an online picture hosting company, but that doesn't mean you can't set up your own website, if you don't already have one. Both options are discussed here.

Publish Your iPAQ Photos on the Web Using an Online Picture Hosting Website

Besides sending your pictures by e-mail or MMS to friends and family, another easy option is to post your pictures on the Internet using an online photo album service. This option is especially effective to allow you to share a bunch of photos at one time with many people—it would be inefficient to e-mail the 439 photos you took at the Montreal Jazz Festival to 60 of your best friends, but sending 60 people a web link so that they can browse your photos on the web makes a lot of sense. Also, you can show off your photos anywhere you happen to be, provided you have access to a web browser. A cross section of online picture hosting sites is listed next, and there are many others:

- Snapfish (**www.snapfish.com**)
- Picture Trail (**www.picturetrail.com**)
- Photo Navy (**http://pnavy.com**)—free
- EZPrints (**www.ezprints.com**)—free online photo sharing
- FotoTime (**www.fototime.com**)

 *If you use an online picture hosting service, remember to only copy your pictures to the website, don't move them. You don't want to risk permanently losing your photos if anything should happen to the service company or their servers.*

Publish Your iPAQ Photos on the Web Using Your Own Website

This section is not intended to provide detailed instruction on how to set up your own website. There are many resources that describe exactly how to publish images and content on the web: you can find informative websites to help get you up to speed, and most bookstores have web publishing guides and reference books.

Following are some great McGraw Hill/Osborne books about HTML and web publishing, whether you are just getting started or are more experienced with web pages. All are available at bookstores or online at either Osborne (**http://books.mcgraw-hill.com**) or Amazon (**www.amazon.com**).

- *Web Design: A Beginner's Guide* by Wendy Willard (2002)
- *HTML and Web Design Tips and Techniques* by Kris A. Jamsa, Konrad King, and Andy Anderson. (includes some advanced topics as well as basics, 2002)
- *Schaum's Easy Outline HTML* by David Mercer (2003)

The key point to understand about publishing your pictures on the Internet is that it is *not* difficult. If you are willing to invest some time into learning the basics, you can do it. The most important thing you need is a company to host your website. Essentially, the web hosting company provides a web server on which you can load your pictures and web pages so that others can view them on the web. There are a lot of options; many of them are free or available at a low monthly cost. If you have a home Internet connection, chances are the company that provides that service also provides web hosting services, and you may even have the service included in your Internet package.

Creating web pages themselves has become very easy if you have the right tools. Web page editing tools have become so easy to use you no longer have to learn HTML in order to publish pages and photos on the Web. There are a lot of choices when it comes to WYSIWYG (What You See Is What You Get, pronounced, "whiz-EE-wig") HTML editors. In fact, most Office document applications allow you to save a document as a web page: Save as HTML or Save as a Web Page. Some examples of web page authoring tools are

- Virtual Mechanics Site Spinner (**www.virtualmechanics.com**), about $50
- Macromedia Dreamweaver for Windows and Macintosh (**www.macromedia.com**), about $400
- Microsoft FrontPage for Windows (**www.microsoft.com**) (some versions of Microsoft Office include Front Page so you may already have it)
- EvrSoft 1st Page 2000 (**www.evrsoft.com**), free

By no means are these the only options you have if you want to easily create web pages—there are hundreds more. You can even create web pages using pure HTML code by using a simple text editor like Notepad, although this is not the easiest way to get going if you are just getting started with web technologies.

Print Your Digital Photos

As you are likely aware, digital photography offers many practical advantages over traditional film photography. One advantage is you can select which photos you print, if any, allowing you to keep the cost of taking and printing pictures down. It is becoming more common to not print photos at all. Many people choose keep photos in digital format and show them only on a computer monitor or projector rather than in printed form.

TIP
Some newer DVD players have the ability to show images that have been stored on recordable DVD/CD disks. This means that if your PC is equipped with a DVD or CD burner you can burn your photos to a recordable DVD/CD and play them back on your TV using your DVD/CD player.

What you do with your photos depends on how you want to use them. When you want to print a digital photo you have several options, and you are not limited to one—you can use all of them, depending on your needs:

- Purchase a photo quality printer to print your own photos at home. HP makes some great photo printers that work very well with your iPAQ, and most other printer manufacturers offer photo printers as well.
- Take digital media storage such as memory cards, CD/DVD, USB drives, and so on to a photo printing shop. This works in much the same way taking film to be developed does.
- Use an online photo printing service that uploads your digital photo files, prints your photos, and sends them back to you. There are so many companies offering this type of service that you may want to do a quick web search to find one that suits your needs.

HP Photosmart Essential or HP Image Zone software installed on your PC allows you to easily use HP Snapfish to share and print photos (covered earlier in the chapter in the section " Use HP Image Zone on Your iPAQ to View, Print, and Send Your Photos."), and many of the same sites that offer photo hosting also offer printing services including:

- **www.snapfish.com**
- **www.shutterfly.com**
- **pix.futureshop.ca** (Canada)
- **www.photobox.co.uk** (United Kingdom)

Wrap It Up

You may not have purchased your iPAQ with the sole intent of taking digital photos, but we hope this chapter has given you a good idea of what a great digital imaging tool your iPAQ can be. We covered a lot of ground, including tips on taking better photos, HP Photosmart and Image Zone software, and sharing your photos.

Chapter 7

Manage Your Home Entertainment with Your iPAQ

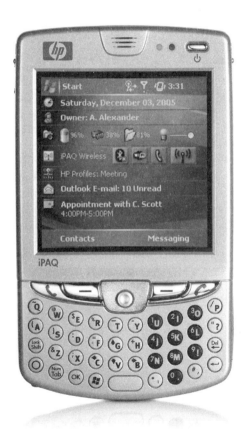

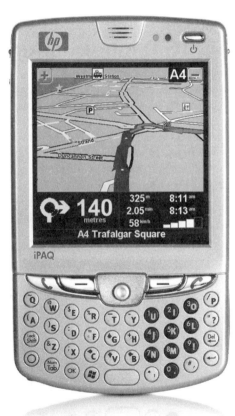

How to…

- Use your iPAQ as a universal remote control for your home entertainment center
- Use your iPAQ to control a Windows Media Center PC and Media Center Extender
- Stream your digital content from your home PC to your iPAQ

This chapter focuses specifically on how your iPAQ can be integrated with your home entertainment system. This chapter will not be a tutorial on Windows Media Player. For that information, please refer to Chapter 5.

In this chapter, we will take a closer look at third-party software that can be used to bring your Pocket PC and your home entertainment closer together.

Turn Your iPAQ into a Universal Remote Control

If your home entertainment centers are like ours, you probably have three to six remote controls floating around. You can simplify that mess by using your iPAQ as a single remote control for everything in your system! This is accomplished using third-party remote control software. A few of the iPAQ models come preinstalled with Nevo Home Control from Universal Electronics. Nevo is by far the best of the universal remote control software applications we tested, but the catch is that if your iPAQ isn't one of the ones that is preinstalled with Nevo, you cannot buy it as a later add-on. For those of you without Nevo, there are several vendors listed at the end of this section. An image of one of these vendors, WinCESoft RemoteControl II (**www.wincesoft.de**) is shown in Figure 7-1. You should look for a vendor with the features that are appealing to you. For example, some of the products are only for TVs, and others have very sophisticated interfaces and can

FIGURE 7-1   Using third-party software, you can use your iPAQ to act as a universal remote control for all of your home entertainment equipment.

control any infrared-controlled device. Some will feature voice commands, allowing you to speak instructions to your Pocket PC, which it will faithfully put into action. This is a rather fun function as you can set your iPAQ in the middle of your coffee table (pointed at your TV) and say things like, "Turn TV on" and have it carry out those instructions!

Making the Software Work with Your TV

In order for you to be able to use your iPAQ to control your TV or other equipment, you must be able to tell it what kind of equipment you have. This can be done in a variety of ways, which can vary greatly from program to program. However, there are generally three methods:

- Use the internal database of the software to select your TV (or other device from the list). This is generally the fastest way to get started, and if you have a common brand of TV, it will likely be in the onboard database of your software.

- Teach the iPAQ what IR codes your device uses. This is generally done by pointing your TV remote control at the iPAQ's IR port (usually on the top, but sometimes on the bottom or side) and then putting your software into Learn mode. Push the buttons on your iPAQ to tell it which button you are "teaching." After that, pushing the button on your remote control will program that button on the software.

- Import a CCF file. A CCF file contains all the codes necessary for managing a specific device. You can download many CCF files from **www.remotecentral.com**, where you will find thousands of CCF files for many different kinds of devices.

Features to Watch for

Many of the third-party products available on the market currently are not the most robust or full featured, so be sure to try out the different ones to find what works best for you. Some are particularly difficult to set up, and if you are not technically inclined, you shouldn't waste your time with these. Some key things to watch for include:

- **User interface**   Some products have a very slick user interface that is easy to navigate, while others are much less intuitive and will likely frustrate you. Many of the applications allow you to customize the interface, but again, unless you are very technically inclined, you probably won't do this.

- **Easy setup for your device**   With many of the applications, choosing your equipment (TV, stereo, VCR, etc.) from a database and getting started right away is very easy. Some will run a wizard when you first start, but others, including the WinCESoft RemoteControl II, are completely counterintuitive when it comes to loading your first TV.

- **Voice control**   Being able to speak to your remote control is a novel feature at the moment only natively supported by PDAWin TV Remote Controller (**www.pdawin.com**) and Vito Remote 4, although you can provide voice support by installing other software add-ons such as Microsoft's Voice Command (**www.microsoft.com/windowsmobile/ downloads/voicecommand/default.mspx**).

■ **Screen display** Make sure that the software works with the screen resolution of your device. If you have an iPAQ where the IR port is not on the top of the device, look for the programs that can be set to paint the screen upside down to make it easy to keep the IR port pointed at the TV while using the Pocket PC. Also, many of the programs support a Full-Screen mode, which removes the title bar and soft buttons from the screen, utilizing 100 percent of the screen for the display of your remote control interface.

■ **Hardware key support** Only some of the programs will work with the hardware keys, meaning that you can use the five-way navigation pad and other hardware buttons to perform functions in the application.

■ **Macros** This feature allows you to preprogram a set of instructions that can be carried out. For example, on some televisions, changing various settings can be several levels deep in a menu. If there are settings that you frequently toggle, you can build macros that will repeat a series of instructions on your behalf to make it easier to repeat complex commands.

■ **Tap and hold support** This is a very important feature in terms of volume control. Be sure that if you press a button and hold it down that the instruction will automatically repeat. If you want to quickly turn the volume down, being able to tap and hold the Volume Down button until the volume is at the right level is very useful. If your software doesn't support tap and hold, you must repeatedly tap the button over and over to get the volume to keep going down.

■ **Price** Most of the products are between $10 and $30 to purchase, and many have free trials or shareware versions with limited functions for you to test them out with.

Some features will be important to you, others may not be, so you should try out some of the different vendors before selecting the one that you would like to buy.

The Vendors

Each of these companies makes software for turning your iPAQ into a universal remote control:

■ **Promixis NetRemote IR (www.promixis.com)** This program has a variety of possible configurations.

■ **UltraMote (www.ultramote.com)** This program has no built-in device database so you will need to set your remote to Learn mode to make it work.

■ **NoviiRemote (www.novii.tv)** This program does not support CCFs or macros.

■ **WinCESoft RemoteControl II (www.wincesoft.de)** This program has a very good user interface, but setting up a device from the onboard database is very challenging.

■ **Griffin Technology Total Remote (www.griffintechnology.com)** In our tests, this was one of the quickest and easiest of the programs to get started with, although it is a little slow switching from device to device. The user interface is simple and easy to use. You can purchase it through Handango's software store (**www.handango.com**).

- **Vito Remote (www.vitotechnology.com)**   We were unsuccessful in getting the Vito Remote product to work with our test Sony television.

- **PDAWin TV Remote Controller (www.pdawin.com)**   This program was among the fastest and easiest to get up and running with. Its biggest weakness is the lack of support for tap and hold (which makes volume control an unpleasant experience) as well as a less attractive user interface.

Managing a Media Center PC

Many home computers are becoming digital home entertainment centers. One of the powerful incarnations of this is the Windows Media Center PC, which can be a full-fledged entertainment system as well as your home PC. Owners of these PCs can now use their iPAQ Pocket PCs as interfaces for connecting to and remote controlling your Media Center PC from anywhere you can get a network connection on your iPAQ. You can accomplish this using the earlier mentioned Nevo software if you have one of the iPAQ models with it built in, or if not, with software from Rudeo (**www.rudeo.com**). This software works best with a Media Center PC but will also work with your regular Windows XP computer running Media Player 10.

Rudeo requires you to first install a server component on your PC and then to install the Pocket PC client on your iPAQ. Once loaded, the client will connect with your wireless network to perform many functions on your Media Center. The first of these functions is to act as a remote control similar to the concept of the software in the previous section of this chapter. Figure 7-2 shows the remote control interface, which will look very similar to the buttons on the physical remote control that came with your Media Center PC. One of the big benefits of this product is that whereas your physical remote is IR and only works when pointing at your Media Center PC, the Rudeo remote

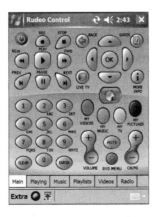

FIGURE 7-2   Rudeo can act as a remote control for your media center PC from anywhere that your wireless network reaches.

FIGURE 7-3   The Playing tab gives you a view into and control over the currently queued media content on your Media Center PC.

control will work anywhere that your wireless network reaches! Now you can control your music from the patio instead of having to be in the living room.

The Playing tab in the Rudeo interface gives you a mini view of the playlist that is currently playing on your Media Center PC. From here you can easily control the volume and see what track is playing as well as the queue of songs, as shown in Figure 7-3.

The Music tab in Rudeo allows you to see all the digitized music stored on your Media Center PC. You can select a specific artist from the top left panel or a specific album from the top right, as shown in Figure 7-4. When you have selected an artist or album, the songs will be displayed in the lower box. You can then check the boxes by the songs you want to select. When you tap and

FIGURE 7-4   The Music tab lets you see the digitized music on your PC and queue up songs to play or add to playlists.

hold the stylus on one of the selected songs, you will have a variety of options, including creating a new playlist of your selected songs, adding the songs to the current queue, or replacing the current queue with the selected songs.

The Playlists tab lets you see and edit all the playlists on your PC, as shown here. You can also queue up on your selected playlist to play on the PC.

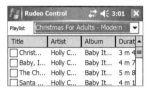

The Videos tab will show you all the video files stored on your PC. These can be queued up to play using the tap and hold menu. The drop-down list at the top of the page lets you choose a specific subfolder or category of video, for example, Recorded TV as shown here.

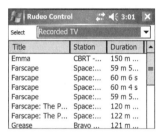

The final tab is the Radio tab, which brings up the list of Internet radio stations you have set on your PC, as shown in Figure 7-5. You can select the radio station of your choice and it will queue up and start playing.

FIGURE 7-5   The Radio tab lets you choose an Internet radio station to play on your Media Center PC.

One of the drawbacks of the Rudeo product is that it doesn't work with Media Center Extenders, which would increase its usefulness significantly if you have installed MCEs into your home theater equipment sets as we have.

Streaming Your Digital Media to Your iPAQ

As you learned in Chapter 5, you can copy your digital media to your iPAQ for your listening and viewing pleasure. But what if you have an extensive music collection on your home PC? Is there a way you can get this content streamed to your iPAQ? Perhaps you want to listen to music while at work through your wireless network, or maybe the gym where you work out has a wireless network you can use. If so, you can stream all of your content to your iPAQ using an amazing free product called Orb (**www.orb.com**). In addition to streaming your music, Orb can also send live television, digital photos, home video, and recorded TV programs to your Pocket PC. Orb works with your Windows XP Media Center edition PC or a standard Windows XP PC. It will stream your content via an agent that you install on your home PC and then through any web browser, including the one on your iPAQ.

In order to use it, you have to set up a free account with Orb. Then you can log in to Orb using the my.orb.com website, as shown in Figure 7-6.

With Orb and your iPAQ you can:

■ **Stream live TV**   You can select a channel from the front page of Orb and stream TV from your PC's TV tuner card right to your Pocket PC. The quality of this image will depend upon the bandwidth you have on both your Pocket PC and your home PC.

■ **Stream recorded video or TV**   This works like live TV but uses video files that have previously been stored on your PC.

FIGURE 7-6   The Orb website will allow you to stream your home digital media to any supported web browser, including the one in your iPAQ.

FIGURE 7-7   You can access all your home media content right through your iPAQ web browser.

- **Browse digital photos**   You can view all the home digital photos that are stored on your PC.

- **Listen to streaming audio**   You'll have access to your entire music collection anywhere that you can get Internet access. As with TV, the quality will depend upon the bandwidth you have, but audio requires much less bandwidth than video, so generally you can get good quality audio from anywhere.

> **TIP**   *You can test drive Orb using a guest account at **http://guest.orb.com**. It is free and easy to try!*

Using Orb is as simple as navigating a web page in your web browser, as shown in Figure 7-7

What Else Can It Do?

With Windows Media Player on board and the connectivity options of your iPAQ, there will likely be more and more tools released to help you make the most of your digital media and your home entertainment center. You can check out the sites referenced in the Appendix B to monitor when new products come to market that you might want to take advantage of.

Wrap It Up

As our home entertainment technology continues to become increasingly integrated with our computers, watch for your iPAQ to continue to grow as a value add component to your home theater and stereo.

Chapter 8

Manage Your Finances on the Go with Microsoft Money or Quicken

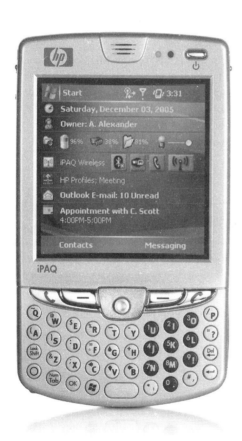

How to...

- Download and install Money for handheld devices or mobile Quicken software
- Manage your accounts
- Work with the account register
- Manage your investments
- Categorize your financial information
- Manage your payees
- Protect your information with passwords
- Set ActiveSync options to sync with desktop Money and mobile Quicken

This chapter focuses specifically on what you can do on your iPAQ with Microsoft Money for handheld devices (which, for the sake of brevity, we will refer to as "Money Mobile") or mobile Quicken software. It is not our intention to teach you how to use Money and Quicken, but rather to show you how your Pocket PC can factor into your personal financial management.

Chances are you will use either Money or Quicken, but not both. To make it easier, we've divided this chapter into two parts, with the first part focusing on Microsoft Money for the Pocket PC (a free download for your iPAQ), and the second part looking at third-party mobile Quicken alternatives for users of the popular Quicken software from Intuit.

What Can You Do with Money Mobile?

Money Mobile does not come preinstalled on your Pocket PC. You must download it from Microsoft in order to install it on your iPAQ (discussed in the next section).

Once you have installed Money Mobile, you'll be able to see a summary list of all your accounts and balances, see the details of a specific account, monitor all of your investments, set and manage categories for tracking your expenses, and manage your list of payees that you make payments to.

Downloading and Installing Money Mobile

You can download Money Mobile for free from the Microsoft website. Because Money for handheld devices is not yet available for Windows Mobile 5–based iPAQs as of this writing, the screen shots in this chapter are all based on Windows Mobile 2003 and may appear slightly different on a Windows Mobile 5 iPAQ. However, the release of Money Mobile for Windows Mobile 5 is imminent, so check the Microsoft website for availability. All the available versions of Microsoft Money for handheld devices can be found at **www.microsoft.com/money/ MoneyForHandheldDevices.mspx**.

Before you download the file, you must have already installed Microsoft Money on your desktop PC, or the two programs will not synchronize properly.

FIGURE 8-1   The Account Manager window shows you the list of all your accounts and the current balance.

Account Manager

The primary window of Money Mobile is the Account Manager, as shown in Figure 8-1. This window lists all your accounts with their current balances. The net balance of these accounts is displayed at the bottom of the window, which, if you have every account entered, will be your approximate net worth. Tapping a checking, savings, or credit card account will take you to the Account Register for that account. Alternatively, you can navigate through the Money Mobile options by using the drop-down menu in the top left of the window, as shown in the illustration.

At the bottom of the Account Manager window is the menu and icon bar that you can also use to navigate through the different Money Mobile windows. Tapping the New command in the Account Manager enables you to set up a new account in Money. The dialog box that opens gives you the opportunity to fill in all the required information for the account:

- **Name**   The name that will let you tell this account apart from the others in your list.
- **Account Type**   Bank, cash, credit card, or line of credit.
- **Opening Balance**   The balance in the account at the time you create it.
- **Credit Limit**   The limit on the account if it is a credit card or line of credit.
- **Interest Rate**   The rate that you are charged or credited on any account balances.
- **Display Account on Today Screen**   This check box allows you to have the account show up in the Today screen with the current balance. This is very useful for tracking your most commonly used accounts.

FIGURE 8-2 Manage individual transactions in the Account Register window.

In addition to the required information, you can include the following optional information: account number, institution name, contact name, and phone number.

Account Register

The Account Register window, shown in Figure 8-2, can be accessed by tapping any account in the Account Manager window. Each entry in the register consists of two lines. The top line shows the date and the amount of the transaction. The second line shows the party involved in the transaction (whom the money was paid to or received from), along with the current balance in the account after the transaction.

The bottom of the window shows you the current balance in the account. You can switch between accounts using the drop-down list in the top-right corner of the window or see the details of any transaction by tapping it with the stylus, which will open the transaction detail dialog box shown here:

The Type field defines the transaction as being either a withdrawal, deposit, or transfer. The Account field lets you put the transaction into any of your existing accounts. The Payee field remembers all of your current payees (managed as a separate list, as described in the section "Payees"). It will automatically try to match what you type in this field with the available list of payees. The Date field lets you enter a date for the transaction. The Amount field stores the amount.

On the Optional tab you can enter or modify additional information about the transaction, including the following:

- **Check Num**   The check number (if paying by check).
- **Category**   The expense or income category for tracking and reporting purposes.
- **Subcategory**   A subcategory for the category selected.
- **Status**   A status of blank, R (for reconciled), C (for cleared), or V (for void).
- **Memo**   Your personal notes on the transaction.

The Split command at the bottom of the Optional tab in the Transaction Detail dialog box allows you to define different categories and subcategories for different elements in the transaction, as shown in Figure 8-3.

In this example, the total Safeway bill of $79.56 has been categorized as $34.56 being Food and $45.00 being Gifts. The Unassigned line shows you the total amount of the transaction that you haven't assigned to a category yet. You can add new subelements by tapping New. If you enter the split amounts and realize that you have entered the total amount of the transaction incorrectly, you can tap Adjust Total and Money Mobile will adjust the total of the transaction to match the sum of your split items. Tapping OK will return you to the Transaction dialog box.

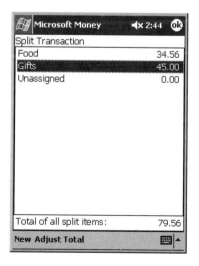

FIGURE 8-3   The Split Transaction window allows you to define different categories and subcategories within a transaction.

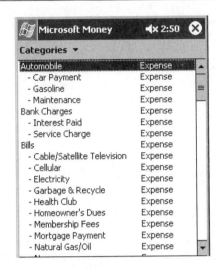

FIGURE 8-4   Display all the categories and subcategories available to you in the Categories window.

Tapping New on the menu bar in the Account Register window will open a blank transaction in which you can enter all the new information on the fly. This is convenient for recording transactions while you are at the checkout instead of trying to remember them all later.

Categories

The Categories window allows you to maintain the set of categories and subcategories used by Money. The full list of categories and subcategories is displayed when you enter the window, as shown in Figure 8-4.

Categories cannot be edited in Money Mobile. This activity is reserved for the full desktop version of Money. In the Mobile version, you are restricted to creating new categories and deleting existing categories.

Tapping and holding the stylus on any category or subcategory will open a shortcut menu enabling you to delete that item from the list. If any transactions exist on your device that utilize this category, you will not be able to delete it. Tapping a particular item in the list will open a dialog box for you to view the properties of the category, as shown here:

TIP

To create a new category, tap New in the menu bar at the bottom of the categories list. This will open a blank version of the window shown in the preceding illustration, allowing you to specify a category name, type (expense or income), and whether it is a subcategory of another category. You can also add a memo to give a longer description of the category.

Investments

If you invest or trade regularly in the stock market, one of the most useful features of Money Mobile is the ability to manage your portfolio from your iPAQ. The Investments window shows the current portfolio of investments that you have chosen to sync to your iPAQ. You can keep up to date on the current prices of your stocks while on the move if you have a wireless connection (for details, see Chapter 3). If up-to-date mobile access to your portfolio valuations is important to you, be aware that Money Mobile is currently the only mobile personal finance software we are aware of that allows this. The various Quicken-related products discussed later in this chapter do not currently offer this functionality.

TIP

You will not see each individual investment account in Money Mobile. Instead, it will sync specific securities that you want to monitor from your iPAQ. You set this up in the ActiveSync options, as described in "Money ActiveSync Options," later in this chapter.

8

Selecting Investments from the drop-down list in the top left of your window, or tapping the Investments icon in the icon bar at the bottom of the window, will open the Investments window, as shown in Figure 8-5.

FIGURE 8-5   The Investments window allows you to track your individual stocks and see how they are performing.

Each investment that you are tracking is shown on its own line. The stock symbol is shown along with the number of shares that you are holding and the last known price. Below that, you will see the current market value of your holdings. At the bottom of the window you will see the total market value of your tracked portfolio as well as when the last price quote update was completed. If you are connected to a computer with a sync cable or have another connection to the Internet (Ethernet card or wireless access), you can get a price update at any time by tapping on the Update icon in the icon bar (the last icon on the right, with a green downward-pointing arrow).

Tapping any specific investment will open a detail dialog box for that investment, as shown here:

You can see the full name of the investment, the last known price, and the number of shares held. You can also flag this particular stock so that it shows up on your Today screen (for those particularly volatile stocks!). Tapping New in the menu bar at the bottom of the Investments window will also bring you to this dialog box so that you can enter a new investment to track. Tapping and holding on a specific investment will give you a pop-up menu allowing you to delete it from your list of investments.

If you delete an investment from your list, it will only be gone temporarily. Next time you synchronize, it will be back. To stop an investment from syncing over to your iPAQ, you must set it not to sync in the ActiveSync options (discussed in "Money ActiveSync Options," later in this chapter). To remove an investment from your portfolio permanently, you must do it from the desktop version of Money.

Payees

Money Mobile keeps your full list of payees synchronized on your iPAQ. You can see this list by selecting the Payees command from the drop-down list on the top left of the window or by tapping the Payees icon in the icon bar (the image of a person). This will open the Payees window, as shown in Figure 8-6.

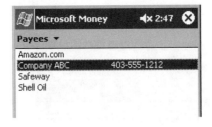

FIGURE 8-6 Open the Payees window to view the complete list of payees synchronized on your iPAQ.

In this list you'll see the name and address of each payee as well as their phone number (if you have one on file) and account number. Tapping any given payee will allow you to see and edit the details of that payee, as shown here for Company ABC.

Tapping New in the menu bar will open a blank version of this window, in which you can enter the information for a new payee.

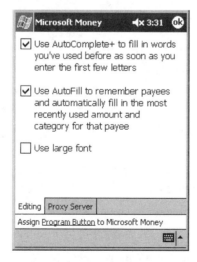

TIP

Whenever you enter new payees in the Account Register window, they will automatically be added as payees in the Payee list. You do not need to add every payee manually before using them in the Account Register.

As with categories, tapping and holding a specific payee will delete that payee; however, if you have used that payee in any transaction (even if the transaction is not synced over to the Pocket PC), the payee will not be permanently deleted and will reappear the next time you sync your information.

Money Options

Selecting Options from the Tools menu will take you to the Money Mobile Options dialog box, shown in Figure 8-7.

8

FIGURE 8-7 The Money Mobile Options dialog box lets you customize how Money Mobile works.

Here you have two tabs to work with: Editing and Proxy Server. The Editing tab lets you set three options:

- **Use AutoComplete**   Selecting this option will cause Money Mobile to try to match any entries that you are entering as they are being typed. This saves you from having to type the whole payee name or category name if it has been used before.

- **Use AutoFill**   Selecting this option will cause Money Mobile to remember the most recently used amount and category for each payee; the next time you enter that payee in a new transaction, Money Mobile will automatically fill in the amount and category. This is useful for regularly occurring transactions such as rent, phone bills, and so forth.

- **Use Large Font**   Selecting this option will cause a larger font to be used in all windows. This makes each window easier to read but reduces the amount of data that can be shown at one time.

On the Proxy Server tab, you can specify whether you want Money Mobile to access the Internet via a proxy server when updating information (such as investment prices). Your system administrator will tell you if this is necessary. In general, it is only an issue if you are working in a protected corporate network. You will need to select the check box to tell Money Mobile to use a proxy server and then fill in the HTTP (HyperText Transfer Protocol) address (such as **http:// sonicproxy.sonicmobility.com**) and the port number to use.

At the very bottom of the Options dialog box is a link that when tapped will allow you to link one of the hardware buttons on your iPAQ to Money Mobile. For example, if you do not use the Voice Recorder button on the side of the iPAQ, you can set it to launch Money (or any other application that you use frequently) instead. The link takes you to the appropriate Settings option to change your hardware button settings.

Setting a Money Password

Your financial information is private and sensitive information. If you have not already secured your iPAQ from unauthorized use by using a device password or one of the other techniques described in Chapter 16, you can add a password specifically to the Money application to prevent unauthorized access (or if you are particularly paranoid, you can use all of these methods for extra levels of security).

To set a password for Money Mobile, in Money Mobile, select Tools | Password. A dialog box will appear in which you can set and confirm the password you want to use. From this point on, you will be asked to enter the password whenever you start Money Mobile.

Money ActiveSync Options

To optimize the use of Money Mobile, you must set up the correct information in the ActiveSync program. Double-click the Microsoft Money line in the Details area of ActiveSync to open the options dialog box, as shown in Figure 8-8.

Did you
know?

Pocket PC Applications
Keep on Running

Applications on a Pocket PC tend to keep running—even when you have tapped OK to close the application, they just become idle. Closing Money Mobile and powering off your iPAQ does not necessarily mean that your password will stop someone from turning your iPAQ on and looking at your accounts. You must specifically close the task in order to log out. This can be done from the Switcher Bar application that comes with your iPAQ.

Also, remember that setting a password will not stop the account balances and information that you have requested from being displayed on the Today page when the iPAQ starts up.

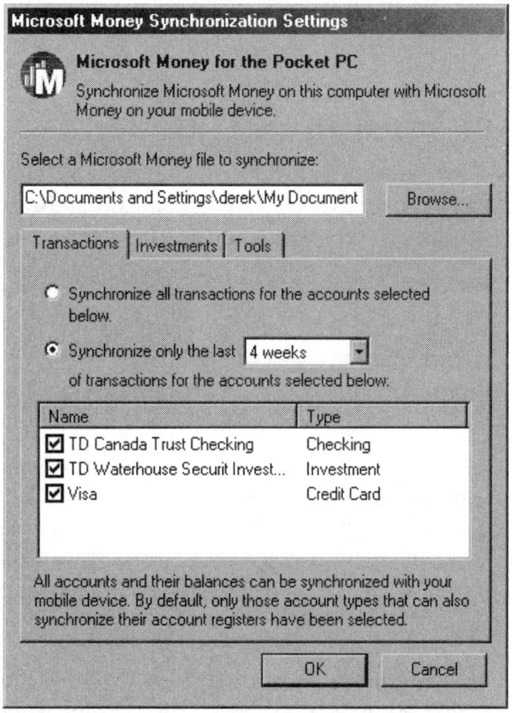

FIGURE 8-8   Use the Microsoft Money Synchronization Settings dialog box to set ActiveSync options.

The most important piece of information in this dialog box is the pointer to the Microsoft Money file that you wish to synchronize with. This path can be changed by clicking the Browse button and navigating to the appropriate file.

In the lower half of the dialog box are three tabs: Transactions, Investments, and Tools. On the Transactions tab, you can select the accounts you want to synchronize over to your iPAQ and choose how to synchronize them. Synchronizing all transactions is time consuming and memory intensive on your iPAQ, so it isn't recommended unless you have very small financial files. Alternatively, you can synchronize only a set number of previous weeks of transactions (from none to 52 weeks of previous transactions; the default is 4 weeks).

On the Investments tab, you can choose to synchronize over to your iPAQ all of your investments or only specific investments selected from the list.

The Tools tab gives you two tools to help you with managing your Money Mobile install. The first tool performs a full synchronization between your iPAQ and your desktop version of Money. If things get out of sync, or if you have changed the file you are using on your desktop, click this to resync all of your data. The second tool allows you to remove all Money Mobile data from your iPAQ. It is important to remove this data before you give your iPAQ to someone else or send it in for servicing. This tab also has a check box to tell ActiveSync to remember your Money password and use it next time you sync data.

What About a Pocket Version of Quicken?

A question we have received ever since the iPAQ began shipping is, "I use Quicken at home. Is there a version of that for my Pocket PC?" Two companies, Landware and Spb Software, have answered the call for a mobile version of Quicken. However, as this software doesn't come from Microsoft and isn't included with your Pocket PC, you must buy one of these products separately:

- Landware (**www.landware.com**) makes a product called Pocket Quicken for the Windows Mobile platform. The product has changed little since the first edition of this book was published, and it is a solid product that works well. Check their website for current information.

- Spb Software (**www.spbsoftwarehouse.com**) had the first mobile Quicken software on the market for Pocket PCs, called Spb Finance (which works with both Quicken and Microsoft Money, incidentally). This product can be downloaded directly from the vendor at the web link. It is reasonably priced and very useful if you do your home finances on the computer.

With both of these products you can see your accounts on your iPAQ, which allows you to check the balances in all your accounts wherever you are. In addition, when you write checks, you can put the entry into your Pocket PC and automatically sync it back into your Quicken file. You can also view graphs of your accounts to see how you are managing your money over time.

Unfortunately, one significant limitation of the Spb Finance product is that it will not track your investment accounts, and thus doesn't allow you to see your portfolios or get real-time stock price quotes as Money Mobile does.

Landware's Pocket Quicken allows you to track your investment accounts, but, like Spb Finance, the current release does not provide real-time stock price updates for your portfolio. If you like to monitor the current trading information for the stocks in your portfolio while mobile, neither of these products will be satisfactory to you.

Both of these products function in a similar way. We will use the Spb Finance product to explain these functions.

Account Manager and Register Tabs

Spb Finance opens to the Account Manager tab. Select a specific account and then tap the Register tab on the bottom of the screen you to see the account register detail for the selected account, as shown in Figure 8-9.

The detail lines of the Register tab show you the same data you are accustomed to seeing in Quicken: date, payee, transaction type, category, reconcile status, and amount. In Spb Finance, you cannot edit any existing transaction; only new transactions or transactions that have not yet been synced with the desktop Quicken can be edited.

When you choose New from the bottom menu, you have the option to create a new payment, deposit, or transfer. This is convenient when you are writing a check at the supermarket or making a transfer at an ATM.

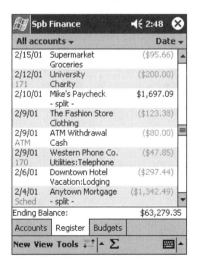

FIGURE 8-9   The Register tab allows you to see all the detailed transactions for a selected account.

8

The View menu gives you the opportunity to view all the categories for classifying your transactions, but in the current version, you cannot add new categories. There are also options for viewing memorized transactions (but again, not editing) and for viewing account balances or income/expense transactions as a graph.

Under the Tools menu, you have access to setting options for regional settings and autocomplete. You can also set Spb Finance to show the balances of specific accounts on your Today screen so that you always know how much money you have in your account before you write that check! There is a password setting under the Tools menu so you can restrict access to this data on your iPAQ.

When you want to sync your iPAQ with your Quicken files, go to your desktop PC where your Quicken files reside. Here, you can set some options in the Spb Finance sync properties (accessed through the ActiveSync window just as with other sync-capable data). From here you can

- Choose which Quicken file to sync with your Pocket PC and, if it is a password protected file, input the password.

- Filter so that only transactions after a specific date will be synced to your iPAQ and choose only a subset of accounts to sync.

- Set the sync schedule to run continuously (this doesn't actually work in the first version), sync once per hour, once per day, or sync only when you manually request it.

The bottom line for managing your finances on your Pocket PC if you are a Quicken user is that the available software is not yet as advanced as the available software for Microsoft Money, and the disadvantage is that you have to pay for it. However, given the rapid growth of the Pocket PC platform and that Quicken is the most popular home finance software, we anticipate improvements in this software very soon.

In closing, we want to add that it would be nice if Intuit, the manufacturer of Quicken, would OEM someone's Pocket PC Quicken software and make it available to all Quicken users for no additional cost. But this seems unlikely in the immediate future. As mobile access to important information becomes more and more important to individuals, the need to buy mobile Quicken software from a third party (at an additional expense) may drive some Quicken users to switch to Microsoft Money instead.

Wrap It Up

With iPAQ you can have your mobile finances at your finger tips at all times, keeping you in much better control of your money.

Chapter 9

Navigate with GPS on Your HP iPAQ

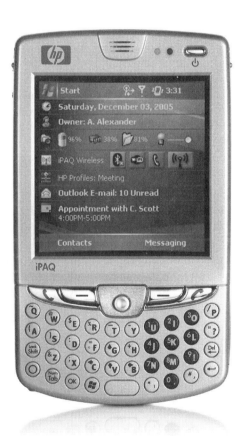

How to...

- Turn your HP iPAQ into a GPS receiver
- Decide which GPS solution is best for you
- Get turn-by-turn driving instructions to any destination
- Never get lost again

Have you ever wished someone were beside you in the passenger seat, guiding you to an unfamiliar address? Or perhaps you've been in a strange city and were trying to find the nearest restaurant or gas station?

Figuring out where you are and where you are going has always been cumbersome and often inaccurate. You can buy a map for a city, but as time passes and things about the city change, it gets less and less accurate. Navigational tools have now been greatly improved courtesy of global positioning system (GPS) technology.

This chapter covers GPS solutions for your HP iPAQ Pocket PC. GPS provides accurate information about your location and speed and, coupled with the appropriate software, GPS solutions can give you turn-by-turn directions to your destination. Some iPAQ models have GPS functionality built-in when you buy them; others can perform GPS with an add-on GPS receiver. Before we discuss specific solutions, we'd like to give you a brief introduction to the Global Positioning System.

The Global Positioning System

On February 22, 1978, a revolution in navigation technology began with the launching of the first Block I Navstar GPS satellite from Vandenberg Air Force Base in California. Declared fully operational in 1995, the U.S. Global Positioning System consists of 24 GPS satellites and five ground stations providing 24-hour instantaneous, precise, and continuous, three-dimensional navigation data via one-way wireless communications to properly equipped military and civilian users, in any weather conditions, anywhere in the world.

GPS signals are precise enough to calculate time to an accuracy of less than a millionth of a second, velocity within a fraction of a mile per hour, and location to within a few feet. GPS was originally designed to provide accurate navigation data to military users, but it continues to expand into the civilian area. GPS is used aboard private and commercial aircraft, ships and boats, and trucks and automobiles. GPS systems are used in search and rescue operations, detailed mapping projects, geodetic surveys, and more.

NOTE

Because they receive signals from satellites, GPS receivers must be able to "see" them (that is, have an unobstructed, line-of-sight view of at least three GPS satellites to receive the necessary information). Since there are 12 satellites above the horizon at any given time, this is usually not a problem. However, if you use GPS in tunnels, canyons, or cities with tall buildings, you may lose the necessary signals temporarily. Note also that it takes a small amount of time for the GPS receiver to find the signals after you turn it on—usually 1–2 minutes. Newer GPS units are usually able to lock on faster, and some iPAQ models actually download into a local database the positions of satellites to speed up the lock-on process.

What Do You Use GPS for?

GPS can be used in a wide variety of ways. The possible uses fall into one of five general categories:

- ■ **Location**   To determine where you are. If you are a hiker, you can use GPS with your iPAQ to find your current position. It can also be used with a wireless service to deliver "location-based services." For example, suppose you were looking for a particular type of shoe. When you walked past a shoe store, your iPAQ's location-based services software could determine if that store has your shoes on sale, in stock, and in your size.

- ■ **Navigation**   To get from one location to another. This is generally why you find GPS systems (such as the Hertz Neverlost system) in more and more rental cars and available as options on many new vehicles. Now you can have this functionality in your pocket everywhere you go. If you like to fish, you can use your GPS to locate and easily return to your best fishing holes!

- ■ **Tracking**   To monitor the movement of people or things. Many trucking companies have adopted GPS to help their central dispatching keep track of where all their vehicles are.

- ■ **Mapping**   For cartography. Almost all modern maps are created using GPS technology for precision.

- ■ **Timing**   For accurately determining the time, GPS satellites can be used as a form of atomic clock, allowing you to get very precise time on your GPS receiver. Every GPS satellite has its own atomic clock on board.

Components of a GPS

GPS solutions originally cost thousands of dollars, but as with any technology, prices have come down. GPS solutions have been available for handheld computers since before the introduction of the first Windows Mobile handheld PCs in 1997, and they have been available for Pocket PCs since their introduction in April 2000. A number of GPS solutions are available for the HP iPAQ.

There are three components to a GPS solution. The first, and by far the most expensive component, is the GPS of satellites and ground stations just described. Fortunately, the U.S. government picks up that bill and there are no hidden GPS service charges. The second component is the GPS receiver, a physical device capable of receiving signals from the GPS satellites. The third is the GPS software that you install on your Pocket PC. This software allows the GPS receiver to interface with your Pocket PC and provides road maps and points of interest (POI) information. You can use Pocket PC GPS solutions to tell you where you are at any time and to provide you with turn-by-turn driving instructions to any destination in areas covered by your GPS maps.

Most vendors sell integrated GPS solutions, which include the GPS software, GPS receivers, and the necessary cables and adapters. They may also sell the GPS receivers and software separately. Although you can mix and match GPS receivers and software, probably the safest way to pick a GPS solution for your HP iPAQ is to look at the software first. Find the software with the features and geographical coverage that you need. Then go with the GPS receiver bundled with the software or suggested by the vendor. We'll use this approach when we look at GPS solutions for HP iPAQ Pocket PCs, but before we do that, we'll discuss GPS receivers.

If you use your iPAQ with a GPS receiver in a vehicle, invest in a cigarette lighter power adapter to keep the iPAQ's battery fully charged and a holder so that you can keep your hands on the wheel!

GPS Receivers

As in most electronic devices these days, the brain of a GPS receiver is a small computer chip that translates the incoming signals into usable information. The chip is attached to a built-in or external antenna and a power source of some kind. GPS receivers come in a number of shapes and sizes and connect to the HP iPAQ in different ways.

Cabled GPS Receivers

These small devices are about half the size of a computer mouse, with a long cable that connects to the sync port on the bottom of the HP iPAQ, as shown in Figure 9-1. This solution is designed mainly for automotive use. The receiver sits on your dashboard and connects to the Pocket PC resting in a dashboard mount.

If you're interested in a cabled GPS receiver, make sure it comes with a cable designed to interface with the connector on the bottom edge of your iPAQ. Also, the digital maps that come with GPS solutions can occupy a lot of file storage space. It's best to place them on a storage card. The advantage to a cabled solution is that it leaves any expansion card slots on the iPAQ available to use for storage cards or other accessories.

Bluetooth GPS Receivers

Shown in Figure 9-2, this type of GPS receiver interfaces with your iPAQ wirelessly via Bluetooth communications. To use this type of receiver, your iPAQ must have Bluetooth capability. This is built-into many of the newer iPAQ devices. If your iPAQ does not have built-in Bluetooth capability, you'll have to add it via a CF or SDIO Bluetooth card.

FIGURE 9-1   A number of cabled GPS receivers are available for the HP iPAQ, including this one from Haicom Electronics. The GPS receiver is to the right of the iPAQ in this picture.

FIGURE 9-2   Bluetooth GPS receivers like HP Navigator, shown here, communicate with the HP iPAQ wirelessly. Your iPAQ must be equipped with Bluetooth wireless communication to use one of the Bluetooth GPS receivers.

9

CompactFlash GPS Receivers

This GPS receiver has a CF card interface that slips into the CF slot of any iPAQ equipped with one (for more detail on CompactFlash slots refer to Chapter 15), as shown in Figure 9-3. It draws a small amount of power from the iPAQ

FIGURE 9-3   Some GPS receivers come with CompactFlash card interfaces like the one shown here from Pharos Science and Applications. They slip into the CompactFlash slot on your iPAQ.

 **Use an iPAQ with a Built-in GPS Receiver**

Some iPAQ models, such as the 6500 and 6900 series, have built-in GPS receivers. The 6900 also comes with Microsoft Pocket Streets preinstalled in the U.S. or with TomTom software in EMEA. These iPAQ models utilize a Quick GPS Connection data file to keep information about the satellite vehicles to help the GPS lock on to the necessary satellites as quickly as possible. You can download this data file by tapping Start | Settings | Connections | Quick GPS Connection icon. An information screen will appear showing if your file has expired: if the GPS Connection Utility icon in the Settings area turns gray, it indicates that your file is out of date and needs updating. Tap the Download Now button to initiate a download of the new file.

On these units, the GPS will also automatically turn on and off when you load up your TomTom or MS Pocket Streets software.

If you are using third-party software, you will likely need to tell the software where to look for your GPS receiver. On the 6900 Mobile Messenger, this is on COM8 (communications port 8) and has a baud rate of 57600 (this is the speed that the software can communicate with the receiver). On the 6500 Mobile Messenger, this is set to COM7 and has a baud rate of 57600.

Using GPS on Your iPAQ

To get a better feel for some of the common functions in GPS navigation, let's take a closer look at what a GPS can do. For these examples, we used the HP Navigation System, which includes the Bluetooth GPS receiver shown in Figure 9-4, but most of the functions will be similar across other GPS packages as well.

 *If you are driving a car, never attempt to interact with a GPS navigation system while the car is in motion. If you need to change an address, you should pull over or allow a passenger to update the information for you. Most GPS software packages will give you audible instructions through your iPAQ's speaker when you need to turn or perform some other action.*

The main interface of your GPS software will likely contain a large map-viewing area, along with a menu or control buttons on one edge, as in Figure 9-5.

Some other common interface elements in the HP Navigation tool include:

■ **Compass** The red arrow on the screen will show you which direction is north. North isn't always up, as the map will rotate to face the direction you are going.

■ **Zoom controls** Below the map area are two buttons that will zoom in or out on the map. They are shown as magnifying glasses with a '+' or '−' in the middle.

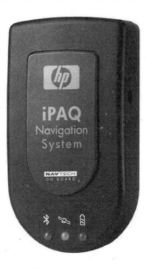

FIGURE 9-4   The HP Navigation System utilizes a Bluetooth GPS receiver.

FIGURE 9-5   The NP Navigation interface contains a large map-viewing window with additional controls at the bottom for changing the view and other options.

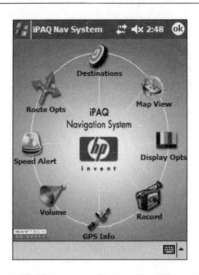

| FIGURE 9-6 | The main HP Nav menu is where you will go to enter destinations and manage all your navigation. |

- **Scale indicator** The bottom center of the map area contains a legend that indicates the scale. This will show the relative distance on the map depending upon what zoom factor you have set. In Figure 9-4, the scale is set at 500 feet (you can choose metric or imperial depending upon your preferences).

- **Menu buttons** The menu buttons are used to launch the HP Nav menu (as shown in Figure 9-6) from which you can switch to the view of the destinations, route options, configuration settings for display and sound, or some interesting settings such as Speed Alert to give you an alarm when you exceed the posted speed limit.

Note that touching the Menu button will open the main HP Nav menu shown in Figure 9-6, which will get you into the other parts of the software that we will be discussing.

Checking GPS Status

Before you can use your GPS, you need to make sure it has locked into the necessary number of GPS satellites. In the menu bar of the HP Nav interface, you will see the GPS Info icon, the one that looks like a small satellite. Tapping this button will tell you the details of how many satellites the system is currently locked into. Incidentally, the GPS transmissions are line-of-sight, so there cannot be obstacles between you and the satellites. Because of this, your GPS generally doesn't function indoors, in parking garages, or in other such locations.

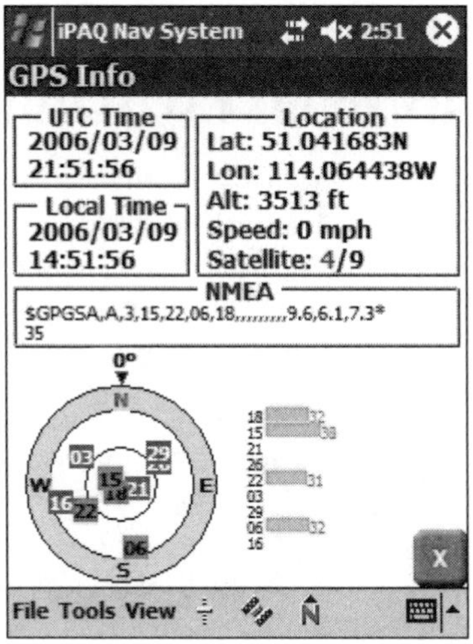

FIGURE 9-7   The GPS Info screen tells you the details of your connection with the GPS satellites.

Selecting the GPS Info icon from the HP Nav menu will open the GPS Info screen, shown in Figure 9-7. This screen tells you important information about your connection with the GPS satellites.

Figure 9-7 shows that we are currently connected to four satellites (the minimum for full functionality—you can get some information with three, but four are necessary to accurately fix your location). The lines connecting to each satellite indicate the strength of the satellite signal. You can also see your current latitude, longitude, altitude, and velocity (if you are moving), as well as the date and time. This is an extremely accurate date and time, as it is based on the atomic clocks aboard each of the GPS satellites you are communicating with. The number that appears beside each satellite graphic is the unique identification number of that particular satellite vehicle (SV).

If you are running your GPS with software and hardware from different vendors, you will need to tell them how to talk to each other. To do this, select Tools | GPS Options. From here you can choose to auto detect the GPS settings (usually your best option) or select the specific COM port and baud rate (communication speed) of your GPS receiver.

Now that you have the hardware and software talking, you are ready to start using your GPS!

Finding Your Current Location

Finding out exactly where you are can be useful if you get lost, if you are hiking in the back country, or if you work in a situation where your physical location is important to coordinating your work activity, as bicycle couriers do. Finding your current location with most GPS software is usually quite straightforward. In the HP Nav software, you will see a small green arrow on the

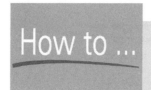

Use Your GPS When You Are Away from Civilization

The ability to find your current location is valuable for hikers, surveyors, marine enthusiasts, and many others. Software like HP Navigation or Destinator is useful for navigating cities and streets, but it's not so useful if you are on the water or hiking in the back country. For these uses, you will need different software like that offered by MapTech (**www.maptech .com**). Their Pocket Navigator product will allow you to load U.S. Geological Survey maps onto your Pocket PC and navigate with them, as shown here.

Of course, if you do plan to use your iPAQ in these kinds of places, you will need to give special consideration to battery life and rugged conditions. The battery life of your iPAQ won't last you through a multiday hike unless you use the GPS very sparingly. Consider carrying spare batteries, an "electric fuel" battery recharger (a chemical battery that can be used to recharge your iPAQ on the fly), or a solar-powered recharger like the Sunsei unit from ICP (**www.icpglobal.com**) or a great new product called Solio from Better Energy Systems Ltd (**www.solio.com**).

If you are traveling in conditions where your iPAQ is going to be exposed to a lot of moisture or dust, you should consider the iPAQ "ruggedized" case or an alternative case to help protect your device when you need it most. More information on these cases can be found at **www.pocketpcmag.com**.

map with a circle around it; this is your current location. If you aren't currently navigating to a destination, the street address will also show in the blue status bar above the menu bar. Some other software packages, such as Destinator (discussed at the end of this chapter) have a Locate option under the Menu button. This will tell you exactly where you are.

Navigating to a Destination

The most common use for GPS on a Pocket PC is to help you find your way from one place to another. We find this particularly useful when we are traveling and have appointments all over town in a city we are unfamiliar with. To navigate to a destination, you must tell your GPS software where you wish to go. You can do this by providing an address, specifying an intersection, or selecting a specific point on a map. In addition, you may set a list of favorite addresses that are places that you go to often, or you can look up a particular contact in your address book to go to their address. Many GPS programs, including HP Nav and Destinator, feature a powerful Points of Interest feature that allows you to get a list of the closest restaurants, banks, gas stations, or many other useful destinations. If you find yourself in an unfamiliar location and want to see all the restaurants within three miles, you can use this feature to do so.

Specific Address

One of the most common ways to navigate is to enter the address of the location you are going to. HP Navigation offers a variety of ways to do this, all of which give the same result. First you select the map that you want to use, and then you narrow that down by city or street on the selected map, as shown in Figure 9-8.

FIGURE 9-8   You can enter a specific address to navigate to with your GPS.

You can select your city or street destination by typing the name of the city or street in the text box at the top. As you type, matches will appear in the scroll box immediately below the entry area, and you can select the destination from the list. After you select your city and/or street, you can enter the building number you are navigating to. If there are multiple choices that match the database, you will be given the list of matching choices to select from, as shown here.

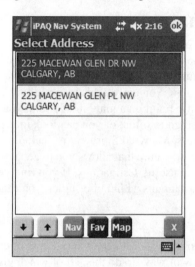

Once you have the address fully entered, press the green Nav button to calculate the best route from where you are to where you want to go. Your next turn or instruction will appear in the box at the top of the map area in green, and your path will be outlined on the map with a bold blue line. As you begin to drive, the maneuvers you need to complete will be displayed one-by-one at the top of the map-viewing area until you arrive at your destination. If you have your iPAQ sound turned on, you will also receive verbal instructions on when to turn and what maneuvers to make. You also have the option to view the list of maneuvers that you must perform, as shown in Figure 9-9.

Intersection

As an alternative to entering a specific address, you can specify an intersection. Entering an intersection is usually faster and easier than entering a full address, and it's useful if you only want to get into a specific area and then plan to navigate manually. This is particularly useful while traveling. Say you're on business in San Francisco and want to meet a friend for dinner in the nearby city of Los Gatos. You know how to get around Los Gatos but not the best way to get there from San Francisco. Just enter a main intersection in Los Gatos and allow the GPS to guide you through San Francisco and onto the best freeway to get you to your destination.

First select the city or street where the intersection is located. This doesn't have to be the same city you are currently in, but it must be on the same map that you currently have loaded. (The Pocket PC generally cannot contain the entire map for most countries in memory at one time,

FIGURE 9-9   In addition to the map view when navigating to a destination, you can also see the Route List to view a list of maneuvers that you must complete to arrive at your destination.

so you must load certain regions.) If your route spans two cities, the software will put you onto the correct highways and calculate the total distance of your trip. After selecting your city, select the two intersecting streets. Most software is smart enough that, after you select your first street, only valid intersecting streets are shown in the list for the second street.

Once you have successfully entered your destination, you can use the Nav button to calculate the route and begin navigation, or use the Map button to show the destination on the map-viewing window.

Favorites

You might find that there are particular destinations you need to get to often, such as your home, office, day care, or other location. You can set the software to remember a group of "favorite" destinations. This is particularly useful when you're traveling in an unfamiliar city and need to drive between a variety of meeting locations and you hotel. After picking up your rental car, just instruct the GPS to navigate you to your hotel. Then you can make the hotel a "favorite" destination so that you do not have to reenter the information every time you want to return to it.

Using the previously mentioned techniques for entering a destination location, you can save that location to the Favorites simply by pressing the small Fav button at the bottom of the address selection screen.

To navigate to a previously saved favorite location, choose Destinations | Favorites. This will open the address selection window shown previously, loaded with all of your favorite destinations.

After you select the favorite location, the Nav button will calculate the route to that destination. The Map button will show you where that location is in the map-viewing window.

Recent

You will find Recent a useful option on the HP Navigation submenu (some GPS software packages call this History). It allows you to see a list of your most recent destinations and simply select from the list to return to that destination.

Contacts

Many of the destinations you might want to navigate to are contained within your current contacts on your iPAQ's Contacts application, which is discussed in Chapter 12. You can select from your list of contacts by choosing Destinations | Contacts. You will then see a list of your contacts, which appears in the same style of selection window displayed when entering cities and streets. When you select a contact, you will see a confirmation of this contact's address, as shown in Figure 9-10. If the contact has multiple addresses, such as both a home and work address, you will see them both displayed and you can select the one you would like.

FIGURE 9-10   You can navigate to the address of any of the contacts stored in your iPAQ Contacts application.

A limitation of many of the GPS software packages that we have tested is that the address must exactly match the way that the software expects the address to be formatted. For instance, in some towns, addresses are divided into quadrants. For example, say you want to navigate to 400 Mount Douglas Close SE. If HP Navigation has this address in its map as 400 Mount Douglas SE Close, it cannot plot the address as you've entered in your Contacts and will bring up an error message saying that the contact you selected does not have an address that matches the current map. Some of the software packages will do a best guess at the address and then allow you to manually correct it; unfortunately, HP Navigation doesn't provide this function and forces you back to your Contacts list.

Points of Interest

The POI feature on GPS navigation products such as HP's is a wonderful, extremely useful feature. It allows you to find the nearest destination from a given category. Imagine you are in an unfamiliar city, and you need to find a gas station or a bank machine. All you need to do is choose Destination | POI. This will open the window shown in Figure 9-11.

Select the type of location you are looking for, and then select if you want to view them by distance (closest being first), alphabetically, or by city, as shown next.

9

FIGURE 9-11   It is easy to find the nearest gas station, bank, restaurant, or other key location with the Points of Interest feature.

Select the destination you would like to navigate to and press the Nav button to calculate the route.

3-D View

An interesting feature in some GPS packages such as Destinator is the ability to switch from the standard map view to a 3-D view. The 3-D view will show you a view as it might appear to the driver moving along the road. Your mapped path will show up in red. Note that this feature isn't currently available in HP's software. The 3-D view of Destinator, an alternative GPS package is shown here as an example:

Loading and Switching Maps

Your iPAQ has a limited amount of memory, and GPS maps are very detailed and need a lot of storage space. If you are planning to do a lot of traveling and need to have a number of maps with you, buying a 64MB or larger SD card or other external storage device is highly recommended. If you only travel to one destination at a time, always returning to home in between, you can load and unload maps as you need them.

All GPS software packages, including HP's, have a complete application for loading and unloading maps. Simply insert the CD into your desktop PC and follow the instructions. The map loader shown in Figure 9-12 will let you select the regions you desire to load by clicking them with your mouse.

9

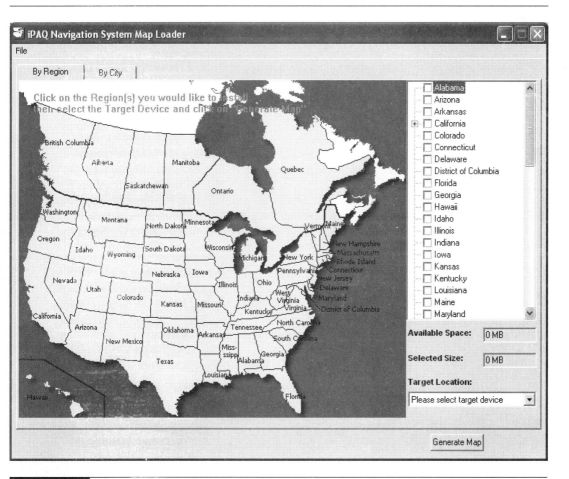

FIGURE 9-12   The map loader allows you to select which maps will be stored on your device.

GPS Solutions for the iPAQ Pocket PC

The rest of this chapter is organized by GPS navigation software available for Windows Mobile devices. We'll describe the software first and then discuss the GPS receivers offered by the software vendor. We'll also comment on the key features of each solution.

Standard Powerful Features Found on the Leading GPS Applications

All of the solutions mentioned in this chapter have some common features. Instead of repeating them, we list them here:

- Current location displayed on moving maps
- Voice guidance that provides turn-by-turn directions and sound alerts for upcoming turns
- Automatic route recalculation when you miss a turn
- Routing options that let you select between quickest and shortest routes
- Turn text directions with distance to destination
- The ability to use Contacts to specify destinations and waypoints
- 2-D, 3-D, and night map viewing
- Extensive POI databases that can help you find hotels, restaurants, nightlife, stores, museums, gas stations, hospitals, airports, and more (POI categories vary for each GPS application)

All of the GPS solutions discussed in the following sections have been certified to work with various iPAQ models. To be safe, ask the vendor if they certify that it does work with your specific iPAQ before purchasing the solution.

HP Navigation System

HP has their own branded GPS navigation kit that comes with a bundled Bluetooth GPS receiver. As of the time of writing of this book, the software hasn't yet been updated for Windows Mobile 5, but the Windows Mobile 2003 version works acceptably on the newer platforms.

HP Software

The HP navigation software cannot be purchased separately, but in our tests it did work with any NMEA-compatible (National Marine Electronics Association) GPS device that can connect to the iPAQ. The main features of the HP Navigation System include:

- Maps of the U.S. and Canada are included
- An easy-to-use interface

- The ability to install maps of specific cities by radius if your device has limited storage
- NAVTECH maps (**www.navtech.com**), one of the most trusted and up-to-date sources of digital maps
- Instant recall of recent destinations
- Safety tools for speed alerts and fog driving

HP GPS Receiver

The HP GPS receiver requires that you have a Bluetooth-equipped iPAQ. The receiver is not sold separately from the software. It uses a rechargeable battery that can be charged from the iPAQ charger so you don't have to carry two chargers with you.

Destinator Personal Navigation System

Destinator Technologies (**www.destinatortechnologies.com**) has offered its GPS solution for iPAQs since the very early iPAQ models and can be purchased as a stand-alone software product or bundled with GPS receivers.

Destinator Software

The Destinator 3 software can be purchased separately and works with any NMEA-compatible GPS device that can connect to the iPAQ. The software can display 3-D maps or 2-D maps. The main features of Destinator include:

- If the GPS receiver is connected, Destinator "knows" where you are; all you have to do is enter your destination, and it will calculate your route.
- The ability to specify roads to be avoided when calculating a trip.
- A voice prompt that tells you when you're speeding or going off route.
- The ability to download maps of any size from "super region" maps that ship with the program.
- NAVTECH maps (**www.navtech.com**).
- An internal address book that lets you store up to 4,000 addresses.
- Instant recall of recent destinations.
- Street-level maps of the United States and Canada are included; Western European maps are available.

Destinator GPS Receiver

Destinator's website lists a variety of software/receiver bundles for the iPAQ models. Check the website for compatibility with your specific model.

9

CoPilot Live

ALK Technologies (**www.alk.com/copilot**) offers its CoPilot Live software separately or bundles it with a Bluetooth or cabled GPS receiver.

CoPilot Live Software

CoPilot Live is one of the easier to use GPS programs available for the Pocket PC. ALK Technologies certifies it to work with any NMEA-compatible GPS receiver that can connect to the iPAQ. It includes the following features:

- Text-to-voice instructions that announce the exact distance to your next turn, the type of turn, and the street name
- A customizable display that lets you select the information you want to see on CoPilot Live's screen, including current road, crossroad, current time, speed, elevation, or nearest town
- Lane change warnings that alert you to upcoming left exits
- Side of street notification that tells you which side of the street your destination is on
- POI alerts that notify you when you're approaching gas stations, restaurants, entertainment, hospitals, or rest areas (alerts may be distance adjusted or turned off)
- Safety screens that minimize graphic information so you can rapidly view navigation information easier and stay focused on the road
- A Waypoints feature that lets you pass through a particular area on the way to your final destination
- The ability to create and organize your own POI database from personal contacts, popular destinations, or other sources
- Regionalized POI capability that lets you download only those POIs within your chosen map area, saving you file storage space
- NAVTECH maps
- Routing options that let you create the quickest and shortest routes for cars and RVs
- Detour and selective routing that lets you navigate around delays and congestion areas
- Auto-zoom that zooms in on the map as you approach your next turn or final destination and zooms back out after you make a turn
- The ability to enter latitude and longitude for Geocaching or other nonaddressed outdoor locations
- User-friendly route entry for new users and live features for advanced users, fleets, or enterprises
- Communication between vehicle and home or office that allows for two-way messaging, vehicle location, and itinerary updates (you need a mobile phone connected to your HP iPAQ and data service from your wireless carrier to use this feature)

CoPilot GPS Receivers

ALK sells the CoPilot Live software by itself or bundled with a Bluetooth GPS receiver. The Bluetooth GPS bundle also includes a universal vehicle mount for your iPAQ and a cigarette lighter power adapter.

TeleType GPS Software

TeleType (**www.teletype.com**) offers its TeleType GPS Software by itself or bundled with a variety of GPS receivers and the necessary accessories. They have been offering GPS solutions since the release of the first handheld PC based on Microsoft mobile software in 1997.

TeleType GPS Software

The TeleType GPS software is one of the most customizable and feature-rich GPS applications available for the HP iPAQ Pocket PC. It takes a little bit more time to master the program, but the extra features and capabilities are worth it. The TeleType GPS software will work with any NMEA-compatible GPS device that can connect to the iPAQ. TeleType GPS software includes the following features:

- Map, speed, altitude, and other information displayed on one screen, as shown previously in Figure 9-7
- Voice command capability
- With the GPS receiver active, uses your current position as the starting point of the trip
- A highly compressed map format that uses less storage space than some competitors
- Start-to-finish trip routing that includes an unlimited number of waypoints, allowing you to pass through specific locations on your way to your destination
- The ability to assign TeleType GPS functions to iPAQ hardware buttons
- The ability to download all maps for a particular state or a selected portion of them using the desktop PC transfer option
- With the GPS receiver active, uses WorldNavigator to automatically load and unload necessary maps
- Trip route recording and replaying
- Metric or imperial units
- The ability to automatically connect to the Internet to download traffic, information, and weather maps
- Voice alerts/directions in Italian, French, German, Dutch, or English
- Maps for Canada and Europe (in the premium bundle)
- Marine and topographical maps (for the United States; worldwide aviation maps are also available)

9

TeleType GPS Receivers

In addition to selling the stand-alone GPS software, TeleType offers WorldNavigator bundles for Pocket PCs. These bundles include the TeleType GPS software, U.S. maps, accessories, and some form of GPS receiver. Bundles with Bluetooth, CompactFlash, or cabled receivers are available. The GPS software will work with a Pocket PC receiving data from any NMEA-compatible GPS receiver.

Mapopolis Navigator

Mapopolis (**www.mapopolis.com**) offers bundles that include the Navigator software and a Bluetooth GPS receiver.

Mapopolis Navigator Software

Mapopolis gives users point-to-point routing and navigation for the entire United States, major Canadian cities, and Western Europe. The Navigator software is available for free at the Mapopolis website, but you must pay for the maps that it uses. Mapopolis Navigator works with any NMEA-compatible GPS device that can connect to the iPAQ. Mapopolis includes the following features:

- With GPS receiver active, uses your current location as the starting point for any trip planning.
- The ability to specify an entry in the optional Place Guide for the starting or ending point. The Place Guide (a $25 option) contains point-of-interest information for the entire United States, including restaurants, convenience stores, gas stations, hotels, and more.
- Sixteen-level zoom-in/zoom-out on maps; fast and smooth map scrolling.
- A Find feature that allows you to search and select cities, streets, and landmarks by name or search and select landmarks by category and name. Street intersections or street addresses can also be located.
- The ability to specify a maximum speed and get an audible warning if you go faster.
- Maps licensed from NAVTECH and TIGER for the entire United States, major Canadian cities, and Western Europe.
- With the GPS receiver active, senses when you are leaving the area of one map and automatically opens the next, providing you with uninterrupted routing throughout the United States.

Mapopolis GPS Receivers

As mentioned, Mapopolis offers their software bundled with a wireless Bluetooth GPS receiver.

Pharos Pocket GPS Navigator

Pharos Science and Applications (**www.pharosgps.com**) offers its Pocket GPS Navigator bundles for a variety of Pocket PCs, as well as notebook and tablet PCs. These bundles include GPS receivers, any necessary accessories, and the Pharos Ostia navigation software.

Ostia Navigation Software

Like the other GPS software solutions, Ostia works with any NMEA-compatible GPS device that can connect to the iPAQ. The software lets you plan trips and get turn-by-turn directions to addresses in the United States and major Canadian cities. Separate packages include complete street-level coverage of the United States and Canada. Some other important software features of the Ostia include:

- Well-designed and easy-to-use interface with large buttons
- The ability to recall up to 11 recent destinations for quick routing
- An onscreen indicator that displays next turn, next street, distance to next turn, distance to destination
- Automatic zoom that zooms in on the map before a turn and zooms out after
- Simulation mode that plays a demo of the route you propose
- The ability to create a reverse route for your return trip
- The ability to save start or destination addresses in Outlook's Contacts, as well as access them from Contacts
- The ability to enter latitude and longitude to navigate to locations without an address (great for geocaching)
- U.S. or Canadian maps
- Smart Navigator, a web-based location and information service that provides real-time traffic maps and POIs and finds and downloads maps (must be connected to the Internet)

Pharos GPS Receivers

Pharos offers the Ostia Navigation Software bundled with Bluetooth receivers and CompactFlash card GPS receivers. They offer a cabled solution for the older iPAQ models, but we did not see one for more recently released iPAQs.

TomTom Navigator

TomTom (**www.tomtom.com**) offers their popular GPS Navigator software in Europe and the U.S. They offer the software as a stand-alone product or bundled with a GPS receiver.

9

TomTom Navigator Software

TomTom's Navigator software is available for all HP iPAQ Pocket PCs. The GPS software for the Pocket PC has an uncluttered user interface and easy-to-use controls. The package includes street-level maps for the entire U.S., and versions with maps of Europe are also available. The software will work with any NMEA-compatible GPS device that can connect to the iPAQ. The Navigator software includes the following features:

- Large onscreen icons and keyboard that are easy to see and use
- Points of interest displayed clearly on map
- Roadblock, which allows instant rerouting around any unexpected obstacles
- A large points-of-interest database that includes gas stations, parking garages, restaurants, hotels, and cinemas
- Customizable menus that let you prioritize the features most important to you
- Demo mode for demonstrating or exploring possible routes
- U.S., Canadian, or European maps; map data from Tele Atlas

TomTom GPS Receivers

TomTom's Navigator software is offered as a stand-alone product and is also bundled with a Bluetooth GPS receiver and the necessary accessories. They have a bundle with a cabled GPS receiver available for the older iPAQ Pocket PCs.

Space Machine PocketMap Navigator

Space Machine (**www.pocketmap.com**) offers PocketMap Navigator as a stand-alone product or bundled with GPS receivers.

PocketMap Navigator Software

PocketMap Navigator software is easy to learn and use and one of the less expensive GPS solutions available to iPAQ users. Like other solutions mentioned here, the software works with any NMEA-compatible GPS device that can connect to the iPAQ. PocketMap's features include:

- A one-touch "next maneuver" feature that allows you to operate the program manually with a touch of the button.
- Automatically zoom before an upcoming maneuver to more clearly display features
- Big button icons that make it easy to operate the program without a stylus
- Automatic loading of maps; displays them for long cross-country routes
- Display of turn-by-turn driving directions with estimated overall drive time and distances along the route

- The ability to create and save up to 300 personalized location points
- The ability to create and save up to 20 complex routes with multiple waypoints for instant recall
- Comprehensive nationwide map database
- The ability to select business listings in 130 major metropolitan areas
- 50-state U.S. coverage, map data from Tele Atlas

Space Machine GPS Receivers

Space Machine offers PocketMap Navigator as a stand-alone product or bundled with Bluetooth, CompactFlash, or cabled GPS receivers. The cabled solutions, which they call PocketMap Navigator Auto GPS kits, are only available for the older iPAQs.

OnCourse Navigator

BuyGPSNow (**www.buygpsnow.com**) offers OnCourse Navigator as a stand-alone product or bundled with GPS receivers. Its features include:

- Voice routing tags that allow you to route to a destination triggered by your voice
- The ability to specify as many waypoints as you like
- Perimeter search, route search, country search for hotels, restaurants, airports, and so on
- Easy-to-read maps that display crossroads and traffic flow (direction) symbols
- Road sign information and display
- NAVTEQ source maps

GPS Receivers from BuyGPSNow

OnCourse Navigator is available as a stand-alone product or bundled with Bluetooth, CF card, and cabled GPS receivers.

TIP   *Streets & Trips 2005, Microsoft's desktop/laptop PC navigation program, includes a user-installable version of Microsoft Pocket Streets. This allows you to export maps from Streets & Trips to your HP iPAQ Pocket PC and use Pocket Streets to view the maps and look up addresses and points of interest. You can zoom in on the map for more detail, or zoom out for the big picture. This latest version of Pocket Streets includes GPS support. If your HP iPAQ is connected to a GPS receiver, Pocket Streets displays your current location on the map. Pocket Streets does not provide turn-by-turn directions or voice prompts. For more information, visit Microsoft's Streets & Trips Web page (**www.microsoft.com/Streets/default.asp**).*

9

GPS for Work and Play

As you've seen in this chapter, Pocket PC GPS solutions are getting more affordable and far more portable. In fact, GPS portability has given rise to a new pastime called *geocaching*. Think of it as a high-tech treasure hunt, where individuals and organizations place small watertight containers with prizes and logbooks inside. Hints, including latitude and longitude, are posted on a variety of websites. The most comprehensive of these sites is Geocaching (**www.geocaching .com**). Just type in your zip code and get a list of the geocaches close to you, along with hints. Then, pull out your GPS-enabled HP iPAQ, and you're off on an adventure.

The cabled solutions are better for vehicle use in your car or RV to help you find that new client's business establishment or your friend's new house. The CF card and Bluetooth solutions also work well in vehicles, but they are portable enough so you can carry them with you in your pocket or backpack when you're out on the trail. Think of it: even in the middle of the Mojave Desert or in a boat in the South Pacific, you can know exactly where you are at any time!

*A variety of additional GPS solutions are available for your HP iPAQ. Check out these products: iGuidance (**www.inavcorp.com**), MobileNavigator5 (**www.navigon.com**), and Street Atlas USA 2006 Handheld (**www.delorme.com**). Also, check out Smartphone & Pocket PC magazine's Encyclopedia of Software and Accessories for other GPS-related solutions at **www.pocketpcmag.com/_enc/encyclopedia.asp**.*

Wrap It Up

Personal navigation is growing by leaps and bounds as people use it for work, vacations, and so much more. Your iPAQ can be a powerful personal navigation tool when combined with the GPS units described in this chapter.

Part III

Work with Your Mobile Office

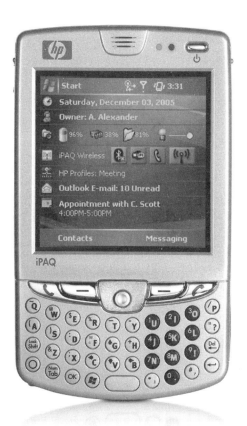 

Chapter 10

Use Word Mobile to Read and Write Documents

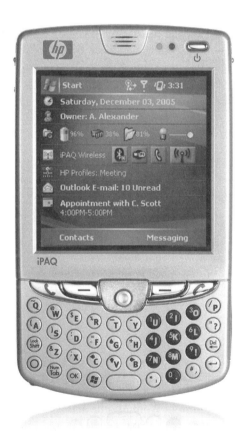

How to...

- Read a Word document on your iPAQ
- Create a Word document on your iPAQ
- Move documents between your iPAQ and your desktop
- Create sketches and drawings
- Capture audio in your documents
- Format a document
- Beam or e-mail a document

One of the most useful features of having a handheld computer running the Windows Mobile operating system is access to scaled-down versions of the popular Microsoft Office software. The most commonly used program in the world for documents is Microsoft Word. Your Windows Mobile 5 device comes with Word Mobile (or if you have an older Windows Mobile device, Pocket Word), which allows you to read, compose, and edit documents on your handheld that are compatible with your desktop version of Word.

In this chapter, we will examine how to use Word Mobile to not only read, but also to write and edit documents. For any of this to be of value, you will need to be able to move documents between your iPAQ and your desktop, so we will also discuss that topic. To make sure that you don't get yourself into any trouble, we will cover exactly which parts of the document you can work with in Word Mobile and which you can't, and what that means for you as a document reader or author.

This Second Edition of this book straddles both the new iPAQ devices equipped with Windows Mobile 5 and the older iPAQ devices equipped with earlier versions of Window Mobile. Some of the earlier versions will feature Pocket Word with a slightly more restricted feature set. The examples in this chapter use Windows Mobile 5 and Word Mobile; however, we will point out the key differences to earlier versions for readers who have earlier releases.

What Word Mobile Can Do

Word Mobile is a scaled-down version of the full desktop Microsoft Word product. As you would expect, it has only a limited set of features, but this doesn't mean it isn't powerful enough to do almost all of what you need while away from your desk.

One of the first differences to point out between the current Word Mobile and its earlier incarnation as Pocket Word is the type of file that it works with on your device. Word Mobile works with the native DOC files that desktop Word creates and uses. However, the earlier version, Pocket Word uses a different file format. When you move the files over to your Pocket PC (either by copying them with Windows Explorer, syncing, or downloading an e-mail attachment), they are automatically converted from the DOC format you are familiar with to the PSW format, which Pocket Word works with. This reduced format supports the most important features of Word, but some information is stripped out. If you are moving your files back and forth between your iPAQ and your desktop, this could become a problem. With Windows Mobile 5 and Word Mobile, you lose less formatting moving back and forth; however, you need to be aware that some features are still unsupported or only partially supported even in the latest version.

NOTE   *A downloaded e-mail attachment isn't actually converted to the Pocket Word format until it is opened. This is an important distinction because otherwise you would be unable to forward the original DOC file to someone via e-mail. If you are running Windows Mobile 5, the file is never converted and stays in its native DOC format.*

The set of fully supported document characteristics includes the following:

- **Standard text formatting**   Consists of bold, italics, underlining, strikethrough, highlight, font type, and font size.
- **TrueType fonts**   Any TrueType fonts you want to use must be installed on your iPAQ (by placing them in the /Windows/fonts folder). By default, Courier New and Tahoma are installed as part of Windows Mobile 5 and Windows Mobile 2003.
- **Bullets**   Any bulleting of text will be supported on the iPAQ.
- **Paragraph spacing and aligning**   Your paragraph spacing and aligning will be retained on the iPAQ.

A number of other characteristics are supported but not fully, or are altered in their implementation:

- **Indentation**   This is altered to make a document more readable on the iPAQ's smaller screen.
- **Images**   The color depth of images is reduced to 256 colors.
- **Numbered lists**   Basic styles.
- **Tables**   With Word Mobile, tables can be viewed, but new tables cannot be inserted into a document. On the older Pocket Word, table data is brought over and inserted as text, and any formatting information is not retained. If you move a document containing a table back to a desktop Word format, the table will appear as simple text aligned with tab stops. Note that new tables cannot be created on the iPAQ.
- **Table of contents and index data**   This information is retained, but as with tables, any formatting is lost.
- **OLE objects**   These objects are not brought over but are replaced by a bitmap placeholder.

10

When a document is transferred onto your mobile device, some document characteristics are preserved but ignored for the purposes of Pocket Word. This means that if you restore the document to a desktop environment, those settings reappear. These characteristics include:

- Annotations and comments
- Columns
- Footnotes
- Frames and style sheets
- Headers and footers
- Margins and gutter settings
- Page setup information
- Paper size settings
- Header and footer vertical locations

It is very important to understand the characteristics that are completely ignored or altered (which may be a big surprise) when you move from the desktop Word environment to the Word Mobile environment, as these settings will return to the default if you ever make a change to the document in Word Mobile, save it, and then move it back to your desktop. These characteristics include:

- Backgrounds.
- Bidirectional text—documents containing bidirectional text can be opened but may not be displayed or formatted properly.
- Borders and shading—page borders are partially supported. If you use the standard line borders, they will be displayed and saved, but if you use graphical images for your borders, they will be converted and saved as lines.
- Metafiles will be replaced by a graphical image but are not saved in the file.
- Revision marks.
- Password protection.
- Shapes and text boxes.
- Smart Tags.

 If you have password protection on a document, you will not be able to move it to your iPAQ. You will need to remove the password protection first.

Even with these limitations, Word Mobile is an excellent way to view attachments to e-mails that are sent to you, edit short documents while you are on the go, or reference important memos without having to carry briefcases full of paper. With applications like Transcriber (described in Chapter 2), Word Mobile becomes a great place to keep your notes while you are on the move if you want to pull them over to your desktop and edit them later. Or, if you are a salesperson on the road, you can edit documents such as contracts while sitting with a client, rather than having to wait until you are back in the office to do it.

> **TIP** *On the Pocket PC, you can set a password to protect the entire unit; however, what if you only want to protect a specific file? This isn't supported on the Pocket PC, so a talented programmer named Francois Pessaux wrote a free application called Lucifer that you can use to encrypt or decrypt any individual file on your iPAQ with DES (Defense Encryption Standard) encryption. If you are technically inclined to tinker, he even provides the source code! To download Lucifer, visit Francois' website at **www.pocketpccity.com/software/ pocketpc/Lucifer-2001-3-21-ce-pocketpc.html**.*

Opening an Existing Document or Creating a New Document

When you tap the icon to launch Word Mobile, you will be presented with a list of documents in the My Documents folder, as shown in Figure 10-1.

To open a specific document, simply tap on it and it will open within Word Mobile. If you are already in Word Mobile, you can open a document by tapping OK in the upper-right corner of the title bar. This will close the document you are in and return you to the document list of Figure 10-1.

10

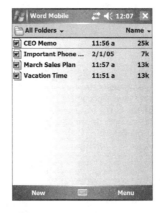

FIGURE 10-1   The document list window shows the Word documents stored on your iPAQ.

At the top of the document selection window, you can see a list of the folders by tapping the All Folders drop-down arrow in the top left, as shown here.

If you have many documents on your iPAQ, you can sort the document list by tapping the drop-down arrow in the top right of the window. As with your desktop version of Windows, you can sort by filename, date, size, or type.

If you want to create a new document, select the New option from the soft button at the bottom left of the document list window. If you are already in a document, you can always select New from the Menu | File soft button at any time to begin creating a new document.

Entering and Editing Text

The essence of working in a document editor is to be able to enter text and information in your document. Word Mobile has changed this procedure significantly. With earlier versions of this software, you could do this in a wide variety of ways including typing the data, writing (where your own writing was captured as an image in the document), drawing (for creating images on the fly), and recording (inserting audio annotations into the document). This was highly flexible, but with the most recent release Microsoft elected to drop the last three and give you only the ability to type your data using one of the standard input methods for all Pocket PC devices in a few different ways.

Entering Text

You enter text through the soft input panel (SIP), the area at the bottom of the screen that appears as a keyboard or as a character recognition area. The soft input panel is covered in detail in Chapter 2.

All entries you make end up as text in the document, just as they do with your standard desktop word processor. Wherever the cursor is, that is where your text will appear. You can move the cursor wherever you like in the text by tapping the appropriate spot with your stylus. Figure 10-2 shows text entered into a Word Mobile document with the Block Recognizer input method selected.

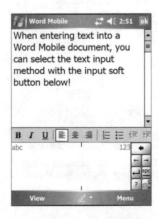

FIGURE 10-2   Typing mode with the Block Recognizer input panel visible

Also visible in Figure 10-2 is the toolbar, the group of buttons above the soft keyboard. The toolbar contains buttons for formatting text. By default, this toolbar is on, but you can turn it off to free up more screen area for viewing your document by selecting Toolbar from the View soft button on the bottom left. The toolbar works much the same way as its counterpart in desktop Word. You select the text that you want and then choose the relevant button to apply formatting to the text. The buttons on the toolbar allow you to select text formatting such as bold, italic, underline, left-justified text, right-justified text, and center-justified text or to start a bulleted or numbered list. These formatting options are discussed later in this chapter.

Formatting Your Document

The amount of formatting that you can accomplish in Word Mobile is limited. Any truly fancy formatting will have to wait until you have transferred the file to a full desktop version of Word. However, you can perform some formatting on the text and paragraphs right on your iPAQ.

Text Formatting

To format text in your Word Mobile document, first you must select the text you want to work with. To select a block of text, tap and hold your stylus just before the first letter that you want to affect. Drag your stylus until just after the last letter that you want to format. This will select all the text between your initial tap and your final release. Then select the Menu soft button and choose Format from the menu. A submenu will appear allowing you to choose whether you want to format the font of the selected text or the paragraph the selected text is in.

Selecting the Font option will open the Format dialog box, shown in Figure 10-3.

In this dialog box you can use the drop-down lists to change the text font, size, and color. You can also set the selected text to be bold, italicized, underlined, highlighted, or struck through.

10

FIGURE 10-3   The Format dialog box allows you to change the characteristics of the selected block of text.

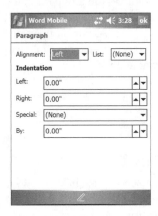

FIGURE 10-4   The Paragraph dialog box lets you change the characteristics of a paragraph.

When you have finished setting the formatting options for the selected text, tap OK in the top right of the dialog box to return to the document.

Paragraph Formatting

To change the formatting of the current paragraph of the document, just place the cursor anywhere in the paragraph by tapping. If you want to affect more than one paragraph at a time, select the text in the paragraphs by tapping and dragging your stylus until all the desired paragraphs are highlighted. To select the entire document, choose Select All from the Edit menu item in the Menu soft button.

Once you have selected the desired paragraphs, choose Edit | Paragraph to open the Paragraph dialog box, shown in Figure 10-4.

In this dialog box you can set the alignment to be left, center, or right. You can also convert the selected paragraphs to a bulleted or numbered list by selecting the appropriate option in the drop-down List field. Set left, right, and special indentations in this dialog box by entering the desired amounts. Special indentations include extra indentation for the first line of a paragraph and hanging indentation.

Saving Your Document

Saving your current document works slightly differently in Word Mobile than it does in the desktop version. Your Word Mobile document will be saved automatically as soon as you tap the OK button in the top-right corner to exit the document. You do not need to explicitly save the document. It will be saved into the folder that you are currently working in, with the name that you last used. If this is a new document that hasn't been saved before, Word Mobile will use the first words in the document as the filename. If you want to use a specific filename, save in a different folder, save to an external storage device (such as a CompactFlash (CF) card),

FIGURE 10-5   In the Save As dialog box, you can change the filename, file type, folder, and storage location of your document.

or save as a different file type, you will need to choose Save Document As from the File menu item on the Menu soft button.

Selecting Save Document As will open the Save As dialog box, as shown in Figure 10-5. Tapping OK will carry out your instructions and make a copy of the document where you have requested.

Remember that if you are editing an existing document and tap the OK button in the top-right corner, your changes will be automatically saved. When you tap this button, Word Mobile will *not* prompt you with a "Do you want to save?" message as the desktop version does; it will assume that you want to save, and the old version will be overwritten. If you have been making edits and decide you don't want to keep them, be careful not to exit the program with the OK button. Instead, use the Revert To Saved command on the File menu. You will be asked to confirm that you want to undo all the changes that you have made since opening the document. If you select Yes, the document will revert to its original state. If you select New after editing a document in Word Mobile, it will prompt you with a message asking whether you want to save, cancel, or save as prior to opening a new document.

Beaming and E-mailing Your Document

Word Mobile realizes that if you are writing documents on your iPAQ, they will likely be short, and you will probably want to be able to transmit them to someone else either by e-mail or by beaming them (transferring information through the infrared port of your iPAQ) to another Pocket PC owner. To make this process as easy as possible, Word Mobile has added Send Via E-mail and Beam commands to the File menu.

Selecting Send Via E-mail from the File menu will create a new e-mail message in your Outbox with your document already attached. You will need to select to whom you wish to send

Setting up to beam a document to another Pocket PC through the infrared port.

the message as well as add a subject line and any text to the message. Tapping the Send button will queue it up to be sent the next time you have an active wireless connection or the next time you connect with ActiveSync.

Selecting the Beam menu item will automatically set up your iPAQ to beam or transmit the document from your infrared port at the top of your unit to a receiving unit that has a physically aligned infrared port. You will see the Word Mobile beaming window, shown in Figure 10-6, which shows the status of the beam. In Figure 10-6 the device hasn't yet located an aligned infrared port that is ready to receive. Once the document has been successfully transmitted, you will see the Results window, as shown in Figure 10-7.

The Results window appears after a document is successfully beamed to another Pocket PC device.

FIGURE 10-8 A document zoomed to 50% allows you to see more information on the screen at one time.

Zoom

The Zoom command on the View soft button menu allows you to change the size of the document view. There are five preset zoom levels: 50%, 75%, 100%, 150%, and 200%. Figure 10-8 shows our sample document zoomed to 50%, the smallest setting, as well as the Zoom command fully expanded.

10

Undo/Redo

Undo and Redo commands are available on the first menu on the Menu soft button. Undo will undo your last action, including formatting, zooming, typing, or deleting. Tapping Undo multiple times will undo multiple previous actions. The Redo command lets you restore the change you just undid. Redo can be useful if you tap the Undo button too many times and accidentally undo more steps than you intended to.

Spell Check

Spell Check is a particularly useful feature because you are much more likely to make spelling errors when entering data on a handheld.

You can start the spell checker by choosing it from the Tools menu under the Menu soft button.

Word Count

You can determine the length of your document by selecting Word Count from the Tools menu. A window will pop up that gives the count of words entered in the document.

Setting Your Options

You can set global options for Word Mobile by selecting Options from the Tools menu. The Options dialog box will open, as shown in Figure 10-9.

Default Template

The Default Template drop-down list allows you to set the standard template that will be used every time a new document is opened using the New command. It is rare that you would want to change this selection from the default Blank Document, unless you find that the vast majority of new documents you create are based on another template. The standard set of templates that install with Word Mobile are

- **Blank Document**   The initial default template is a completely blank document.
- **Memo**   This template contains a title and the standard fields To, CC, From, and Date.
- **Meeting Notes**   This template contains a title, subject, date, attendees, and action items headings.
- **Phone Memo**   This template contains a title, caller, company, phone, date and time, and message headings.
- **To Do:**   This template contains a title and a list of blank bullets for entering to-do items.

Alternatively, to start a document with a specific template, you can select the Templates folder from the document list window discussed in the section "Opening an Existing Document or Creating a New Document" earlier in this chapter.

FIGURE 10-9   You can set Word Mobile options in the Options dialog box.

You can add new templates to this default set by creating a template you want and putting it in the Templates folder. For example, if you are a real-estate inspector and find that you use your iPAQ for doing inspections in the field, you could set your default Word document template to be a blank inspection report. Just remember to use the Save Document As command to avoid overwriting your initial template. (We recommend keeping an extra copy of all your templates in a different folder, because at some point you will likely accidentally overwrite your template.)

Save To

The Save To list box allows you to save your documents by default to the main memory of your iPAQ or to an external storage location. External storage locations can include Secure Digital (SD) cards and CF cards. Various iPAQ models feature different combinations of these slots, which are discussed in greater detail in Chapter 15.

Display In List View

The Display In List View command allows you to select what types of files appear in the document list window that opens when you first launch Word Mobile. By default this list will show all known file types. You can restrict this list to show only Word documents, Rich Text files, or Plain Text files.

Synchronizing with Your Desktop

10

Synchronizing your data with ActiveSync is covered in detail in Chapter 2, and if you are in need of detailed instructions you should refer to that chapter. Note that keeping a synchronized document on both your Pocket PC and desktop system can be a great convenience. Every time you make a change on your Pocket PC or desktop, the document will be synchronized with the other system. If you reference and update this document frequently, then this capability could save you a great deal of time. However, keep in mind that if you modify the document on both the desktop and the Pocket PC between synchronizations, the next time you ActiveSync with your iPAQ, you will have to resolve the conflict by selecting one of the documents to overwrite the other.

An Alternative to Word Mobile

For the serious mobile writer, the feature set of Word Mobile might prove disappointing. If you want the ability to create and edit your Word DOC files in their native format with full functionality, you should purchase TextMaker from the German software vendor SoftMaker (**www.softmaker.com**). It is an impressive program that allows you to create and edit full Word documents. It includes full support for images, tables, headers and footers, and more (for example, see Figure 10-10). TextMaker can use its own native file format as well as support Microsoft Word, RTF, Pocket Word, and HTML files. If mobile access to and editing of documents is important to you, this software is a must-have addition to your Pocket PC.

FIGURE 10-10　TextMaker allows you to work with full unconverted Microsoft Word documents, including many advanced features.

Writing Resources

Many writers like to keep a dictionary and thesaurus close at hand. However, your iPAQ won't come with these installed by default. You can check out some of the following sources for reference materials that are compatible with your Pocket PC.

TomeRaider

TomeRaider (**www.tomeraider.com**) is an e-book reader that allows you to view a wide variety of reference material such as encyclopedias, dictionaries, thesauri, guides, religious works, philosophical texts, and much more. A dictionary entry is shown in Figure 10-11. It is compact and responsive, allowing you to look up important reference information quickly and easily without consuming all of the storage space on your iPAQ. You have to purchase the software for a nominal charge, but the reference materials are free. A vast library of TomeRaider books is available at **www.memoware.com**.

Lextionary

Lextionary, by Revolutionary Software Front, is both a dictionary and thesaurus. It contains almost 140,000 words available for lookup. It is more limited than TomeRaider in that it is a single-purpose stand-alone application instead of a generalized reference reader. You can download a free trial copy from the Revolutionary Software website at **http://revolution.cx/Pocket-PC-Dictionary.htm**.

FIGURE 10-11   Many portable reference books are available to load separately on your Pocket PC.

Microsoft Reader References

You can also find a variety of free Microsoft resources such as the Encarta Encyclopedia and a Pocket Dictionary directly from the Microsoft website at **www.microsoft.com/reader/ downloads/default.asp**.

Wrap It Up

The Word Mobile platform is a powerful tool that allows you to read and compose documents anywhere you like greatly enhancing your mobile lifestyle!

Chapter 11

Use Excel Mobile to Work with Numbers

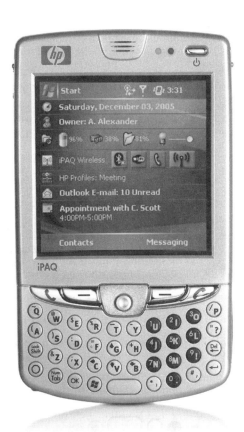

How to...

- Open and work with an Excel workbook on your iPAQ
- Create an Excel Mobile workbook on your iPAQ
- Move workbooks between your iPAQ and your desktop
- Create a template
- Format cells and workbooks
- Use formulas in a workbook
- Beam or e-mail a workbook

Like Word Mobile, Excel Mobile is part of the unique capabilities of the Pocket PC–based handhelds like the iPAQ. Excel Mobile allows you to view, create, and edit spreadsheets on your handheld that are compatible with your desktop version of Excel.

In this chapter we will examine how to use Excel Mobile to not only view, but also to compose and edit spreadsheets. As we did in Chapter 10 on Word Mobile, to make sure that you don't get yourself into any trouble, we will cover exactly which parts of the spreadsheet you can work with in Excel Mobile and which you can't and what that means for you as a spreadsheet reader or author.

What Excel Mobile Can Do

Excel Mobile is a scaled-down version of the full desktop Microsoft Excel product. As you would expect, it has only a limited set of features, but this doesn't mean it isn't powerful enough to do almost all of what you need while away from your desk.

As with the earlier version of Word Mobile, Pocket Word, the earlier version of Excel Mobile was called Pocket Excel. The files that Pocket Excel worked with were converted versions of the XLS files that are on your desktop. The converted Pocket Excel workbook extensions are .pxl for workbooks and .pxt for templates. The current version of Excel Mobile works by default with the standard XLS files that the desktop version of Excel uses.

 *Excel Mobile files are limited to 256 columns and 16,384 rows. This is a pretty big file, but the desktop version of Excel can handle much larger ones. If the Excel spreadsheet you are moving to your Pocket PC is larger than this, it will be automatically truncated. Any formulas that refer to rows beyond 16,384 will be replaced with the #REF! error.*

When you move the files over to your Pocket PC (either by copying them with Windows Explorer, syncing, or opening an e-mail attachment), they will move in their standard format and will be the same size they are on your desktop. (Note that if you are running Pocket Excel on an older iPAQ, the files are automatically converted to the correct format. This reduced format supports the most important features of Excel, but some information is lost.) If you save the contents of a workbook you have been working with on your iPAQ, you will lose any unsupported formatting or formulas that were in the original workbook. If you are moving your files back and forth between your iPAQ and your desktop, this could become a problem. You shouldn't notice any significant problems with basic spreadsheets, but some that utilize more sophisticated functions could operate differently in Excel Mobile. To help you understand the details of what is and isn't supported, we've produced lists of the different features and characteristics.

This is the set of fully supported spreadsheet characteristics:

- **Standard text formatting** Bold, italics, underlining, highlight, font type, font color, and font size formatting are fully supported.

- **TrueType fonts** Note that any TrueType fonts you want to use must be installed on your iPAQ. By default, Courier New and Tahoma are preinstalled. Any fonts that are in an Excel spreadsheet but not loaded on your iPAQ will be displayed to the closest matching font on your iPAQ, but the original font is preserved so that if this workbook is transferred back to your desktop the data will be displayed in the original font.

- **Cell formatting** Standard and custom formats are supported for cells including General, Number, Currency, Accounting, Date, Time, Percentage, Fraction, Scientific, Text, and Custom. Note that any numbers formatted using the Excel 97 version of Excel and the conditional formatting feature will be displayed in Number format.

- **Cell alignment** Horizontal and vertical alignment options are supported, along with word wrap within a cell; however, vertical text in a spreadsheet appears horizontal.

- **Charts** New to Excel Mobile are charts, which were unsupported in previous versions of this application. Not all chart formats are supported, but all standard formats will work fine.

- **Row heights and column widths** Adjustment of row heights and column widths are supported.

A number of other characteristics are supported, but not fully or are altered in their implementation:

- **Formulas with arrays, external links, and intersection range references** You cannot use any of these features in your formulas. When you copy a spreadsheet that contains one of these features from your desktop, the cells containing the formulas will be converted to values in Excel Mobile.

- **Formulas with unsupported functions** Many of the functions in Excel are supported in Excel Mobile, but not all. We won't list all the functions here. More functions are supported in Excel Mobile than in the older Pocket Excel. For example, the Round() function is available in Excel Mobile, but not Pocket Excel. You can see a full list of supported functions in both Excel Mobile and Pocket Excel from the Insert Function command on the Tools menu. When you copy a spreadsheet that includes unsupported functions from your desktop, those functions will be converted to values.

11

■ **Pivot tables**   Pivot tables are not supported in Excel Mobile, and, like the unsupported formulas, will be changed to values if brought over from desktop Excel.

■ **Borders**   Borders are supported, but not if you try to be fancy. You can only create borders with single lines. Any different borders that are brought over from desktop Excel will be converted to single-line borders.

■ **Vertical text**   Vertical text is not supported and will be changed to horizontal text if brought over from a desktop file.

■ **Hidden names**   Any hidden names that are brought over from a desktop file will be displayed.

■ **Passwords**   Although Pocket Excel allowed you to set a general password for your spreadsheet, Excel Mobile no longer supports this feature, which is very disappointing. You must remove the password protection in desktop Excel and then sync the file over to your iPAQ.

■ **Protection**   You can use protection features on the desktop version of Excel, and these features will be preserved in Excel Mobile; however, they are disabled.

■ **Zoom**   The normal Excel feature of allowing you to have different Zoom levels on different pages of a worksheet is not available in Excel Mobile. You can set a Zoom level, but it applies to the entire workbook and is not retained when the workbook is saved.

When a spreadsheet is brought onto your mobile device, one characteristic is converted but is ignored for the purposes of Excel Mobile: cell shading. This means that if you restore the spreadsheet to a desktop environment, the cell shading originally assigned to a cell reappears.

It is very important to note which characteristics are completely unsupported when you move from the desktop Excel environment to the Excel Mobile environment, as these settings will return to the default if you ever move the spreadsheet from Excel Mobile back to the desktop. These characteristics are

■ Graphics (images, object charts, picture controls, drawing objects, and so on)

■ AutoFilter

■ Add-ins

■ Data validation

■ Cell notes

■ Cell patterns

■ Scenarios

■ Text boxes

■ Hyperlinks

■ VBA scripting

Excel Mobile is a very handy way to whip together quick calculations, write up expense sheets while on the go, gather sports statistics at the park, calculate a tip at the restaurant, and more.

Opening an Existing Spreadsheet or Creating a New Spreadsheet

When you tap the icon to launch Excel Mobile, you will be presented with a list of workbooks in the default folder, as shown in Figure 11-1.

To open a specific workbook, simply tap it and it will open within Excel Mobile.

If you are already in Excel Mobile, you can open a workbook by tapping OK in the upper-right corner of the title bar. This will close the workbook you are in and return you to the list shown in Figure 11-1.

One of the folders in the list is the Template folder. Templates are preformatted read-only documents. A Vehicle Mileage Log template comes preloaded as part of Excel Mobile. Templates retain their same base formatting forever, which is great for standard forms that you need to fill out often, such as expense sheets.

If you have many workbooks on your iPAQ, you can sort the list by changing the Sort By setting. To change the sorting method, tap the drop-down arrow in the top right of the window, shown here, and make a selection from the list. As with your desktop version of Excel, you can sort by filename, date, size, or type.

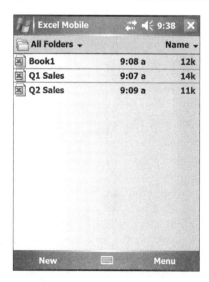

FIGURE 11-1   The workbook list window shows the Pocket Excel workbooks stored on your iPAQ.

If you want to create a new workbook, select the New soft button at the bottom of the screen. If you are already in a workbook, you can always select New from the Menu | File soft button at any time to create a new workbook.

Entering Data and Formulas into Cells

The benefit of spreadsheet software like Excel Mobile is that you can analyze groups of numbers or information by entering the data into the spreadsheet and then building formulas to calculate and manipulate the values automatically. Typical examples of this include tracking expenses, tallying up sales for a group of stores, keeping sports statistics, or any other numerical activity. For non-numeric activities, the software might contain items like your grocery list or Christmas gift list.

Selecting Cells

Before you can enter data into a cell, you must select the cell or group of cells that you want to work with. To select a single cell, tap the cell you desire with your stylus as shown in Figure 11-2.

If the cell you want is not visible, you can scroll using the scroll bars on the right and bottom, or you may use the Go To command in the Edit menu that is available from the Menu soft button. Selecting Go To will open the dialog box shown here, allowing you to specify a particular cell (which you can name by its cell address, H9, for example, or if you have named ranges in your workbook you can use that name).

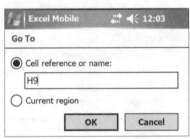

The Go To Current Region command will select a rectangular cell range around the currently selected cell bordered by blank rows or columns, as shown in Figure 11-3.

 **Insert Graphs with Pocket Excel**

If you don't have the current Excel Mobile and are limited to Pocket Excel, you will notice that Pocket Excel doesn't support graphs, but if you need to display graphs on your older Pocket PC, you can do so with a third-party application such as AutoGraph from Developer One (**www.developerone.com**). It is easy to use. You copy the range of cells you want to graph into the clipboard by selecting the range and choosing Edit Copy from the Pocket Excel menu. Next, you start Pocket AutoGraph and paste the cells. You can now choose your graph format and display a picture of your information. Next time you are on a plane with the sales manager and you want to show the sales trend for the East Coast region, you know how to do it!

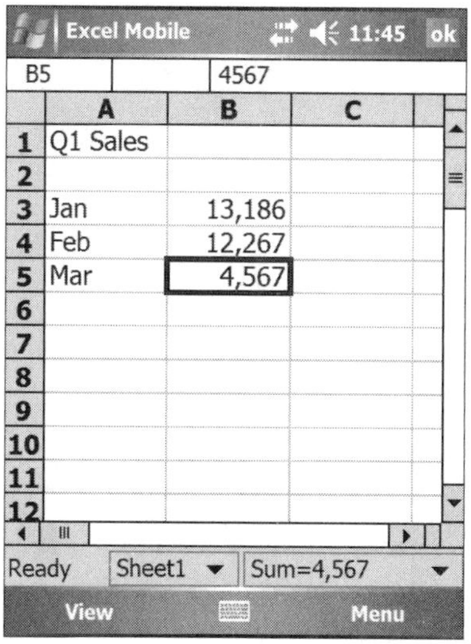

FIGURE 11-2   Before you can enter data into a workbook, you must select the cell or cells you want to work with.

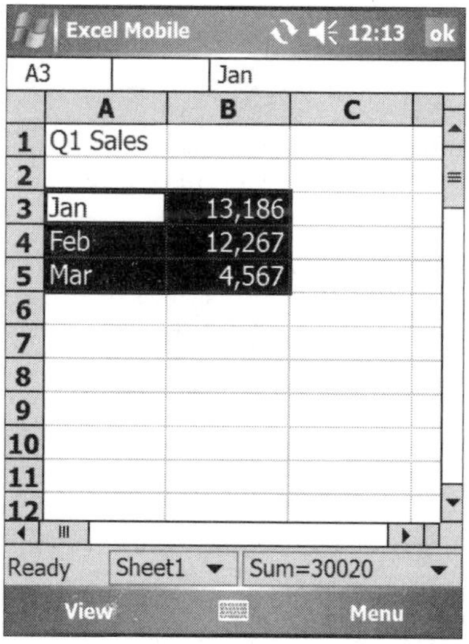

FIGURE 11-3   The Go To Current Region command will select the set of all cells around the current cell that contains data.

11

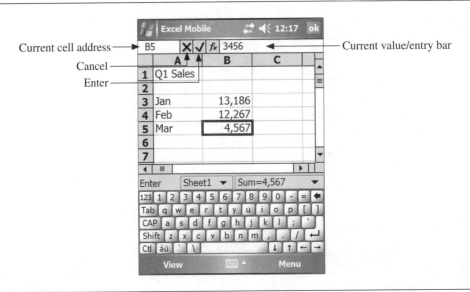

FIGURE 11-4 Data that you enter appears in the cell value box with buttons to cancel or accept your entry.

You can also select a range of cells by tapping with the stylus and dragging the rectangle so that all the cells you desire are contained within the shaded area.

Entering Data into a Cell

Once you have selected a cell or range of cells, you can enter data, labels, or formulas into the current cell. You can enter data in the standard ways, through the character recognizer, keyboard, or Transcriber.

When you start typing characters, they will appear in the entry bar where the current cell value is displayed, as shown in Figure 11-4. To the left of this bar you will find the address of the current cell, a button to cancel your entry and a button to complete your entry (which is the same as pressing ENTER on the keyboard). There is also a button for creating formulas, which is addressed later in this chapter.

The difference between using the Enter button on the entry bar and ENTER on your keyboard is that tapping the Enter button will leave you in the current cell, whereas pressing ENTER on the keyboard will accept your entry and will make the cell below the current cell the new current cell. The latter action is convenient for entering a long list of data.

Entering a Formula

Being able to enter formulas to perform calculations on numbers is where the real power of a spreadsheet program like Excel becomes evident. Usually you are after more than just a list of numbers. You need to be able to add up those numbers, find an average, or perhaps perform a net present value calculation. All of this is possible with Excel Mobile formulas.

To enter a formula, first select the cell in which you want the result of your formula to be displayed. To tell Pocket Excel that you are creating a formula, enter an equal sign (=) in the cell value box. Next, type in the formula that you desire along with any information that it needs to make its calculation, as shown next. (Note that the three buttons between the cell address and the cell value only appear when you are editing a specific cell.)

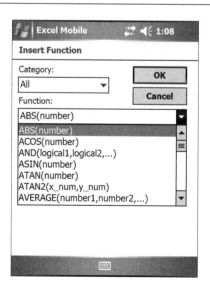

This illustration shows an example of one of the most commonly used formulas, the Sum formula. It is very likely, if you are a frequent user of Excel, that you will know the most common formulas such as Sum, Average, and Count, but you may not know all the other functions that are available. To access these, you can go to the Insert | Function menu item under the Menu soft button, or tap the *fx* button to the immediate left of the cell value area (note that the *fx* button appears only when you begin to enter data into a cell, otherwise it is hidden). Any of these actions opens the Insert Function dialog box, shown in Figure 11-5.

FIGURE 11-5 You can select from a list of all available functions in the Insert Function dialog box.

To select which subset of functions you want to look at, make a selection from the Category drop-down list. The default setting is to show all functions, but you can choose to view subsets of Financial, Date and Time, Math and Trigonometry, Statistical, Lookup, Database, Text, Logical, and Informational.

The Function list shows all the available functions that match the category you selected. The arguments that the function expects are presented in parentheses. When you select a function in the list, a brief description of it will appear beneath the list. To list every function in detail is beyond the scope of this book, but if you have access to the desktop version of Excel, you can look up the details of each function; they work the same way in Excel Mobile as they do in the desktop version.

Once you have selected the function you desire, tap OK to return to the cell value box where the selected function will be pasted into place. Next, simply replace the argument placeholders with the values that you desire. In addition to typing in the cell addresses by hand, you can tap specific cells to enter them into your formulas or, to enter a range, tap and hold a cell and then drag the stylus over the range of cells you would like to select.

Tapping and Holding a Cell

If you tap your stylus and hold it on a cell without moving the stylus, you will be presented with a pop-up menu to make it easier to perform common functions on a specific cell, as shown here.

From this pop-up menu you can easily cut or copy the selected cell (or cells) into the clipboard, from which they can be pasted elsewhere in the spreadsheet. You also have commands to open the Insert Cells or Delete Cells dialog boxes.

The Delete Cells dialog box works the same as the Insert Cells dialog box except that rows are shifted either left or up, or entire rows or columns are deleted.

Use the Format Cells command on the pop-up menu to edit the formatting of the selected cells. New to Excel Mobile is the Insert Chart menu item allowing you to graphically display information in a chart inside your workbook.

Formatting Cells

The amount of formatting that you can accomplish in Excel Mobile is limited when compared with that available in the desktop version. Any truly fancy formatting will have to wait until you have transferred the file to a full desktop version of Excel. Nevertheless, you can still format a number of items in Excel Mobile.

When you select Format Cells from the tap-and-hold pop-up menu, or from the Cells command under the Format menu, the Format Cells dialog box will open. Along the bottom of this dialog box are five tabs to choose from: Size, Number, Align, Font, and Borders.

Size

You can format the row height and column width of the currently selected cell on the Size tab in the Format Cells dialog box, as shown in Figure 11-6. Only these two properties may be edited.

Row height is measured in points, and column width is measured in characters based upon the standard font. Row height can be set anywhere from 0 to 409. A value of 0 will make the row a hidden row. Column width can be set anywhere from 0 to 255 characters (decimal points are allowed) based upon the standard character font. Setting the column width to 0 will hide the column.

Number

You can change the data type of the number in a cell on the Number tab of the Format Cells dialog box. The Category list box contains a list of all the valid formats for Excel Mobile.

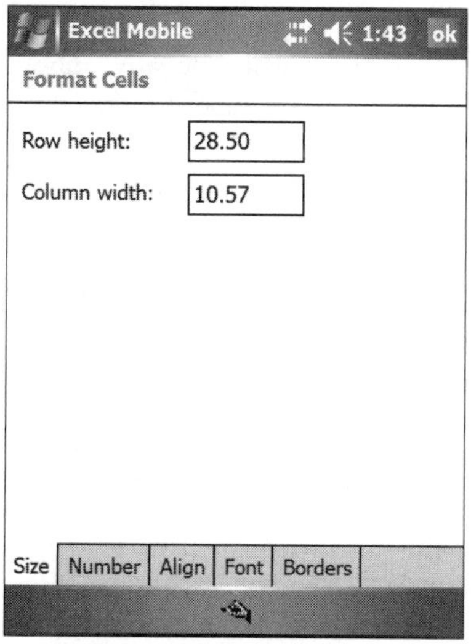

11

| FIGURE 11-6 | The physical size of the selected cell(s) can be adjusted by setting the Row Height and Column Width values on the Size tab of the Format Cells dialog box. |

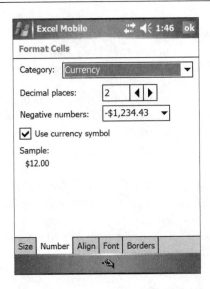

FIGURE 11-7   You can select the data type for a cell with the Number tab of the Format Cells dialog box.

You can scroll through this list and select the format that is appropriate for what you are doing. When you select a format, appropriate formatting options for that data type will appear below. For example, in Figure 11-7 the Currency data type has been selected; the options for this data type are the number of decimal places, how to display negative numbers, and whether you want the currency symbol to be shown. A sample of a number formatted as this data type is displayed below the options.

The format types available are General, Number, Currency, Accounting, Date, Time, Percentage, Fraction, Scientific, Text, and Custom.

Align

The Align tab is used to set the alignment properties of the currently selected cell. From here you have the option to set the horizontal alignment to General, Left, Center, Right, or Center Across Selection. You can set the vertical alignment to Top, Center, or Bottom. Also, a check box will allow you to wrap text onto multiple lines within a cell, as shown in Figure 11-8.

Font

On the Font tab you can select from the drop-down lists to change the selected cell's font, color, and size. You can also set the cell to be bold, italic, or underlined, as shown in Figure 11-9.

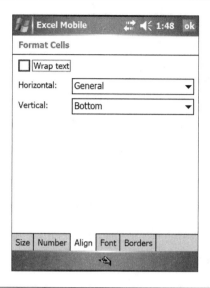

FIGURE 11-8   Use the Align tab to set options for horizontal and vertical alignment as well as word wrapping within a cell.

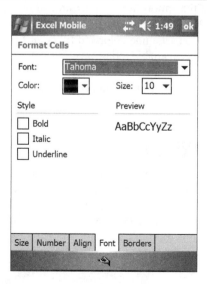

FIGURE 11-9   You can format the font settings for the selected cell on the Font tab.

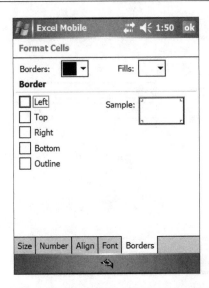

FIGURE 11-10   You can format the borders for your cells with the Borders tab.

Borders

On the Borders tab you can select the options for a border around the currently selected cell or cells. You can only create one style of border—a single line—unlike desktop Excel, which has many line weights and types. You can set a line color and fill color for the cell from the drop-down lists. Given that all Pocket PCs available today have full-color screens, the use of colors in a spreadsheet can be very effective. You can also set which side of the cells you want to see a border on by checking the appropriate boxes for Outline, Left, Right, Top, and Bottom, as shown in Figure 11-10.

Formatting Rows and Columns

Under the Format menu are commands to set specific formatting for rows and columns. These do not deal with colors or fonts of the rows and columns, but rather allow you to either hide or show the selected rows/columns or set them to AutoFit. AutoFit means that the row height or column width is adjusted to automatically accommodate the widest or tallest data in the row/column.

Working with Sheets

Workbooks in Excel Mobile accommodate multiple sheets, just as the desktop version of Excel does. When you create a new workbook, it is automatically created with three sheets. You can see what sheet you are currently in by looking at the Sheet area of the status bar (immediately above the menu), as shown in Figure 11-11.

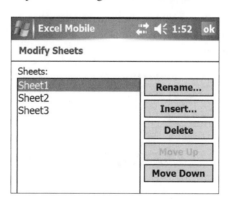

Displays the current sheet. To change the sheet select from the drop down list

See or change the current worksheet with the sheet box in the status bar.

You can add, remove, reorder, or rename sheets in your workbook by selecting Modify Sheets from the Format menu, which opens the dialog box shown next.

Using the AutoCalculate Feature

The status bar in Excel Mobile also contains a box for automatically showing calculated values on the currently selected range of cells. For example, if in the spreadsheet shown in Figure 11-12 we wanted to see the total of sales across both the East and West regions for January, we would

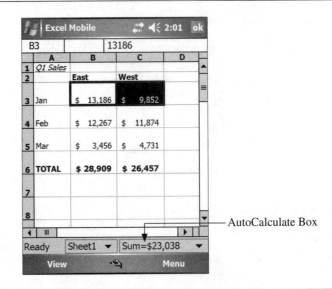

AutoCalculate Box

FIGURE 11-12 The AutoCalculate feature will perform automatic calculations on a selected range of cells.

select the relevant range of cells, and the AutoCalculate box in the status bar would show that the total sales are $23,038 as the figure shows.

To change the kind of calculation being performed, tap the drop-down arrow in the box and make a selection from the list of calculations. The choices are Average, Count, Count Nums, Max, Min, and Sum, as shown here.

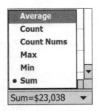

Using AutoFilter

Sometimes you have a large set of data, and you want to be able to easily jump between subsets of that data. For example, if you have a list of all your employees across the country, you might want to be able to quickly filter the list to only show those employees in a given city. You can do this using the AutoFilter command on the Tools menu. To use AutoFilter, select a cell in the title or header row of your spreadsheet and then select AutoFilter. Drop-down arrows will then appear in all the columns of your row, as shown here.

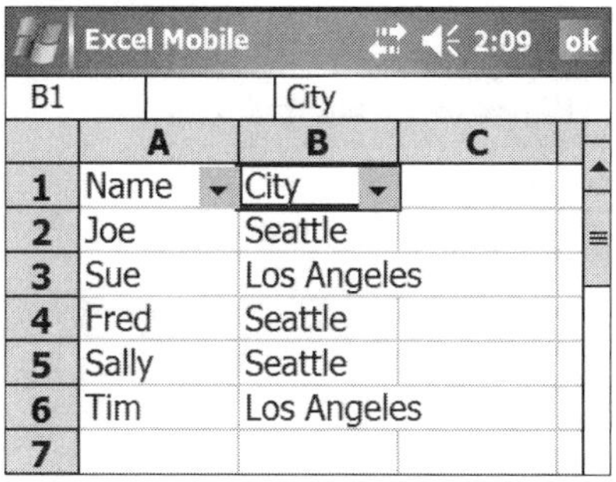

Click the drop-down arrows in any column and select from the list to filter for a specific column value, get all the data, see the top ten items, or set a custom filter, as shown here.

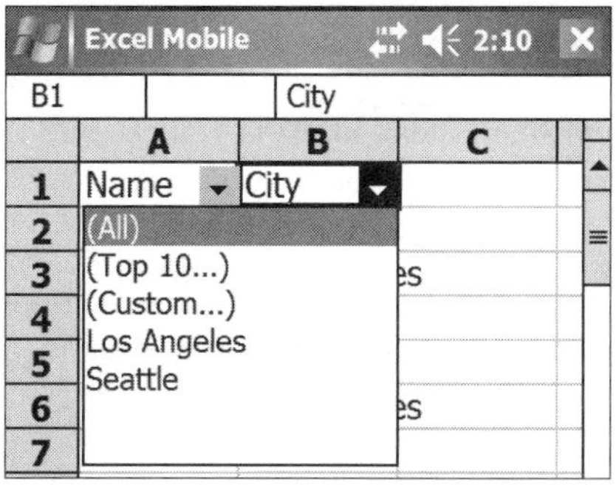

The following shows the result of filtering an employee list for a specific city, in this case, Seattle.

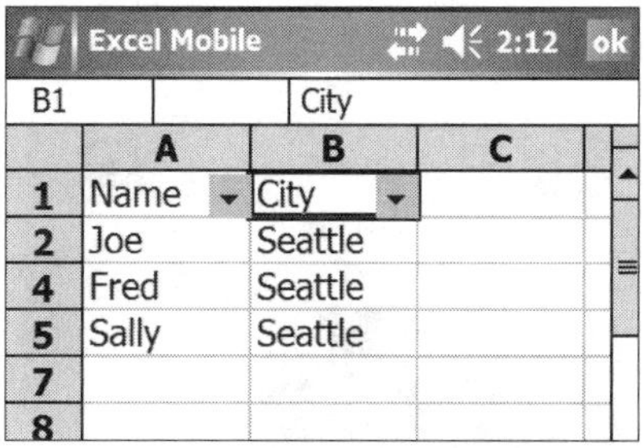

Selecting Custom opens the Custom AutoFilter dialog box, as shown in Figure 11-13. This dialog box allows you to set custom filter criteria. You can select one or two conditions where the selected column is equal to, not equal to, greater than, less than, greater than or equal to, less

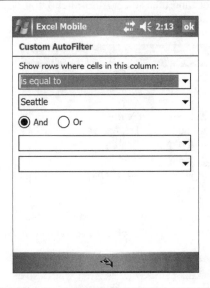

FIGURE 11-13   With the Custom AutoFilter command you can build complex filter criteria
with up to two elements that can be joined by an AND or OR condition.

than or equal to, or begins with a value that you enter in the second field. You can then set an
AND or OR condition with a second criteria that you can choose.

Sorting

When you are working with lists of data and numbers, the ability to sort the information in a
meaningful way is critical. To sort data in Excel Mobile, first select the range of cells that you
want to sort, as shown here. (You can include or exclude the header row; you have the option of
excluding it later in the Sort dialog box.)

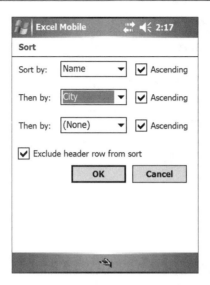

FIGURE 11-14 The Sort dialog box allows you to select which columns to sort by.

Once you have selected the cells you want, choose Sort from the Tools menu. The Sort dialog box will open, as shown in Figure 11-14. You have the option to sort by up to three columns. If the first column you select has two values that are the same, then the second column will be evaluated when choosing which row of data to place first, and so on, with the third. The check box to the right of each column allows you to specify whether you want to sort in ascending or descending order.

The check box at the bottom of the dialog box allows you to exclude the header or title row if you included it in your selection. If this box is selected, the column title will appear in the drop-down lists that currently show Column A, Column B, and so forth.

Inserting Symbols

If you find that you need to insert special characters in your text, you can do that with the Insert Symbols command on the Tools menu. Typical examples of special characters include currency characters such as pound (£) or yen (¥) and letters with special accents and certain characters from the Latin alphabet as well as characters from the Hebrew, Arabic, Cyrillic, Greek, and other alphabets. When you choose Insert Symbols, the Insert Symbol dialog box opens, as shown in Figure 11-15.

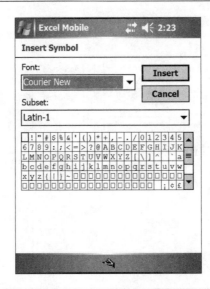

FIGURE 11-15 Use the Insert Symbol dialog box to insert special characters into your worksheet.

From here you select the font that you want to work with from the drop-down list, as shown here.

Then you can select the subset of the font. For example, the subsets available for Courier New include a few Latin choices, some special formatting and spacing characters, Greek, Cyrillic, Hebrew, Arabic, Armenian, Devanagari, Gurmukhi, Gujarat, Oriya, Tamil, Telugu, Kannada, Malayalam, Thai, Lao, Basic and Extended Georgian, Hangul Jamo, and many more special sets of characters, drawing symbols, pictograms, and others.

The display of characters that you can select is larger in Windows Mobile 5 than it was in previous versions. However, the graph that displays all the characters is somewhat small and, if you have poor eyesight, will be difficult to read. You can see the character better by selecting it. This will show an enlarged version of the selected character, as shown here.

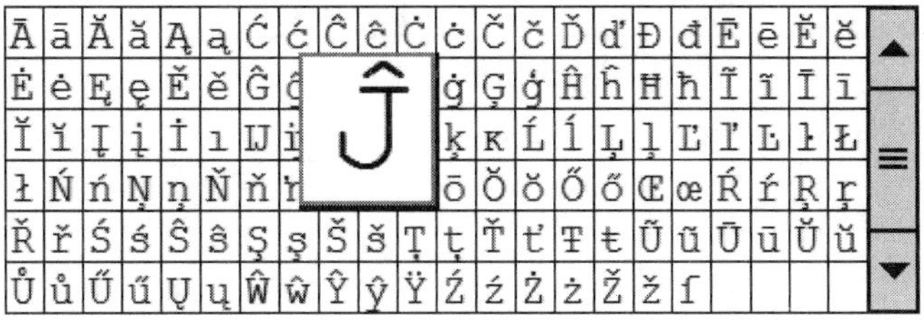

Now tap the Insert button, and that character will be inserted into your workbook at the point where your cursor is.

Defining Names

A seldom-used feature of Excel is the ability to assign a name to a cell or range of cells. This allows you to reference the cell by name when using it in formulas instead of having to remember the cell's address every time you want to use it. This technique can be very useful for large spreadsheets that contain a number of formulas. For example, if we take our list of sales by region, we can add names to the regions and then use those names in our formulas. To define the name for a region, we first select the region. In the following illustration, we selected all the sales for the East region. To give this range of cells a name, we select Define Name on the Insert menu to open the Define Name dialog box, as shown in Figure 11-16. In this dialog box you can enter a name for the selected region. In our example, we call this region EastSales. Tapping Add adds the name that you enter to the list of defined names. The Refers To field below the list allows you to see which cell or range is included in the selected name.

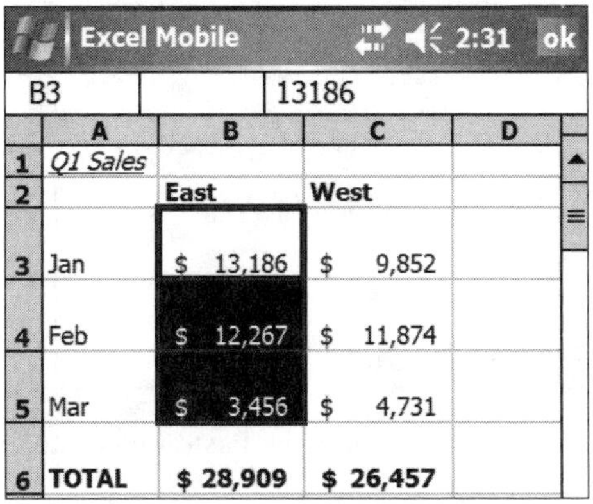

11

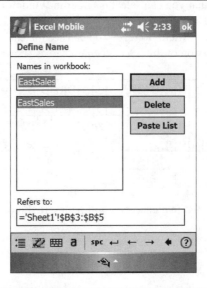

In the Define Name dialog box you can give a name to your selected cell or range of cells.

Once a name is defined, you can substitute it for any cell reference (if it names a specific cell) or any cell range in any formula. In our example, we named a range of cells EastSales. In the formula in cell B6, as shown here, we are summing the range of cells from B3 to B5. This is the same range we named EastSales, so we can substitute the range in the formula with EastSales, and Excel will perform the correct calculation.

A final feature to mention in this section is the Paste List button shown previously in Figure 11-16. If you make extensive use of defined names, you may want to have a list somewhere in your workbook of all your defined ranges for reference. You can create such a list by placing your cursor where you want the list to be inserted and then opening the Define Name dialog box and selecting Paste List. A list of defined names that looks something like this will be pasted into your workbook:

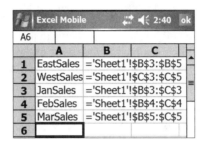

Using the Fill Feature

The Fill feature of Excel allows you to fill a range of cells with data quickly and easily. Fill can be used for static copying of data from an existing set of cells or can include filling the range with a series or data that is different in each cell, such as an increasing number or date. To perform a copy type of fill, you must select the cells that you want to copy and then, at the same time, select all the cells that you want to fill in with the copied data. The original data must be on one edge of the selection range. This can be any of the top, bottom, left, or right edges. Once the data and range are selected, you choose the Fill command from the Edit menu to open the Fill dialog box, as shown in Figure 11-17.

11

FIGURE 11-17   The Fill dialog box allows you to fill a selected range of cells with data.

To perform your copy, you simply indicate which row the original data is in by choosing your fill direction from the list of Down, Up, Left, or Right. The fill type in this case will be Copy. Once you've made your selections, tap OK to copy the original data into the range.

It's likely you will also use the Fill command to fill a range of cells with series data, such as a range of numbers or dates. When building a series, it helps to think in advance about what cells you need to select. For example, if you want to produce a list of days of the week on the left of your worksheet, you can enter the first day **Mon** on the first line. Then you select the Mon cell along with the six cells beneath it, as shown here.

Select Edit | Fill, and in the Fill dialog box select a Direction of Down, a Fill Type of Series, and a Series Type of Autofill, as shown in Figure 11-18.

FIGURE 11-18 You can set the options in the Fill dialog box to produce an Autofill of days of the week.

Autofill instructs Excel to examine the data in the selected range and to extend the range. In the example, entering **Mon** on line 1 tells AutoFill to fill the lines in the range with the subsequent days of the week. Tapping OK will produce the results shown here.

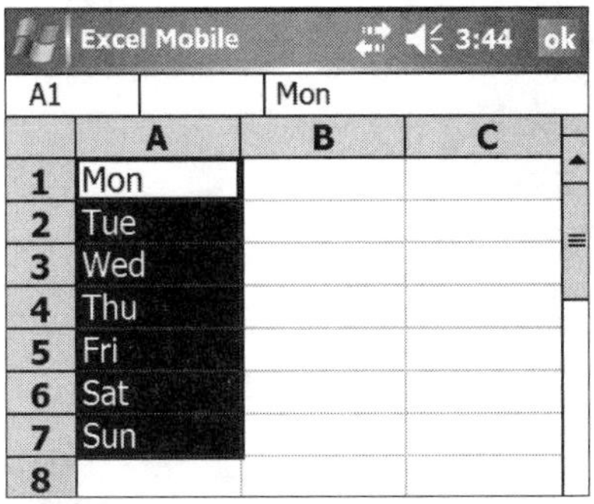

The other Series types that you can select are Date and Number. Selecting one of these means that the primer data you have entered in the fill range includes only the starting point for the series (that is, the first day or number that you want). For the rest of the information, you will indicate what you want to fill in (days or numbers). If you choose days you must choose the type of date information that you want to fill in: Day, Month, or Year. Then, with either option, you must choose the increment or step value. This is the number that the Fill function will increase each subsequent line or column in the fill. For example, to fill a range with the first day of each week, you would put your first date such as **Jan 1** on the first line in your range. Then in the Fill dialog box you would select a Fill Type of Series, a Series Type of Date, and a Step Value of 7. Tapping OK would produce a worksheet like the one shown here.

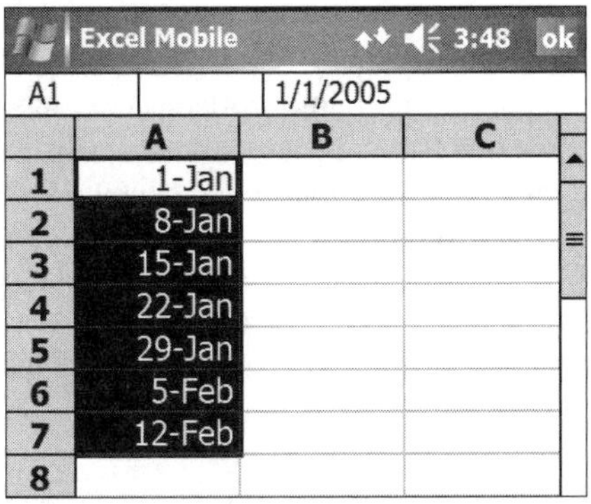

Zoom and Full Screen View

The Zoom command on the View soft button allows you to change the view of your worksheet to make the workspace larger or smaller. This useful feature allows you to see more of your worksheet at one time or focus on a small area of it, although you might sacrifice resolution and readability,

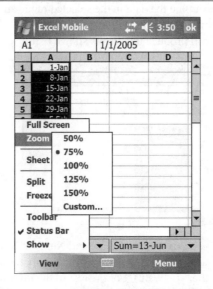

FIGURE 11-19 A worksheet zoomed to 75% allows you to see more information on the screen at once.

depending on the scale you select. There are five preset zoom levels you can select from—50%, 75%, 100%, 125%, and 150%—or you can choose Custom to set your own zoom percentage. Figure 11-19 shows a sample worksheet zoomed to 75% with the Zoom command fully expanded.

Panes/Splitting

If you want to view two different parts of the same worksheet at the same time, you can split your screen into panes. This can be done so you can look at two different sets of data or to keep certain information fixed at the top and left of your worksheet while you scroll around in the main part of the worksheet. Figure 11-20 presents an example of a divided screen where we have split our regional sales spreadsheet to allow us to scroll through the data section while keeping the column and row headers in place.

To break a spreadsheet into panes, select the cell where you want the split to occur. Then select Split from the View menu. To remove the split from any worksheet you are in, select Remove Split from the View menu.

The Freeze Panes command under the View menu works in a very similar way. The difference is that in a split, you have the ability to scroll anywhere on the spreadsheet within any of the panes. With a freeze, only the main "unfrozen" area freely scrolls in all directions. When you hit the boundary of a frozen pane, the cursor will automatically jump into the correct pane for editing purposes. Another difference is that frozen panes are displayed with a single, static line rather than the double, movable line used with a split screen. Choosing Unfreeze Panes from the View menu turns off the Freeze Panes command. An example of frozen panes is shown in Figure 11-21.

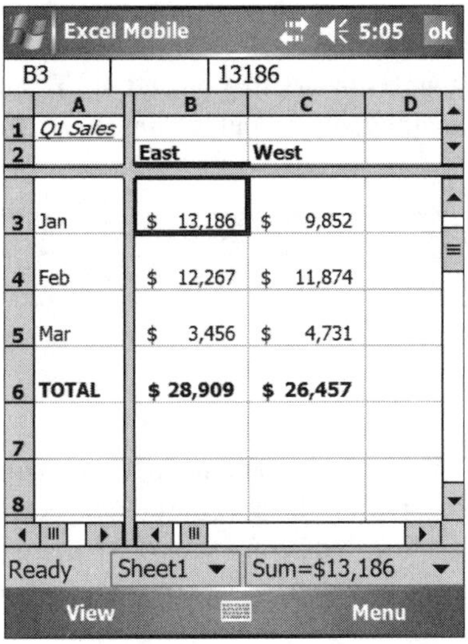

FIGURE 11-20 Windows can be split into panes to allow you to work with different sections of a worksheet at the same time.

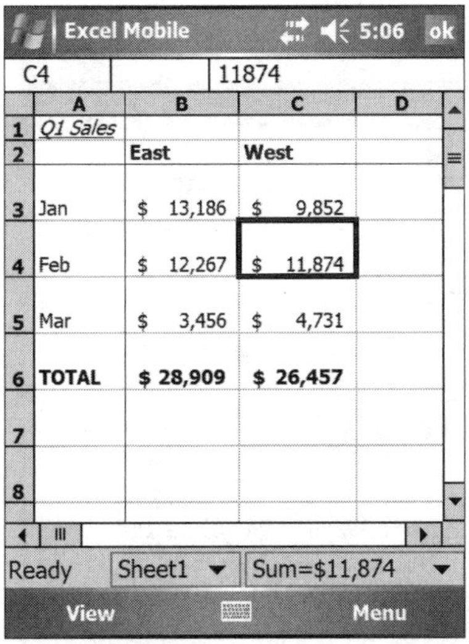

11

FIGURE 11-21 Frozen panes are displayed with a solid, static line.

The Toolbar

By default, the toolbar for Excel is hidden, but you can make it appear by selecting Toolbar from the View soft button menu. This toggles the toolbar on and off. From the toolbar, shown next, you have quick access to cell formatting, alignment, common functions, number formatting, and a button to toggle through all the zoom settings.

Undo/Redo

Undo and Redo commands are available on the Edit menu. Undo will undo the last action that you took, including formatting, zooming, typing, deleting, or other action. Tapping Undo multiple times will undo multiple previous actions. The Redo command will let you restore the change that you just undid. This feature can be useful if you tap the Undo button too many times and accidentally undo too many steps.

Find and Replace

To locate any specific text in your workbook, you can use the Find/Replace command on the Edit menu. Selecting this command opens the Find dialog box, shown in Figure 11-22.

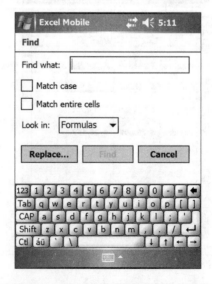

FIGURE 11-22 The Find dialog box allows you to search for and replace text strings in your workbook.

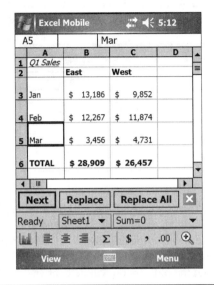

FIGURE·11-23   In the middle of a Find/Replace action, you will have an additional toolbar on your worksheet that includes Find and Replace commands.

Enter any text string that you are looking for in the Find What box. Then you can set options to require it to match case or to only match if the entire cell content matches your text. You must then select whether you would like to search in cells that contain formulas or cells that contain values. If you like, you can specify a value to replace the search text with by tapping the Replace button. In the new dialog box that opens, you specify your replacement string.

If you tap the Find button, Excel will find and make current the first cell after your current cell that contains the string. A new toolbar will also be displayed, as shown in Figure 11-23. This toolbar allows you to move on to find the next instance of your text string, replace the text (using the replacement text that you specified), or replace all instances (it will stop asking you to confirm each one). You may cancel your Find/Replace action by tapping the X button.

Saving Your Workbook

Saving your current workbook is slightly different in Excel Mobile than in the desktop version. Your Excel Mobile workbook will be saved automatically as soon as you tap the OK button in the top-right corner to exit the workbook. You do not need to explicitly save the workbook. It will be saved into the current folder you are in, with the name that you last used. If this is a new workbook that hasn't been saved before, the filename of the workbook will be Book1, Book2, and so on, depending on how many workbooks you have in the directory that have already been named that way. If you want to use a specific filename, save in a different folder, save to an external storage device (such as a CompactFlash or Secure Digital card), or save as a different file type, you will need to choose Save

Workbook As from the Tools menu. Also, if your spreadsheet was last modified in desktop Excel and you are now saving it for the first time with Excel Mobile you will see this warning dialog:

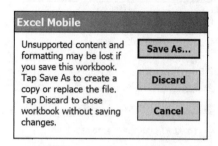

Selecting Save Workbook As opens the Save As dialog box, shown in Figure 11-24. Tap OK to carry out your instructions and make a copy of the workbook where you have requested.

Remember that if you are editing an existing workbook and you tap the OK button in the top-right corner, your changes will be saved automatically. When you tap this button, Excel Mobile will *not* prompt you with a "Do you want to save?" message as with the desktop version. It will assume that you want to save, and the old version will be overwritten. If you have been making edits and decide you don't want to keep them, be careful not to simply exit the program with the OK button. Instead, use the Revert To Saved command on the File menu. You will be asked to confirm that you want to undo all the changes that you have made since opening the workbook. If you select Yes, the workbook will revert to its original state.

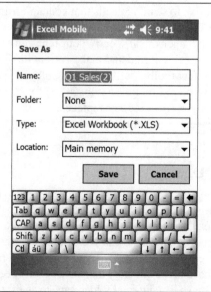

FIGURE 11-24   In the Save As dialog box you can change the filename, file type, folder, and storage location of your workbook.

How to ...   Create Custom Templates

If you want to create your own templates for documents you use often (such as expense sheets, telephone contact logs, purchase orders, and so on), you can do this during the Save As process. At the stage where you are specifying the filename and location, you have the option to save the document as a Excel Mobile template. You can save it anywhere, but it would be convenient to save it in the Templates subfolder.

If you select New after editing a workbook in Excel Mobile, it will prompt you with a message asking whether you want to save, cancel, or save as, prior to starting a new workbook.

Beaming and E-mailing Your Workbook

Excel Mobile realizes that if you are writing workbooks on your iPAQ, they will likely be small, and you will probably want to be able to transmit them to someone else either by e-mail or by *beaming* them (transferring information through the infrared port of your iPAQ—discussed in more detail in Chapter 2) to another Pocket PC owner. To make this process as easy as possible, Excel Mobile has added Send Via E-mail and Beam commands to the File menu.

Selecting Send Via E-mail creates a new e-mail message in your Outbox with your workbook already attached. You will need to select to whom you wish to send the message as well as add a subject line and any text. Tapping the Send button will queue it up to be sent next time you have an active wireless connection or next time you connect with ActiveSync.

Selecting Beam will automatically set up your iPAQ to beam the workbook from your infrared port at the top of your unit to a receiving unit that has a physically aligned infrared port. The Excel Mobile Beaming window, shown in Figure 11-25, will appear, showing the status of the beam. In Figure 11-25, the device hasn't yet located an aligned infrared port that is ready to receive. All versions of the HP iPAQ are set to receive incoming beams automatically.

Once the workbook has been successfully transmitted, you will see the results message box, as shown in Figure 11-26.

Protecting Your Workbook with a Password

Like Word Mobile, Excel Mobile is not able to use passwords to protect your workbook. This is different than in earlier versions of Pocket Excel where workbook passwords were supported. Now you must utilize third-party software to provide this level of protection, as discussed in Chapter 10.

11

FIGURE 11-25   Setting up to beam a workbook to another Pocket PC through the infrared port.

FIGURE 11-26   The results message box appears after a workbook is successfully beamed to another Pocket PC device.

Synchronizing with Your Desktop

Synchronizing your data with ActiveSync is covered in detail in Chapter 2, and if you need detailed instructions, you should refer to that chapter. Note that keeping a synchronized workbook on both your Pocket PC and desktop system can be a great convenience. Every time you make a change on your Pocket PC or desktop, the workbook will be synchronized with the other system. If you reference and update this document frequently, this capability could save you a great deal of time.

Wrap It Up

Having Excel Mobile built into your iPAQ is an extremely handy tool. Whether you are recording your golf scores, looking up a bus schedule, reading a sales report attachment on an email, or some other use, you will undoubtedly find this to be a key part of your iPAQ.

11

Chapter 12

Use Outlook Mobile to Take Control of Your Mobile Life

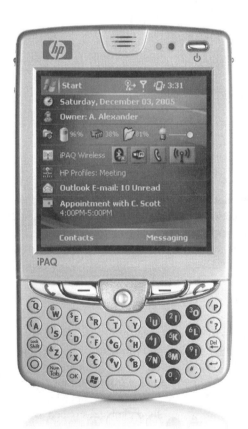

How to…

- Use and customize the Today page
- Manage appointments with the Calendar
- Create new appointments
- Set reminders and categories and invite meeting attendees
- Navigate and manage contacts
- Create new contacts
- Customize the Contacts manager
- Read and compose e-mail
- Set up inboxes and connect to a mail server
- View attachments
- Attach files to an e-mail
- Read, edit, and compose tasks
- Read, edit, and compose notes
- Beam information
- Set up ActiveSync for all Outlook functions

The single most useful thing the average person does with an iPAQ is to keep track of personal information such as contacts/address book, appointment book, personal notes, to-do lists, and, of course, e-mail. These activities fall into a general category called personal information management (PIM). Microsoft Outlook has become the most widely used e-mail and PIM tool around today. On your iPAQ, a pocket version of this popular tool is preinstalled.

What Is Outlook Mobile?

Outlook Mobile isn't a single application. It is actually five applications, each of which performs a different part of the PIM job, but all interact and synchronize with your desktop version of Outlook. Outlook Mobile doesn't have all the bells and whistles of the desktop version, but it has everything you need when you are on the move and is extremely effective. Speaking from personal experience, until we started using Outlook Mobile, we carried our Palm Pilot PDAs and paper-based day planners. After using Outlook Mobile for the first time, we went fully digital and stopped using paper day planners.

The five applications that make up Outlook Mobile are

- **Calendar** Lets you schedule appointments and events to make sure you don't double-book and are in the right place at the right time.

■ **Contacts**   Keeps a database of all of your contacts and their relevant information. At your fingertips is complete contact information for anyone you know: phone numbers, e-mail address, notes, pictures, audio narratives, and more.

■ **Notes**   Allows you to take notes on your handheld instead of scratching them on little pieces of paper that you can easily lose track of. We use it to keep track of an incredibly diverse range of miscellaneous information.

■ **Tasks**   Provides a convenient to-do list that lets you prioritize your tasks. It also includes check-off boxes so you can mark tasks off your list when they are completed.

■ **Inbox**   Allows you to receive your e-mail on your handheld, read your messages, and respond to them while on the go. You can create new messages, attach files, and do everything you would do from a full-sized PC. If you are wirelessly enabled, you can send and receive your e-mail from anywhere at any time (for details, see Chapter 3).

See What's Up with the Today Page

The Today page is the jumping-off point to any of your personal information that is handled by Outlook Mobile. It allows you to see at a glance what appointments you have upcoming today, how many unread messages are in your Inbox, and how many unfinished tasks are on your to-do list, as shown in Figure 12-1.

Tapping any line item will take you to the appropriate application to view the item selected. You can modify the Today page in a number of ways.

Tapping the time line will bring you to the Settings window for the clock, where you can set the current time for your home time zone or for the time zone you happen to be in if you are away from home, as shown in Figure 12-2.

12

FIGURE 12-1   The Today page lets you see all of your important information.

FIGURE 12-2   The Settings window for the clock lets you set both your current time and a second time zone for when you are traveling.

You can customize the appearance and functionality of the Today page by going to the Settings command under the Start menu and choosing the Today icon. This opens the Settings window shown in Figure 12-3. From here you can select different themes for your Pocket PC. The theme changes the picture behind the Today page and the Start menu.

You can select any theme you like from the list of available themes. The default theme and one or two others, depending on which model of iPAQ you own, will be preloaded on your Pocket PC. You can download new themes from a variety of websites. There are two sites, which you can access at no charge, that are solely devoted to Pocket PC themes: **www.pocketthemes.com** and **www.pocketpcthemes.com**. Both sites have additional information such as links to software for

FIGURE 12-3   The Settings window for the Today page allows you to select different themes for your Pocket PC.

building your own themes and much more. Microsoft also has a website where you can download themes at **www.microsoft.com/windowsmobile/downloads/themes.mspx**. To download a theme, you simply copy the theme file to your My Documents directory on your iPAQ. It will automatically appear in the list of available themes.

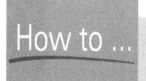

*Do you want to personalize your iPAQ and maybe create your own personal theme? You can do this with software from BVRP called Pocket Theme Manager, which helps you manage your theme collection, create your own themes, and more! You can try it out for free at **www.bvrp.com**.*

How to ...   **Customize Your Today Page**

At the bottom of the Settings window, you will find another tab, the Items tab. From here you can select what items appear on the Today page, as shown here.

The list of all the items that can appear on the Today page is shown with check boxes, allowing you to select which items you want on the Today menu. You can also adjust the settings to cause the Today page to appear if the device is used for a specific time period.

Some of the items in the list also have options you can configure, such as the Calendar. If you tap the Options button after selecting Calendar, you will see the options shown here,

If you want to share a theme with a friend, you can select the theme and tap the Beam button to send it to another Pocket PC user via the infrared port. You can also select any picture to be your theme by selecting the Use This Picture As The Background check box and then browsing to find your picture file.

Keeping Your Appointments with the Calendar

The Calendar application is an absolutely invaluable tool that can immediately make the purchase of your iPAQ worthwhile. If you're like us, you probably struggled with appointments, double-booking yourself, or losing track of where you were supposed to be for a specific appointment. Paper day planners are cumbersome and too much effort to keep up-to-date (not to mention they are large and heavy to carry around). Now, with your iPAQ in your pocket, if someone asks you whether you are free for a meeting next week, you can pull it out, see your schedule, pick a mutually convenient time, and enter the meeting into your timetable. Back in the office, the new appointment is automatically synced with your desktop Outlook calendar application, which is likely hooked into Microsoft Exchange. Everyone in the office can share calendars, so anyone who would like an appointment with you can see whether you are busy at that time. We can practically guarantee that the number of appointments you miss or double-book will drop dramatically, making you much more effective not only at work but also in your personal life.

TIP
Although the built-in Calendar application is everything most people will need, if you want to take it up a level, check out Agenda Fusion from Developer One (www .developerone.com). It features improvements in appointment viewing and scheduling, including drag and drop functionality and color coding. It also has enhancements to other PIM applications like Contacts, enabling you to dial a contact phone number (with the appropriate phone integration).

Starting the Calendar Application

You can launch the Calendar application on your iPAQ in a number of ways. First, when looking at the Today page, you can tap the calendar icon and be taken directly to today's appointments. You can also get to the Calendar application by selecting Calendar from the Start menu. The iPAQ provides four small hardware buttons to launch specific applications. These buttons are configurable, but in their default out-of-the-box configuration, the leftmost button will launch the Calendar application, giving you a quick and easy way to access one of the most-used applications on your iPAQ.

Viewing the Calendar

After you open the Calendar application, what you see will depend on the view that you last used. If this is your first time accessing the application, you will see the Agenda view. The Calendar has five different methods by which you can look at your data. It is always the same data, but it's shown in different levels of granularity. The five views are

- Agenda view
- Day view

- Week view
- Month view
- Year view

The Agenda view, shown in Figure 12-4, contains a list of all of today's appointments and their times. All of the views share most of the standard navigation icons and options shown in Figure 12-4.

The top-left corner always shows the current day, date, month, and year being viewed. Immediately to the right of that are the days of the week, which can be tapped to jump to that specific day of the week. If a day other than the current date is being viewed, the current date will appear with a white square around the day's letter. Tap the icon to the right of the day of the weeks letter (the white square with a curved arrow) to jump immediately to today's date. The left and right arrows on the far right will scroll ahead or back within the calendar. In the Agenda, Day, and Week views, it will scroll by one week. In the Month view, it will scroll by a month, and in the Year view, it will scroll by a year.

The five different views can be accessed using the View menu item from the Menu soft button. You can also change the view you are currently looking at by pressing the hardware Calendar button. Each press changes the view down one level of granularity. The navigation dial on the hardware of the iPAQ is also useful with the calendar. It allows you to move from the current date being viewed to the next date by pressing the disc to the right or down. Pressing the disc to the left or up will move you to the previous day.

Tapping any item in the list in the Agenda view will open the details of that appointment, as shown in Figure 12-5. If you want to edit the appointment or add notes, tap the Edit menu. This will open the appointment in an editable window where you can change all the information such as subject, date, time, location, or notes.

12

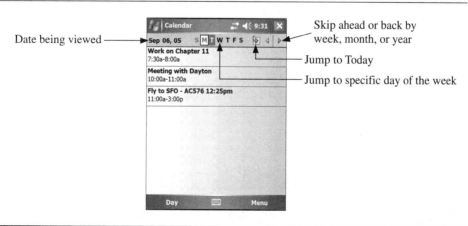

FIGURE 12-4   The Agenda view, featuring a list of today's appointments, contains many standard navigation items found in all views.

Tapping the Edit soft button when viewing an appointment detail will allow you to edit the appointment.

The Day view looks more like a traditional day planner and like the desktop version of Outlook. It shows a single day divided into one-hour blocks with all of your appointments recorded in their relevant time slots, as shown in Figure 12-6.

All of the controls work the same as they do in the Agenda view, but here you will use the scroll bar on the right to scroll through the entire day. In all views, when looking at a specific appointment, you can tap and hold your stylus on the appointment to open a shortcut menu, as shown here. This enables you to move or copy an appointment to another point in your calendar.

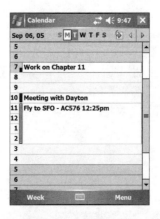

The Day view divides the entire day into one-hour slots where all of your appointments are shown.

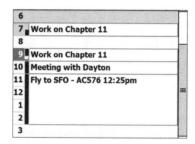

Looking at Figure 12-6, if we wanted to make another appointment to work on Chapter 11 before our meeting with Dayton, we would tap and hold to open the shortcut menu and select Copy to copy the appointment to the clipboard. Then we would select another time slot, tap and hold to open the shortcut menu, and paste the appointment into the new time. The new schedule would look something like this.

In the Day view, you will also see any relevant icons beside the appointment if this option has been turned on in the Options dialog box, as shown here.

You might see the following icons:

- **Bell**   Indicates that a reminder alarm has been set for this appointment
- **Circle with arrows**   Indicates that this is a recurring event
- **Note page with pencil**   Indicates that this event has notes
- **House**   Indicates that this event has a specified location
- **Key**   Indicates that this is a private event
- **Heads**   Indicates that others are invited to this event

12

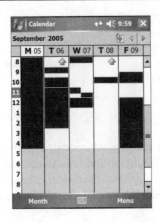

The Week view enables you to see your schedule for the entire week at a glance.

The Week view, shown in Figure 12-7, displays all of your appointments for a week. By default, the week is defined as seven days, but you can customize this setting to show a five-day or six-day week by selecting the Options command under the Tools menu.

All of your appointments show up in the Week view as blue blocks in their appropriate date and time slots. You can easily see where you have free time and where you do not. To view the details of a specific appointment, tap the blue block. This will open a small box at the top of the screen, which will display the details of the appointment, as shown here.

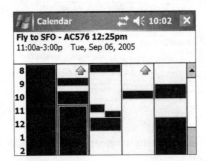

After ten seconds, the box will disappear, returning you to the default Week view. Tapping in the appointment box before it disappears will open the appointment details permanently in a window like the one shown earlier in Figure 12-5.

The Month view, shown in Figure 12-8, enables you to see at a glance your entire month and on what days you have appointments. Each square in the view represents a day. If the current date is in the month you are viewing, that day will be outlined in red.

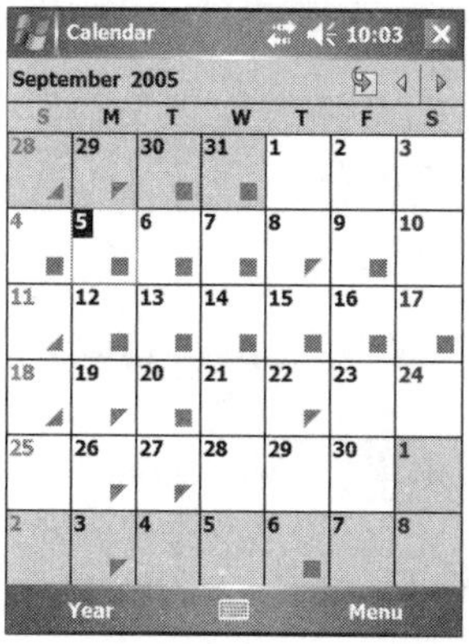

FIGURE 12-8   The Month view shows you an entire month's appointments in one window.

The Month view uses icons to give you a quick feel for how busy that day is. Each day will display one of the following icons to indicate the density of appointments:

- **No icon**   Indicates there are no appointments for the day
- **Triangle (pointing to top left)**   Indicates at least one appointment in the morning
- **Triangle (pointing to bottom right)**   Indicates at least one appointment in the afternoon
- **Dark square**   Indicates appointments in both the morning and afternoon
- **White square**   Indicates an all-day event

12

NOTE *If you are unable to get the white square to appear for an all-day event, it is because it will only show up if the appointment option Show Time As (on your desktop version of Outlook, or Status as it is called in Outlook Mobile) is set to Busy or Out Of Office, which is not the default setting for an all-day event. If you change this on your desktop version of Outlook and re-sync(or change the Status field in the appointment on your iPAQ), the white square will show up. This trick also works for multiple-day events. Tapping any specific date in the Month view will take you to the Day view for the day you selected.*

The Year view will display the entire year calendar on your screen at once, as shown in Figure 12-9. The current date will appear in reversed type. (In Figure 12-9, the current date is September 5.) Tapping a specific date will take you to the Day view for the selected day.

The Year view shows you an entire calendar year at a glance.

Entering a New Appointment

To begin entering a new appointment or event into your calendar, tap the New Appointment menu item from the Menu soft button. Alternatively, you can tap and hold the stylus on a time in the Day or Week view, and when the shortcut menu appears, select New Appointment. Whichever of these options you choose will open the New Event dialog box.

Entering Details

You enter the details of your new appointment or event in the New Event dialog box, shown in Figure 12-10. You can fill in as many or as few details as you choose. The minimum information

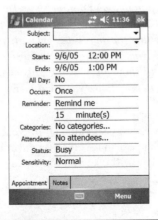

The New Event dialog box is where you can enter the details for the new appointment.

required to create a new event is a subject and a time. The subject line includes a drop-down arrow, enabling you to select from commonly used words for appointments, such as Meet with, Lunch, Visit, and Birthday. You use the onscreen keyboard or other input mechanism to enter the text for the rest of the subject.

You can also enter a location and a start and end time for the appointment. On the Type line in the desktop version of Outlook (or the All Day line in Pocket Outlook), you can choose to make the appointment an all-day appointment. The Status line will change how this appointment appears to anyone who looks at your public calendar through Microsoft Exchange. You can set the time to appear as Free, Busy, Tentative, or Out Of Office. The Sensitivity line enables you to mark the appointment as Private, which means that someone looking at your public calendar will not see the subject line of the event. Instead, they will simply see Private as the subject. Thus, you can keep your medical appointments and other personal information private from outside observers.

Setting Reminders

The Reminder line in a new event allows you to specify whether you would like an alarm and pop-up reminder about an event. You can set a reminder to occur anywhere from minutes in advance of an appointment to months. For example, you might set reminders for events such as birthdays a week in advance so there is time to buy a gift and card. For events such as internal meetings, you might set reminders at five minutes.

On the Reminder line, you can select from one of two options in the drop-down list: None and Remind Me. If you select Remind Me, you will have to select the time before the event to remind you by first selecting whether you want to be reminded minutes, hours, days, or weeks in advance, as shown here.

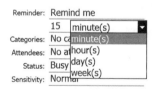

Once you have selected the units, you select the quantity by tapping the number to the left of the units. You can select from the drop-down list or type in your own quantity. Setting a reminder will cause an alarm bell icon to appear beside the event in the Day and Agenda views.

Setting Categories

You can also select a category for the appointment. This enables you to view only appointments related to a specific subject at one time. By default, the Calendar will display the appointments for all categories, but you can choose Categories from the Tools menu to open a dialog box similar to the one shown in Figure 12-11. From this dialog box you can check the categories that you would like to show.

You select a category by tapping the Categories line in the event detail dialog box. You can choose multiple categories for a given appointment. If the category you want hasn't been created yet, you can add a category (or remove one) via the New soft button at the bottom of the category selection dialog box.

12

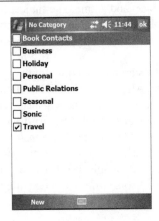

FIGURE 12-11   You can select the categories you want to be visible in the Calendar to see subsets of your events.

Inviting Attendees

As in the desktop version of Outlook, you can invite individuals to meetings or other events in the Calendar. In Outlook Mobile you do this on the Attendees line in the event detail dialog box. Tap the Attendees line to open a dialog box showing the list of attendees currently invited to your event. If there are no attendees you will see instructions that you should push the Add soft button to select a name from your list of contacts. The list of contacts is shown here.

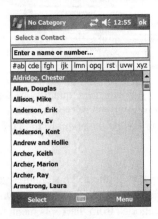

You can select as many attendees as you like by selecting them one at a time and adding them to your list. Once you have all the contacts you want, tap the OK box in the upper right. A Microsoft Exchange event invitation (or if you don't use Microsoft Exchange, a text-only meeting invitation) will be mailed automatically to each of the selected individuals. In order to invite an individual to an event, they must have an entry in your Contacts list with a valid e-mail address.

FIGURE 12-12   You can attach any text you like as notes for your event.

Adding Notes

You can add notes to any appointment by selecting the Notes tab at the bottom of the event detail dialog box. From here you can add any notes you want by typing in the input area, using a transcriber, or using a keyboard as shown in Figure 12-12.

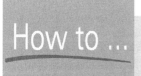   **Set Up a Recurring Appointment**

Many appointments that you schedule will occur on a regular basis, such as weekly status meetings and birthdays. You can set these appointments to recur automatically. Tapping the Occurs line in the event detail dialog box opens a drop-down list of the most common recurrence options, shown here.

From this list, you can select the option to make this event repeat every week, on the same day every month, or annually. If the recurrence pattern for your event is not listed, choose Edit Pattern. Doing so will open the first of three windows that make up the Recurrence Wizard, shown here.

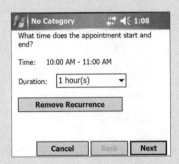

Here you set the duration of the appointment and have the option to remove the recurrence of the event. Once you have set the duration, tap the Next button to open the second window of the wizard, shown here.

In the second window you can choose the following options:

- **Daily** You can set the recurrence as every *X* number of days or every weekday.
- **Weekly** You can set the recurrence as every *X* week(s) and also specify any combination of days of the week you want the event to occur on.
- **Monthly** You can select which day of the month to have the event recur and then set it to recur every *X* month(s). Alternatively, you could have it occur on a specific day of the week in a month every *X* month(s), such as the third Tuesday of every month.
- **Yearly** You can select which day of the year you want the event to recur on. Alternatively, you can have it occur on a specific day of the week in a specific month. For example, Mother's Day occurs on the second Sunday of every May.

The third window in the wizard is where you set the start and end dates for the pattern, as shown next. You can choose to have the pattern not end, end on a specific date, or end after a certain number of occurrences of the event.

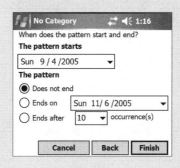

Beaming an Appointment

Imagine you are sitting with someone, planning a meeting together. You can enter the details of the meeting into your Calendar. Then, by tapping and holding a specific appointment, you can choose Beam Appointment from the Menu soft button. This will start the process of searching for and transmitting the appointment to a Pocket PC with an aligned infrared port. The receiving Pocket PC device will be given the option of accepting the beamed appointment. Beaming to non-Pocket PC devices is also possible. For details about beaming outside the Pocket PC universe, see Chapter 2.

ActiveSync Settings for the Calendar

As covered in Chapter 2, you can adjust ActiveSync options on your PC. There is only one option you can set in ActiveSync on your desktop PC to change what information is shared in the Calendar application. This option is to choose how much historical data you want to keep in your calendar. You can choose to keep all of your previous events; however, this setting can lead to a lot of memory consumption. You can alternatively keep on the past 2 weeks, 1 month, 3 months, or 6 months of appointments. What you choose will depend on how often you want to be able to go back into the past to see what you did on certain dates.

Managing Your Contacts

The other personal information management task that is right at the top of the list with the Calendar is keeping track of all your contacts. The Contacts application in Pocket PC is extremely useful and flexible. In addition, it seamlessly synchronizes with the contacts in your desktop version of Outlook, enabling you to access this crucial information both at your desk and when you are on the move.

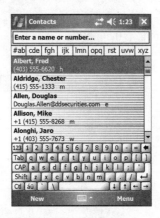

FIGURE 12-13   The Contacts window is your personal address book for your iPAQ.

Navigating Your Contacts

You can launch into the Contacts application by pressing the hardware button for opening Contacts (second from the left in the default configuration) or by selecting Contacts from the Start menu. Either action will open a window similar to the one shown in Figure 12-13.

By default, you will see a list of all your contacts sorted in alphabetical order. If you are like us, you probably have hundreds of contacts. There are many ways to make it easier to sort through your reams of associates. Using the Menu soft button you can apply a Filter to select a subset of your contacts to view. In the categories list, you can choose to see All Contacts (the default), Recently Viewed (the most recent contacts you have looked at), or a subset based on the category you have given each one. In order to do this, you need to have assigned one or more of the static categories in Outlook to each of the contacts or assigned a category when you edited the contact on your iPAQ.

In the box at the top of the window you can type specific text that you want to search for in your list. Any text that you enter will be matched against the first or last name of the contact. For example, with our set of data, entering **b** in the text search box will cause it to filter the list to show Bush, George (a last name match), as well as Clinton, Bill (a first name match), as shown next.

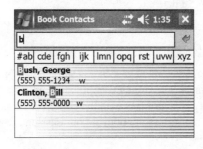

Immediately below the search text box you will see a series of boxes, each containing three letters of the alphabet. Tapping any one of these boxes once will cause the view to scroll to the appropriate subsection of the contacts list. If you are currently viewing your contacts sorted by last name, then tapping the ijk box will cause the list to scroll to show those contacts with last names starting with *I*. If you are viewing your list sorted by company name, it will scroll to show company names beginning with *I*. If you tap the box again, it will scroll the second letter in the box, *J*. A third tap will scroll to *K*; the same method applies to the rest of the letter boxes.

You can use the three techniques for narrowing your list of contacts alone, or together. For example, you could select Government from the drop-down list of categories, type a **b** into the text search box, and tap the cde box to get a list of all the contacts who are categorized as Government with first names starting with *B* and last names starting with *C*.

You can also navigate through your list of contacts with the scroll bar on the right side of the window if your list of contacts won't fit in one window (they almost never do), or you can use the five-way navigation disc in the lower center of the iPAQ. You can also use the hardware navigation disc and press up to scroll up your list or down to scroll down your list. If you hold the button down, a large box will appear and cycle through all the letters of the alphabet, enabling you to scroll to the specified letter, as shown in Figure 12-14.

By default, when you enter the Contacts application, you are looking at a view of your contacts sorted by name. You can change this to see a list of companies instead, if this is your preferred method of navigation. Change your sort rule by selecting View By | Company menu item under the Menu soft button. The resulting window will look something like this illustration. The number in parentheses after the company name is the number of contacts that you have in your list who work for that company.

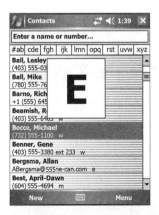

FIGURE 12-14   Holding down the hardware navigation disc will enable you to scroll through all the letters of the alphabet.

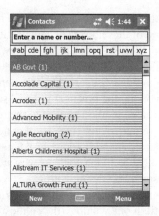

In your list of contacts, you will see a letter to the right of each entry's contact information. This letter tells you what type of contact information is being shown. For example, a small *e* indicates an e-mail address, a *w* is a work phone number, an *f* is a work fax number, an *h* is a home number, and so on. Tapping any contact name or phone number in the list will open the contact's detail information, as shown in Figure 12-15.

The Summary tab shows all the contact information you have for the contact. The Notes tab contains any notes that you have for the contact. Notes can include text, drawings, images, and sound recordings. Tapping the Edit soft button will enable you to enter and change any of the information displayed here. Tap the Menu soft button to change your zoom (on the Notes tab only), edit the contact, delete the contact, or transmit the contact to another Pocket PC via beaming (infrared) or wireless (Bluetooth, if so equipped).

FIGURE 12-15 Tapping a contact name or number will open that individual's contact detail.

Some of the lines in the contact detail will cause an action to occur if they are tapped. For example, you can see Send E-mail is listed by George's e-mail address in the detail in Figure 12-15. This will create a new e-mail to this contact that will be sent the next time you synchronize.

Tapping and holding any name in your list of contacts will open a shortcut menu from which you can copy or delete the contact, send an e-mail to the contact, or beam the contact to another Pocket PC.

Entering a New Contact

To add a contact to your list, tap the New soft button at the bottom of the Contacts dialog box to open the new contact form, shown here.

From this window you can enter an entire range of information. These fields mirror the fields found in the desktop version of Outlook, allowing seamless synchronization of information.

A number of the fields are contractions of information held in multiple fields. For example, the Name field is a combination of the Title, First, Middle, Last, and Suffix fields. As you enter a name, Contacts will try to place the appropriate names into the appropriate fields. If it is unsure, it will display a red icon with an exclamation mark at the end of the line. All combination fields include a drop-down arrow at the end of the field. If you tap the arrow, all the subfields involved will be displayed, and you will be able to enter the data into each subfield, as shown here.

12

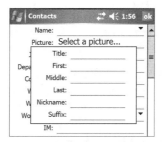

Date fields, such as Birthday and Anniversary, enable you to select a date from a drop-down calendar, as shown in Figure 12-16. If no date is selected, the field will show None. The drop-down calendar also has options below the specific dates to select Today or None.

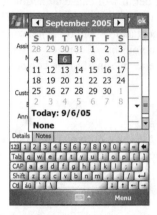

FIGURE 12-16 Date fields include drop-down calendars to make entering a date easier.

The Categories field is another unique field. It displays the category, or categories, that you have assigned this contact to. When you tap the field, it will open a separate form in which you can select all the categories you want to apply to this contact from a list of categories. You can select multiple categories by selecting multiple check boxes, as shown next.

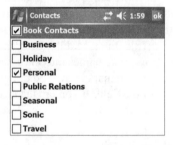

If the category that you want isn't in the list, you can add a category using the New soft button at the bottom of the categories dialog box.

Categories in Outlook Mobile are synced over from your desktop Outlook installation. Setting up and managing your categories is easier on the desktop, so you should do the bulk of your organizing there instead of on your iPAQ.

Customizing the Contacts Manager

Even on the Pocket PC, you can customize a few options in your software. This list is limited in the Contacts application, but you can change a few items in the view as well as some default information for when you are entering details.

Selecting the Options menu item from the Menu soft button will open the Options dialog box, shown next, where you can make changes to your Contacts application.

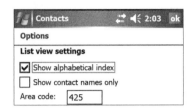

The two check boxes allow you to show or hide the alphabetical index (these are the "ABC boxes") and show contact names only (that is, don't show phone number or e-mail address).

You can also change the default area code, which is automatically included with every new contact you enter.

With the most recent version of ActiveSync (version 4), you are not able to set any sync options for Contact synchronization. If you are running an older iPAQ with an older version of ActiveSync, there are three options you can set in ActiveSync on the desktop PC for your contacts:

- **Sync All Contacts**   This default setting will ensure that any modifications made to contacts in either your iPAQ or your desktop are all up to date.

- **Sync Only The Following Contacts**   This option enables you to choose only specific contacts to synchronize. This is very limiting because any new contacts added to your iPAQ will not be automatically sent over to your PC.

- **Sync Only Selected Categories**   This setting enables you to select only specific categories of contacts to synchronize. This can be useful if you synchronize with multiple desktop systems or if several people are sharing the same iPAQ.

Keeping in Touch

For the Internet, e-mail is the killer application. It was e-mail that drove people to get Internet connections to every corporate desktop and in every home. Many PDA experts expected that being able to get e-mail anywhere, anytime would be the driving force that would cause millions of people to adopt PDAs. This ended up being a pipe dream, as most PDAs, particularly up until now, were not wirelessly connected, and so e-mail could only be sent or received while your PDA was attached to your computer with a sync cable.

Out of the box, your iPAQ may or may not be wirelessly enabled, but even without wireless connectivity, it can sync your Outlook Inbox with its own Inbox application, allowing you to take your e-mail with you. If your iPAQ is not wireless, with some simple wireless add-in products, you can easily extend your iPAQ to allow you to send and receive your e-mail anywhere, at any time. For details about wireless iPAQ, see Chapter 3. This section will focus on the specifics of using the Inbox application, whether you are wirelessly connected or not.

12

Setting Up Your Inbox and Services

There are two ways to work with e-mail on your Pocket PC: through your ActiveSync connection or by connecting to an external mail server.

E-mail with ActiveSync

ActiveSync will keep a copy on your Pocket PC of the messages in your current desktop Outlook folders. All of the setup for this is done in your ActiveSync application on your PC. With each synchronization, the appropriate messages are transferred to your iPAQ so that you can read them when you are disconnected. You can also compose replies to the e-mail you read, and these will be sent by your desktop version of Outlook the next time you synchronize your iPAQ.

 *Remember that your Inbox will only synchronize with one desktop Outlook partnership, so if you are syncing with multiple desktops make sure you set up your partnerships correctly and sync with your Inbox partner first.*

To set up ActiveSync synchronization of your desktop, open ActiveSync on your PC and select the check box beside E-Mail, as shown in Figure 12-17. After selecting the check box, you will want to adjust the settings for your mail synchronization. Click the Settings button to open the E-mail Synchronization Settings dialog box, shown in Figure 12-18.

From here you can specify which subfolders you want to be synchronized with your iPAQ. Click on the Select Folders button, then select the check box before the name of any subfolder whose messages you want copied to the Inbox program on your iPAQ. Then you can specify whether

FIGURE 12-17   To synchronize your E-mail between your desktop PC and your iPAQ select the E-mail check box in the ActiveSync options.

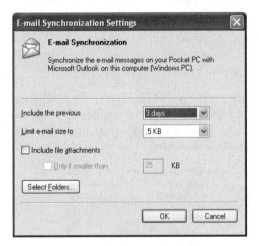

FIGURE 12-18   The E-mail Synchronization Settings dialog box allows you to select what messages will be stored on your iPAQ.

you want only a limited amount of each message to be copied to your iPAQ. The purpose of this is to reduce the amount of data stored on the device so you don't run out of room. However, we recommend not selecting this option because if, just once, you receive an important long message, and it is truncated, you might get so annoyed you will toss your iPAQ into the nearest dumpster. Instead, we recommend keeping only a limited number of days of messages. By default, the system will only synchronize three days of messages. We find that even three days of messages is sufficient, unless we are on the road for an extended period of time.

The Include File Attachments option enables you to automatically copy file attachments to your Pocket PC or leave them unless you request them. Attachments can quickly fill up the memory of your device, so by default this option is turned off, and we would usually recommend that you leave it off. You can request to have attachments downloaded from your iPAQ as needed. Alternatively, if you really want to keep all your attachments, you can use the Storage tab under the e-mail Options menu item to set attachments to be stored on an external storage card.

The Drafts folder cannot be synced with your desktop Outlook program.

Connecting to a Mail Server

Your iPAQ can also be configured to connect to other types of mail servers and bypass your desktop Outlook program altogether. In order for this configuration to work, your iPAQ must be able to connect to the Internet. You can connect your iPAQ to the Internet in one of three ways:

■ **Wireless connection**   Through the built-in wireless modem, a third-party wireless modem, Bluetooth connection, or WiFi network card, you can connect to the Internet from almost anywhere.

- **Wired connection** Through a third-party Ethernet network card, you can get onto a corporate or home network with an Internet gateway.
- **ActiveSync connection** If the desktop PC that you ActiveSync with has an Internet connection, you can use this option to cause it to connect via the PC Internet connection to sync with an outside mail server.

You must set up the properties of the outside mail server by configuring a new service on your iPAQ. From the Menu soft button, select the Tools menu item and then New Account. This will open the E-mail Setup Wizard, which will help you configure your service. The first window asks you for your e-mail address, as shown here.

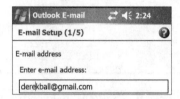

Enter your e-mail address in the box provided, and then tap the Next soft button to bring up the second window of the wizard, as shown next.

Here the wizard will attempt to automatically configure your e-mail service by reading from an XML configuration file kept on the Microsoft servers. A number of the major ISPs are referenced there. If you are not using a major ISP, do not have a currently connected Internet connection, or cannot be configured automatically, you can tap Skip to configure the service yourself. Tap Next to open the third window of the wizard, shown here.

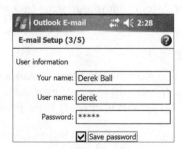

In this window you will enter your user information, including your full name, username, and password. You have the option to save the password and not be prompted each time it tries to synchronize your e-mail. When you have entered all our information, tap Next to open the fourth window of the wizard, as shown here.

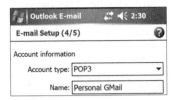

In this window you will configure your server type and name for this service. There are two types of servers you can connect to: POP3 and IMAP4. The name you choose for the service can be anything you like but should be descriptive enough to let you differentiate it from your other mail services (if you are connecting to more than one).

Almost every mail server that you might connect to supports POP3. It is an older protocol but widely supported. With POP3, your e-mail is copied down to your device. There is little intelligence in the protocol for handling folders or synchronization with the server.

It is very likely that the mailbox being accessed by your handheld is also accessed from one or more desktops. In this case, it is probably better to use the newer, more efficient, IMAP4 protocol. In Derek's situation, he has an office e-mail service that is run from a Microsoft Exchange server. At work, his desktop accesses the Exchange server through Outlook. He has a computer at home with a cable modem that keeps synchronized with his mail server using IMAP4. This way, no matter which desktop system he is using, when he reads, composes, deletes, or files messages, it is in one common message store that all his systems share. When he chose to connect his iPAQ to this message store, IMAP4 was the obvious choice, as it would participate in this tidy little family of e-mail handlers by synchronizing with the central Microsoft Exchange message store.

When you have entered the relevant account information, tap Next to open the wizard's final window, as shown next.

The fifth and final window of the wizard (unless you choose to set options!) is where you will specify the Internet address of your mail server. You must specify the address of your POP3 or IMAP4 server in the Incoming Mail box. Mail is always sent using a specific protocol called SMTP (Simple Mail Transfer Protocol). In order to send mail, you must have an address for an SMTP server,

12

which is the one that you will enter in the Outgoing Mail box. Usually this server will be the same as your incoming mail server, but not always. Check with your ISP or system administrator if you do not know what to enter in these boxes. If your mail server uses a network connection that requires a specific domain to connect to, you will enter that value in the Domain box.

From this window you can access an additional three options windows to configure such items as changing the time intervals for downloading new messages, downloading attachments, and limiting what portion of a message is downloaded. Tap the Options button to open the first window, as shown here.

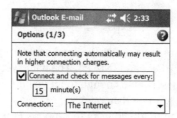

The first Advanced Options window enables you to set the frequency to check for new messages. By default it will check every 15 minutes. You can clear the check box to have the Inbox only check for new messages when you specifically request it. Tap Next to move to the second window of the Advanced Options, as shown next.

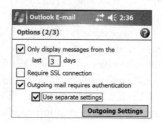

In this window you can select to only display messages from a specified number of days. You can also choose to require an SSL connection when connecting to this mail server, which provides a greatly enhanced level of security if your mail server supports this. If your outgoing e-mail server requires authentication, you can select that check box. Authentication requirement is becoming more and more common as the problem of junk e-mail continues to grow. You can also specify a connection and different connection information by which to send outgoing messages by selecting the Use Separate Settings check box and tapping the Outgoing Settings button.

The third Advanced Options window, shown here, lets you set how much of the message you want to download from the server. The drop-down list enables you to choose whether you want to download only the message headers or a full copy of the message. If you are downloading only the headers, you can choose to include a specific amount of the message. By default you will download the first 2KB (approximately 2000 characters), but you can download more (or less) by changing the number in the box. When you have finished setting these options, tap Finish to end the wizard.

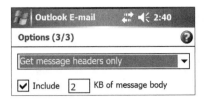

Your new e-mail service is now fully configured and ready to use.

Navigating Your Inbox

When you open the Inbox application, it will open the inbox of the last e-mail service you used. You will see the list of e-mail messages, as shown in Figure 12-19.

If an e-mail message has been read, it appears in normal text; an unread message appears in bold. You can see whom the message is from, the time/date received, the size, and the subject. The envelope icon to the left of any message provides a great deal of information about the message as well:

- If the bottom-right corner of the envelope is missing, this means that the message has not been downloaded from the server. If it is there, then the message has been downloaded.

- Closed envelope indicates an unread message. An open envelope indicates the message has been read.

- Paper clip attached to the envelope means that the message includes attachments.

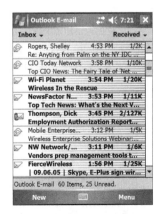

FIGURE 12-19   Opening the Messaging application will show you the messages from the last e-mail service you used.

At the top left you can tap the drop-down arrow to choose which e-mail service and inbox you want to look at, as shown here.

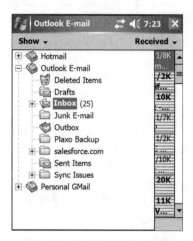

Tap the drop-down arrow on the top right to change how the messages in the current folder are sorted. By default they are sorted by received date, but you can also choose to sort by the sender, message type, or subject, as shown next.

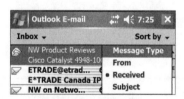

The very bottom of the window contains a status bar that indicates what operation is currently being performed. If no operation is being performed, it will indicate which mail service you are viewing, the total number of messages, and the number of unread messages.

Below the status bar are the left and right soft buttons. From the Menu soft button you can perform most standard e-mail functions including Reply, Reply All, Forward, Move, Mark As Unread, and Download Message (for messages where you do not have the entire message on your iPAQ yet). You can also initiate a Send/Receive of e-mail, switch e-mail accounts, and access tools for managing your mailboxes.

Reading a Message

To read a message, tap it with the stylus. This will open the message details, as shown in Figure 12-20. The top section of the window contains the header of the message. It is scrolled to show you who the sender is and the subject. You can scroll up using the scroll bar on the right to see who it was addressed to and the date and time it was sent.

FIGURE 12-20   An open e-mail message.

You can read the message by using the scroll bar on the right side of the window to move up and down within the message. Alternatively, you can use the hardware control disc to scroll the message up or down.

The Menu soft button contains several commands:

- **Mark As Unread**   This command returns the message to bold in the message list, as though it had never been read.

- **Download Message**   This command causes the entire contents of the message to be downloaded from the mail server the next time you are connected.

- **Move...**   Use this command to move the message to a folder.

- **Languages**   This command enables you to select the language font for the message. This is useful if you receive messages in other languages. By default, Windows Mobile will attempt to auto detect the correct language font to use.

- **Save To Contacts**   This will save the sender to your Contacts list.

Handling Attachments

E-mail attachments are used all the time to send Word documents, Excel spreadsheets, and more. Being able to receive, read, and work with these attachments on your Pocket PC makes it a very powerful tool. Attachments to e-mail messages appear in the header of the message, as shown in Figure 12-21.

If an attachment has not been brought down to your iPAQ, it will appear as a torn sheet of paper icon. Once you tap this icon, a green arrow will appear indicating that the message is set

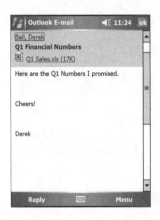

FIGURE 12-21 E-mail attachments appear in the header of the message.

to download on your next connection. Once fully downloaded, the full icon for the attachment will appear. You can tap and hold the stylus on the attachment to perform a Save As operation if the attachment has been downloaded.

 *Once an item is flagged for download, it is not actually downloaded until your next send/receive cycle. You can manually initiate this cycle by tapping the Send/Receive menu item in the Menu soft button.*

Composing a Message

To create a new message, simply tap the New soft button at any time. This will open the New Message window, as shown in Figure 12-22. The top box contains a minimalist header row with only From, To, and Subject fields. You can enter the e-mail address of the person to whom you want to send the message, or you can select a contact from your Contacts application by tapping the To field. You can keep repeating this to add as many recipients as you like. You can also get there by choosing Add Recipient from the Menu soft button.

At any time, you can tap in the message body and enter the text of your message. A slick trick is to record a quick voice memo and e-mail it to someone as a WAV file. You can do this by tapping the record icon (the cassette tape) on the menu bar, which opens the full record toolbar, as shown in Figure 12-23. From here you can use the built-in iPAQ microphone to dictate a quick message, which will be attached as a WAV file to your e-mail message. What a great way to whip out a quick note to someone when you don't have time to write it down. We can all talk much faster than we can write or type, especially on a miniaturized virtual keyboard!

When you have finished composing your message, tap the Send soft button to send your message to your Outbox for transmission next time you are connected to your service.

FIGURE 12-22   Tapping New will open a window for creating new messages.

Using My Text Messages

Many e-mail messages can be replied to with a very short message. Outlook Mobile has a handy
function called My Text Messages, which helps you respond quickly to your e-mail. My Text
Messages provides a list of common replies, which you can select with one tap and drop into your
message. To access My Text Messages, tap My Text in the Menu soft button to open a pop-up list

FIGURE 12-23   Voice attachments are a great way to send a quick note to someone when you are
on the move and don't have time to type.

12

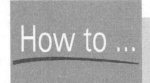 **Enter Extended Header Information**

To enter extended header information, you scroll the scroll bar on the right side of the message window up. This will show the full header area and will provide you with CC and BCC rows to enter recipient names in. The expanded header area is shown here.

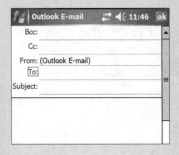

of standard messages, as shown in Figure 12-24. The list includes convenient short responses such as "I'm running late." and "Where are you?"

You cannot change the total number of items in this list, but you can change ones that you don't use often into something that may be more useful to you. To do so, select Edit My Text

FIGURE 12-24   A set of standard responses can be inserted into your message with the My Text command.

Messages from the bottom of the list of messages. This will open the My Text Messages dialog box, shown next, where you can select any item and change it.

Your messages in My Text Messages are shared between the MSN Messenger client and the Inbox application.

Customizing Your Inbox

You can edit or modify a number of areas in the Messaging application. One thing to keep in mind is that if you need to change the basic properties of your e-mail service, you cannot do this while you are connected to it. If you need to change the name of a mail server or something fundamental, you must be disconnected from your service; then you can go to the Tools menu and select Options. This will open the dialog box shown in Figure 12-25. From here you can select any service in the list to modify. You will notice that ActiveSync is not in the list. This is because that is the one mail service that is set up from the PC, not from your iPAQ.

12

FIGURE 12-25   To edit the base properties of a service, select it from the list in the Options dialog box.

FIGURE 12-26 The Message tab lets you set behavior when working with messages, such as what to do after a delete and how to reply.

Notice the four tabs at the bottom of the Messaging Options dialog box. These tabs let you open other dialog boxes with other settings. On the Message tab, shown in Figure 12-26, you configure options for what part of the message body to include when replying. You can choose to keep a copy of sent messages in the Sent folder and what action to take after deleting a message.

The Address tab, shown in Figure 12-27, enables you to customize how the Messaging application does address lookups. It can select addresses from all e-mail fields in your Contacts folder or only a specific field. You can also set it to look up e-mail addresses against a Contacts folder on a mail server (if the mail server supports this action).

FIGURE 12-27 Customize the way addresses are looked up with the Address tab under Options.

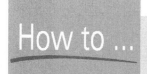 **Do Name Lookups Against an External Mail Server**

If you want to perform name lookups on a mail server that isn't one of your base e-mail services, tap the Add button on the Address tab of the Messaging Options dialog box. This will open the following dialog box. You must specify the directory and server to search for the names. There is a very good chance that the server may require you to log on and authenticate. If so, select the authenticate check box and fill in your username and password.

The final tab of the Messaging Options dialog box, Storage, simply allows you to select a check box to store attachments to e-mail messages on an external storage card if you have a CompactFlash or Secure Digital storage card.

Keeping on Top of Your Tasks

If you are like Derek, you have many tasks that always seem to run in parallel; keeping track of those tasks can require a Herculean effort. In fact, Derek found that every time he had something to add to his task list, he couldn't find the list, so he would start another one. Next thing he knew, he had several to-do lists going at the same time!

Now he keeps all of his to-do tasks organized in his iPAQ, which seamlessly integrates them with his desktop version of Outlook. Life is good!

Navigating Your Tasks

You open the Tasks application by tapping Tasks icon in the Programs area (accessible from the Start menu), or by navigating to it from the Today page by tapping the Tasks item in the list. Either action opens the main Tasks window, shown in Figure 12-28.

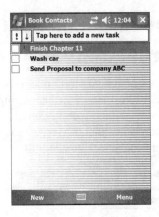

FIGURE 12-28   Keep track of all your to-do items in the Tasks application.

Choose the Filter option from the Menu soft button to view a subset of tasks. Your choices include the following:

- **All Tasks**   A list of all tasks.
- **Recent**   A list of tasks you have looked at most recently.
- **<Category>**   A list of all the categories that you have assigned to tasks. You can view any single category you select.
- **No Category**   A list of any tasks that do not have specific categories assigned.
- **Active Tasks**   A combination with one of the above lists to show only the subset of tasks that are active.
- **Completed Tasks**   Like the Active option, this works with the other list items to further subcategorize by completed items only.

NOTE   *By default, only active items are kept on your iPAQ so that when you next sync your device, any completed items will be removed, although a full record is still kept in your desktop Outlook.*

Tap the Sort By menu item from the Menu soft button to sort the list of tasks. By default they are sorted by priority. You can also choose to sort by Status, Subject, Start Date, or Due Date.

The check box to the left of each task allows you to mark a task as completed, thus changing its status.

Tapping a specific task will allow you to view the details for that task.

There is a line about one-third of the way down the page. Above this line are the details of the task properties. Below the line are any notes that you have entered for the task. You can tap Edit to change any of the task properties, or to enter notes for the task. The Menu soft button contains commands to delete the task or beam it to another device.

Creating a New Task

You can add a new task to the list by tapping New in the menu bar or by using the entry bar. The New command will open the new task dialog box, shown in Figure 12-29.

You can enter information in the following fields in the New Task dialog box:

- ■ **Subject** The name of the task that you need to perform.

- ■ **Priority** Normal (default), High, or Low. Selecting High will cause a red exclamation mark to be displayed next to the task in the list. Selecting Low will cause a blue down arrow to be displayed next to the task.

- ■ **Status** Either Completed (active) or Not Completed.

- ■ **Starts** Defaults to None but can be set to any date when the task should become active. This allows you to put future tasks on your list that you don't want to appear until a specific date. Note that if you assign a start date to your task, it will also automatically receive a due date.

- ■ **Due** Defaults to None but can be set to any date when the task needs to be finished. If the current date is past the due date, the task will appear in red in your task list.

- ■ **Occurs** Allows you to set recurrence for a task, just as you do for an appointment. For example, Derek gives his dog medication on the first of every month, so he could set a recurring task that starts on the first of November and recurs on Day 1 of every month, which will make that task appear on his task list on the first of every month.

12

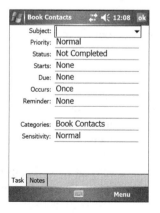

FIGURE 12-29   Use the New Task dialog box to add a task to your to-do list.

■ **Reminder**   Enables you to set a reminder alarm so that your iPAQ will announce a task and remind you to finish it. This can only be set if your task has a due date. After choosing the Reminder option, you can tap the date to select a date from the calendar.

■ **Categories**   Enables you to place this task in a category. The categories will be the same as those that you have set up for appointments and contacts. All Outlook Mobile programs share the same categories list. You can assign multiple categories to a task. This is particularly useful if you have a very large number of tasks in your list and need to see the various subsets. You can enter all the groceries you need to pick up as separate tasks and then categorize them under a group called Shopping List.

■ **Sensitivity**   Normal (default) or Private. Setting this as Private means that if you are sharing your calendar with people on a Microsoft Exchange server, they will not be able to see the details of this task. They will merely see that a task exists and that it is private.

■ **Notes tab**   This is a separate tab where you can add any notes you like to a task. When you are finished setting up your new task, tap OK in the upper-right corner to have the task added to your list.

An alternative way to add tasks is to change the standard interface to show the entry bar. To view the entry bar, select Options from the Menu soft button. Making this selection again will hide the entry bar. When you use the entry bar, you simply enter a new task by entering the task name into the edit box. You can select the priority by tapping the exclamation mark or down arrow icon to the left of the entry box. Tapping in the list area will cause your new task to be created. We like this feature because it makes it easy to add new tasks to your list on the fly as they come to mind. When you create tasks this way, all the other properties of the task are defaulted (normal priority, no recurrence, no due date, normal sensitivity, and so on).

Keeping Track of Your Notes

The Notes program is another useful tool for helping to eliminate the scraps of paper in your life. If you need to jot something down, or find yourself in a meeting for which you must take notes, or need to make a quick dictation, you can do all of this with Notes.

Navigating Your Notes

The Notes application can be accessed from the Start menu. Launching Notes will open a list showing all the Notes files in your My Documents folder, as shown in Figure 12-30.

Notes are shown with their first words as their title (which can be modified after saving the note the first time), the date or time they were created, and their size. The icon on the left will show you if it is a regular note or an audio file. If the note is an audio file, its size will show as the number of seconds of the recording. To open and view a particular note, simply tap it with your stylus. If you

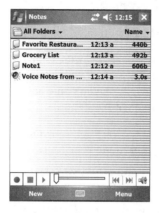

FIGURE 12-30   Each note is stored as its own file in the My Documents folder on your iPAQ.

tap and hold a note, the shortcut menu gives you the option to create a copy of the note, delete the note, select all the notes, e-mail the note, beam the note, or rename/move the note.

An open note can be edited at will. The Menu soft button have commands that enable you to perform operations such as cut, copy, paste, undo, redo, clear, and select all. You can tap the cassette tape icon to embed an audio recording within a text note. You can also use the stylus to write your own script and drawings right on the page. The Note will be saved as an image of what you have drawn. If you handwrite text, you can select the text and choose Recognize from the Tools menu to have the handwriting interpreted into text. If the Recognizer gets a word wrong, you can tap and select the word and then choose Alternates from the Tools menu to see a list of alternate words to select from.

The Tools menu also includes commands to e-mail or beam the note, to change the current zoom factor from 75 percent to 300 percent, and to rename, move, or delete the note.

Creating a New Note

To create a new note, you can tap New on the menu bar at any time. Or, from any application, at any time, you can press the hardware Record button on the iPAQ to begin creating a new voice note immediately.

Your new note will open in the default entry mode that you have chosen. Out of the box, your iPAQ is configured to be in Writing mode, where you can draw and write characters on the screen. The default mode can be changed in the Notes Options dialog box. Once you have created the note you desire, you can tap the OK button to save the note. By default it will be saved in the My Documents folder using the first words that you entered as the filename.

Syncing with Outlook Express, Lotus Notes, or Other PIMs

If you want to sync your data on your Pocket PC with something other than Outlook, you can do this with third-party add-in software. There are a wide variety of applications available (at a wide variety of prices and available support). Depending on what information is important to you, and which platform, you can check out some of these links:

- SyncData's product SyncExpress 2002 will sync Outlook Express only, for $16. You can download it at **www.syncdata.it** (a free trial is also available).

- Companion Link (**www.companionlink.com**) has sync software available for Outlook Express, Lotus Notes, ACT!, and Goldmine in the $50 to $75 price range.

- Handango (**www.handango.com**) also provides a category for sync software that has some other alternatives.

- Intellisync (**www.intellisync.com**) allows synchronization with Outlook Express, Lotus Notes, Act! Goldmine, and additional features with Outlook. Intellisync was acquired by Nokia at the end of 2005, so the future of these products is somewhat uncertain.

Getting Hotmail on Your iPAQ

If you use a Hotmail e-mail box, it is now automatically available to you on your iPAQ! Just choose Pocket MSN from the Programs area or from your Today screen to get your Hotmail messages as well as your MSN Instant Messenger.

If you have an iPAQ prior to Windows Mobile 5, there are two ways you can get your Hotmail:

- If you have your iPAQ connected to the Internet (as explained in Chapter 3), you can access your Hotmail account through a special Pocket PC-compatible mobile section on MSN. Open Internet Explorer and go to **mobile.msn.com/pocketpc**. You will find a conveniently formatted Pocket PC interface waiting for you.

- If you want to sync your Hotmail so it is available on your Pocket PC while you are disconnected, you will need to purchase a third-party utility to do it for you. Handango (**www.handango.com**) has a list of the most popular utilities. Currently leading the pack is Pocket Hotmail, which costs $5 and has a free trial available.

Wrap It Up

Working with email on the go is one of the most important applications of your iPAQ. If you have a device with wireless connectivity you are now truly empowered to communicate while you are mobile. The nature of mobile connectivity will continue to grow more and more pervasive as we see more and more iPAQs with WiFi or cellular data connections.

Chapter 13

Take Your Presentations on the Road with Your iPAQ

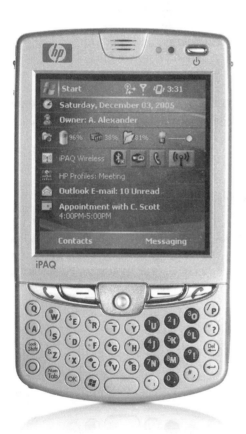

How to...

- Use MS PowerPoint Mobile on your iPAQ
- Use ClearVue Presentation on your iPAQ
- Move PowerPoint presentations from your PC to your iPAQ
- Display your iPAQ screen on an external monitor or projector
- Use third-party software to create and edit presentations on your iPAQ

Microsoft PowerPoint is the dominant tool allowing you show off numbers, graphics, and textual information in presentations and meetings. PowerPoint is actually capable of much more than most people use it for, however: with it, you can add custom builds and slide transitions, add animations, and even embed sound and video. The ability to view and work with PowerPoint presentations on your iPAQ is very handy. In fact, if you have the right configuration, you only need to bring your iPAQ to your presentation instead of lugging around your laptop, miscellaneous cords, and 15 pounds of accessories.

Being able to view PowerPoint files on your iPAQ is cool, but to be ultimately useful you must be able to connect your iPAQ to a projector or monitor to show your presentation to a group of people. Hardware is available that allows you to do exactly that, and the tools you need are discussed later in this chapter.

View Microsoft PowerPoint Mobile on Your iPAQ

Right out of the box your iPAQ should arrive preconfigured and ready to view PowerPoint slideshows. Most iPAQs running Windows Mobile 5 arrive preinstalled with Microsoft PowerPoint Mobile, while Windows Mobile 2003 SE iPAQs ship with ClearVue Presentation from Westtek (**www.westtek.com**). We will discuss PowerPoint Mobile and ClearVue Presentation first and then discuss some of the other iPAQ presentation options later on.

> **TIP** *How Do I Get My PowerPoint Files onto My iPAQ? As with transferring any file onto your iPAQ, there are several ways to get your PowerPoint files onto your iPAQ. The fastest is to move the files from your desktop PC using Microsoft ActiveSync and a sync cable. ActiveSync is covered in detail in Chapter 2. Other ways to get a file onto your iPAQ include downloading the file as an e-mail attachment through your e-mail program, downloading the file from the Internet, or copying the file to your iPAQ using a removable storage card.*

Use Microsoft PowerPoint Mobile on Your iPAQ

This section relates specifically to Windows Mobile 5 as PowerPoint Mobile isn't available for Windows Mobile 2003. PowerPoint Mobile allows you to view PowerPoint slideshows in either PPT and PPS file formats that were created with PowerPoint 97 or later versions. Presentations in

HTM and MHT file formats won't run in PowerPoint Mobile. PowerPoint Mobile is a functionally reduced version of the full Windows PC-based PowerPoint software and allows you to view slide elements such as slide transitions, animations, and time slide advances for timed slideshows. If your slideshow contains website addresses, you can even click the URL to launch the web page on your iPAQ.

> **TIP**
>
> *What PowerPoint features won't play using PowerPoint Mobile? There are a few PowerPoint features that work just fine when you run the presentation on your PC but won't show up on your iPAQ including Notes written for slides and rearranging or editing slides. PowerPoint Mobile only allows you to view presentations and won't allow you to edit them.*

Copy a Slideshow from Your PC to Your iPAQ Using a Sync Cable

As mentioned earlier, there are several different ways to get a PowerPoint file onto your iPAQ, including downloading the file as an e-mail attachment through your e-mail program, downloading the file from the Internet, or copying the file to your iPAQ using a removable storage card. For this example, we will use the method of attaching your iPAQ with a sync cable to your desktop PC. This is as simple as copying any file from one place to another locally on your PC. Using ActiveSync on your PC is covered in Chapter 2, but here are the basics.

1. Your PC must be running the latest version of Microsoft ActiveSync, and your iPAQ must be connected to your PC with a sync cable. ActiveSync comes packaged with your iPAQ on a CD and is available for free download from Microsoft.com.

2. Important: turn off the file conversion setting in ActiveSync. By default when you copy a PowerPoint file to your iPAQ using ActiveSync, the file will be converted from a PPT file to a PPV file. PowerPoint Mobile can open a PPV file, but some other PowerPoint viewers such as ClearVue Presentation can only open a native PPT file. To turn the file conversion off follow these steps:

    a. If you are using ActiveSync 4.1 connected to a:

        ■ Windows Mobile 2003 iPAQ, on your PC, launch ActiveSync and select the Options button, as shown in Figure 13-1. Then select the Rules tab and select the Conversion Settings button, as shown in Figure 13-2.

        or

        ■ Windows Mobile 5 iPAQ, on your PC, launch ActiveSync and select Tools | Options button. Then click Tools | Advanced Tools | Edit File Conversion Settings.

    b. Ensure that the Convert Files When Synchronized, Copied Or Moved option is unchecked, as shown in Figure 13-3.

3. On your PC, use the File Explorer to locate the PowerPoint file you want to move to your iPAQ, right-click the file and select the Copy option from the menu.

13

FIGURE 13-1   ActiveSync Options.

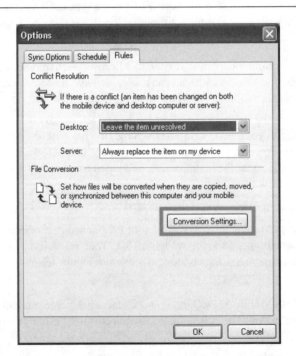

FIGURE 13-2   ActiveSync Options Rules tab.

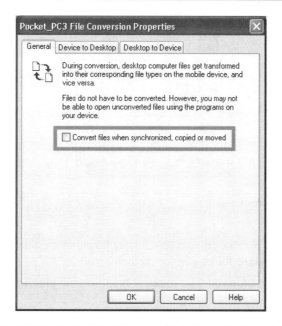

FIGURE 13-3   Uncheck the conversion option in ActiveSync.

4. Still on your PC, open the MS ActiveSync program and select Tools | Explore Pocket PC option, as shown in Figure 13-4, to open the file folders on your iPAQ. Find the folder you want to copy the PowerPoint file to, right-click in the right panel, and choose Paste.

5. The PowerPoint file will now be copied to that folder on your iPAQ.

13

FIGURE 13-4   ActiveSync Explore on the iPAQ.

FIGURE 13-5 File Explorer icon.

6. To open the PowerPoint file on your iPAQ, simply Launch the File Explorer, as shown in Figure 13-5, and find the folder you copied the file to.

7. Select the PowerPoint file you want to open, as shown in Figure 13-6, and PowerPoint Mobile will open the file.

The next section discusses some of your options when working with presentations; later in the chapter, your options to display your presentations on projectors or monitors are also discussed.

Use PowerPoint Mobile to View Your PowerPoint Presentations

PowerPoint Mobile is a PowerPoint viewer that comes preinstalled on iPAQ handhelds running Windows Mobile 5. You can control the display of your PowerPoint presentations while you are

FIGURE 13-6 Select file.

FIGURE 13-7   PowerPoint onscreen icon.

viewing a presentation by clicking the onscreen menu button, as shown in Figure 13-7. Depending on the background of your presentation, the icon may be difficult to see, but once you know where to look for it, it should be obvious.

The PowerPoint Mobile Menu

When you click the menu icon, you will see a menu, as shown in Figure 13-8.

The options available to you, depending on where you are in the slideshow are

- **Next**   Advances to the next slide. You can accomplish the same thing by tapping the iPAQ screen.
- **Previous**   Takes you to the previous slide.
- **Go To Slide**   Pops up a list of slide titles from which you can select where you want to jump to.

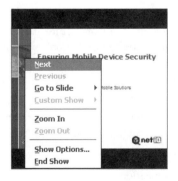

FIGURE 13-8   PowerPoint menu.

FIGURE 13-9 Zoom.

- **Custom Show** Allows you to show different slides to different groups of people by defining a Custom Show. For example, for the Sales group you want to show them slides 1 through 10 and for the Support group you want to show 1 through 5 and 11 without having to jump around between slides.

- **Zoom In** Allows you to zoom into a specific part of the screen. This feature is an excellent addition specifically for the small iPAQ screen. When you click the Zoom In option from the menu, you will see a display cut out at the bottom right of the screen, as shown in Figure 13-9. By moving around the red box, you can change the part of the screen that is magnified. The buttons on the right allow you to zoom in, zoom out, or close the zoom option. You cannot navigate to another slide until you zoom out.

- **Zoom Out** Works in a manner similar to the Zoom In option.

- **Show Options** Allows you to configure the way you want the presentation to look when you are playing it on your iPAQ with some features designed specifically for the iPAQ screen, Orientation and Playback:

  - **Orientation** Allows you four different options to change the way the screen shows up on your iPAQ and on a projector or monitor if you are connected to one. The two Landscape modes allow you to turn the presentation on its side for better use of screen real estate, and you can choose which way you want the screen to show. (If you choose one landscape mode and it appears upside down, simply choose the other one.)

  - **Playback** Allows you to configure which presentation features to use and which ones to ignore when playing on your iPAQ including:

    - Show without animation
    - Show without slide transition

PowerPoint's Beam File option.

- ■ Use timings, if present
- ■ Loop continuously (especially effective when used with timed slideshows to provide a moving background for down time in meetings or trade shows)
- ■ **End Show**   Ends the presentation and closes the PowerPoint Mobile program.

Other Useful PowerPoint Mobile Features

In addition to the standard move and rename types of File Explorer functions, you can also send a presentation file using e-mail or beam a presentation file using the infrared port to send the file to another infrared-capable device. Both of these options are available from the menu that is available before your open a PowerPoint file, as shown in Figure 13-10.

Use ClearVue Presentation on Your iPAQ

If your iPAQ is running Windows Mobile 2003 SE, it may be preloaded with ClearVue Presentation software rather than Microsoft PowerPoint Mobile. ClearVue is available for Windows Mobile 5 as well as 2003 SE and even if your iPAQ didn't include the software, it can be purchased separately from Westtek (**www.westtek.com/pocketpc/presentation/**) for about $9;and there is also an upgraded Professional version that costs about $30. and the basic ClearVue Presentation software allows you to open and view Microsoft Office and PowerPoint files and even includes support for timed transitions, animations, charts, graphs, text, and images. The Professional version allows you to edit PowerPoint presentations on your iPAQ as well as the ability to view presentations and also features the ability to print PowerPoint presentations from your iPAQ. We really like some of the additional features that are available ClearVue Presentation that are not included in Microsoft PowerPoint Mobile.

    If you are already familiar with using MS PowerPoint on your PC, then ClearVue Presentation will be straightforward, so we won't discuss every feature and function. However, we will talk about some of the more interesting features that help make this product a very good choice.

13

FIGURE 13-11 ClearVue slide sorter view.

The general layout of the application is intuitive and the slide sorter view is shown in Figure 13-11.

All of the options are accessible within ClearVue Presentation using the menus.

Onscreen menu - The onscreen menu available during a presentation is accessed in much the same way as in PowerPoint Mobile, by tapping the icon on the screen, shown in Figure 13-12.

The onscreen menu allows you to do several operations while you are actively running a presentation, as shown in Figure 13-13, including:

- **Next** and **Previous** slide
- **Go to...** Allows you to jump to a specific slide in the presentation.
- **Pen...** Allows you to draw on the slide while it is being shown.
- **Pointer** Allows you to use an onscreen pointer to point to specific information.
- **End show**

FIGURE 13-12 ClearVue icon.

FIGURE 13-13 ClearVue onscreen menu during a presentation.

Slideshow menu - Different menu options are available to you when you are not actively showing a presentation such as setting up show parameters, defining customs shows, or setting up external video; the menu is shown in Figure 13-14. This menu allows you to configure your slideshow and video output preferences including:

- **View Show** Selecting this option launches the presentation.
- **Set Up Show...** Allows you to configure how you want the presentation to run, including using timed advances, looping the presentation, or viewing the presentation in landscape mode, as shown in Figure 13-15.
- **Custom Show...** The custom show option is a great feature that allows you to define different slide shows for different audiences, where you want to use some of the

13

FIGURE 13-14 ClearVue menu when you are not showing a presentation.

ClearVue Set Up Show screen.

same slides for both audiences. For example, you want to use the same presentation for the CEO and for the sales group but you don't want to show the financial slides to the sales group so you can define a custom show for the sales group that skips the financial slides.

■ **External Video**   This option is where you configure settings to output your slideshow to a projector or external monitor using a CFXGA/U graphics card. More on this topic is covered later in this chapter when we discuss third party hardware.

One of the other nice features in ClearVue is the ability to use Notes. The notes feature allows you to make and see notes yourself for a specific slide without the audience seeing them, as shown in Figure 13-16.

ClearVue slide Notes view.

Other Third-party Presentation Software

In this section, we will discuss software other than PowerPoint Mobile and ClearVue Presentation that you may find more appropriate to your needs. One of the major reasons you may want to use something different from the PowerPoint viewing software that came preinstalled on your iPAQ is to modify your presentations on your iPAQ. The basic versions of PowerPoint Mobile and ClearVue Presentation are viewers, and don't allow you to edit your files.

What You Should Know about Video Drivers and Connecting Your iPAQ to a Monitor or Projector

It is important to understand if you intend to use hardware (generally, a third-party removable card) that allows you to connect your iPAQ to a monitor or projector, you need to be running a compatible VGA (video) driver on your iPAQ. Some presentation software has built-in VGA support, while others require VGA driver software in addition to the presentation software.

Different vendors take different approaches to solving the same problem, and presentation tools tend to fall into one of a few different categories:

- Viewing software that only allows you to view PowerPoint presentations but not modify or update the slides

- Software that allows you to both view and modify PowerPoint files

- Packages that allow you to view and modify PowerPoint files and include hardware that allows you to connect your iPAQ to an external projector or monitor

- Hardware-only solutions that allow you to project your iPAQ screen to an external projector or monitor

What You Need to Project Presentations Using Your iPAQ

Ultimately you need the following to project your PowerPoint from your iPAQ onto an external projector or monitor:

- PowerPoint viewing software, which may also include other functionally but must at least offer viewing capabilities.

- VGA driver software, which may be included with viewing software but isn't always.

- A method to connect your iPAQ to an external projector or monitor—you can use either a CompactFlash card that has a VGA/SVGA connector or Bluetooth or infrared to make a wireless connection. Both options are discussed in the "Hardware to Display Your iPAQ Screen on a Projector or Monitor" section of this chapter.

We won't discuss every alternative scenario, but you do need all three of these things to work. Before you choose your tools, ensure that you have all of the pieces you need.

13

Pocket Slides from Conduits Technologies

Pocket Slides from Conduits Technologies (**www.conduits.com/products/slides/**) converts presentations on the fly using ActiveSync and gives you the ability to hide and show slides, view slide thumbnails, and control slide transitions. One of the reasons you may want to use Pocket Slides instead of the built-in iPAQ PowerPoint software is that it allows you to edit your presentations right on your iPAQ, including editing speaker notes, text, images, and animations. You can also use the stylus to highlight information onscreen. This product is certainly a favorite for people that rely on PowerPoint.

Pocket SlideShow

Pocket SlideShow from CNetX (**www.cnetx.com/slideshow/**) is a PowerPoint viewer application that offers different viewing options and supports VGA cards but does not allow you to edit your PowerPoint files. Like some of the other PowerPoint offerings, Pocket SlideShow uses ActiveSync to convert PowerPoint presentations but it uses a proprietary format, a PSS extension.

Periscope

Periscope by Pocket PC Creations (**www.pocketpccreations.com/periscope**) does not allow you to edit PowerPoint files but allows you to perform PowerPoint viewing tasks as well as remote desktop tasks. This product is unique because it enables you to control a PowerPoint presentation running on either a desktop or a laptop using your iPAQ. You can do this either through the serial/USB port or wirelessly. If you want to use the wireless option, your iPAQ and the PC you want to connect to must share the same wireless technologies such as Bluetooth or WLAN. These technologies are covered in Chapter 3.

Hardware to Display Your iPAQ Screen on a Projector or Monitor

There are several reasons you may want to display your iPAQ screen on an external projector or monitor. Although this chapter focuses on PowerPoint presentation software, you will also need hardware that allows you to display your iPAQ screen on an external source. There are two primary ways to project your iPAQ screen on a monitor: with a CompactFlash VGA/SVGA expansion card or using a Bluetooth or infrared connection. Some of the major vendors that support the HP iPAQ are discussed here. CompactFlash cards expand your iPAQ so you can connect it to a standard VGA or SVGA monitor. It is the same type of physical connector that allows you to connect a desktop PC or laptop to a projector or monitor. You simply insert the CompactFlash card into the appropriate card slot on your iPAQ and connect a VGA connector cable to it. (By the way, this type of hardware works to display most anything that is on your iPAQ screen, not just PowerPoint.)

iPAQ VGA/SVGA Connector Hardware Vendors

The vendors discussed here simply allow you to expand your iPAQ by adding a VGA/SVGA connector so you can connect directly to any VGA/SVGA monitor or projector.

Flyjacket from LifeView

LifeView's FlyJacket (**www.lifeview.com**) uses a slightly different approach to expanding your iPAQ output capabilities. It is an expansion sleeve you put on your iPAQ to expand the multimedia connection functionality to connect to a projector, VGA monitor, TV, video, DVD, digital camera, and so on. The product offers a built-in CompactFlash slot, a pen-shaped remote control that can be also used as a laser pointer, and an ICAM module that can turn the FlyJacket into a digital still and video camera. The FlyJacket's main use is for presentation or demonstration purposes, but you can also use it with video sources.

Voyager CompactFlash VGA Adapter by Colorgraphic

Voyager (**www.colorgraphic.net**) allows you to present PowerPoint, Excel, and Word files and "mirror" your LCD display on a projector. This product also comes bundled with ClearVue Suite from Westtek, which is discussed earlier in this chapter. Voyager works with NTSC/PAL broadcast standards and includes a multifunction remote for wireless presentations. The product is easy to use: just connect your iPAQ to your PC, install the appropriate driver on your iPAQ, insert the CF card, and connect to the projector or monitor. The card works with Type I or Type II CompactFlash slots or Type II PCMCIA slot with the included PCMCIA adapter.

Bluetooth and Infrared Presentation Products

Most iPAQ devices have a CompactFlash slot and will work with the CF products discussed in this chapter but another connection alternative is Bluetooth and infrared.

infraBLUE IRMA Bluetooth/IR Presenter

InfraBLUE (**www.corporatekeys.com**) offers two wireless products for the iPAQ to display presentations, one using infrared and the other using Bluetooth (similar to the Pitch Duo, discussed next). Bluetooth and infrared technologies are discussed in Chapter 3, but the important thing to know is that, assuming your iPAQ offers both Bluetooth and infrared, infrared is a line-of-sight technology that must be aligned with the projector/monitor infrared port and can't be moved, while Bluetooth allows the iPAQ to be anywhere within the 30-foot range.

Mobility Electronics iGo Pitch Duo

Mobility Electronics iGo Pitch Duo (**www.mobilityelectronics.com**) uses Bluetooth to communicate between an iPAQ and an external projector or monitor. The iGo Pitch Duo is a physical Bluetooth device that you connect to a projector or monitor and accepts a connection from your iPAQ. The product includes:

- Pitch Duo hardware
- AC adapter

13

■ SVGA cable
■ CD with drivers and software

Wrap It Up

As iPAQs become increasingly powerful, they are beginning to become the tool of choice for out-of-office business. A laptop is still the dominant mobile computing platform, and for good reason: they tend to offer a full-size screen, lots of processing power, and memory to run applications and store data. However, there are certainly times when it is much more convenient to be able to go to a meeting armed with nothing but your trusty iPAQ. One of the major tools that is used almost universally in meetings and presentations of all kinds is Microsoft PowerPoint. This chapter covered several different topics relating to your iPAQ and PowerPoint and discussed both software and hardware options to help you facilitate effective presentations with your iPAQ while leaving your laptop on your desk.

Chapter 14

Use Your iPAQ in Your Enterprise

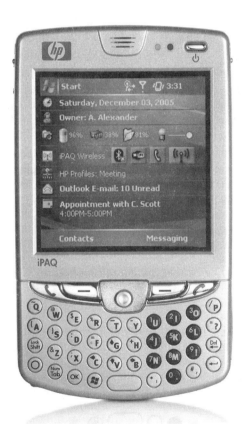

How to...

- Anticipate challenges of rolling out iPAQs in your organization
- Identify the right iPAQ e-mail solution for your organization
- Use Terminal Services on your iPAQ to connect to a host Windows computer
- Use third-party applications on your iPAQ that help you and your company
- Find more information about enterprise iPAQ applications

For many of you, your iPAQ has become the preferred tool to use in situations where a laptop and cell phone used to be required. We know that we would much rather clip our iPAQs to our belts than lug around our laptop bags, charging cords, and various accessories from meeting to meeting, although our chiropractors are less enthusiastic about the evolution.

There is certainly a convenience factor to carrying a small, powerful iPAQ, but there is also fact that that HP iPAQ is proven technology that allows you to be more productive. Now, this means many things but for the enterprise (companies and business organizations), this means productivity can go up. If you are more productive, you accomplish more in a day, and if several more productive iPAQ users work for one organization, then theoretically the organization also accomplishes more as a result. It is a win-win situation.

Much of the content in this chapter is slightly biased toward iPAQs that are wirelessly connected using Bluetooth, WiFi, or cellular networks, but there are certainly many enterprise applications that run locally on your iPAQ that don't need a wireless connection to work properly. In fact, more and more applications function both using wireless connectivity as well as in a disconnected state. Disconnected applications synchronize data with your PC or with an application server when the iPAQ is reconnected through ActiveSync or using a network connection.

Deploying iPAQs in the Enterprise: Some Things to Consider

Smart mobile devices such as your iPAQ are commonly used in day-to-day business to help you better perform your job. Some industries have seen a surprising adoption rate, such as health care, government, military, and finance, but there is scarcely any industry that is not reaping the benefits the mobile devices offer to one degree or another. There is a perpetual stream of new enterprise applications that help solve specific problems for specific user groups in new and interesting ways.

Supporting iPAQ Users

There are a few good reasons why iPAQs and other mobile devices can end up being a big pain in the neck for the IT people in your company, especially if your organization has hundreds or thousands of users. It is tough enough keeping track of all of your company's hardware and software, enforcing IT policies and rules, ensuring security measures are met, supporting end users to keep them up and running, and keeping up with the latest technology and the hundreds of other responsibilities that they have, let alone worrying about a bunch of handheld devices. It is enough to keep the poor IT folks up at night.

This is something to keep in mind when you talk to your company's computer and network people about setting up your iPAQ on the network. Some of the challenges specific to support iPAQ handhelds include:

- Tracking who has what device and which hardware accessories

- Tracking which software a particular iPAQ user is using

- Enforcing policies (making sure that iPAQ users have password protection enabled, for example)

- Tracking service contracts with cellular providers and ensuring that each user has an appropriate voice and data plan

- Supporting the iPAQ users to ensure they have all of the information they need to effectively use their device

Keep in mind that, although you may require help setting up your iPAQ with the correct software and configuration, often the IT department has a different set of challenges when it comes to mobile devices such as your iPAQ.

Accessing Corporate E-mail on Your iPAQ

Much of this chapter is devoted to corporate e-mail and your iPAQ. The ability to send and receive e-mail while mobile is an exceedingly valuable innovation. It allows you to be more responsive, more educated about what is happening, and even more productive. The downside, if there is one, may be that you end up spending more after-hours time dealing with e-mail. Specific enterprise e-mail options are discussed later in this chapter, but the built-in e-mail application, Microsoft Outlook Mobile, formerly known as Pocket Outlook, will do everything most iPAQ users need. Using MS Pocket Outlook is discussed in detail in Chapter 12. That said, MS Pocket Outlook will not work for every type of corporate e-mail system, and, even if MS Pocket Outlook does work for you, you may find that you have some specific or additional requirements. For that reason, other iPAQ e-mail client options as well as some of the most successful e-mail software is presented in this chapter.

14

Security and Enterprise iPAQs

One of the most significant concerns for organizations that choose to rule out HP iPAQs or other mobile devices to employees is usually related to security. After all, the very attributes that makes the iPAQ so useful, such as being highly portable, able to store large amounts of information, being capable of running sophisticated software, and having the ability for wireless networking, are exactly the same attributes that cause concern for IT professionals in most companies. Chapter 16 discusses security, including simple tasks you can do to make your iPAQ more secure as well as more sophisticated options and solutions.

E-Mail—the Killer Wireless Application for Your iPAQ

E-mail has revolutionized the way we communicate, and in many cases e-mail has even altered the way we do business. Extending e-mail into the wireless realm has enabled us to be connected no matter where we are. Of course, not everyone thinks this is a good thing, but for many it offers freedom from the constraints of the office environment while still allowing you to be involved and in touch. The iPAQ lets you send and receive e-mail in many different ways as well as perform tasks usually relegated to the desktop, such as managing contacts and viewing attachments. Regardless of how many other applications you use on your iPAQ or how often you play games or listen to MP3s, if you use your iPAQ for e-mail, you will likely use e-mail almost as much as anything you do on your iPAQ.

Understand the Most Common E-mail Account Types

The type of e-mail account you have determines the type of software you will need to run on your iPAQ to receive and send e-mail. The type of software you need also determines how you will need to configure your iPAQ to send and receive e-mail. The important thing to keep in mind is that different types of e-mail require specific software on your iPAQ to work properly. Some e-mail client software for your iPAQ supports more than one e-mail protocol and, generally, e-mail accounts fall into one of four categories:

- **Corporate e-mail such as MS Exchange with Exchange ActiveSync, Non-EAS MS Exchange or Lotus Domino**   If you have an e-mail account provided by your employer, chances are it's one of these. (EAS stands for Exchange ActiveSync and is included in recent MS Exchange Service Packs on the server side.)

- **POP3 (Post Office Protocol 3)**   If your Internet service provider (such as EarthLink, AT&T WorldNet, BellSouth, Shaw, Telus, Comcast, O2, Orange, SBC, or Verizon) hosts your e-mail account, it is likely a POP3 account.

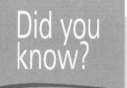

iPAQ Phone Users: Got Data?

If you are just getting started in the world of wireless data, it is important to know that your wireless service provider, the company you are paying to use your iPAQ as a phone, classifies e-mail as data. Not all mobile phone contracts include data service by default. If you know that your contract includes data service, great! If you are not sure, you may want to take a look at your contract to find out or give your service provider a call. In order for your iPAQ to send and receive e-mail, you must have data service included with your iPAQ phone plan. This topic is covered in more detail in Chapter 3.

■ **IMAP (Internet Message Access Protocol)** This is a method of accessing electronic mail or bulletin board messages that are kept on an e-mail server. IMAP permits a client e-mail program on your iPAQ (or PC) to access remote e-mail message stores as if they were local. For example, e-mail stored on an IMAP server can be manipulated from a home desktop computer, a workstation at the office, or a notebook computer while traveling, without the need to transfer messages or files back and forth between these computers. Many corporate e-mail account types support IMAP e-mail.

■ **Web-based e-mail such as Hotmail, Yahoo!, Google, Netscape, Lycos, and Excite** You typically use this type of e-mail account by going to a web page and logging in to your account to send and view e-mail.

Find Out What Type of E-mail Your Organization Uses

If your e-mail account is hosted and managed by the organization you work for, then there is a high likelihood that it is Microsoft Exchange, Novell GroupWise, or Lotus Domino. The built-in e-mail client on your iPAQ is Pocket Outlook and works with Microsoft Exchange but not with Lotus Domino or Novell GroupWise e-mail servers. Fortunately, there are several companies that offer such software for your iPAQ.

> **TIP**
>
> *Ask your IT department for help - If you have a corporate e-mail account that you would like to begin using on your iPAQ, asking for help from your corporate IT department is a good idea. We know that asking for help is a lot like asking for directions. Nevertheless, asking the proper people the right questions can save you a lot of time and frustration. The fastest way to find out information about your e-mail account is to call up the support desk of the organization that provides your e-mail. Usually just introducing yourself, explaining why you're calling, and asking whether your e-mail account is a POP3 account will start you down the right path. If, on the other hand, the company you work for provides your e-mail, great! Go bug the e-mail or systems administrator; you may even be able to persuade them to set up your iPAQ for you—something well worth the price of a venti soy latte, if you find that a little bribery is necessary.*

About Microsoft Exchange ActiveSync

Exchange ActiveSync is a relatively new addition to the Microsoft Exchange Server 2003 e-mail server product. It allows handhelds running Microsoft Windows Mobile to access corporate information on a server running Exchange Server. Exchange ActiveSync is an over-the-air data synchronization service that enables mobile users access to their e-mail, calendar, and contact information both online and offline.

> **TIP**
>
> *Is MS Exchange ActiveSync the best choice for you? If you know that your corporate e-mail server is MS Exchange and you choose to use the built-in Pocket Outlook as your iPAQ e-mail client on your iPAQ, this combination is likely all you need to send and receive e-mail as well as synchronize your calendar and contacts with the corporate e-mail server. The one other requirement that you will need to ensure has been met is that the MS Exchange Server has been upgraded to MS Exchange 2003 Service Pack 2.*

14

Choose an Appropriate E-mail Client for Your iPAQ

Several different technologies and configurations allow you to send and receive e-mail on your iPAQ, so it's important that you understand the available options and what their differences are before you get started. If you already have an e-mail account or many e-mail accounts, your options are relatively straightforward because you don't have to consider all of the available options. The four major types of e-mail accounts you can use with your iPAQ are Microsoft EAS (Exchange ActiveSync); POP3; corporate e-mail including Non-EAS Exchange and Lotus Domino, IMAP; and web-based e-mail. Each e-mail type is described in more detail later in this chapter.

 If you have only a corporate e-mail account that you want to use on your iPAQ, then skip directly to the section entitled "If You Have a Corporate E-mail Account."

Use MS Pocket Outlook on Your iPAQ

Your iPAQ likely arrived with Microsoft Pocket Outlook preinstalled. Pocket Outlook allows you to use several types of e-mail accounts including IMAP, POP3, and Microsoft Exchange. If your e-mail account uses one of these technologies, then MS Pocket Outlook is a good choice for sending and receiving e-mail on your iPAQ. Using and configuring Pocket Outlook is covered in detail in Chapter 13.

 Most users will be very satisfied with MS Pocket Outlook because it works with most types of e-mail at no additional cost to you. However, if your company has already selected a mobile e-mail solution and does not allow you to use Pocket Outlook or if your corporate e-mail does not work with Pocket Outlook (such as Lotus Domino or web mail), the following sections are aimed at you.

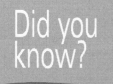

What Is Push E-Mail?

Push e-mail is sent to your iPAQ without requiring any action from you other than turning the wireless connection on. E-mail simply shows up when you are not looking because it is pushed to your device from the e-mail server. Non-push e-mail, on the other hand, requires you to actively request to send or receive e-mail before your iPAQ will connect to the e-mail server to send any pending e-mail and check for new e-mail. To further confuse the issue, many e-mail clients that are technically classified as non-push applications automatically connect to the e-mail server to check for new messages (often called "polling") on a scheduled basis and, if there are new messages, they are downloaded to your iPAQ. To most users, there isn't much practical difference between a true push client and a client that polls the e-mail server, but there still seems to be heated debate among e-mail vendors on the matter.

Alternative iPAQ E-mail Clients

If you choose not to use the included Microsoft Pocket Outlook e-mail client or just want to know what other options you have, this section covers some of the most popular options available.

MS Exchange iPAQ E-mail Client Options

The following products allow you to receive e-mail if your organization uses MS Exchange; each is covered in more detail later in this chapter:

- GoodLink
- BlackBerry Connect for Windows Mobile
- Visto
- Seven

Lotus Domino iPAQ E-mail Client Options

The following products will allow you to receive e-mail if your organization uses Lotus Domino; each is covered in more detail later in this chapter.

- Visto
- BlackBerry Connect for Windows Mobile
- Intellisync Mobile Suite

Novell GroupWise iPAQ E-mail Client Options

The following products allow you to receive e-mail if your organization uses Novell GroupWise; each is covered in more detail later in this chapter.

- GWAnywhere
- Notify

Additional Information Regarding Alternative iPAQ E-mail Clients

The preceding section simply lists which e-mail clients work with the various enterprise e-mail servers including MS Exchange, Lotus Domino, and Novell GroupWise. Note that regardless of which corporate e-mail a product supports (Exchange, Domino, or GroupWise), all support POP3 and IMAP e-mail protocols as well. This section discusses each option in more detail and lists website addresses so that you can review the latest product information online.

In addition to support for specific corporate e-mail servers (MS Exchange, Lotus Domino and Novell GroupWise) you will likely find that push e-mail products look very similar and, if your company hasn't already selected one, the major difference will probably come down to price.

14

BlackBerry Connect for Windows Mobile   If your company has a BlackBerry Enterprise Server and your company uses Lotus Domino and Microsoft Exchange for e-mail, then BlackBerry Connect for Windows Mobile (**www.blackberry.com**) is worth a look. BlackBerry Connect allows Windows Mobile–based devices such as your iPAQ to leverage the benefits of BlackBerry wireless services, including BlackBerry Enterprise Server and BlackBerry Internet Service. BlackBerry Connect allows you to synchronize data on your iPAQ such as e-mail and other data applications. Some of the highlights of the product include:

- Advanced security features
- Attachment viewing—the ability to open and view e-mail attachments in popular formats such as Microsoft Word, Microsoft Excel, Microsoft PowerPoint, Adobe PDF, and Corel WordPerfect, as well as HTML and ASCII
- Wireless e-mail reconciliation—the ability to manage e-mail with automatic wireless synchronization of device and desktop mailboxes
- Remote address book look-up—the ability to look up contact information stored in company directories over the air
- Wireless calendar synchronization
- Centralized management and IT control
- Ability to access personal and/or business e-mail
- BlackBerry push technology, where e-mail is delivered automatically to the iPAQ
- Wireless extension to existing mailboxes that seamlessly integrates with up to ten supported e-mail accounts, such as POP3/ISP e-mail, Microsoft Outlook, and Lotus Notes.

Intellisync Mobile Suite   Intellisync Mobile Suite (**www.intellisync.com**) offers support for Microsoft Exchange and Lotus Domino as well as IMAP and POP3 and offers over-the-air push e-mail and PIM synchronization, including wireless e-mail, calendar, and contacts. Some of the other features include:

- XML platform that opens wireless e-mail to easily access customer relationship management software, sales force automation software, and collaboration software.
- File and web content distribution—Intellisync File Sync automates distribution of files or Intranet content to mobile devices.
- Security and device management—Intellisync Mobile Systems Management lets you manage mobile devices with features such as over-the-air deployment and automatic device backups.

GoodLink   GoodLink (**www.good.com**) currently supports MS Exchange but has been talking about support for Lotus Domino as well. Similar to the other offerings, GoodLink offers synchronized over-the-air e-mail and PIM (Personal Information Management) information. Some of the other features include:

- MS Outlook–like functionality
- Attachment viewing for Word, Excel, PDF, and PowerPoint files
- Advanced handheld security with GoodLink Compliance Manager with role-based administration
- Availability in English, French, Italian, German, and Spanish
- World-wide coverage with Global Connect
- Ability to be installed, upgraded, and managed entirely over the air
- IT management tools including role-based administration
- Good Monitoring Portal, which allows the monitoring of mobile devices including software version installed, device type, radio status and carrier
- AES encryption for over the air data
- Remote erase capability
- Ability to show PowerPoint presentations directly from a mobile device
- Ability to receive faxes in TIFF format
- Ability to print documents using Bluetooth connectivity

Visto   Visto Mobile Enterprise Server (**www.visto.com**) works with both Microsoft Exchange and Lotus Domino. Visto provides over-the-air e-mail, calendar, and contact synchronization to your iPAQ, including attachment viewing capability. The Visto Mobile Enterprise Server allows IT administrators to control user provisioning and profiles and can generate reports and log files to help track device usage. Key features include:

- Ability to manage e-mail from your iPAQ including reading, writing, responding to, forwarding, and deleting messages
- E-mail, calendar and contact updating in real-time to your iPAQ so you're always up to date without requiring a cradle
- Ability to create, edit, and delete appointments on your device and synchronize with your calendar over the air
- AES data encryption
- Ability to download and view attachments on your iPAQ including Word, Excel and other Office documents

Seven   Seven Enterprise Edition (**www.seven.com**) supports Microsoft Exchange e-mail and is designed to be operator-hosted (that is, hosted by cellular service providers). Seven may

14

appeal more to either large enterprises that are highly distributed or to organizations that want to outsource IT projects. Some of the features of this product include:

- No requirement for middleware or a server in your network—mobile devices are provisioned via a web-based management console
- Data encryption that uses configurable AES, 128-bit SSL and VPN connectivity
- Push synchronization that allows real time e-mail access without the need for desktop cradles
- Over-the-air software that automatically pushes upgrades to all end-user mobile devices
- Real-time Data Obliteration that erases data from misplaced iPAQs to reduce security risks
- Over-the-air synchronization of e-mail, calendar, contacts, and documents

NotifyLink   NotifyLink (**www.notifycorp.com**) supports Novell GroupWise and MS Exchange, as well as IMAP4 e-mail systems. NotifyLink provides wireless access and management of e-mail, calendar, contacts, and tasks.

GWAnywhere   GWAnywhere (**www.gwtools.com**) supports Novell GroupWise and offers synchronization in multiple modes: offline synchronization, live connect push, or online real-time synching. GWAnywhere provides e-mail as well as PIM data.

Solutions to Allow Your Organization to Manage Their iPAQs

As discussed earlier in this chapter and in Chapter 16, there are some unique challenges associated with managing a bunch of highly mobile, highly powerful mobile devices such as the HP iPAQ relating to deployment, support and security. There are a few companies that have tackled these problems to allow your IT department to keep a better leash on all of those mobile "network assets."

SonicSentinel

Avocent Corp. (**www.avocent.com**) is relatively new to the world of mobility but has a strong history as a leader in data center management as the market leader in KVM (keyboard video mouse) technology. Avocent acquired a company called Sonic Mobility in 2004 because they understand the opportunity that mobile device management presents. Avocent is also the vendor that makes SonicAdmin, a tool specifically for the IT Administrator folks discussed later in this chapter.

SonicSentinel is designed specifically to help the corporate IT and network security deal with all of those difficult-to-track-and-secure mobile devices like the iPAQ. Some of the key features include:

- Real-time device status and uptime tracking. An agent that is installed as a background application on the iPAQ routinely sends diagnostic information back to a central server for analysis and alert generation and reporting.

- Real time monitoring and device tracking to determine which devices are online and functioning properly. On the console, you can monitor current and historical information for any device including device type, OS version, battery strength, signal strength, connectivity patterns, installed software, and memory usage.

- Ability to track up-to-date asset management information such as device type, service provider, assigned user, serial number, IMEI, and ESN.

- Automatic alert generation. You receive notifications and alerts when specific events occur such as critical device battery levels or key mobile devices going off-line for a specified period of time.

- Real-time control and security. This protects vital corporate and personal data with the ability to remotely wipe data on the device or lock a missing device to prevent corporate or personal data from being misused.

- Ability to enforce mobile device policies, including password protection and prevention of the installation of unauthorized software through software blacklists.

Some other vendors that offer software to secure and manage iPAQs and other mobile devices include:

- Intellisync (**www.intellisync.com**)
- Xcellenet (**www.xcellenet.com**)

Enterprise iPAQ Applications

14

This section deals with enterprise software for your iPAQ *other* than e-mail and device management software. E-mail is obviously an extremely valuable function of wireless iPAQs, but once it's working, the next question is usually, "What else can I do with my iPAQ?" There are now countless software applications for the Pocket PC/Windows Mobile Operating System, which is both fantastic and a little overwhelming. The types of software range from free applications that allow you change your iPAQ interface colors or convert imperial measures to metric measures, for example. There are also the types of software commonly categorized as *enterprise solutions*. This type of software helps organizations perform day-to-day tasks more efficiently to get the job done and "add shareholder value."

Industry and Job-specific Software

Each industry tends to have specific challenges and business requirements. This section covers some solutions targeted at the specific industries of finance and health care. Also listed in this section are tools for IT professionals and sales professionals since many (although not all) industries have sales and IT people.

Software for Health Care Professionals

The medical industry is an exemplary example of an industry that recognizes the value of mobile technology. There are many types of software designed for your iPAQ that assist health care providers manage information about medicine, nursing, coding/billing, and patient tracking, drug guides, calculators, medical references, and study aids. There are even utilities to help time contractions (useful for the expectant parents as well as doctors and nurses), track blood glucose levels, track patient hospital rounds, and track medications. There are so many different software solutions for health care professionals that we will only provide a brief example of what is available here.

- **DrugGuide (Davis's DrugGuide for Nurses) powered by Skyscape (www.skyscape .com)** Costs about $40 and includes over 5000 trade and generic drugs, with more than 150 drug classifications, over 1000 drug monographs, and 700 commonly used combination drugs, including the dosage amount of the active generic ingredient. Skyscape also offers many different Windows Mobile software products specifically designed for health care professionals including doctors, nurses, and even students and residents.

- **CCS Treatment Guidelines for Medicine and Primary Care, 2002 Edition (www .ccspublishing.com)** Costs about $37. This is a reference book you can run on your iPAQ that is essentially a handbook containing a compilation of current diagnostic and treatment guidelines for patient management in primary care including the New American College of Physicians guidelines. The handbook outlines the diagnosis and therapy for common problems encountered by family physicians, internists, and other primary care providers. This reference is intended for physicians, medical students, nurse practitioners, and physician's assistants.

- **DiagnosisPro for Pocket PC by MedTech USA Inc. (www.medicalamazon.com)** Costs about $315 and is an interactive tool that allows medical professionals to quickly generate differential diagnoses based on multiple entries by entering findings such as signs, symptoms, lab values, and x-ray or EKG results. DiagnosisPro generates a hierarchical list of diseases from a database of 10,000 diseases, 25,000 findings, and 250,000 relationships. The software then provides a detailed review of each disease, including clinical presentations, abnormal lab values, rule-outs, complications, and treatments. It also includes 15,000 ICD codes, and you can also compare the characteristics of any two diseases side by side.

Software for Sales Professionals

Sales professionals are often highly mobile and need to be available at all times and have immediate access to data. Contact information for a particular account is obviously important, as well as other data such as products the contact has bought, any open support issues, unique requirements, and even the names of the contact's family members. The ability to get at recent product information is also extremely valuable information. The unique requirements of sales and field service professionals makes mobile technology such as the HP iPAQ important.

Some of the leaders in sales force automation include:

- **SalesForce (www.salesforce.com)**   An online hosted service that has had some excellent success in the market. This service stores all contact and sales data centrally on a server that you can access on your iPAQ; you can also synchronize data using a wireless connection.

- **Sales Everywhere by IT Everywhere (www.pocketgear.com)**   A tool for the mobile sales person that runs standalone/offline on your iPAQ without requiring over-the-air connectivity, as shown in Figure 14-1. The application allows you to keep track of contacts, accounts, actions related to accounts, contacts, calendar, products, pricelists, sales history to track sales, and forecasting information.

Software for Finance Professionals

Time and money are closely associated for those who make their living in the finance sector. Whether just keeping in touch, being able to access financial data, or being able to receive real-time

FIGURE 14-1   Sales Everywhere.

14

data about transactions or the status of the stock market, time and information are very important. Fortunately, the iPAQ is made for this kind of thing.

- **Microsoft Money 2006 for Windows Mobile-based Pocket PC**   Covered in Chapter 8, this essentially allows you to coordinate and synchronize your accounts with your desktop PC and see your balances on your iPAQ Today screen; you can update your investment portfolio on the fly and find up-to-date quotes by synchronizing your device with your desktop or by downloading information directly from the Internet.

- **Loan, amortization, and tax calculators**   There are several types of calculator applications designed specifically for financial professionals. Check out **www .pocketgear.com** or **www.pocketpccity.com** for examples.

- **Stock market software**   It seems like everyone is "in the stock market." The trick is to be informed enough to make quick decisions to buy and to sell your stocks at just the right time. What do you do if you are not at your PC? Simple: you take your iPAQ. There are two main methods to get real-time stock market quotes on your iPAQ: install an application designed for stock quotes, or use the iPAQ browser to view your favorite stock market or financial website.

  - PocketStockMonitor by Pockettx Software Inc. (**www.pocketx.net**), shown in Figure 14-2, is one example of software you can install on your iPAQ to view stock quotes either when your iPAQ is in a cradle connected to an Internet-connected PC or using a wireless connection to connect to the Internet.

  - To access stock quotes with your iPAQ browser, you can essentially use whatever stock or financial website you normally use on your desktop on your iPAQ. Whether you use Yahoo finance, **www.bloomberg.com**, or **www.etrade.com**, you can view them all on your iPAQ using the wireless connectivity or even while cradled and connected to your Internet-connected PC. Many of the financial sites also offer web pages specifically designed for the smaller screen of your iPAQ.

FIGURE 14-2   PocketStockMonitor.

TIP

*One of the best ways to ensure that you are up to date with the latest market news is to use real-time financial streaming audio to tune into one of the Internet radio stations specializing in financial news. A good example of this service is Bloomberg Radio (**www.bloomberg.com**); using your iPAQ to listen to Internet radio is covered in Chapter 5.*

Software for Information Technology Professionals

The people in IT are a special breed. These are the men and women who are responsible for ensuring that all of the network users are up, working, and happy. It might seem pretty simple to those who don't have the responsibilities of the IT people: all they have to do is keep the PCs, networks, and servers up and running secure, virus free, fast, and efficient and be on call 24 hours a day to respond to events that are interrupting the technical harmony of it all. Easy. Right? For these hard-working people, virtually every time a user or manager contacts a systems administrator it isn't to visit, it is because something is wrong or broken and it needs fixing immediately.

Many of the statistics that track what people do during an average day suggest that network and systems administrators tend to spend only 30 percent to 40 percent of their time in front of a PC or server. In addition, IT people are virtually guaranteed to carry one or a combination of cell phone, Pocket PC, or pager to help ensure that when something goes wrong you can contact them. So, if you can always contact them but they are not always in a convenient place to fix the problem, what do they do? In the olden days they had to either drive back to the office or find a computer so that they could try to get remote access to the network and if that didn't work they had to drive to the office.

With the wide availability of wirelessly connected HP iPAQs and cellular networks and some special software, nowadays when the IT person receives notification about a problem on their iPAQ by either phone or e-mail, they can use their iPAQs to log in to the network to diagnose and fix the problem. This allows the IT people to be much more responsive, which means users are up and working more, and allows them to be much more productive.

SonicAdmin by Avocent Corp.   SonicAdmin (**www.avocent.com**) has been available for over four years and allows IT people to securely access their back-end servers and networks to do day-to-day maintenance and quickly respond to high-priority emergencies. If you are not a member of the IT community, this may not seem that impressive, but for IT people this power is golden. SonicAdmin has a lot of features so we won't list them all but the highlights are

- Microsoft Windows management:
  - **User management**   View all users; add, edit, and delete users; edit a user's properties (as shown in Figure 14-3); use SMTP user e-mail; create user groups; and use Active directory organizational units.
  - **Event logs**   View events and save and clear logs.
  - **DNS management**   View DNS zones, add and delete DNS records.
  - **Print service management**   View printer status and job lists, kill or restart jobs.

FIGURE 14-3   SonicAdmin User Details screen.

- **File Explorer functionality**   View, move, cut, copy, and paste files; e-mail files from a managed server, as shown in Figure 14-4.

- **The ability to view and edit text files remotely**   Edit boot.ini, batch files, html, and more.

- **Services and server processes**   Stop, start, restart, or pause services; modify service log on properties; kill bad processes.

FIGURE 14-4   SonicAdmin File Explorer screen.

- **Statistics**   View operating system and service pack details and system uptime, CPU, memory and disk space information; view process count and auto refresh statistics for real-time monitoring.

- **Server and device management**   Log off, shut down, or force-reboot any server; generate and run custom scripts and batch files; control power to any external devices including servers, switches, routers, hubs, modems, lights and more.

- Product integrations:

  - **Microsoft Exchange administration**   Includes management of contact e-mail addresses, SMTP proxy addresses, delivery options, storage limits, and queues.

  - **TelAlert (www.telalert.com) integration**   Browse, view, create, and respond to alerts.

  - **NetIQ AppManager (www.netiq.com)**   Filter, search for, and manage computers, events, and jobs.

  - **RSA SecurID (www.rsa.com)**   Integrate with RSA SecurID two-factor authentication.

- Telnet/SSH interface that allows you to manage non-Windows systems and applications such as Linux, Unix, databases, network hardware, and so on, as shown in Figure 14-5.

MS Terminal Services for Windows Mobile   Windows administrators tend to be familiar with Terminal Services, but now that mobile devices have evolved to the point where the screens are of high enough quality and wireless networks are much faster than they used to be, Terminal Services (also called Remote Desktop) can be used on all of the recent iPAQs. The steps to set up and begin using Terminal Services on your iPAQ are covered later in this chapter under the

14

FIGURE 14-5   SonicAdmin Telnet screen.

heading "Use Microsoft Remote Desktop, included with Windows XP Professional." That section deals specifically with connecting to a PC, but the steps are essentially the same for connecting to a Windows server.

Cross-industry Software for Your iPAQ

In this section, we discuss a few products we thought would be good to mention that don't easily fit into a particular industry but would certainly be useful for most organizational iPAQ users.

Mobile Credit Card Order Entry

If your business is one of the many has to be able to accept a credit card for payment such as courier, taxi driver, pizza delivery, or what have you, the ability to accept and verify the card is very valuable indeed. There are a few vendors that specialize in this type of software. A vendor that provides embedded credit card verification is Merchant Anywhere's Pocket Verifier (**www .merchantanywhere.com**); another option is to use an online credit card verification service using your iPAQ browser. Many vendors provide that service, and you will need to set up a merchant account that also integrates with your bank. Likely the best solution is to contact your bank to find out if they have a preferred provider of an online credit card transaction service that they recommend.

Mobile File Access

Anyone who has carried an iPAQ for a length of time has likely been in the situation where it would have been ideal to have access to a specific file or information that is sitting back at the office on your PC or on a file server. For example, say you are visiting a client at their office and they express interest in a particular product you have and want to talk about the technical specifications. However, you haven't memorized all of the engineering data. You really need to be able to hand the client a document that contains all of the information they need, but it is back at the office. Of course, you can always just send the document when you get back to the office, but this is less than ideal if you are on road trip or if you are in hurry to close this client's business this quarter, which happens to end in two days. Wouldn't it be great to be able to use your iPAQ to access that file and give the information to the client right then?

As with any problem that needs a software solution, new product offerings are perpetually entering the market, and the list presented here is a very small portion of what is available. Expect to find others as you look.

> TIP
> *When considering any technology that allows you to access one networked device with another, such as accessing a PC over the Internet with your iPAQ, it is very important to consider potential security risks. Obviously, you don't want to expose your PC or computer network to anyone but you, so it is wise to understand the unique security implications of using this type of software.*

- **Microsoft Remote Desktop**   A good remote access solution, provided you have Windows XP Professional on your work or home PC. This topic is covered in more detail in this chapter under the title "Use Microsoft Remote Desktop, included with Windows XP Professional."

- **File4ward by Penokio (www.penokio.com)**   An application that allows you to browse the files on your home or work PC using any web browser by using the browser on your iPAQ. Penokio offers a free version that is limited by the number of downloads and file sizes. They also offer inexpensive upgrades if you need more flexibility (these cost around $10–$15).

- **FilePoint Exchange by Bachmann Software (www.bachmannsoftware.com)**   Costs about $40 and has a free trial download. This tool allows you to wirelessly access your desktop PC or network from your iPAQ, including the ability to browse folders and files; download documents, spreadsheets or other files; search your remote computer for files using Google Desktop Search; access frequently needed files with FilePoint Favorites; and configure access to multiple computers on different home or office networks.

Use Microsoft Remote Desktop, Included with Windows XP Professional

If you are running Windows XP Professional on your work or home PC, you can use MS Remote Desktop (also known as Terminal Services) to connect your iPAQ to your computer to access all of your programs, files, and network resources in the same way you can when you are sitting in front of your PC. This is very handy for a bunch of reasons and especially valuable if you have forgotten something or just don't have a particular file on your iPAQ that is on your PC.

> TIP
>
> *What's the difference between Remote Desktop and Terminal Services? They provide similar type of functionality, but Remote Desktop is available on your Windows XP-based PC and is based on the Terminal Services technology that first appeared in the Windows NT Server operating system. This technology gives you the ability to log on to a remote computer from an intranet or over the Internet to operate or administer the PC remotely. This same technology is called Terminal Services on your iPAQ. It is a little confusing, but by either name it is very useful technology.*

Key Elements that You Need to Use Terminal Services on Your iPAQ   The following steps to set up the host PC are based on the host running Windows XP and Remote Desktop software. Similar steps allow you to set up a Windows server as a Terminal Services client (the largest difference is the names).

1. Microsoft Windows XP Professional must be installed on your PC or the computer containing the files and programs that you want to access from an HP iPAQ. This PC is known as the host.

2. If the host PC is behind a firewall, port 3389 must be open to TCP traffic. If you are accessing a host PC on a corporate network, you will likely need to discuss your requirements with your IT department. Also, there may be Network Address Translation (NAT) settings that need to be changed. Once you explain what you want to do to your friendly IT people, they should have the expertise to get it all working.

3. Your iPAQ must be running Terminal Services client software to connect to a Remote Desktop host PC. Your iPAQ is known as the client. If your iPAQ doesn't have Terminal Service running, you can download it for free from Microsoft at **www.microsoft.com/ windowsmobile/downloads/terminalserver.mspx**.

4. Both the PC that you want to connect to and your iPAQ must be connected to the Internet.

Set Up the Remote Desktop on Your Windows XP PC (the Host)   The host computer can be either your home or your work PC.

1. Verify that you are signed in as the administrator. This may be a temporary show stopper if you are using your work PC as the host because your network ID and/or PC privileges probably don't have administrator privileges. You will have to get your corporate IT people to modify your PC logon privileges to give you "administrator" rights on your PC.

2. On your PC, select Start | Control Panel. If the screen is not already set to Category View, switch to that view by selecting the Category View option, as shown in Figure 14-6.

3. Select the Performance and Maintenance icon, as shown in Figure 14-7.

4. Select the System icon, as shown in Figure 14-8.

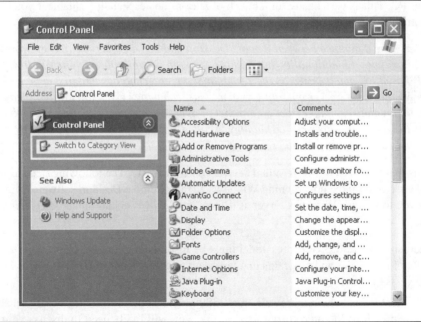

FIGURE 14-6   Remote host switch to Category View.

FIGURE 14-7   Remote host Performance and Maintenance icon.

5. Select the Remote tab and select the Allow Users To Connect Remotely To This Computer check box, as shown in Figure 14-9. Click the Apply button and then the OK button.

6. You need to set the Windows XP firewall to allow a Remote Desktop connection, so once you are back on the Performance and Maintenance screen, select the Back button on the top left. Back on the Pick A Category screen, choose the Security icon, as shown in Figure 14-10.

7. You should now see the Security Center screen. Select the Windows Firewall icon and, when the Windows Firewall dialog box comes up, select the Exceptions tab, as shown in Figure 14-11. Ensure that the Remote Desktop option has a check beside it. Select OK and close the Security Center window.

14

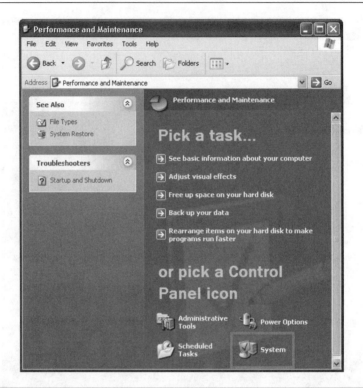

FIGURE 14-8   Remote host System icon.

8. Your PC is now ready to accept a connection from your iPAQ, but first you need the network name of your PC. To get that, you need to go back to the Performance and Maintenance tab and select System, then select the Computer Name tab, as shown in Figure 14-12, and write down or remember the computer name.

That's it. Remember to keep your PC running and connected to the Internet; it is also a good idea to lock it while you are not using it.

Set Up Remote Desktop on Your iPAQ (the Client)   The steps to ensure that your Windows XP computer is ready to accept connections from your iPAQ are listed in the previous section. In this section, we will discuss what you need to do to begin using Terminal Services/Remote Desktop functionality on your iPAQ.

1. Ensure that you have a network connect to the Internet or intranet that will be capable of providing the connection path to the host computer; in this example, a Windows XP desktop computer.

2. On your iPAQ, select the Start menu button and then select Programs.

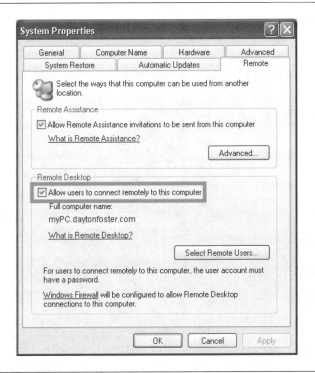

FIGURE 14-9 Remote host Allow Users to Connect.

3. On the Programs screen, find and select the Terminal Services Client icon, as shown in Figure 14-13. If you don't have the Terminal Services Client icon, you can download the Terminal Services client application for free from Microsoft at **www.microsoft.com/ windowsmobile/downloads/terminalserver.mspx**.

4. You should now see the screen shown in Figure 14-14. Using the onscreen keyboard, enter either an IP address or a fully qualified domain name for the remote computer to connect to.

5. After you've entered the computer address in the Server field, select the Connect button. If the remote computer is reachable, you'll soon see its desktop and a logon prompt. If you get a connection error, verify that the remote computer has Remote Desktop or Terminal Services enabled, and if a firewall is in between, ensure that port 3389 is open in the firewall.

6. You will be prompted to log on to the host PC. Do so.

14

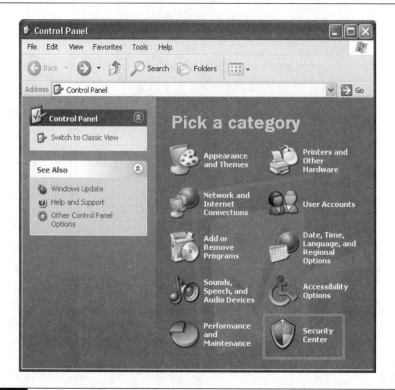

FIGURE 14-10 Remote host Security icon.

7. Once you are connected and logged on to the host computer with Terminal Services, you will see a small version of the screen of the host PC. You will need to use the scroll bars to navigate around the screen to do the type of things that you need to do. Using Terminal Services, you can interact with your PC or a server in much the same way that you can when you are sitting in front of it, although the performance will likely be slower and, of course, you can't see the entire screen very well at one time.

A couple of tips to help you use Terminal Services on your iPAQ:

- Dialog boxes often pop up in the middle of the host computer screen. If your iPAQ is not focused on the center of the screen, you may not see the dialog until you scroll around. If it seems like you can't do anything on the host PC, it may be that it is waiting for you to close a dialog, so remember to scroll around to ensure that isn't the case.

- Buttons at the bottom of the iPAQ Terminal Service client, as shown in Figure 14-15, allow you to quickly refocus the screen on specific sections of the screen instead of using the scroll bars.

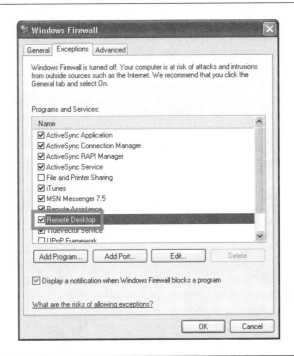

Remote host XP Firewall settings: Remote Desktop option.

Where to Find More Corporate Applications for Your iPAQ

As smart mobile devices such as your wonderful HP iPAQ continue to gain in popularity, more and more software developers will release software for Pocket PC/Windows Mobile. There are a lot of iPAQ fan websites that cover all sorts of topics relating to your iPAQ. In addition, there are also excellent resources for finding enterprise software. A few examples are listed here:

- Pocket PC Magazine Enterprise Solutions Section (**www.pocketpcmag.com/_top/enterprise.asp**)

- Microsoft Windows Mobile Business Solutions Website (**www.microsoft.com/windowsmobile**)

- Pocket Gear Business Software list (**www.pocketgear.com/software_browse.asp?cat=3**)

14

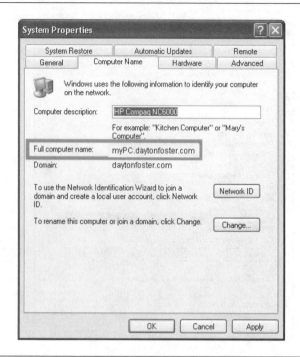

FIGURE 14-12   Remote host: record the Computer Name.

FIGURE 14-13   iPAQ Terminal Services Client icon.

FIGURE 14-14   iPAQ Terminal Services screen.

Wrap It Up

The HP iPAQ has become a valuable tool in the technology toolbox of many modern businesses. The benefits of mobility are clear, and HP is leading the way (with a little help from Microsoft, of course). Only a few years ago, mobile devices and networks were designed specifically to allow users to make and receive wireless phone calls. The iPAQ offers a quantum leap forward in mobile technology. Microsoft has extended tried-and-true mobile phone technologies to allow us to send and receive e-mail from virtually anywhere. The promise of a true mobile office has never been closer.

Arguably, getting the e-mail functionality set up on your iPAQ for the first time may be the most confusing and challenging part of configuring your iPAQ. However, armed with the information in this chapter, you should be well on your way.

As soon as your e-mail is configured, you might want to begin finding out what other neat and useful stuff you can use your iPAQs for. This chapter covered just a fraction of the types of enterprise software that you can run on your iPAQ, including software for IT people, financial professionals, and salespeople, as well as some software that can be useful to anyone that works in an office.

14

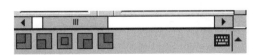

FIGURE 14-15   iPAQ Terminal Services navigation buttons.

Part IV

Optimize and Secure Your iPAQ

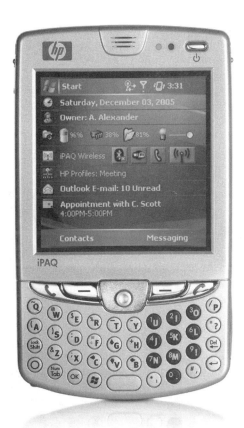

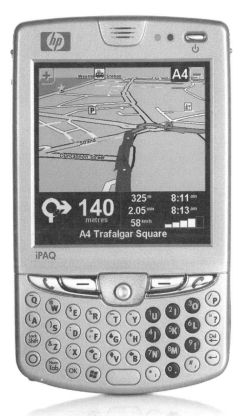

Chapter 15

Optimize Your iPAQ

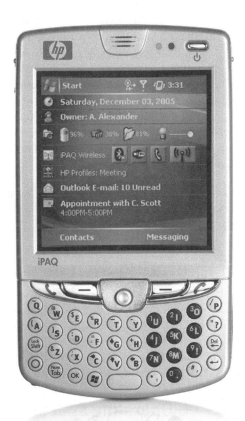
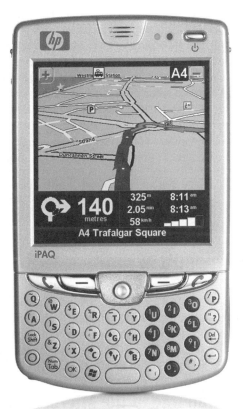

How to...

- Identify key differences between Windows Mobile 5 and previous versions
- Manage your iPAQ memory
- Increase the memory capacity of your iPAQ with removable memory cards
- Maximize the battery life of your iPAQ
- Find third-party applications to help optimize your iPAQ

Virtually everything around you is more effective under certain conditions than in other circumstances; even people get more accomplished under some conditions than others, and technology is no exception to the rule. There are ways you can help your technical assets perform at optimal levels. There are specific actions you can take to ensure your iPAQ is performing as well as it can. Assuming you use a home or work PC, you are likely painfully aware that certain things slow your PC down. Things like running too many applications at once, using all of the available memory, or inadvertently collecting viruses or spyware applications from the Internet, all of which use system resources and can affect how your PC runs.

This chapter discusses some of the primary ways you can get the most out of your iPAQ through memory management, file management, and battery life extension. Some of the steps you can take to optimize your iPAQ involve using tools, tips, and tricks in the Pocket PC/Windows Mobile operating system, and others involve using third-party tools for assistance.

If you don't need it, delete it—or at least move it to your PC. As a general rule, if there are files or programs you don't use on a regular basis, it is a good idea to delete them or move them to your PC with ActiveSync to free up memory on your iPAQ.

The Microsoft Windows Mobile 5 Operating System

There are so many versions and models of the iPAQ on the market that is difficult to effectively cover every idiosyncrasy between the models. That said, the latest iPAQ models will ship with Windows Mobile 5 operating system, including the hx2190, hx2490, hx2790, and the 6500 series. If you have Windows Mobile 5 on your iPAQ or your iPAQ did not ship with Windows Mobile 5 installed but is upgradeable to Windows Mobile 5 (HP offers Windows Mobile 5 upgrades on specific iPAQs including the hx2100, hx2400, hx2700, and hx4700 series), then this section is for your information.

The Timeline of the Microsoft Pocket PC Operating System

In case you are interested in history, following is the timeline of the continuing evolution of the Windows Mobile operating system.

- **Late 2005** Windows Mobile 2005 upgrade available for hx2100, hx2400, hx2700, and hx4700 iPAQs
- **May 2005** Windows Mobile 2005 ships

- ■ **March 2004**   Windows Mobile 2003 Second Edition update released

- ■ **June 2003**   Windows Mobile 2003 released

- ■ **October 2001**   Pocket PC 2002 released

- ■ **April 2000**   Pocket PC 2000 (Palm-size PC v2) released

- ■ **January 8, 1998**   Palm PC v1.0/1.2 released; three months later, "Palm PC" was renamed to "Palm-size PC," so both names refer to the same operating system.

About Persistent Memory in Microsoft Windows Mobile 5

A key improvement included in the Windows Mobile 5 operating system is the inclusion of "persistent storage," which is just one way to name "memory that doesn't get deleted when the battery runs dead"; that is, it persists. If you have an iPAQ or experience with handhelds that did not have persistent storage, you likely have had the unfortunate experience of the handheld going dead or resetting, only to have to resynchronize all of your PIM (Personal Information Management) information and reinstall your applications. This process can be time consuming and inconvenient. (You may use other words to describe the experience if you like.) It has only taken six iterations and eight years for Microsoft to evolve the Windows Mobile operating system enough to deal with this problem. (Not to be too harsh on Microsoft—there are good reasons it was not dealt with earlier.) The good news is that Windows Mobile 5 offers persistent storage to help prevent you from losing your iPAQ data and applications.

The net effect of persistent storage on your iPAQ is your personal data, user-installed applications, and updates are stored in nonvolatile flash ROM (Read Only Memory) and that RAM (Random Access Memory: essentially short-term memory that is only 'remembered' when the iPAQ has power) is now reserved only for running programs, in much the same way it works on your desktop PC. This means that applications can no longer be installed in RAM. The big advantage is you don't lose your data, your installed programs, or your system configuration if your iPAQ battery runs dead.

Before Windows Mobile 5 and persistent storage, up to 30 percent of the battery power was allocated to the task of saving data. Persistent storage frees up the 30 percent of battery power that was formerly used to keep data in RAM.

TIP

RAM or Random Access Memory, is a type of memory chip referred to as "volatile" memory. Volatile memory requires a constant flow of electricity to retain the data stored within it. RAM is the type of memory in your desktop PC and is used to run programs and to store active data files. When you turn off your desktop PC, the power to RAM is shut off, and when you turn your PC back on, part of the boot process moves data back to the empty RAM.

TIP

ROM or Read Only Memory is "nonvolatile" memory. Nonvolatile memory does not require a constant power source to retain its data. This is the type of memory that is found in removable memory cards such as CompactFlash and Secure Digital cards. The data stored in ROM memory is only lost when it is purposely deleted.

15

A Reiteration of How Persistent Memory in Windows Mobile 5 Is a Benefit

To summarize the key points presented in this section, there are two benefits of persistent memory relating to how it allows our iPAQs to run better and longer:

■ Data, user-installed applications, and iPAQ settings are not lost when the battery runs dead, which is what happens in previous versions of the Windows Mobile operating system.

■ Battery life is longer than with previous versions of the Windows Mobile operating system because battery power is no longer required to keep data, user-installed applications, and iPAQ settings in RAM.

Manage Your iPAQ Memory Using Windows Mobile

Built in to the Microsoft Windows Mobile 2003 Second Edition operating system are some excellent built-in tools to help you allocate and manage the memory on your iPAQ. For example, the Memory Control screen allows you to:

■ View how much memory is in use versus how much is free in both the iPAQ RAM memory and on SD/CF memory cards.

■ Change how much memory is allocated to file storage and how much is allocated to program use.

■ Find the largest files in memory.

■ View the Running Program List; this allows you to see what is running at a specific time and stop applications you are not using to free up system resources.

Manage Memory Using the Memory screen

To access the Memory screen, simply follow these steps:

1. Select Start | Settings.

2. Select the System tab, then select the Memory icon, as shown in Figure 15-1.

3. In the Memory screen, three tabs allow you to optimize how your iPAQ is using memory, both the iPAQ RAM memory and any removable memory cards that are in your iPAQ. Removable memory cards are covered in this chapter under the heading "Increase the Memory of Your iPAQ."

View and Manage How Your iPAQ RAM Memory Is Allocated

You have the flexibility to change how much memory is allocated to file storage and how much is allocated to program use. Figure 15-2 shows that Dayton's iPAQ has a total of 57.78MB of main memory available to programs and file storage.

FIGURE 15-1 Memory icon.

You can adjust the ratio of memory allocated to file storage versus that available to programs by clicking and dragging the slider on the screen, as shown in Figure 15-3. The default setting is 50:50, so on Dayton's iPAQ, 29MB is allocated to files and the other 29MB is allocated to programs, but he can change the allocation any time.

Why would you want to change the memory allocation to favor either file storage or programs? The answer really depends on how you use your iPAQ. For example, if you don't run third-party applications other than what your iPAQ shipped with and you store a lot of Word, Excel, or music files in memory, it would likely be beneficial to allocate more of your memory to storage.

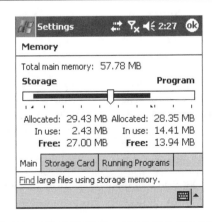

FIGURE 15-2 Memory, main tab.

15

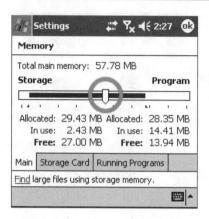

FIGURE 15-3 Memory slider.

However, the reverse may be true: if you store all of your data files on removable storage cards but download every new piece of software that shows up on Handango (**www.handango.com**) and play music while you are reading e-mail or taking photos, then your iPAQ would likely run better if you allocate more memory to programs. Ultimately, you may need to try a few different settings to find the optimal setting to match the way you use your iPAQ.

 If you are receiving Out of Memory or Program Memory Low errors, it is important to consider what you or your iPAQ is doing when the error occurs so you can troubleshoot to overcome the problem. For example, if you are installing an application and you receive an Out of Memory error, depending on how much total free memory you have on your iPAQ, you may be able to overcome the situation simply by allocating more memory to programs and then trying to install the program again. Keep in mind, however, that this reduces the memory that is available to file storage.

View Available Memory

The Storage Card tab in the Memory Settings allows you to see how much memory is available on your Secure Digital (SD) and/or CompactFlash (CF) removable memory cards, as shown in Figure 15-4. You can see that Dayton's SD card has only 156MB out of 332.25MB left available. This is good information to know before you try to download a file to the card.

Find the Largest Files in Memory

You can find the largest files that are stored in memory; in fact, you can find files with several different criteria. For example, as shown in Figure 15-5, you can search for any files larger than 64KB in size.

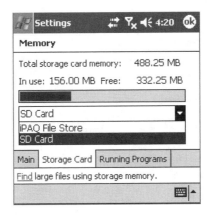

FIGURE 15-4 Memory, Storage Card tab.

TIP

One reason that the Help option is available in the Find screen Type drop-down list is that help files can take up a significant amount of memory. The Find screen allows you to quickly find help files and frees up memory by deleting the help files we don't use.

This allows you to see which large files you have in memory. If you don't need them, you can either delete them or move them to your PC the next time you ActiveSync.

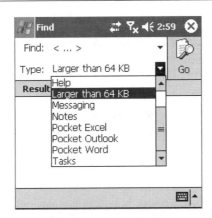

FIGURE 15-5 Find File Larger than 64KB.

15

FIGURE 15-6   Running Programs.

View the Running Program List

Often programs run in the background that you are not actively using. It makes sense to run only the programs you want to use at a given time in order to free up memory and system resources, such as processing time, to ensure your iPAQ is running the best it can.

This allows you to see what is running at a specific time and stop applications you are not using to free up system resources. To see which programs are running, follow these steps:

1. If you are not already on the Memory screen, select Start | Settings.

2. Select the System tab, then select the Memory icon.

3. Select the Running Programs tab; you will see a screen that looks like Figure 15-6.

In the Running Programs screen, you can see all of the programs that are running. You have several options: Activate, Stop, or Stop All.

- **Activate** When you select an application from the Running Program List and select the Activate button, the Memory screen will close and the selected application will be brought up.

- **Stop** When you select an application and select the Stop button, the application will be stopped or shut down.

- **Stop All** Selecting this option shuts down all running applications and leaves you with only the operating system running.

Increase the Memory of Your iPAQ

Your iPAQ has limited onboard memory and depending on how you use your iPAQ on a day-to-day basis, you might find your iPAQ runs out of memory. Once this happens, it will likely be a regular nuisance. The ability to store data on removable memory cards has some significant advantages:

■ Removable memory cards are persistent memory, which means they don't require power to retain information. Even if your iPAQ battery completely drains, your memory card will not "forget" its information, while data stored in the iPAQ RAM memory may be lost in this scenario. Note: MS Windows Mobile 5 has persistent memory, which removes some of this risk.

■ Memory cards are relatively inexpensive and highly portable. You can even swap cards between any device that supports the card format (CF or SD), such as other mobile devices, cameras, and even some laptops.

■ Memory cards offer the ability to organize your files. As a simple example, you can keep similar types of music MP3 files on different cards (hip-hop on one card, R&B on one card, and rap on another card, for example.)

■ By storing applications and files on memory cards, you are able to free up your on- device memory to take care of whatever memory your iPAQ needs at a given moment.

TIP *If you store an application on a memory card, when you run that application it will be copied temporarily to the iPAQ RAM memory where it will be run. When you are finished with the application, it will be removed from temporary iPAQ RAM memory to free up the memory for other purposes.*

Most iPAQs have at least one slot for removable memory cards. The two most common types of cards for the iPAQ are the CF and the SD cards. The types of data you can store on a removable memory card include:

■ Pictures

■ MP3 and other audio files

■ Movies, recorded TV, and other video

■ Games

■ E-books

■ Applications

■ Databases

The following list contains a few iPAQ models and the memory card compatibility for each one. The list does not cover every iPAQ model; if your model isn't listed, refer to your user guide or check the Hewlett Packard website (**www.hp.com**) to find out what type of card you need.

15

1700 Series	Secure Digital slot
2200 Series	Secure Digital and CompactFlash slots
2700 Series	Secure Digital and CompactFlash slots
2400 Series	Secure Digital and CompactFlash slots
3100 Series	Secure Digital slot
3700 Series	Secure Digital slot
4100 Series	Secure Digital slot
4300 Series	Secure Digital slot
4700 Series	Secure Digital and CompactFlash slots
6300 Series	Secure Digital slot
6400 Series	Secure Digital slot
6500 Series	Secure Digital slot and mini SD slot

Secure Digital vs. CompactFlash Cards

Your iPAQ may have a slot for at least one type of removable memory card, and some models
have two card slots. The three types of cards that iPAQ devices use are SD, mini-SD, and CF,
cards. If you don't already own an appropriate memory card, check your iPAQ user guide
to see which one(s) your iPAQ uses. SD and CF cards are not compatible, so ensure you are

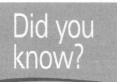

What You Need to Know about Secure Digital and Multimedia Memory Cards

If your iPAQ has a SD card slot, you should know about another card type called
Multimedia (MMC) cards. Even though your iPAQ user documentation states your iPAQ
is compatible with SD cards, it can also use MMC cards. What is the difference? The cards
are the same size and look about the same, but inside they are very different. The SD
card standard evolved from the MMC card specification and includes new technology
such as the ability to encrypt the data stored on the card. This is specifically designed for
copywritten material such as music and movies, as well as other media and programs.
Another improvement included in SD cards is that SD cards have at least a four times faster
data transfer rate than MMC cards. One of the most significant differences between the two
cards is price. Generally speaking, MMC cards are a fraction of the cost of SD cards. Pricing
is changing constantly as technology improves, but we recommend comparing the prices
between comparable MMC and SD cards before you spend your hard earned money.

buying the correct format for your iPAQ. There is also a third type of memory card called a MMC that you should be aware of if your iPAQ uses SD cards. MMC cards are discussed in the Did You Know box, "What You Need to Know about Secure Digital and Multimedia Memory Cards."

Copy Files and Applications to a Removable Memory Card

To free up memory in your iPAQ RAM, you can move files and applications to a removable memory card. There are a couple different ways to do it; here is one way that is very similar to how you move files on a PC with the added twist of using the tap and hold method that is unique to devices such as your iPAQ.

1. On your iPAQ, if you are not already in File Explorer, select the Start button.
2. Select Programs | File Explorer.
3. Browse to the file you want to move.
4. Tap and hold on the document you want to move (you can also do this with menus).
5. When the pop-up menu comes up, select Cut.
6. Select My Device to browse a complete list of folders.
7. Select either the storage card or CF card.
8. On the screen, tap and hold in the new destination folder.
9. When the menu pops up, select Paste.

Change Your Camera Settings to Automatically Save Photos to a Memory Card

Your iPAQ is likely equipped with a SD and/or CF Card slot(s) that allows you use removable memory cards. Your iPAQ has a limited amount of available onboard memory for files, applications, and pictures, so the ability to expand the memory is extremely useful. In fact, SD/CF cards are commonly available in sizes as small as 64MB and as large as 8GB. Another advantage to them is that if you ever have to perform a hard reset on your iPAQ, all of the memory will be wiped out, but anything stored on your SD/CF memory cards will remain intact. Digital photos and configuring your iPAQ camera are covered in Chapter 6, and the steps to save photos to a memory card are covered there under the heading "Automatically Save Photos to a Memory Card."

There are at least four reasons why storing photos and other data on memory cards is a good idea:

1. You will almost certainly be able to store more photos on a memory card than in local memory on your iPAQ, especially since large cards of several gigabytes are constantly coming down in price.
2. You can easily swap memory cards when one gets full or organize photos into different categories.

15

3. Memory cards are more stable than on-device memory. If for some reason there is a problem with your iPAQ and you lose data, photos and data stored on a memory card will likely not be affected.

4. If you have a card reader for SD or CF cards you can easily pop out the memory card from your iPAQ to read the photos from the card without needing to synchronize your iPAQ. This can be a much faster method of transferring photos.

Maximize the Battery Life of Your iPAQ

There are some simple ways you can prolong the battery life of your iPAQ by adjusting some of the settings in Windows Mobile.

Save Your Battery by Configuring Your iPAQ Settings

Your iPAQ offers several configurable options regarding your screen settings to help you maximize your battery life including Power, Backlight, and Beam settings.

Configure Your Power Settings to Save Your Battery

Windows Mobile allows you to configure your power settings. In addition to being able to see how much battery strength you have and approximately how much more time you have left before it runs dead, you can also do such things as:

- Define how much time passes when the iPAQ is inactive before your iPAQ goes into Standby mode, both when it is plugged into AC power and when it is on battery power.

- Change your Standby settings. Standby is also called Suspend or Off and is the state that the iPAQ is in when it looks like it is powered off. In reality, the iPAQ is not off, it is just not being used and the battery power is still being consumed to keep user data and programs in RAM. This means that as long as the Standby period has not elapsed, your data and programs that are in nonpersistent memory (RAM), will not be lost. However, when the Standby period has elapsed the battery power will no longer be used to maintain memory, and you will lose anything stored in RAM.

- Configure whether you want charging to be fast or slow when your iPAQ is charging through a USB cable.

Steps to Access and Modify Your Power Settings   The Power configuration screens are found under Settings and can be accessed by following these steps:

1. Select the Start menu or button.

2. Select Settings and the System tab.

3. Select the Power icon, as shown in Figure 15-7.

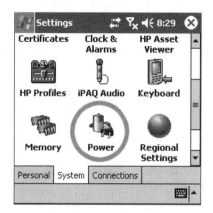

FIGURE 15-7 Power icon.

4. Once the Power screen is open, you will see four tabs:

   a. Main Allows you to see how much battery you currently have left, as shown in Figure 15-8.

   b. Advanced Allows you to define how much time will pass when your iPAQ is inactive before it goes into Standby mode, both when charging and when on battery power. A lower time interval will preserve your battery better than longer intervals.

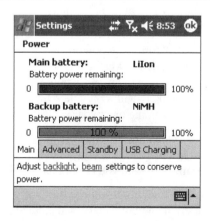

15

FIGURE 15-8 Power, Main tab.

c. **Standby**   Allows you to define how long your iPAQ will use battery power to keep data and programs in RAM. When this time interval has elapsed, battery power will no longer be used to keep data in RAM and you will lose data but, provided you have more battery power left, your iPAQ will still function. A low standby interval will allow your iPAQ to go longer between charges but you will more quickly lose data not stored in ROM (essentially only includes the programs your iPAQ shipped with).

d. **USB Charging**   This relatively straightforward tab allows you to define whether you need fast or slow charging when charging your iPAQ though a USB synchronization cable.

Configure Your Backlight Settings to Save Your Battery

Another effective way to slow the drain of your battery and prolong the life of your iPAQ, between charges anyway, is to change the configuration of your backlight settings. Backlight is a fancy way of referring to the screen light intensity. The screen on your iPAQ has significant power requirements, and minimizing when it is on and how bright it is when it is on will help prolong your battery life. You can access the Backlight settings on your iPAQ by following these steps, which also include some descriptions of the settings:

1. Select Start, then select Settings.

2. Select the System tab and select the Backlight icon.

3. In the Backlight screen you will see three tabs:

   a. **Battery Power**   Includes two check boxes:

       i. The first check box ("Turn off backlight if device is not used for") allows you to define how much time should pass when your iPAQ is not being used before the screen automatically turns off. A lower setting helps keep power consumption down, but if it is too low you may find it annoying so you may want to play with the setting to find the best setting for you.

       ii. The second check box ("Turn on backlight when a button is pressed or the screen is tapped") allows you to define whether the screen should automatically turn back on when you touch the screen or press a button. If you regularly carry your iPAQ in a pocket or case you likely will want to turn this flag off as it will prevent your iPAQ from accidentally turning on in your pocket or in your case.

   b. **AC Power** (may also be called the External Power tab)   Essentially the same settings as on the Battery Power tab but they are applied to when your iPAQ is charging and don't do much to help you prolong battery life.

   c. **Brightness**   This feature is an important one because, as mentioned earlier, your screen is a significant drain on your battery, and reducing the brightness reduces how much power is required to run. The first time you turn down the brightness you may feel like it is too dark, but give it a shot, you will likely find that after a while you don't even notice the difference. Of course, like most of the other settings on your iPAQ, a little trial and error is likely in order to find the optimal setting.

Other Ways to Save Your Battery

There are a few less obvious ways you can slow your battery drain:

■ **Save your battery by minimizing how often your e-mail application polls for new messages**   If you have an e-mail application on your iPAQ, it likely checks for e-mail on a regular basis. It is a good idea to make sure that it isn't checking for e-mail (also called polling) too often. Every time your e-mail application polls your e-mail server, it drains your battery. When you think about it, most of us don't really need to receive e-mail on a real time basis and a 15 minute lag isn't really noticeable.

■ **Save your battery by using dark colors for your user interface**   Your iPAQ uses much more power to display white and light colors than it does to display black or other dark colors. By changing your user interface colors from the default to darker colors you can slow the drain on your iPAQ battery. There are a ton of applications that allow you to modify your iPAQ user interface colors, and a quick search for something like "Pocket PC Themes" or "Pocket PC Theme generator" in your favorite Internet search engine will likely turn up several. You can also check out **www.handango.com** or **www.windowsmarketplace.com** to see what they have to offer. We have seen theme software as inexpensive as free, or $1 to $30.

■ **Turn off the Receive All Incoming Beams feature on your iPAQ**   Pocket PCs equipped with IR (infrared) ports are capable of sending and receiving beamed data wirelessly at close, point-to-point, distances. By default your iPAQ is configured to receive all incoming beams. The problem with that is that sunlight can cause an iPAQ to start trying to accept an incoming message over the IR port. This effort requires extensive processing power and can drain your battery faster than you would like. To disable this setting, launch the Start menu, select the Settings menu, select the Connections tab, select the Beam icon, and uncheck the Receive All Incoming Beams check box. You will have to remember to enable this feature when you want to receive a beam in the future, but this will prolong your battery life.

What Other Tools Are Available to Optimize Your iPAQ?

As we have said many times in this book, one of the best things about the iPAQ community is that there are always enterprising software developers identifying opportunities to add value for the legion of iPAQ users. Tools to help you help your iPAQ to run better are available for download at reasonable prices. These third-party tools tend to fall into three broad categories:

15

■ Tools that help you manage your system resources such as memory and applications

■ Tools that allow you to compress files stored on your iPAQ so that the files take up less room allowing you to store even more data

■ Tools that help you maximize your battery life

We have listed a few of the available tools to help you optimize your iPAQ. As always, keep in mind that new products are released constantly, so it is a good idea to search the Web when you are ready to try software out. In addition, it is always a good idea to try products and read user reviews before you buy. User reviews can be helpful but are usually best when taken with a little salt as we all have a slightly different perception on what good and bad mean, and we also have different technical experience and background, obviously.

Tools That Allow You to Compress Files Stored on Your iPAQ

It seems that one thing you never have enough of, besides time, is memory on your PCs and iPAQs. Some software developers recognize this reality and have built tools to make your life easier (for a price, of course):

- **SpaceMaker by dmdSOFTWARE** Available online from such websites as **www.handango.com** or **www.pocketgear.com**; costs about $7. This automatically begins working on system restart to help you identify and delete temporary files by monitoring things that can unnecessarily take up memory such as:

  - Internet Explorer trash, cookies, and cache
  - ActiveSync trash
  - Windows CE and other application temporary files
  - "Trash" on storage cards

- **Resco Explorer 2005 for Pocket PC by Resco (www.resco.net)** Costs about $25 and provides you with File Explorer functionality that allows you to compress files with built-in Zip tools, encrypt files, view registry entries, and view text and image files. This application has won awards from *Pocket PC Magazine* and been nominated for awards by Handango (**www.handango.com**).

- **WinMobileZip by ADISASTA (www.adisasta.com)** Costs roughly $20 and offers two primary functions, serving as a file compression utility to save storage space and as a security tool to safe guard your sensitive data using Advanced Encryption Standard (AES)

- **Pocket Mechanic by Omega One Software (www.omegaone.com/pocketpc)** Costs about $15 and is a utility designed to optimize removable memory storage cards. The software allows you to perform maintenance on your removable memory cards and iPAQ including:

  - Formatting, defragmenting, scanning, repairing, and testing for physical errors
  - Deleting files
  - Using a storage card benchmark that measures raw card read/write speed
  - Performing system cleanup such as deleting unused temporary and cached files
  - Securing the delete feature by overwriting your sensitive data before deleting to guarantee your privacy

Tools That Help You Maximize Your Battery Life

Extending how long you can use your iPAQ between charges largely determines how useful your iPAQ is. In addition to the built-in tools for maximizing battery life in the Operating System setting as discussed earlier in this chapter in the section "Manage Your iPAQ Memory Using Windows Mobile," there are several third-party software utilities that help you manage and reduce your battery power use. We only list one of these utilities here so you get an idea of what is on the market, but a quick Internet search will give you a better idea of all of the tools that are out there. As usual, they range in price from free to about $20.

Battery Pack Pro by Omega One Software (**www.omegaone.com**) costs about $30 and, among other things such as deleting unused data and closing unused applications, the software equips you with an application bar on your Today page, shown in Figure 15-9. This allows you to take several actions right from the Today page such as:

- Closing programs

- Displaying battery, memory, and storage card life

- Automatically removing unwanted files

- Adjusting Calendar, Task, and Alarm sounds to repeat or change volume (useful in a theater or other venue where you don't want your iPAQ to make noise)

- Launching detailed graphical battery, memory, and storage card information

- Activating a function called "Power Light," designed to turn your iPAQ screen into an impromptu flashlight, which can be effective for finding a keyhole in a dark alley, for example

15

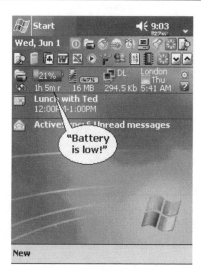

FIGURE 15-9   Battery Pack Pro.

Wrap It Up

After reading this chapter, you should have a keen understanding of some of the new features in Windows Mobile 5 that help optimize your iPAQ. You also learned ways to configure your iPAQ using the Settings functions to manage your memory, power usage, and screen settings, among other things. We discussed removable memory cards in both CompactFlash and Secure Digital formats and talked about why they are powerful must-have tools for the iPAQ user. Last, we talked about just a few software utilities designed to help optimize your iPAQ with regard to efficient use of memory and battery power. Many of the topics presented here are tools to add to your tool belt. As with any tool, you may need to play with the settings a bit to find the best configuration to suit the way you use your iPAQ. The biggest step may simply be to understand which iPAQ settings and behaviors we can change.

Chapter 16

Secure Your iPAQ

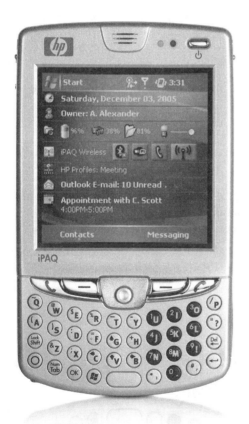

How to...

- ■ Identify security risks
- ■ Take precautions to minimize security risks for both noncorporate and corporate iPAQ users
- ■ Use third-party software to secure your iPAQ data and connections

This chapter discusses both personal and corporate security topics because many risks are common to both corporations and individual iPAQ users. The topics common to both individuals and corporations are discussed first in the chapter; topics that are more relevant to corporations are discussed later in the chapter. It is a good idea to understand the potential risks as well as the steps you can take to reduce the risks and therefore your exposure.

How This Chapter Is Laid Out

Security is a broad topic, but it need not be overly complicated. This chapter is basically divided into two sections:

1. Security precautions that all iPAQ users should consider
2. Security precautions that corporate iPAQ users and corporate security professionals should consider

To understand the difference between a corporate iPAQ user and a noncorporate iPAQ user for the purposes of this chapter, see the box "Our Definition of a Corporate iPAQ User."

Many of the security risks listed in this chapter pertain more to iPAQs that have wireless capability, but the topics covering on-device security and virus protection certainly apply to nonwireless iPAQs as well.

Our Definition of a Corporate iPAQ User?

The corporate iPAQ user uses their iPAQ to connect to a corporate or organizational computer network; the way they connect may range from connecting an iPAQ to a work PC through a synchronization cable to using company WiFi networks and company e-mail on their iPAQ.

What Are the Security Risks Associated with Your iPAQ?

Portable mobile wireless devices like your iPAQ continue to be hot topics in the press, and not all of the press is positive. Interestingly enough, the primary qualities that make mobile devices like your iPAQ so useful and convenient are the same attributes that make them open to security risks. Your iPAQ is small and portable, which means it is easy to misplace or have stolen. Your iPAQ is capable of storing large amounts of personal and corporate information, which means that the consequences of losing it can be significant if it gets into the wrong hands. If your iPAQ has wireless connectivity, you have the benefit of being able to send and receive e-mail, browse the Web, play games, and perform countless other tasks, but this also means there is a relatively unguarded path for malicious programming code to be inadvertently transferred onto your iPAQ and possibly on to your PC.

There are two general categories of security risks:

- Damage caused by personal or corporate information falling into the wrong hands. This is typically a result of losing an iPAQ or memory card, or having it stolen.

> **NOTE** *There is a much smaller risk of having data scanned out of the air when using a wireless connection. One of the security concerns with wireless is that there exists the possibility that a device designed to intercept data as it is sent from one wireless device to another over a wireless network, may intercept and misuse the information. Fortunately, this risk is significantly lower than in the past as most networks incorporate encryption so that even if your data is intercepted, it will be incomprehensible.*

- Damage caused by viruses and other malicious or poorly engineered software,

The Risk Associated with Your iPAQ Being Lost or Stolen

As stated earlier, the two primary qualities that make your iPAQ so useful and convenient are the same attributes that make these devices possible security risks. Your iPAQ is a compact, powerful device with enough memory to store between 25 and 152MB of data in memory and, if you have Secure Digital (SD) or Compact Flash (CF) memory cards, it is capable of storing up to 8GB of additional data per card. This is a significant leap ahead in mobile computing, but it also means that if your iPAQ is lost or stolen, your e-mails, documents, spreadsheets, pictures, and other data are in grave danger of being misused.

So what's the big deal? Most of us feel that our personal data would not be very useful to anyone else or damaging to ourselves, but personal information can be very damaging if it gets into the hands of people who know how to use it for their benefit. If you use your iPAQ for work as well as for personal data, the security risk can be many times higher than the risk for someone who uses the iPAQ strictly for personal data; the level of risk depends on the nature of your work.

The security risks are usually much greater for companies, and these risks, as well as preventive measures that should be taken, are presented later in this chapter under the heading "Other Security Measures Specifically for Corporations."

16

Research information collected by David Melnick, Mark Dinman, and Alexander Muratov for the book *PDA Security: Incorporating Handhelds into the Enterprise* (McGraw-Hill/Osborne, 2003) collects feedback from executives around the U.S. who reveal the types of information commonly stored on wireless mobile devices:

- **Network passwords**   Obviously, your iPAQ is a very convenient place to store those hard-to-remember usernames and passwords. The risk is that if the wrong person gets a hold of this information, there can be a gateway into your entire network, critical data, and systems to which you have access.

- **Customer information**   According to many executives, customer information getting into the wrong hands is a public relations nightmare and possibly a lawsuit waiting to happen. In the financial services sector, if customer data leaks, the company is legally obligated to contact every customer to inform them that their personal information may have been compromised. And wouldn't it be less than ideal if a competitor somehow got your customer list and contact information?

- **Press releases**   If your organization routinely shares pre-press release information via e-mail, or if an employee works on public relations documents on their iPAQ, there is the risk of private information being released to the public long before it was intended to be released. This is especially risky if your company is publicly traded. In the U.S., the Securities and Exchange Commission (SEC) has very strict rules about releasing information before public distribution. Remember Enron and Martha Stewart?

- **Bank account numbers and credit card information**   This type of information is commonly stored on mobile devices, even though many of us know better. But it is just so darned convenient. A user is even more likely to store this information as Internet purchasing and banking transactions become more common. The risks here are relatively obvious: if an unscrupulous person gets your credit card number, there is a good chance you may be financing something like a world-class collection of a rare Beanie Babies for someone you don't even know.

- **Corporate financial information**   E-mail is generally the way most organizations share information. Users routinely exchange spreadsheets and other documents as attachments. You may be surprised at just how much inside information you keep in your e-mail inbox. Whether it's an in-progress annual report or the internal projections for next quarter's sales, the inadvertent leak of financial data may have a serious and long-lasting impact on your organization.

- **E-mail**   Again, there is no telling what kind of information a mobile device user has conveniently stored in their e-mail. When you stop to consider it, there is likely a significant amount of information you'd prefer to keep private.

- **Intranet access**   Are you familiar with the term "The keys to the castle?" Users who work for companies that have corporate intranet sites, websites not meant for use by anyone outside the company, often store username and password information on their mobile devices. This risk is relatively obvious, but the other risk is that many web browsers allow the cache of login information. This means that anyone who picks up an iPAQ can access a corporate intranet by simply choosing a shortcut or web favorite and clicking "login." This provides an ultra-convenient way for someone to gain insider knowledge about an organization.

- **Price lists**   Consider this scenario. Your best salesperson just finished a meeting with a valued long-time customer, and when she left the meeting she forgot her iPAQ on a chair in the boardroom. The customer picks up the iPAQ to return it and notices some interesting information on the screen: the prices that a major competitor has been paying your company for products. "My largest competitor is getting a better deal than I am?!" This situation may cause irreparable damage to the relationship and cost the organization dearly.

- **Employee information**   Privacy legislation does not look favorably on an organization publicly sharing employee information, whether it is an intended disclosure or not. If employee information is publicized, the potential costs include litigation and the significant negative impact of bad publicity.

- **Medical (HIPAA) information**   This point is aimed directly at organizations that are involved in health care. The U.S. Health Insurance Portability and Accountability Act of 1996 (HIPAA) deals with the privacy of patient records and other health care information. Mobile devices are very popular with doctors and health care workers, because there are many applications designed specifically for medical information uses. If a mobile device containing patient information is lost or stolen and HIPAA rules are violated, the fines can be upwards of $50,000. The negative backlash that could occur because of a security breach could be devastating for a health care organization. After all, if you can't trust your doctors and nurses, who can you trust with your private information? More information about HIPAA is available at **www.cms.hhs.gov**.

See the section in this chapter called "Enterprise Network Authentication and Encryption Solutions" for solutions to help minimize these risks.

The Risk of Damage Resulting from Viruses and Malicious Code

You are likely familiar with viruses that spread through the Internet. Examples of well-known viruses include Mydoom, Chernobyl, and Anna Kornakova, but new viruses are released many times per day. If you have ever had the misfortune of having your PC infected by a virus, you understand the amount of inconvenience that can be caused. For example, Dayton once sat in an office with a coworker who had his entire hard drive erased by a version of the Chernobyl virus. It is an understatement to say that it was not a fun day for him. In fact, he permanently lost a significant amount of data, not to mention the time he lost rebuilding his laptop. In addition to the inconvenience factor, viruses can be very expensive for the organizations that fall victim to them.

Wireless Mobile Device Sold on eBay for $15.50 Reveals Bank's Secrets?

A former vice president from a major financial services firm decided that he no longer needed his wireless mobile device. He had bought the device with his own money and had been using it to send and receive e-mail messages through his corporate e-mail account. The person who won the eBay auction paid $15.50—plus shipping—and received not only a wireless device but also more than 200 corporate internal e-mails. These e-mails included guarded financial secrets and a database of more than 1,000 names, job titles from vice presidents to managing directors, e-mail addresses, and phone numbers (some of them home numbers) for the company's executives worldwide. The major financial corporation was understandably unhappy and is still receiving negative press about the matter, but who was really at fault?

If you have an iPAQ that is capable of wireless connectivity through cellular, WiFi, or Bluetooth, your iPAQ has the powerful ability to transmit messages and data using over-the-air networks. Wireless connectivity is an extremely useful feature that allows you to stay connected and stay mobile. But this also means that there are many ways that a virus can be transmitted to your iPAQ. Depending on your model, a virus can be contracted through the voice phone channel, the GPRS/CDMA data channel, Bluetooth, the infrared port, and even infected memory expansion cards. Wireless data is easy to intercept, and your information may be scanned right out of the air.

This topic is covered in much more detail in the section "Specific Security Measures for Corporate iPAQ Users," and antivirus options are listed later in this chapter.

What You Can Do to Mitigate Security Risks

For simplification purposes (perhaps oversimplification purposes), we divided this section into two separate categories. Depending on how you use your iPAQ, you may fall a little bit into both, but most of us fall more clearly into corporate or noncorporate iPAQ users. See "Did You Know" box for our definition of a corporate iPAQ user which will help you decide which one fits you.

Security Measures All iPAQ Users Should Consider

Depending on your situation, there are different ways you can protect the information stored on your iPAQ as well as your PC. Fortunately, there are some great tools that allow you to protect your data, and many security features are built right into your iPAQ operating system. This section covers on-device security (both built-in and third-party software)and antivirus software for both your iPAQ and your PC, among other topics.

On-Device Security

On-device security refers to steps you can take to

- Restrict access to your iPAQ by requiring a user ID and password
- Automatically encrypt data that is stored on your iPAQ or on memory cards, so that if your iPAQ is misplaced or stolen (combined with password protection) your data is not accessible to unauthorized use

Use the Built-in iPAQ Security Features

Hewlett-Packard understands security issues related to your iPAQ and strives to provide necessary tools to help mitigate the risk. HP recommends a suite of technologies for use with your iPAQ including HP ProtectTools, Biometric Fingerprint Reader (available on the iPAQ hx2700 only), and VPN (Virtual Private Network) and WEP (Wired Equivalent Privacy) encryption technologies.

Set a Password on Your iPAQ   While having to enter a password before you use your iPAQ may be a bit of a pain, you will be more than glad you did if you leave your iPAQ in a taxi or coffee shop. You can even define how long it takes before your iPAQ locks and requires you to enter your password again. The steps to set your password are very simple (these steps work on Windows Mobile 2003 but are similar on other versions):

1. On your iPAQ, press the Start menu.
2. Select Settings from the menu.
3. On the Personal tab, select the Passwords icon.
4. On the Password screen, as shown in Figure 16-1, check the Prompt If Device Unused For check box.
5. Select the time interval before your iPAQ locks, between 1 minute and 24 hours. We find that 5 minutes is a good start; you can adjust it depending on how you use your iPAQ.

FIGURE 16-1   Set a Password screen.

16

6. Choose the password type; you can choose simple or complex formats.

7. Enter your new password to match the format you have selected.

8. Select the Hint tab and enter a hint that will serve to remind you of what your password is in case you forget it.

HP ProtectTools

HP ProtectTools are based on the same technologies used by Credant Technologies (as discussed later in the section "On-device Security Software") and provide a layer of security requiring PIN or password access. A second layer of protection involves data encryption of the data on your iPAQ. Many models of iPAQ ship with ProtectTools already installed, but if yours didn't, HP has ROM updates available for download on HP.com. A ROM update replaces your entire Pocket PC operating system and applications, so the process isn't entirely trivial.

HP ProtectTools encrypts e-mail, attachments, contacts, calendar, notes, My Documents, and other files. These are then automatically protected whether stored on the device or on a memory card. It you forget your PIN or password, you can regain access by entering an answer to a preselected question.

If your iPAQ is lost or stolen, failsafe actions can be automatically invoked to hard reset the iPAQ to factory defaults after a predetermined number of incorrect password attempts.

Special Features of the iPAQ hx2700. If usernames and passwords are not enough for you, you may be interested in the iPAQ hx2700. HP makes the hx2700 series iPAQ with a built-in fingerprint reader you can configure to use only a fingerprint, a PIN, a password or to require various combinations. HP says that this type of identification is virtually foolproof, as fingerprints are a unique form of biometric identification that belong to only one person. A key difference between passwords and fingerprints is that it is unlikely you will ever forget your fingerprint.

Antivirus Software

Antivirus software for your iPAQ falls into one of two main categories:

■ Software that runs on your desktop PC and protects your PC and network by scanning files for viruses during and after an ActiveSync operation

■ Software that runs natively on your iPAQ and operates in the background to scan for viruses and malicious programs.

Each type of software offers protection and, if you can, it is a good idea to run antivirus software on both your PC and your iPAQ. All of the major software companies offer antivirus virus protection for PCs that will detect known viruses if they are found in your iPAQ ActiveSync files.

Antivirus Software for Your iPAQ   The Internet is a public network and therefore results in inherent security and privacy challenges. It is an extremely effective way to distribute software viruses that

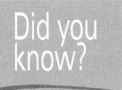

How Antivirus Software Protects Your iPAQ?

Antivirus software generally refers to single-purpose applications that scan your iPAQ or PC for any pattern that may indicate a malicious computer program. The patterns that the software looks for when it scans your device or PC can be very complex. When malicious code is identified, the code is quarantined to prevent damage, and if the software "knows" how to patch the damage, it will do so. Antivirus vendors are constantly working on ways to identify and fix viruses as soon as they are known, and program update files are loaded to your PC or iPAQ on a regular basis over the Internet to ensure that you always have the latest virus protection.

aim to disrupt services, cause user frustration, and inflict financial pain on people and organizations all over the world. This is great if you are a hacker or virus programmer but not so great if your Internet connected technologies are vulnerable. Computer viruses have unfortunately become commonplace. Most viruses target specific application weaknesses in technologies such as operating systems, databases, web servers, and e-mail servers. For the most part, mobile devices have not been popular targets yet, but you can bet that this will change as mobile devices become more popular and hackers and virus programmers become motivated to attack devices such as your iPAQ. After all, if your iPAQ has wireless connectivity, it is likely connected to the Internet just like any home PC or corporate web server.

Fortunately, there are companies that offer software to help protect your iPAQ from malicious virus attacks.

How Viruses Can Get Onto Your iPAQ?

The most common types of viruses are distributed via e-mail, and destructive commands are generally stored within e-mail attachments. Most viruses cannot infect your iPAQ unless you open the attachment. While most viruses are not designed to directly target your iPAQ, the most significant risk may be to your PC and your network. A virus can be easily transferred from your iPAQ to your PC and network when you ActiveSync with your PC. This is one reason that antivirus scanning on your PC is extremely important.

As mobile devices like your iPAQ become more popular, more software vendors are offering virus scanning and other security products designed for them. The two largest companies in the antivirus protection market are Symantec and McAfee, and both offer antivirus software that runs on your iPAQ to scan for viruses and other malicious programs.

The products listed here run natively on your iPAQ and run in the background to scan your iPAQ files, looking for signatures of viruses and Trojan horses and worms; they also prompt the user if malicious code is detected. Depending on the product, updated virus definition files are either loaded to your iPAQ during synchronization with your PC or over the air directly to your iPAQ using the wireless Internet connection. Some of the following vendors offer software for earlier versions of the Pocket PC (Windows Mobile) operating system and are in the process of releasing more recent versions for your iPAQ that run the latest versions.

- F-Secure AntiVirus for Windows Mobile (**www.f-secure.com**)

- Symantec AntiVirus for handhelds (**www.symantec.com**)

- McAfee System Protection McAfee VirusScan PDA Enterprise 2 (**www.mcafee.com**)

Antivirus Software for Your PC: Windows, Mac, and Linux   The most common type of antivirus protection is software that runs on your PC to prevent viruses from infecting your computer and the network and to prevent viruses from spreading to others through your computer. When you synchronize data from your iPAQ to your PC, the files will be scanned to prevent malicious programs that you may have picked up from e-mail or Internet activity on your iPAQ from infecting your PC or network.

Following is a cross-section of Windows antivirus vendors, but there are many more to choose from, and some, like AVG Control Center, offer free versions to noncommercial users:

- McAfee, a Network Associates Company (**www.mcafeeb2b.com**)

- Symantec (**www.symantec.com**)

- Aladdin Knowledge Systems (**www.ealaddin.com**)

- FRISK Software International (**www.f-prot.com**)

- F-Secure Corp. (**www.f-secure.com**)

- GFI Software Ltd (**www.gfi.com**)

- Panda Software (**www.pandasoftware.com**)

- Trend Micro, Inc. (**www.trendmicro.com**)

- AVG (**www.grisoft.com**)

A cross-section of vendors that provide antivirus software for Macintosh personal computers follows, and there are also others:

- Norton AntiVirus for Macintosh (**www.symantec.com**)

- Sophos AntiVirus for Mac (**www.sophos.com**)

■ Intego (**www.intego.com**)

■ McAfee Antivirus for Mac (**www.mcafee.com**)

While Linux is not yet a common platform for desktop computers, it is worth mentioning that companies such as AVG (**www.grisoft.com**) and Alwil Software (**www.avast.com**) offer antivirus software for Linux systems.

Third-Party Security Software for Your iPAQ

Several companies provide software tools to allow you to better secure your mobile device, but marketing documents you can find on the Web concerning these products can occasionally be confusing. Most of these tools fall into one of two categories: on-device security that usually includes authentication and data encryption and is excellent for all models of iPAQ, and over-the-air technologies that allow you to wipe or lock a mobile device and really only benefits those iPAQs that have cellular phone functionality.

Companies such as PointSec (**www.pointsec.com**), PDA Defense (**www.pdadefense.com**), and Credant (**www.credant.com**) offer solutions that run on your iPAQ and allow you to password-protect your iPAQ, while products that provide over-the-air wiping and locking capability include Avocent SonicSentinel (**www.avocent.com**) and Microsoft ActiveSync combined with Exchange Server 2003 Service Pack 2 and up.

On-device Security Software   On-device security products are installed on your iPAQ and provide tools for authentication (password protection) and data encryption so that if your iPAQ is lost or stolen it will be very difficult, if not impossible, to get at the data stored on your iPAQ. The leading products on the market seem to be Credant Mobile Guardian, PDA Defense, and PointSec. (We don't discuss PointSec here because is a product intended for enterprise wide deployments, but if that is what you need, we recommend taking a look at their product as well.)

■ **Credant Mobile Guardian (www.credant.com)**   Provides three versions of their Mobile Guardian product, in order of decreasing functional capability: CMG Enterprise Edition, CMG Group Edition, and CMG Personal Edition (Personal Edition is only available as a preinstalled version and cannot be purchased separately). Prices vary depending on the functionality you need, from around $20 to over $70 for the enterprise type of functionality. The basic functionality of Mobile Guardian includes:

   ■ Authentication

   ■ Policy enforcement

   ■ Device lockdown

   ■ Encryption of on-device data

   ■ Logon/logoff capability

■ **PDA Defense (www.pdadefense.com)**   Helps defend your iPAQ data against unauthorized access by enforcing password protection, encrypting data, and managing connection types, such as the ability to disable the infrared port on a iPAQ. This software

16

is a cost effective way—about $35 for a single-user license—to help ensure your data is protected in the event you lose or misplace your iPAQ. PDA Defense includes the following features:

- 128-512-bit encryption including memory card encryption support
- A bitwiping bomb and time-sensitive bitwiping bomb
- Auto-lock to automatically lock your iPAQ when not in use
- Data transfer disabling/infrared port disabling
- Encryption key erasure
- Password history tracking
- Password masking
- Temporary password unlock, in case you forget your password
- Application launch protection

Over-The-Air Security Software—for Justifiably Paranoid Organizations   As mentioned earlier, over-the-air security solutions are intended to help secure those mobile devices with cellular phone capability. They have the capability to send commands to your iPAQ using the cellular wireless network to lock (require a password) or wipe the device (delete all data). These solutions really benefit organizations that have a bunch of mobile device users and are worried about corporate data being misappropriated; they may not be particularly useful to the average iPAQ user. Obviously, this type of functionality won't be important to everyone, but specific industries such as military/defense, finance, and health care will be interested in having this level of control.

- **Avocent SonicSentinel 2 (www.avocent.com)**   Allows you to actively monitor your devices in real-time and send commands to your mobile devices over the air. It accomplishes this through an agent that runs on your iPAQ and periodically collects diagnostic information about the device status and sends it back to the SonicSentinel server. The data is analyzed for anomalies and stored and can generate notifications based on defined criteria and send commands to the iPAQ such as wiping data (including memory cards) and locking the device. It has the added benefit of being able to enforce policies such as password protection and software blacklists, which prevent unauthorized software from being installed. A screenshot of the server console is shown in Figure 16-2.

- **Microsoft ActiveSync with Microsoft Exchange Server 2003 Service Pack 2 and later**   Microsoft's update for their Microsoft Exchange Server 2003 e-mail server, Service Pack 2, allows for push e-mail and Personal Information Manager (contacts, addresses, calendar, etc.) synchronization with Exchange and Windows Mobile 5 iPAQs and other handhelds. If your iPAQ is not already running Windows Mobile 5, HP offers Windows Mobile 5 upgrades for the HP iPAQ hx2100, hx2400, hx2700, and hx4700 series of handhelds. Once you are running Windows Mobile 5, you need Messaging & Security Feature Pack for Windows Mobile 5, which is available as a free download from Microsoft (**www.microsoft.com/windowsmobile**), as well as an appropriately upgraded

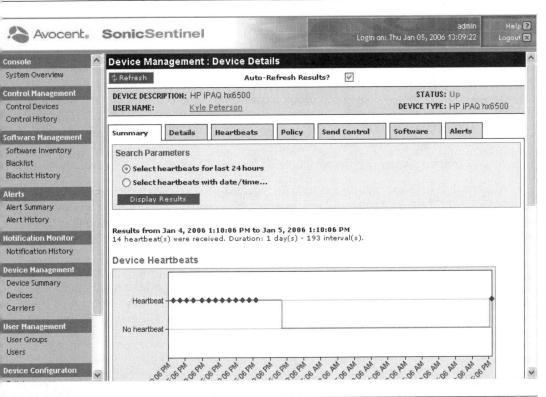

FIGURE 16-2   Avocent SonicSentinel 2.

MS Exchange Server. In addition to e-mail and PIM synchronization, MS Exchange Server Service Pack 2 allows you to send security commands to your iPAQ from the Exchange Server including:

- Policy setting that lets you unlock a device with a password
- Local wipe that lets you configure how many incorrect logon attempts are permitted before your iPAQ data is wiped
- Remote wipe that lets you reset devices remotely over the air in the event that one is lost or stolen

WiFi Security: Wired Equivalent Privacy and WiFi Protected Access

This section applies to you if your iPAQ has WiFi wireless network capability (also known as WLAN, Wireless Local Area Network, and 802.11). Getting connected via WiFi with your iPAQ is covered in more detail in Chapter 3.

16

NOTE
WiFi Encryption: WEP vs. WPA. WEP (Wired Equivalent Privacy) is a security protocol for wireless local area networks (WLANs) as defined in the 802.11b standard. WEP is intended to provide the same level of security as a wired LAN using network cables. LANs are inherently more secure than WLANs because LANs are somewhat protected by the physical attributes of their structure, which has the benefit of having the network inside a building that can be protected from unauthorized access. WLANs, which depend on wireless networking, lack the same physical structure and therefore are more vulnerable. WEP was designed to provide security by encrypting data before it is sent over the air. WEP was once the WLAN/WiFi/802.11 (which all mean the same thing) standard, but now it is generally acknowledged that it isn't perfect. This has led the introduction of WPA (WiFi Protected Access), which is deemed more secure then WEP. Both are discussed in this chapter.

The Wired Equivalent Privacy (WEP) and the WiFi Protected Access (WPA) security protocols are specified in the IEEE 802.11 standard and attempt to provide security to wireless LAN (WLAN) networks comparable to a typical wired LAN. WEP and WPA encrypt data transmitted over the WLAN to protect the vulnerable wireless connection between the iPAQ (the client) and wireless access points (APs).

Both of these standards depend on the type of wireless AP hardware you have. You must install the correct client software on your iPAQ for it all to work properly. The Microsoft Pocket PC or Windows Mobile operating system usually includes both WEP and Virtual Private Network (VPN) clients, so you will need to check to see if the built-in clients will work with your network infrastructure.

TIP
Many Wireless Access Points have WEP/WPA turned off by default. If you are concerned about data security and/or unauthorized use of your WLAN, ensure that your access point is configured to require WEP or WPA.

Virtual Private Network Technologies

VPN technologies are more important for those users who have an iPAQ with cellular phone connectivity and who use applications with a server or database component behind their corporate network firewall. As an option to sending data over the air in unencrypted formats, VPN are valuable tools because they allow you to securely connect to a remote network and then encrypt all of the data that is passed between your iPAQ and the remote network. Most carriers provide some level of data encryption, but it may be weaker protection than what you need, so be sure to check with your carrier. This is extremely important when you are connecting over the public wireless networks, as wireless data packets are easily scanned out of the air. If the information is encrypted by a VPN solution, the data packet will appear as a bunch of scrambled random characters that are useless to the would-be hacker or eavesdropper. The following two vendors provide VPN solutions for Pocket PC/Windows Mobile platforms, and expect more to enter the marketplace as devices such as your iPAQ become more popular and the market grows:

■ Check Point: VPN-1 SecureClient (**www.checkpoint.com**)

■ AnthaVPN by Worldnet21/Anthasoft (**www.anthavpn.com**)

Many of the companies that manufacture network routers provide VPN client software for Pocket PC mobile devices to work with their routers, including Cisco and Nortel. If you are a corporate user, you may want to check to see if your IT department knows of any VPN clients that will work with your company's network infrastructure.

Enterprise Network Authentication and Encryption Solutions

Many organizations are understandably concerned about the risks associated with allowing a wireless mobile device to connect to the corporate network over a wireless network. Some of the solutions that address these risks are mentioned in the "Virtual Private Network Technologies" section and other parts of this chapter. One of the ways to help ensure that a user who is attempting to remotely connect to the corporate network is really who they claim to be is by using one of the sophisticated user authentication solutions. These products use more than just a username and password to authenticate a user and make unauthorized access very difficult even if someone has stolen your iPAQ. These types of solutions are called "strong authentication" or "two-factor authentication" systems and involve both a clientside application installed on your iPAQ and a serverside application installed on a server in your computer network that serves as the gateway to the network. Of course you have to authenticate before you can get through the gate. A couple products available for your iPAQ are

- RSA Security SecurID (**www.rsa.com**) is used in conjunction with a RSA ACE Server, and it works by using a one-time-use SecurID access code that automatically changes every 60 seconds.

- WiKID (**www.wikidsystems.com**) is two-factor authentication that uses asymmetric encryption instead of the more standard shared-secret architecture.

Specific Security Measures for Corporate iPAQ Users

You are likely aware of some of the technical security risks that too often are topics in the press. This section provides an overview of the potential security risks of your iPAQ and wireless handhelds in general for companies.

Much of the talk about corporate security risks and what should be done to defend against attacks amounts to nothing more than technical fear mongering. Despite the attempts to guess dollar values for security attacks that have not yet occurred, the fact is that the actual cost of a security breach cannot be known until after it has already happened. This does not mean that precautions are not warranted; in fact, ideally, you don't ever want to find out how much an attack costs your organization. The best way to avoid incurring costs is to understand the risks and protect yourself and your organization.

In an article published by CNNMoney.com on December 29, 2005, CNN said that 2005 saw the most computer security breaches ever. "Over 130 major intrusions exposed more than 55 million Americans to the growing variety of fraud as personal data like Social Security and credit card numbers were left unprotected, according to *USA Today*. The Treasury Department says that cyber crime has now outgrown illegal drug sales in annual proceeds, netting an estimated $105 billion

16

in 2004, the report said. At the same time, the Department of Homeland Security's 2005 research budget for cyber security programs was cut 7 percent to $16 million. It is difficult to gauge the true number of security failures because many companies are unaware they've been hacked, the paper said."

In addition to the financial costs, there are some costs that are more difficult to value. For many companies, the costs associated with destroying the confidence of customers and business partners is devastating. The larger an organization is, the more a negative public impression will cost the company in the long run. Many organizations work hard to create positive public perception, and even a small security problem that becomes public can erase years of effort and negatively impact a company's bottom line.

The security risks associated with wirelessly connected mobile devices can be divided into a few general categories: theft or loss of a device, interception of wireless data, and the threat of damage caused by viruses and malicious code.

Minimize the Risk Involved with Using Wireless Mobile Devices

The following are specific precautionary steps that should be followed by every organization that has employees using mobile devices. This section is directed at the corporate IT or security person responsible for network access and data, but the information is valuable for any mobile device user, as it can help avoid unnecessarily risking company assets.

1. **Research and understand the risks** The first step is to understand how employees are using their iPAQs and other wireless mobile devices. Answering these questions will allow you to understand some of the risks and the scope of any potential issues:

   - How many employees use wireless mobile devices?

   - What devices are being used?

   - Do the users synchronize their devices with network computers?

   - What type of data do users store on their devices?

   - What applications do users use on their devices?

2. **Create or modify security policies** In addition, ensure that wireless handheld devices are within the control of the organization and clearly convey the policies to staff.

   - Often, many of the devices in an organization are personally owned, rather than supplied by the company. It is crucial to define policies that effectively define how these personal devices interact with corporate data and systems. The policies should include sections that cover situations in which employees have their own mobile devices. Issues like whether or not the organization will allow employees to synchronize devices with work computers should be included. Another item that should be included is a detailed list of specific security concerns regarding particular devices or software.

   - Convey the very important point to users that they must use the password protection that is built into their devices. Users often turn off this protection for the convenience of being able to use their iPAQ without having to log on, but the cost to the organization could be significant if the device is lost or stolen. Some of the software options to help enforce this security policy are listed earlier in this chapter in the section "Enterprise Network Authentication and Encryption Solutions."

3. **Track mobile devices (also known as asset management)**   Most organizations take time and effort to ensure that they have an up-to-date inventory record of each server and workstation that is being used by the company. Usually this information includes hardware and software configurations, as well as network addresses, and which user is assigned to specific hardware. Doesn't it make sense to do the same thing for mobile devices? Gartner Group estimates that companies with more than 5,000 employees could save between $300,000 and $500,000 per year by tracking, tagging, and storing contact information about their wireless mobile devices.

4. **Dictate standard security software that mobile users must use**   Requiring mobile device users to use antivirus and VPN software can go a long way toward protecting your network assets. It is also important to ban any software that may be a security risk. For example, some organizations ban certain document applications because of the security vulnerabilities they cause.

Wrap It Up

After reading this chapter, you should have a firm understanding of some of the security risks that may be associated with wireless mobile devices such as your iPAQ. This chapter was not designed to scare you but to make you aware of possible risks and the best ways to minimize those risks. Of course, any risks are generally more significant for some groups of users than others and are dependent on how you use your iPAQ and who you work for. Clearly the FBI is more concerned about security than many of us so need to be, so it is only necessary to take precautions where appropriate. The most important precaution that you can take is to ensure that you are using a password to access your iPAQ and that your data is encrypted so that if you misplace your iPAQ no one will be able to use or abuse your information.

Part V

Appendixes

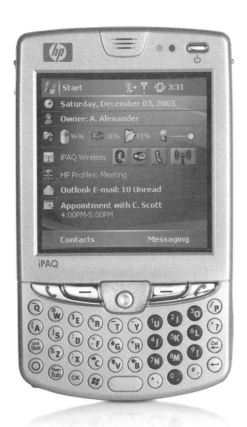
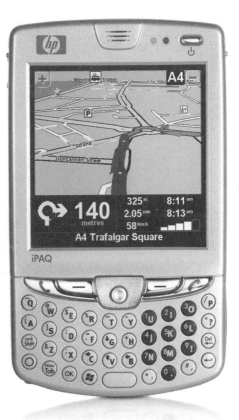

Appendix A

Troubleshoot Your iPAQ

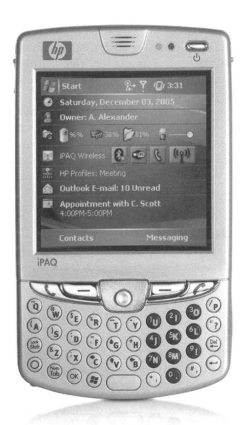

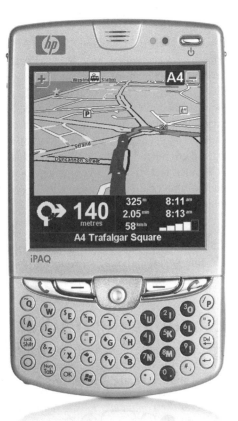

How to...

- Troubleshoot battery issues
- Troubleshoot speaker issues
- Troubleshoot ActiveSync issues
- Troubleshoot phone quality issues
- Troubleshoot wireless connectivity problems
- Troubleshoot camera and photo issues
- Troubleshoot GPS issues
- Troubleshoot memory issues

HP has designed and engineered your iPAQ with the utmost attention to detail to ensure that your experience with your iPAQ is as painless and trouble-free as possible. That said, there are a few user and technical scenarios that may cause problems for you, your iPAQ applications, or the iPAQ itself. This chapter serves to help you overcome the most common known issues that you may encounter. The chapter is divided into functional categories to help you quickly locate answers to the most common questions. According to Jackie Dillemuth, the Manager of iPAQ Total Customer Experience and Marketing Services at HP, the most common user troubles encountered are related to synchronization (setup, installation, troubleshooting issues, syncing tasks, Calendar, and so on), power management (optimization, unnecessary battery drain, and expectations about battery life), and wireless connectivity (WiFi and Bluetooth) and Global Positioning Satellite (GPS) challenges are also becoming more common.

How to find out which operating system is running on your iPAQ: the Windows Mobile or Pocket PC operating system has evolved over the past few years and each has subtle differences, and it is a good idea to know exactly which version of the operating system is on your iPAQ. To find the OS version, click the Start | Settings | System | About.

Troubleshooting the iPAQ Battery

Your iPAQ has a built-in, state of-the-art lithium ion battery that generally doesn't require maintenance. However, there are a few tips to help you troubleshoot battery challenges. This section lists some potential battery problems and their solutions.

Several recommendations to help you get the most out of your battery between charges are discussed in Chapter 15.

My iPAQ Battery Doesn't Seem to Charge

Is the power adapter plugged in correctly? Make sure that it's hooked up to an active power outlet and that all connections are tight. If the connection to your iPAQ seems a little loose, try disconnecting it and reconnecting it again. To check if your device is charging, select Start |

Settings and select the System tab and the Power icon. If you see a lightning bolt symbol over the battery, it is charging properly. If you have had your iPAQ for more than a year, it is also possible that your battery died and you need to order a new one from HP.

One other thing to try is to let the battery drain entirely before trying to recharge it again. Before you do this, ensure that your iPAQ is fully backed up (synchronized with your PC) so you don't lose any files when you let the battery die.

iPAQ Sound and Speaker

Your iPAQ has a built-in speaker on the back of the device. It also has a jack for an earbud or headphones to allow you to listen to the sounds of games, music, video, and so on.

The iPAQ speaker is designed to play system sounds like ringtones and applications beeps. It is not designed to play loud music, so if it is buzzing you are likely playing too much volume through it. Like any other speaker, it can be damaged if too much volume is pushed through it. Here are some steps to help you avoid damaging the built-in speaker:

- **Use headphones**   You can use any type of headphone you want with your iPAQ provided they have a 2.5mm connector (even if the connector is not 2.5mm, you can probably find an adaptor to downsize it to 2.5mm).

- **Don't use MP3 volume boost**   Some MP3 encoders allow you to boost the volume of a song by as much as 15dB. If you are encoding MP3s for use with your iPAQ, do not boost the volume when encoding. More information should be available from the company that developed your MP3 or in the documentation.

Troubleshooting Synchronization with ActiveSync

Your iPAQ is best used in conjunction with a PC to allow you to synchronize data between your iPAQ and your personal computer. Synchronization is covered in Chapter 2. Before you can synchronize your iPAQ with your PC, you will have to install the ActiveSync software on your PC; the ActiveSync CD-ROM should be included with your iPAQ.

Troubleshoot Synchronization Problems

Most ActiveSync USB connection problems are caused by Windows desktop firewall applications or applications that manipulate your PC network traffic. These applications conflict with the TCP traffic between your iPAQ and your PC, which causes data transfer and connection issues. There are several symptoms that may suggest that you are having problems with the ActiveSync synchronization process when you connect your iPAQ to your home or work PC with the USB sync cable.

TIP   *If your iPAQ is running Windows Mobile 5 you should upgrade to the latest version of ActiveSync, at least version 4.1. This will minimize ActiveSync issues for your device. ActiveSync is available as a free download from Microsoft at* ***www.microsoft.com/ windowsmobile/downloads/.***

A few things that may indicate synchronization problems include:

- If you get the error message "Unable to ActiveSync due to system error," on your PC then skip to the section "I Keep Getting 'Unable to ActiveSync Due to System Error' When I Try to Sync."

- ActiveSync makes the connection and begins the synchronization process but synching stops before it is complete. This is also indicated if the ActiveSync icon begins spinning but stops and turns gray before synchronization fully occurs.

- No ActiveSync chimes sound, and there is no activity in the ActiveSync window on your PC when you connect your iPAQ to your PC.

- ActiveSync continues to search for a connection but can't make the connection: when you connect your iPAQ to your PC the ActiveSync icon spins but can't make a connection to your iPAQ.

- ActiveSync disconnects before synching can start: when you connect your iPAQ to your PC the ActiveSync icon swirls and the Retrieving Settings message appears, but the ActiveSync connection is dropped before the partnership is established.

If you are experiencing any of the preceding symptoms, follow these troubleshooting steps to help you get the ActiveSync process working correctly. Any one of these steps may allow you to isolate the problem so it is important to test ActiveSync when you make a change to see if the problem has been overcome.

NOTE *If your iPAQ is running Windows Mobile 2002 or 2003, you should be using MS ActiveSync 3.8.*

1. Confirm that you are running ActiveSync on your personal computer. Your iPAQ should have come with an ActiveSync CD containing the software but if you don't have it, you can download the latest version from Microsoft: **www.microsoft.com/ windowsmobile/downloads/pocketpc.mspx**.

2. If you are running ActiveSync 4 or later and you are running a software firewall such as Sygate Personal Firewall, TrendMicro PC-cillin Internet Security 2005, Norton Personal Firewall, McAfee Personal Firewall, or ZoneAlarm, ensure that you add MS ActiveSync to the firewall program's exception list. Each firewall program is slightly different so you will have to check the user manual or on the manufacturer's website to find how to do this. If ActiveSync is not in the firewall exception list, the firewall won't allow ActiveSync make a connection to your iPAQ.

3. If your PC has more than one USB port, it is likely that ActiveSync will only work on one of the ports. Change which port you are using to see if that works.

4. On your PC, ensure that USB is selected in ActiveSync as a connection method. To check the setting, launch ActiveSync on your PC and select File | Connections Settings. Ensure that the Allow USB Connections check box is selected, as shown in Figure A-1.

FIGURE A-1   ActiveSync: Allow USB Connections.

■ If you don't need to connect to a Microsoft Exchange Server to synchronize e-mail, contacts, and other Exchange data, then ActiveSync should not be configured to try to connect to an Exchange server. To check the configuration, follow these steps:

1. Connect your iPAQ to your PC with the sync cable and wait for ActiveSync to connect.

2. On your PC select Start | All Programs | Microsoft ActiveSync to launch ActiveSync.

3. In the ActiveSync application, select Tools | Options, then select the Sync Options tab.

4. Ensure that the check box for Enable Synchronization With A Server is disabled, as shown in Figure A-2.

Specific Synchronization Issues and Troubleshooting

The issues listed in the previous section discuss general synchronization troubles; this section discusses slightly more specific issues and resolutions.

Syncing a Windows Mobile 5 iPAQ with a Windows XP PC

Some users have experienced a problem using a Windows Mobile 5 iPAQ with a Windows XP PC running ActiveSync 4.1: ActiveSync doesn't seem to recognize that your iPAQ is connected, which makes syncing impossible. This is a frustrating experience because there really isn't any indication of what is causing the problem.

A potential cause for this behavior is that Windows XP doesn't recognize your iPAQ as a mobile device but instead recognizes it as a different type of network connection and won't allow TCP/IP connectivity. ActiveSync requires TCP/IP connectivity to communicate with your

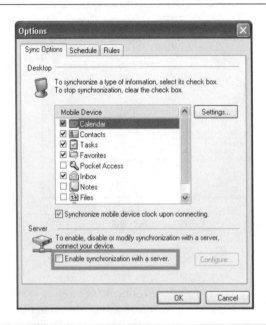

FIGURE A-2   ActiveSync: Enable Sync With Server.

iPAQ, so this may be your problem. To check if this is the problem, follow these steps on your Windows XP computer running ActiveSync 4.1:

1. Select Start | Control Panel | Network Connections.

2. If you have a Local Area Network connection that doesn't make sense, as shown in Figure A-3, this could be the problem.

3. Right-click the mysterious Local Area Network connection icon and select Properties.

4. On the properties screen, select the check box beside Internet Protocol (TCP/IP), as shown in Figure A-4.

Syncing Media to Your iPAQ

It is a good idea to use a removable storage card such as a Secure Digital (SD) or CompactFlash (CF) in your iPAQ and then synchronize files to the card. Synchronizing to your iPAQ RAM or File Store can cause problems for certain iPAQs.

If you plan to synchronize protected files such as music songs purchased from an online store, such as MSN Music, Napster, or iTunes, it is a good idea to sync while your memory card is inserted into your iPAQ. If you synchronize protected content to a memory card while the card is inserted into a storage card reader, the licenses will not copy correctly and Windows Media Player 10 Mobile will not be able to play the protected files.

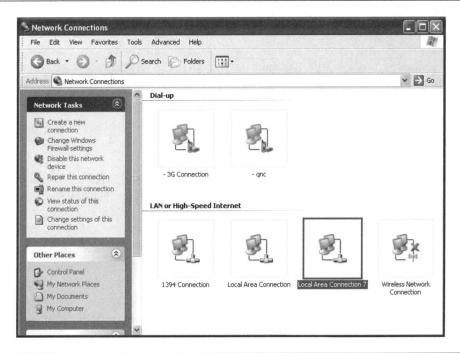

FIGURE A-3 Network Connections.

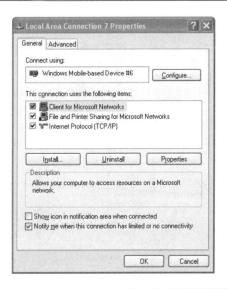

FIGURE A-4 Connection Properties.

I Keep Getting "Unable to ActiveSync Due to System Error" When I Try to Sync

This error may occur when you try to perform a ActiveSync operation at the same time that your iPAQ is on an active call of any type. Examples include making a voice call, sending or receiving e-mail, browsing the Internet, or downloading files from the Internet at the same time that you are trying to make an ActiveSync connection. There are a few things to try to overcome this error:

- Make sure that your iPAQ is not currently making a voice call, connected to the Internet, or downloading files from the Internet, then try to ActiveSync again by disconnecting the USB cable and reconnecting.

- One other potential cause of the error is that your e-mail application may be checking for e-mail in the background without it being obvious. If this error seems to happen infrequently, then this may be the problem. You can test this possibility by disabling automatic e-mail checking in your e-mail application, retrying the ActiveSync operation, and turning automatic e-mail checking back on. You may have to check the documentation for your specific e-mail application to find out how to configure this setting.

If you have tried the prior suggestions and ActiveSync still won't sync, turn your iPAQ wireless mode off as in the following steps, perform the ActiveSync operation, and turn it back on again. With the wireless mode off, there is no chance that an application is performing Internet functions without you knowing about it.

1. On your iPAQ, select the Start button, select Settings, select the Connections tab, and select the iPAQ Wireless icon, as shown in Figure A-5.

2. On the iPAQ Wireless screen, select the Phone button to turn the phone off, as shown in Figure A-6, wait 10 seconds or so, and tap the button again to reconnect the phone to the cellular tower.

FIGURE A-5   iPAQ Wireless icon.

| FIGURE A-6 | iPAQ Phone button. |

Troubleshooting the iPAQ Phone

Mobile phone technology has been mainstream technology for many years and is relatively mature; however, there can still be issues.

I'm Not Happy with the Sound Quality on My Phone

There are many factors that can cause problems with the sound quality that you hear, or that the person you are speaking to hears, when you are talking on your iPAQ phone. Factors that can cause problems include:

- Phone of the person you are talking to

- Signal strength and the quality of the connection between the phones

- Environment: weather, background noise, solar flares, and so on

- Wireless network issues

Some things you can do to maximize the sound quality of your phone conversations are listed here:

- **Hold your iPAQ correctly**   Position the iPAQ handset closer to your ear to prevent sound from leaking back to the microphone. Be sure you're holding the iPAQ so that your hand is not near the microphone hole in the back. Your hand—or any other reflecting surface—will tend to conduct the speaker sound down to the microphone and cause echo on the recipient's end.

- **Turn down the phone volume**   Try decreasing your iPAQ volume to avoid coupling, or feedback, on the receiver's end. (Coupling occurs when the receiver hears their voice as it goes through your speaker, which is picked up by your microphone and gets sent back to the receiver with a slight delay as it travels through the network.) This applies to both speaker phone and the built-in ear speaker.

When Talking on My iPAQ I Hear Echo, Echo, Echo...

If you are hearing your own voice echo when you are talking, the echo is originating at the other person's phone, not at yours. You can ask the other person to either turn down the volume on their phone or hold the speaker closer to their ear to minimize feedback.

I Am Hearing Static When I'm Talking on My iPAQ Phone

Static is generally caused by a barrier between your iPAQ and the cellular tower to which your iPAQ is connected. For example, there is a barrier when you get into an elevator while talking on your phone. There is not too much you can do except to be aware of barriers and avoid talking on your phone when you are driving though a tunnel, for example.

Troubleshooting Wireless Connectivity

Your iPAQ, as you know, is equipped with wireless radio components to allow you to make wireless phone calls and/or send and receive wireless application data. Due to the complexity of this feature, and depending on whether or not your iPAQ arrived perfectly configured, you may need to do a little troubleshooting to ensure that your iPAQ is set up correctly. If you are having problems with WiFi or Bluetooth, rather than cellular voice and data connectivity, this is also covered.

Why Does My Cellular Service Disconnect Periodically?

You may have experienced intermittent service as you move around within your city, state, or province. Wireless networks do not yet cover every square mile of surface area, and many areas have better connectivity than others. If you are disconnected, it may be because you are in an area without wireless coverage.

Some mobile service providers log off wireless users after a given period of time—from hours to days, depending on carrier. This is another possible explanation for being unexpectedly disconnected from the network. You may be automatically disconnected regardless of whether you have been using your connection during the defined time period.

How Do I Reestablish My Wireless Connection?

Provided that you are in an area with cellular coverage, launch an application that requires a data connection, such as a web browser or an e-mail application. Your connection should be established automatically, but you may have to approve the connection when prompted. If you are roaming, you may occasionally have to reset your iPAQ to get it to connect to the cellular network. The steps to reset your iPAQ are covered in this appendix in the section "Reset your iPAQ."

What Should I Do if I Can't Connect to the Internet at All with My iPAQ Using My Cellular Connection?

If wireless applications such as e-mail and the Web will not work, here are some steps to help get you going:

- **Check your wireless service contract**   If you have never been able to use e-mail or the Web on your iPAQ, check to see whether your wireless service contract includes General Pocket Radio Service (GPRS) data services. Not all service contracts include data services by default, and it is possible that you are only covered for voice data and not other forms of data. To make sure that your GPRS service is enabled, contact the company who holds your contract. The contact information of the major carriers that host iPAQs is listed at the end of this chapter. If you have your service contract handy, the contact information should be provided there as well.

- **Find out if the correct wireless service is provided in your area**   Specific cellular networks do not offer coverage everywhere, and it is possible that the type of network (CDMA, GSM, and so on) that is used by your iPAQ is not provided in your area. This may not seem like a particularly useful point, but sometimes a user buys a device from a source other than from the local service provider. For example, Dayton bought his iPAQ on eBay because the carriers in his area were not selling them yet when he wanted to buy one. Obviously, you can't use GSM, CDMA, and so on if it is not supported in your area.

- **Be sure that your username and password are correct**   Some wireless service providers require that you enter a username and password to allow you to connect to their wireless network. This information is stored in your iPAQ wireless settings, and your iPAQ should have been preconfigured with this information. If it wasn't, your iPAQ will not be able to authenticate with the wireless network and you will have to contact your service provider to find out what your username and password are.

- **Turn your wireless mode off and on again**   By following these steps to turn your wireless mode off and then on again, your iPAQ will try to re-authenticate with the network and will often fix a broken connection:

  1. On your iPAQ, select the Start button, select Settings, select the Connections tab, and select the iPAQ Wireless icon, as shown in Figure A-7.

  2. On the iPAQ Wireless screen, select the phone button, as shown in Figure A-8, to turn the phone off, wait 10 seconds or so, and tap the button again to reconnect the phone to the cellular tower.

- **Contact your wireless service provider for assistance**   If none of these steps helped, contact your wireless service provider directly for assistance. Remember, wireless data services are still a relatively new technology, and the support and configuration kinks are still being worked out in many areas. Therefore, problems often originate with the carrier rather than directly with you or your iPAQ.

FIGURE A-7   iPAQ Wireless icon.

Troubleshooting Bluetooth Troubles

We will discuss some specific Bluetooth troubles here, but for a Bluetooth primer see Chapter 3, where the subject is covered in detail. Bluetooth wireless technology is a wireless standard and specification that HP, among many other product manufacturers, has built into their products. In doing so, HP produced the Bluetooth-enabled iPAQ in compliance with the industry standard; that said, each product manufacturer tends to integrate Bluetooth in their own unique way, so ultimately HP is the best source of support for HP Bluetooth troubles.

FIGURE A-8   Phone button.

About Bluetooth Profiles

Every Bluetooth capable device such as a printer, laptop, and headset supports specific Bluetooth profiles. A profile is a unique way to describe the Bluetooth functionality of different devices. Because the Bluetooth wireless technology is used for many different types of applications, it is necessary to describe how the different devices and their applications should connect and function together; this is the profile. Supported profiles will be listed in the user manual for each device. For example, a Bluetooth mouse that supports the HID (Human Interface Device) profile will not work with your iPAQ because the iPAQ does not currently support HID. It is important to ensure that whichever Bluetooth device you want to connect your iPAQ to supports a profile that is the same as your iPAQ.

Bluetooth is a short-range wireless network and requires at least two Bluetooth-capable devices to form a network. A few steps to check if you are having difficulty getting two Bluetooth devices to "talk":

NOTE   *If you find some of the terminology here confusing, see Chapter 3 for a Bluetooth overview.*

1. Ensure that the same Bluetooth profile exists on both Bluetooth devices.
2. Ensure that both devices have Bluetooth connectivity turned on.
3. Ensure that both devices are paired with each other (Pairing is not necessary if you are only transmitting vCards or business cards using Bluetooth).
4. Initiate a communication session.

If the two Bluetooth devices still don't communicate, here are some more specific things to try:

- **Ensure that the profiles match**   In order for the Bluetooth devices to connect, it is important that each device that communicates shares a common profile. For example, to connect a Bluetooth headset to your iPAQ you will need to have an identical headset profile for each device, or to print from your iPAQ to a Bluetooth-enabled printer, both devices typically will need the BPP (Basic Printing Profile).

- **Ensure that Bluetooth functionality is on**   This is fairly obvious but it is certainly worth checking. To turn your iPAQ Bluetooth radio on, select the Start button, select Settings, select the Connections tab, and select the iPAQ Wireless icon. If Bluetooth is off, press the Bluetooth menu to turn it on, as shown in Figure A-9.

FIGURE A-9   Bluetooth button.

■ **Ensure that the devices are paired**   For security reasons, two Bluetooth devices always need to be initially paired before they can begin to exchange data. The term *pairing* (also known as *bonding*) essentially means that two Bluetooth devices are exchanging protected passkeys. Once the devices are paired, all of the information sent over the wireless Bluetooth connection is encrypted and will only be able to reach devices that are paired. Pairing is discussed in Chapter 3.

■ **I cannot pair my iPAQ with another Bluetooth device**   If you went through the pairing steps in Chapter 3 and still can't get the devices to connect, the most common problems are

■ **The device cannot be found**   This can occur if Bluetooth is off or the other device is not in discoverable mode. You will need to ensure that device that you are trying to connect to is configured to be visible, or discoverable, by enabling it on the appropriate menu.

■ **You receive a "Pairing unsuccessful" message**   If you see this message it's usually a symptom that the wrong password or PIN was entered when the pairing was first attempted.

■ **Pairing succeeded but the connection still doesn't work**   If this seems to be what is happening, it may be that both devices don't share a common profile that allows them to communicate. As mentioned earlier, both devices need to support the same profile in order to be able to connect. This information is generally in the device user manual and some applications, such as the Bluetooth manager application on a Bluetooth-capable laptop, will list the supported profiles as well.

About Bluetooth Pairing

The concept of pairing can be a little confusing, but it serves a specific purpose. Pairing, also known as bonding, is a concept that was introduced to create a first-time recognition of which devices are allowed to communicate with each other. The initial pairing process is required to allow each Bluetooth device to recognize each other and begin communicating. It is a security feature embedded in Bluetooth that effectively prevents a nonauthorized Bluetooth device from connecting to your iPAQ.

Troubleshooting the iPAQ Camera

Taking photos with your iPAQ camera is covered in detail in Chapter 6. Here are a couple of common scenarios that can cause user frustration.

Why Doesn't a Digital Image Transfer from My Desktop to My iPAQ When I ActiveSync?

This scenario can occur if the settings in the ActiveSync program running on your PC are not set to automatically synchronize your photos. Microsoft and HP have made this task exceedingly simple, provided your PC is running a Windows operating system. If your PC is a Mac, then some of your options are discussed in Chapter 6. Essentially, all you need to do is install Microsoft ActiveSync on your PC and connect your iPAQ to your PC with a synchronization cable or cradle. Microsoft ActiveSync is included on the companion CD that came with your iPAQ and is available as a free download from Microsoft.com. The link to download ActiveSync Version 4.1 is **www.microsoft .com/windowsmobile/downloads/activesync41.mspx**.

When ActiveSync is installed on your PC and you synchronize your iPAQ with your PC, your pictures will be moved to your PC. Whether this happens automatically or requires you to start the synchronization process manually depends on your ActiveSync settings. (ActiveSync configuration is covered in detail in Chapter 2.) Once your iPAQ is synchronized with your Windows PC, you can easily browse to your photos on your PC by following these steps:

1. Open MS ActiveSync and select the Explore button as shown in Figure A-10. This will launch a file explorer window as shown in Figure A-11.

2. Open the My Pictures folder, and you will see your iPAQ photos. You can view, move, rename, e-mail, edit, and do anything else you want to do with your photos once they are on your PC.

FIGURE A-10   ActiveSync Explore button.

FIGURE A-11   ActiveSync Mobile Device folders.

ActiveSync for Windows can be configured to synchronize continuously, when connected, or only manually when you decide to synchronize your iPAQ with your PC. If the manual option is selected, synchronization won't occur until you click the Sync button. To check the settings on your PC:

1. Launch the ActiveSync program (Start | Programs | ActiveSync).

2. Select Tools | Options.

3. Select the Schedule tab and select the When Connected To My PC, Sync drop-down menu, as shown in Figure A-12. Select which option you want. The easiest method is Continuously, but it may slow down your PC, especially when you connect your iPAQ after not doing so for more than a couple of days and a lot of data needs to be synchronized.

Why Does the iPAQ Camera Preview Image Look Fuzzy?

It is important to keep in mind that your iPAQ screen resolution is likely lower than the actual capability of the camera. This means that your resulting photos will likely be much higher quality

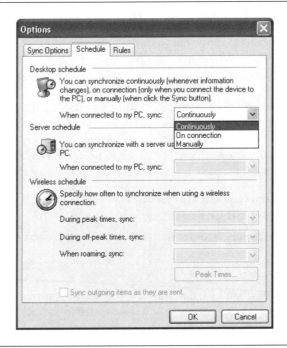

FIGURE A-12   ActiveSync Sync Schedule.

when you view them on your PC than when you view them on your iPAQ screen. Don't be too critical of the photos on the preview screen until you have had the chance to view them on a PC.

Why Do My iPAQ Pictures Have Blue Spots on Them?

Blue spots on your photos indicate that the lighting isn't sufficient for your camera to capture detail and ultimately take a good photo. If your iPAQ is equipped with a flash, you should try using it to see if the contrast improves. Unfortunately, your options are limited if you can't improve the lighting on your target.

Troubleshoot iPAQ GPS Problems

As with any technically complicated technology, there are bound to be some issues, especially when you are talking about as many moving parts as is required for GPS to work correctly. GPS requires your iPAQ to be working correctly, as well as GPS software and network connectivity, not to mention that the satellites themselves all have to be working correctly for GPS to work. GPS is covered in detail in Chapter 9 and contains information regarding how to choose, set up, and use GPS.

Troubleshooting iPAQ Memory Problems

Your iPAQ has limited on-board memory that you will likely find gets used up fairly quickly as you take photos, run programs, receive e-mail, and perform other day-to-day tasks. One of the best ways you can free up memory is to use a removable memory card(s) to store your programs and files.

Sometimes device instability can cause memory issues, for example, if a program has created a memory leak and is causing your iPAQ to lock up. In this case you may need to perform a soft reset of your iPAQ to free up memory (see the section "Perform a Soft Reset" later in this chapter).

Chapter 15 covers memory optimization topics such as using built-in Windows Mobile tools to help you allocate and manage the memory on your iPAQ. See Chapter 15 to learn how to:

- View how much memory is allocated versus how much is free in both the internal storage memory and on SD/CF memory cards.
- Change how much memory is allocated to file storage and how much is allocated to program use.
- Find the largest files in memory.
- View the Running Program List; this allows you to see what is running at a specific time and stop applications you are not using to free up system resources.
- Move files and programs to a removable storage card to free up your iPAQ memory.

How to Reset Your iPAQ

If you have been a PC user for a while, you are likely familiar with the reality that your PC periodically needs a reboot, or restart, when it is having difficulties. In order to keep us comfortable with new technology, HP and Microsoft have done an excellent job of ensuring that most of the experience of using a desktop or laptop computer translates your iPAQ. This includes the need to periodically reset your iPAQ. However, there are some key differences to be aware of Such as that there are two types of resets: a soft reset and a hard reset. Depending on the type of iPAQ behavior you are trying to remedy, you need to choose the correct option. The primary difference between the two is that a hard reset returns your device to factory settings. This essentially means that your iPAQ will return to exactly the same state as when you first received it new from the manufacturer. Therefore, any files, music, photos, programs that you installed as well as configuration settings and anything else that you added, will be lost. This means of course that you will want to use this option as a last resort.

Perform a Soft Reset

A soft reset is conceptually the same as rebooting your home or work PC. The iPAQ restarts, and all of your data and settings remain intact. If you are experiencing some ongoing erratic behavior on your iPAQ and can't seem to get it to stop, a soft reset will often fix the problem.

To perform a soft reset, all you need to do is use your stylus, or a paperclip, and stick it into the Reset button that is usually on the bottom of your iPAQ. The reset button looks more like a tiny hole than a button. If you are not sure where it is, it is a good idea to look at your iPAQ documentation before sticking pointy things into random orifices to ensure that you don't inadvertently break something. (This seems obvious, but we once saw a fellow jam a paper clip into his iPAQ speaker by accident.)

Perform a Hard Reset

Windows Mobile 5 and Windows Mobile 2003 each deal with a hard reset a little differently. Windows Mobile 5 has persistent memory that survives a hard reset, while Windows Mobile 2003 does not. That said, performing a hard reset in either version of the operating system still results in your configuration settings being deleted. However, in Windows Mobile 5, any file or application stored in persistent memory will not be lost.

If your iPAQ is not running the Windows Mobile 5 operating system, a hard reset returns your device to factory settings, which essentially means that your iPAQ will be returned to exactly the same state as when you first received it new from the manufacturer. Therefore, any files, music, photos, programs that you installed, as well as configuration settings and anything else that you added will be lost. If your iPAQ is running the Windows Mobile 5 operating system, a hard reset will delete your configuration settings but not the files and applications that are stored in persistent memory.

If you can, it is a good idea to synchronize your iPAQ with your PC before you perform the hard reset and/or move any files and programs that are in the iPAQ File Store memory to a removable Secure Digital or CompactFlash memory card.

To perform a hard reset, use your stylus or a paperclip and stick it into the Reset button that is usually on the bottom of your iPAQ while simultaneously pressing and then releasing the power button on your iPAQ. Keep in mind that the reset button looks more like a tiny hole than a button. If you are not sure where it is, it is a good idea to look at your iPAQ documentation before performing these steps.

Perform a Clean Reset (Windows Mobile 5)

The concept of a clean reset is something new in Windows Mobile 5. A clean reset is similar to a hard reset in previous versions of Windows Mobile because it clears all of your user installed settings, programs, and data and returns your iPAQ to the way it was when it was shipped from the factory. You will notice that it unlikely that you would accidentally do a clean reset.

To perform a clean reset on iPAQs with phone capability:

1. Press and hold down all three of the buttons Answer/Send, Power, and End call buttons.

2. While holding these three buttons down, use your stylus to press the Reset button on the bottom of your iPAQ until the iPAQ restarts.

3. When you see it begin the restart process, release all of the buttons.

To perform a clean reset on iPAQs that don't have phone capability:

1. Press and hold the Calendar and iPAQ Wireless buttons at the same time.

2. While holding down these buttons, use the stylus to lightly press the Reset button on the left side of your iPAQ for a couple of seconds.

3. When your iPAQ screen begins to fade, release the Calendar and iPAQ Wireless buttons first, and then remove the stylus from the Reset button.

4. Plug the device into the AC Adapter or press the Reset button again.

Your iPAQ will now be good as new.

Recover Your Data after a Hard Reset

Windows Mobile 5 and Windows Mobile 2003 each deal with a hard reset a little differently. Windows Mobile 5 has persistent memory that survives a hard reset while Windows Mobile 2003 does not. That said, performing a hard reset in either version of the operating system still results in your configuration settings being deleted. However, in Windows Mobile 5 any file or application stored in persistent memory will not be lost.

After you perform a hard reset, assuming you had time to backup your data to either a removable Secure Digital or CompactFlash memory card or had the time to synchronize your iPAQ with your PC, all you have to do is re-sync your iPAQ with your PC or use files and programs that are stored on your removable memory card.

Where to Find More Information about Troubleshooting

There are several excellent sources to help you find information to solve iPAQ problems:

- **Hewlett Packard**   Since HP designed and manufactured your iPAQ, they certainly know a lot about it. HP offers up-to-date self-service online help, as well as telephone and e-mail support (**www.hp.com**).

- **Microsoft**   Microsoft made the operating system running on your iPAQ, and the Microsoft site generally has very good information to help you troubleshoot issues and also offers tutorials and FAQs (**www.microsoft.com/windowsmobile/**).

- **Ask your wireless service provider**   Contact your wireless service provider's support department for assistance. The following is a list of contact information for the largest providers:

  - AT&T Wireless (**www.attws.com**), 1-800-888-7600
  - Cingular Wireless (**www.cingular.com**), 1-866-246-4852
  - Sprint PCS (**www.sprintpcs.com**), 1-800-974-2221
  - T-Mobile (**www.tmobile.com**), 1-800-937-8997
  - Orange (**www.orange.com**), +44 (0) 207 984 1600

  Another option is to search the Web for user feedback, forums, and Pocket PC fan sites such as:

  - **www.pocketpcthoughts.com**
  - **www.pocketpcmag.com/forum**
  - **www.pocketpcaddict.com**

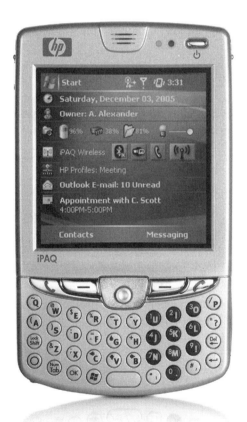
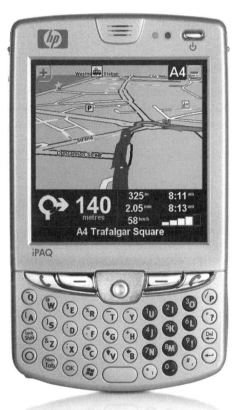

This book is not the only game in town. A wide and wonderful variety of resources are available to users of HP iPAQ Pocket PCs, and most of them can be accessed for free right on the Web. Most of the software and hardware accessories available for the iPAQ are available online, and most of your questions can be answered there as well. You might also check out some of the non-Web-related resources towards the end of this appendix.

Websites

We've organized the online resources in this chapter in sections that first describe the type of sites discussed and then list the better examples in the category.

 *HP's website (**www.HP.com**) has an online store where you can buy iPAQ Pocket PCs and HP accessories for them. In addition you can find support information, ROM upgrades, and other very useful information.*

iPAQ-specific Websites

Although there were once more than a dozen websites specifically dedicated to the iPAQ, many of them have switched to being general mobility websites. Currently the only dedicated independent iPAQ website that we are aware of is **www.ipaq.net**, which hosts a variety of content including articles, tips and tricks, and forums for discussion. It is free to sign up and there is a great deal of useful content there for the iPAQ owner.

General Pocket PC Websites

These sites provide a variety of information about Pocket PCs in general. Much of it is useful to iPAQ users.

www.microsoft.com/windowsmobile/default.mspx

Microsoft's Windows Mobile site focuses on devices that use the Windows Mobile operating system, including the Pocket PC. It thoroughly describes the available devices and the Microsoft software built into the Pocket PC, it has a number of FAQs that answer questions about the Pocket PC, and more. It has an extensive "resources" section with links to downloads for the Pocket PC, hardware accessories, support communities, technical articles, white papers, case studies, and a lot more.

www.pocketpcmag.com

This site contains archives of *Smartphone and Pocket PC* (formerly *Pocket PC* magazine) articles, including reviews of most Pocket PCs and the major third-party accessories and applications. It has a searchable Encyclopedia of Software and Accessories and a Buyer's Guide that lets you compare models feature by feature. It has a relatively new, but very busy, user forum with a section devoted to the HP iPAQ.

www.pocketpcthoughts.com

Pocket PC Thoughts is one of the most popular Pocket PC websites available. It presents a daily log of new and interesting information and ideas relating to the world of Pocket PCs. The information is brief but with links to additional detail. The site also includes articles, columns, links, and an online user forum with a busy section on the HP iPAQ.

www.pocketpcfaq.com

This is probably the oldest and one of the richest websites devoted to the Pocket PC. Webmaster Chris De Herrera has been working with what is now known as the "Windows Mobile" operating system since 1996, and his site has been around almost that long. It includes news, FAQs, bug lists, reviews and commentary, a decent e-book library, a list of newsgroups for the Pocket PC, and a Pocket PC forum that does not include a specific iPAQ section but does include an active questions and comments section.

www.brighthand.com/ppc/

Brighthand is a general mobile computing website with a strong Pocket PC section that includes news, commentary, device reviews, and a very active discussion forum that includes sections for the HP iPAQ Pocket PCs.

News Sites

Some of the general sites mentioned earlier are also excellent sources of news about Pocket PCs and the HP iPAQ, especially Pocket PC Thoughts. In addition, you should check out the following sites:

- **www.pocketpctalk.com**
- **www.pocketpcwire.com**
- **www.infosyncworld.com**
- **http://pocketpc.pdablast.com**
- **www.ppcsg.com**
- **www.bostonpocketpc.com**
- **www.theunwired.net**
- **www.pocketpccanada.com**
- **http://pocketpc.pdablast.com/news.html**
- **www.pocketpclife.co.uk/news.asp**

Commercial Software Sites

These sites focus predominantly on commercial software for your HP iPAQ or any Pocket PC. Most commercial software is also available in free trial versions. You get to use a trial version for 15 or

30 days, or five times—something like that—to see if you like it. Then you have to buy it if you want to continue using it. In addition, these sites may have some freeware and shareware available.

- **www.handango.com**
- **www.pocketgear.com**

 iPAQs use Intel PXA processors, which are in the ARM processor family. Most, but not all of the software developed for Pocket PC devices will work with the iPAQ Pocket PCs. However, we strongly suggest that you download the demo version of a product and test it on your iPAQ before you buy the commercial version, especially if you have an iPAQ with a VGA screen. If a demo is not available, visit the vendor's website and make sure they certify that the software will work with HP iPAQs running the Windows Mobile 2003 or Windows Mobile 5 operating system. This advice applies to all software you install on your iPAQ.

Download Sites

These sites have a variety of commercial software, shareware, freeware, and free demos of commercial Pocket PC software. Also, check the general Pocket PC and the commercial websites listed earlier. Many of them have download sections.

- **www.handango.com**
- **www.pocketgear.com**
- **www.pocketpcsoft.net**

Freeware Sites

These sites specialize in freeware for the Pocket PCs but may also have shareware programs. They may link to other sites for downloading software.

- **www.pocketpcfreewares.com/en/index.php**
- **www.freewareppc.com/**

Media Sites

These sites provide or have links to sites that provide e-books, audio books, video, and music for Pocket PCs.

Free and Commercial E-books

To read e-books on iPAQ Pocket PCs you may need to install a reader program. See Chapter 5 for details.

- **www.mslit.com**
- **www.blackmask.com**

- **http://etext.virginia.edu/ebooks/ebooklist.html**
- **www.pocketpcfaq.com/scripts/linkman/linkmat.cgi**
- **www.ereader.com**
- **www.fictionwise.com**

Free and Commercial Audio Books

Most audio books are available in MP3 or WMA formats, which can be played by Media Player Mobile. In the case of Audible.com, you have to install a download manager on your desktop PC.

- **www.audiobooksforfree.com**
- **www.audible.com**

Movie/Video Download Sites

Most videos are available in WMV or MPEG formats. You can view the former with Media Player Mobile. You need to install Pocket TV (**www.pockettv.com**) to view the latter.

- **www.pocketmovies.net**
- **www.pocketrocketfx.com**

Music Download Sites

Most music is available in MP3 or WMA format. You can play this on Media Player Mobile. There are a variety of music download sites online, including **www.napster.com**, **www.mp3 .com**, and others.

TIP

You can use an online search engine like Google.com to find thousands of sources for music, video, e-books, and more. However, you might have to wade through pages of links or use the advanced features of the search engine to find the material you are looking for.

Accessories Sites

These focus mainly on hardware accessories for Pocket PCs, although some of them may have software sections.

- **www.hp.com**
- **www.mobileplanet.com**
- **www.expansys.com**
- **www.pocketpctechs.com**

Support Forums

These are interactive forums where iPAQ users can post questions and comments and get feedback from other users and experts.

- www.microsoft.com/windowsmobile/communities/pocketpc/newsgroups.mspx
- www.pocketpcmag.com/forum
- http://forums.pocketpcfaq.com/
- http://discussion.brighthand.com
- http://discuss.pocketnow.com
- www.pdastreet.com/forums
- www.pocketmatrix.com/forums/

> **NOTE**   *The list of interactive forums changes frequently and new sites pop up all the time. Check some of the more active websites such as **www.pocketpcmag.com** for new sites.*

Price Comparison/Online Auction Sites

Looking for a bargain on accessories or a used iPAQ? Try one of these sites:

- www.pricegrabber.com
- http://shopper.cnet.com/
- www.streetprices.com
- www.shopping.com
- www.ebay.com

Sites Formatted for the Smaller Pocket PC Screens

More websites are offering "mobile" versions of their sites, formatted for optimum viewing on the smaller screens found on mobile devices. *Smartphone and Pocket PC* magazine's Mobile Best Sites web page (**www.pocketpcmag.com/mobile.htm**) has a list of some of the better mobile site directories available online, including two of the better portal sites with extensive directories of other mobile sites:

- www.pdahotspots.com
- www.evmo.com

RSS Feeds

RSS is an XML format that allows a website to publish its content. With the help of an RSS aggregator program like PocketRSS (**www.happyjackroad.net**), your iPAQ can have news, sports, weather, stock information, and other content delivered to the iPAQ every time you sync. *Smartphone and Pocket PC* magazine's Best Sites web page (**www.pocketpcmag.com/_top/ bestsites.asp**) has a list of Pocket PC–related sites that offer RSS feeds.

Publications

A number of U.S. magazines write about handhelds, but two focus entirely on handhelds and issues involving them.

Smartphone and Pocket PC **Magazine (formerly** *Pocket PC* **Magazine)** **(www.pocketpcmag.com)**

This publication focuses entirely on Windows Mobile Pocket PCs and Smartphones. It includes news, product reviews, articles on how to use your Windows Mobile device, tips and tricks, new product announcements, and enterprise issues. You will find many articles by one of this book's authors, Derek Ball, who is a regular contributor to this magazine.

Pen Computing **(www.pencomputing.com)**

This publication focuses on a variety of handhelds, including Pocket PCs, Palm OS, Psion/EPOC devices, and tablet PCs. They have a strong Pocket PC section that includes editorials and reviews.

Conferences

Conferences are a great place to meet fellow users as well as hardware and software developers. Many have smaller sections that deal with handheld devices that include Pocket PCs.

CTIA Wireless

This is the biannual conference for the CTIA (Cellular Telecommunications Industry Association), the major international association for the wireless telecommunications industry. There's usually a small but reasonable amount of Pocket PC–related exhibits and discussions. However, the show is targeted toward enterprise users and developers—not end-users. More information is available on the CTIA website (**www.ctia.org/conventions_events/index.cfm**).

The folks at Pocket PC Summit (**www.pocketpcsummit.com**) usually host an "Enterprise Mobility Pavilion" at CTIA Wireless, which often has some focus on Windows Mobile solutions for the enterprise.

The Consumer Electronics Show (CES)

CES is a large event covering all areas of consumer electronics. It's a lot of fun, and there is some direct coverage of the Pocket PC at the show. More information is available at the CES website (**www.cesweb.org**).

Microsoft Professional Developers Conference

Sponsored by Microsoft, this conference focuses on developer issues. It has a variety of educational sessions and technical content, with presentations from Microsoft and a variety of developers. It also has a vendor expo. More information is available on Microsoft's website (**http://msdn.microsoft .com/events/**).

User Groups

The real Pocket PC experts are the people who use them day in and day out. One of the best ways to get the most out of your HP iPAQ is to network (and we're not talking about WiFi or LAN here). Find a friend or group of friends that share your interest in the Pocket PC.

Microsoft Pocket PC Clubs List

- www.microsoft.com/windowsmobile/communities/pocketpc/localclubs/default.mspx

Pocket PC Magazine User Group List

- www.pocketpcmag.com/_top/User_Groups.asp

Index